Franz Joseph and Napoleon III

1852 - 1864

Franz Josep

CHARLES W. HALLBERG

nd Napoleon III

1852-1864

A STUDY OF AUSTRO-FRENCH RELATIONS

OCTAGON BOOKS

A DIVISION OF FARRAR. STRAUS AND GIROUX

New York   1973

Reprinted 1973
by special arrangement with Twayne Publishers

OCTAGON BOOKS
A DIVISION OF FARRAR, STRAUS & GIROUX, INC.
19 Union Square West
New York, N. Y. 10003

*This book has been reproduced from an original in the
Brown University Library*

Library of Congress Cataloging in Publication Data

Hallberg, Charles William, 1899-
    Franz Joseph and Napoleon III, 1852-1864.

    Reprint of the ed. published by Bookman Associates, New York.

    Bibliography: p.
    1. Austria—Foreign relations—France. 2. France—Foreign re-
lations—Austria. 3. Franz Joseph I, Emperor of Austria, 1830-
1916. 4. Napoléon III, Emperor of the French, 1808-1873.
5. Europe—Politics—1848-1871. I. Title.
[DB49.F8H3 1973]   327.436′044   73-9704
ISBN 0-374-93380-4

Printed in USA by
Thomson-Shore,Inc.
Dexter, Michigan

Franz Josep

CHARLES W. HALLBERG

nd Napoleon III

1852-1864

A STUDY OF AUSTRO-FRENCH RELATIONS

BOOKMAN ASSOCIATES

New York

Manufactured in the United States of America
Printed by Record Press, New York

To

Eleanore and Ingrid

Preface

WHILE THERE ARE a number of excellent works dealing with various aspects of Austrian and French policies during the middle period of the nineteenth century, little has been done to set forth the rela tion of these policies to each other, which is the aim of the present study. Its treatment is diplomatic and no pretense is made to discuss economic, psychological or social factors. During the years 1852 to 1864, in both Austria and France, diplomacy was controlled from the top. Public opinion had not yet attained the place it was to occupy after the Franco-Prussian War. It is true that in both countries, and especially in France, there existed certain groups whose attitude could not be ignored. But although exerting an influence on foreign policy, neither these groups nor the public in general had any real control over it. The formulation of policy and its execution was the work of the rulers and their ministers.

The author wishes to express his gratitude to the officials of the Archives des Affaires Étrangères in Paris and the Haus-, Hof-, und Staatsarchiv in Vienna, especially to the late Dr. Lothar Gros, for their unfailing courtesy and cooperation; and to Professor Lynn Case of the University of Pennsylvania and Professors Gaudens Megaro and Martin A. Weinbaum of Queens College for their many valuable suggestions. He also wishes to thank the following publishers or proprietors of copyright for permission to quote from copyrighted books: Ernest Benn Limited for *Conversations with Napoleon III*, edited by Sir Victor Wellesley and Robert Sencourt; Longmans Green & Company, Ltd., for *Later Correspondence of Lord John Russell*, edited by G. P. Gooch; University of California Press for *England and the Straits Question, 1844-1856* by V. J. Puryear; and Mrs. Gertrude Redlich for *Emperor Francis Joseph of Austria* by Joseph Redlich.

CHARLES W. HALLBERG
Queens College
May 1954

Contents

The End of the Metternich System and the Emergence of New Leaders

THE STRUGGLE BETWEEN France and the Hapsburgs forms an important chapter in the history of Europe. For three hundred years, from the days of Francis I and Charles V to the final defeat of Napoleon at Waterloo, this struggle went on with few interruptions. Emerging from the Hundred Years' War with her territories unified and her government centralized, France sought to break through the ring which the Hapsburgs had thrown around her, to defeat and humiliate the Holy Roman Empire, and to increase her power and prestige. The Hapsburgs, on the other hand, endeavored not only to keep France within bounds but to unify the Empire by pursuing a vigorous German policy. The obstacles, however, were far too great for the Hapsburg rulers. Not only was their power weakened by internal difficulties in the Austrian dominions, but the rise of Protestantism culminating in the disastrous Thirty Years' War, the jealousies and ambitions of the German princes, the intervention of France and Sweden, and the wars with the Turks, marked the definite decline of their influence in central and southeastern Europe. Louis XIV engaged the Empire in a series of tilts in his efforts to reach the Rhine and give France her "natural frontiers." The War of Spanish Succession at the beginning of the eighteenth century, while placing a Bourbon on the throne of Spain and thus establishing the basis for a close dynastic alliance, at the same time enlarged and enriched the Hapsburgs by the acquisition of former Spanish territories in Italy and the Belgian Netherlands. The "diplomatic revolution" of

1754, which brought Austria and France into an alliance against England and Prussia, was but an interlude in the now traditional struggle. In 1792 France declared war on Austria and for the next twenty-three years carried the tricolor to all parts of Europe. Several times Napoleon defeated the Hapsburg armies but in the end they managed to be on the winning side.

By 1815 a new era had dawned in Europe—an era of reaction against the principles of the French Revolution and the dominance of Napoleon. After months of bickering, the statesmen gathered at the Congress of Vienna worked out a settlement designed to give peace and security to a war-scarred continent. Talleyrand, the shrewd, calculating diplomatist of France, who had turned his back on the Emperor, introduced the principle of Legitimacy to bolster the cause of his new master, Louis XVIII. This principle was used to restore a number of princes driven from their thrones and also some of the states which had been brought under the sway of the insatiable Bonaparte. Certain states having suffered losses were compensated by additions of territory; others, like Holland, were strengthened in order to serve as barriers against a new French aggression. On June 9. 1815, six days before Waterloo, the Final Act of Vienna incorporating the various settlements was signed, and the Congress came to a close.

The principal powers in the new Europe were Austria, England, Prussia and Russia. By a treaty concluded at Chaumont on March 9, 1814, they had agreed to continue the war against Napoleon until their objects were attained and to make peace in common. The allies had dictated the First Treaty of Paris, May 30, 1814, which thrust France back to her boundaries of January 1792. But the escape of Napoleon from Elba and the Hundred Days necessitated a new arrangement and on November 20, 1815, France signed the Second Treaty of Paris. Her boundaries were now pushed back to those she held in January 1790; she was ordered to pay an indemnity of 700,000,000 francs and to submit to military occupation. On the same day the allies renewed their alliance and agreed to meet periodically in order to check the spread of revolutionary principles. France was made an outcast among the nations and the author of her woes was sent to the rocky island of St. Helena.

The Age of Reaction, following the downfall of Napoleon, was likewise the Age of Metternich. The Austrian Chancellor emerged from the Congress of Vienna as the foremost statesman of the continent. In the eyes of his enemies, he became the personification of the reactionary spirit. His policy of the *status quo* was dictated, more or less, by the conditions existing within the Austrian Empire. Although the Hapsburg possessions were larger and more compact than before the Revolution, they constituted a hodge-podge of nationalities. Any development along the lines of nationalism and liberalism might threaten their existence. Hence, Metternich was determined to maintain the structure created at Vienna and to prevent liberal ideas from coming to the fore. Not only were such ideas to be kept out of the Hapsburg dominions; they were likewise to be barred from Germany and Italy where Austrian influence was dominant. Metternich was the watchdog of central Europe.

Success attended the efforts of the Austrian Chancellor for a number of years. France, once the hotbed of revolution, became respectably conservative under her new Bourbon ruler, Louis XVIII, and in 1818 was received into the European Concert.[1] The Tsar Alexander I of Russia, who had once wished to be regarded as a liberal and whose Polish Kingdom was created along liberal lines, was gradually "converted." By 1820 Metternich had imposed his system upon the German states and in the same year the Congress of Troppau drew up a protocol which proclaimed it to be the right and duty of the powers to intervene in any state of Europe for the purpose of putting down revolution. This doctrine of intervention, designed to strengthen the monarchical principle, was applied to revolutions in Italy and Spain, and it was France, incidentally, which put down the latter. England refused to support the new doctrine,[2] for although she was reactionary at home, she favored liberalism abroad in the interests of her trade and the balance of power. Her attitude gave encouragement to revolutionary elements in the various European states.

In 1830 the Metternichean system was rudely shaken. The July Revolution in France which overthrew the reactionary Charles X and brought to the throne the Orleanist Louis Philippe, was the signal for uprisings in Belgium, Italy, some of the German states, and

Poland. The Belgians cast off the shackles imposed at Vienna and won freedom from the House of Orange, but the Poles saw their Kingdom destroyed and their liberties swept away by Nicholas I, who had succeeded his brother Alexander I in 1825. Having troubles of their own, the rulers of Austria, Prussia and Russia were unable to intervene in Belgium. Three years later, these rulers renewed their faith in the doctrine of intervention[3] and thereafter, for the next decade and a half, the Holy Alliance was the jealous guardian of the conservative and monarchical principles in Europe.

Although the forces of liberalism and nationalism were momentarily driven underground, they continued to grow and in 1848 produced a revolutionary movement which swept the continent like a tidal wave. Once more it was France that took the lead against the established order. The government of Louis Philippe had alienated all but the upper bourgeois class whose interests it served. Discredited by corruption and by the weakness of its foreign policy, the July Monarchy was overthrown in February and was succeeded by the Second French Republic. Within a short time the fires of revolution had spread to other parts of the continent. Everywhere reform became the order of the day, and one after another the rulers of central Europe bowed before the storm. Cries of independence and unity reverberated throughout Italy and Charles Albert of Piedmont placed himself at the head of a crusade to drive the hated Austrians from the Peninsula. The enthusiasm was no less in Germany where concessions were hastily granted. The King of Prussia promised a constitution, while a constituent assembly was summoned to meet at Frankfurt to give liberty and unity to Germany. But it was Austria, the bulwark of the conservative system, which experienced the worst agitation. The weak but obstinate Ferdinand I was forced to part with Metternich, who fled to Holland and later to England. In Hungary the Diet passed a number of reforms known as the March Laws. At the same time the Slav nationalities of the Empire won concessions conforming to their aspirations. By the end of March the revolution was everywhere successful. Then slowly the tide began to turn. In June Prince Windischgrätz subdued Bohemia; on July 25th Charles Albert was defeated at Custozza, while Vienna surrendered the last day of

October. But in Italy, Hungary and Germany the revolution was still unconquered.

In both Austria and France the revolutions of 1848 produced important changes. New leaders appeared who were destined to exert considerable influence upon the course of future developments. On November 21, 1848, the Emperor Ferdinand appointed as his Chief Minister Prince Felix zu Schwarzenberg,[4] an uncompromising foe of revolution. Schwarzenberg, in turn, found Ferdinand an obstacle and prevailed upon him to abdicate. On December 2nd Ferdinand's nephew, Franz Joseph, a youth of eighteen, son of Archduke Francis Charles, who had renounced his rights of succession, ascended the throne. A week later, on the 10th, the people of France elected as their President Prince Louis Napoleon, the son of the former King Louis and Queen Hortense of Holland, and a nephew of the great Emperor.

Determined to restore the power and prestige of the Hapsburgs, Prince Schwarzenberg applied himself vigorously to the task of putting down the revolutions. He refused to recognize the liberal constitution drawn up after much debate by the Frankfurt Assembly and ordered the Austrian delegates to withdraw. Frederick William IV of Prussia, who had been proclaimed hereditary Emperor of Germany, was informed of Austria's attitude and induced to reject the crown. The Frankfurt Assembly was dissolved and by the end of June 1849 the agitation in Germany was suppressed. In Italy, General Radetzky inflicted a disastrous defeat on the Piedmontese at Novara (March 23, 1849) and Charles Albert, discouraged by his failure to free the Peninsula from Austrian control, abdicated in favor of his eldest son, Victor Emmanuel II. The Bourbon King of Naples reconquered Sicily which the revolutionaries had wrested from him, while the Austrians overthrew the Florentine Republic and restored the Grand Duke of Tuscany. In April, Louis Napoleon sent an army to occupy Rome where Mazzini and Garibaldi had set up the Roman Republic. French troops entered the Eternal City on July 3rd where they remained, with a single brief interruption, for the next two decades. At the same time, parts of the Papal territory were occupied by Austria and the Pope was restored. In August, Austrian troops put down the

Venetian Republic controlled by Daniel Manin and the last strong-hold of the revolution in Italy was conquered. There remained Hungary which, on April 14, 1849, proclaimed its independence with Louis Kossuth as dictator. Because of the situation in Italy, Franz Joseph was unable to subdue the Magyars with his own forces and appealed to Tsar Nicholas of Russia for aid. In May a strong Russian army crossed the Hungarian frontier and by the middle of August the Magyar cause was lost. The revolutions thus came to an end and reaction was once more the order of the day.

The swift and vigorous manner in which Schwarzenberg directed the fight against revolution made a lasting impression upon the young ruler, Franz Joseph. For the next three years, Schwarzenberg was the most important figure in Austria and, indeed, throughout central Europe. "His was the really decisive influence. He was, from the day he formed his government to that of his death, the real leader of the whole policy of the empire. He dominated everything at court. The Emperor listened to him as he did to no one else." [5]

No sooner had the revolutionary ferment subsided than Schwarzenberg turned his attention to the German problem. Although Frederick William IV of Prussia had rejected the crown offered by the Frankfurt Assembly, he had not abandoned hope of wresting from Austria the leadership in the Bund. In his attempt to form a German league under Prussian influence, however, he was outmaneuvered by Schwarzenberg, who succeeded in reconstituting the old Diet of the Confederation under Austria's presidency. The refusal of the King to recognize the Diet as the legal authority in the Bund and his support of irregular troops operating in Holstein against Danish rule, brought on a crisis. A showdown between the two German powers was reached when Schwarzenberg prevailed upon the Diet to dispatch troops to Hesse where the reactionary Elector had been driven out by his irate subjects. When Frederick William sent several of his own army corps to Hesse, Schwarzenberg demanded their removal within forty-eight hours. Rather than risk war, the Prussian King decided to yield and directed Manteuffel, who had succeeded Radowitz as Prime Minister, to meet the Austrian representative at Olmütz. The "Humiliation of Olmütz" (November 29, 1850) checked Prussian ambitions to dominate German affairs.

Following this tussle with the Prussian King, Schwarzenberg came forth with his own plan which was designed to give Austria control over the Diet and permit the admission of all her territories into the Confederation.[6] He submitted this plan to a congress of German states convened at Dresden in December 1850 under his presidency.

The proposal to include all the Austrian territories in the Confederation was opposed by Louis Napoleon who held that it would upset the balance of power in Europe and thus constitute a danger to France. "It will," he said to Hübner, the Austrian Minister at Paris, "transform Austria and Germany into a single empire extending from the Po to the Baltic Sea. We cannot consent to it without knowing what compensation Austria will give us, what she will give Europe."[7] He insisted that it was a violation of the treaties of Vienna and hence required the consent of the signatory powers. On March 5, 1851, the French Government addressed a circular to all the signatories of the treaties of 1815 declaring that no change could be made without their approval.

Schwarzenberg denied that his proposal was in violation of the Vienna Settlement. The latter, he pointed out, was not a treaty as such but a general instrument in which were registered the results of numerous negotiations concluded since the First Treaty of Paris, May 30, 1814. In signing the Final Act, the signatory powers did not thereby become parties to the special treaties. The Federal Act which established the German Confederation was a special treaty entered into by the princes and Free Cities of Germany and therefore did not require the approval of the powers for its modification. In other words, Schwarzenberg maintained that it was for the Diet alone to decide whether or not the Austrian provinces should be admitted. There was, he declared, no danger of upsetting the balance of power in Europe since Austria would acquire no additional territory.[8] Hübner was directed to point out to Louis Napoleon that the admission of the Austrian provinces would offer new guarantees against the revolutionary spirit and socialism and would be the means of strengthening the Hapsburg Monarchy, which all statesmen should consider "an imperative need of society." [9]

It was unlikely that the heir to the Napoleonic legend would agree to a scheme which would strengthen the Hapsburgs, traditional enemies of France and defenders of the order established in 1815. Yet, he did not give an outright refusal but instead suggested to Hübner the possibility of a new European settlement whereby Austria would join England, France and Russia in redrawing the map. In return for this, he promised that France would adopt the institutions of Austria and become a conservative power. The price was far greater than Schwarzenberg was willing to pay. "It is needless to say," he wrote, "that we cannot follow M. Bonaparte on the terrain where he tends to push the question." [10] He believed that the opposition of France and England was due to their fear of seeing Austria's position strengthened in Italy. "In the interest of his personal policy, the President of the Republic regrets to see the eventual disappearance of the chance to possess Savoy by indemnifying Piedmont at our expense in Lombardy. From his side, Lord Palmerston does not as yet appear to have renounced the hope of retaking at an opportune moment the project he pursues with so much ardor of founding a strong military power in the northern part of the Peninsula, equally to our detriment, submitting to the exclusive influence of England, and of making it at the same time the active instrument of the constitutional propaganda to which the Principal Secretary of State likes to deliver himself without regard to time, place and circumstance . . ." [11]

Recognizing the futility of forcing through his plan, Schwarzenberg abandoned it. However, had Lombardy-Venetia been admitted to the Confederation, the events of 1859 might conceivably have been different. On May 15, 1851, the Dresden conference came to a close after adopting a proposal to reëstablish the old Diet at Frankfurt.

Schwarzenberg did obtain one important advantage at Dresden. During the conference, on March 10th, Manteuffel wrote to the Austrian Minister suggesting a mutually defensive alliance between Prussia and the entire Austrian Empire. Schwarzenberg replied on the 17th that the question should be deferred until the close of the conference. Finally, on May 16, 1851, a secret treaty of alliance was concluded for a period of three years. Each power promised to give full assistance to the other in case of an attack upon any of its territories inside or outside the Confederation. Thus, the Prussian threat was removed, at least for the time being, and the power and prestige of the Hapsburgs appeared as great as ever before. The revolutionary movement had been crushed and Austria had regained her dominant position in Italy and Germany. For the next three years Prussia's military support was assured in the event of an attack against any part of the Hapsburg territories. Schwarzenberg had established himself as a worthy successor to Metternich.

But already a new power had appeared on the banks of the Seine. Perhaps it is an irony of history that the revolutionary upheaval produced not only the savior of the Austrian Monarchy but also one who was to be counted among its greatest enemies. During the Metternichean era France was never able to offer a serious challenge to the Vienna Settlement. The Bourbons, Louis XVIII and Charles X, and the Orleanist, Louis Philippe, were more concerned with the consolidation of their power at home than with victories abroad. Indeed, the July Monarchy had pursued a policy of "peace at any price." [12] Yet, the great mass of French people remained unreconciled to the "humiliations" of 1815 and wanted to break the chains which bound them to a position of inferiority in European affairs. In Louis Napoleon they found their champion.

The nephew of the great Napoleon was born in 1808 and twenty-four years later became head of the Bonaparte House.[13] Convinced that he was destined to rule France, he attempted to seize power in 1836 at Strasbourg but was arrested and exiled to the United States from where, however, he shortly returned. Four years later, he made a second attempt at Boulogne which led to his imprisonment in the fortress of Ham, in northern France. Escaping in 1846, he went to England and at the time of the Chartist agitation in 1848, was enrolled as a special constable. The February Revolution paved the way for his future career. He was elected to the Constituent Assembly and in December 1848 defeated General

Cavaignac, Lamartine and Ledru-Rollin for the presidency of France. Three years later, on December 2, 1851, he executed a *coup d'état* and through the revision of the constitution obtained absolute power.

The exciting adventures of the new dictator of France, as an alleged Carbonaro,[14] as conspirator and captive, undoubtedly exerted a strong influence on his character. A conspirator he remained, with a love for petty intrigues and small contrivances, preferring the mysteries of backstairs diplomacy to open negotiations, and secret agents to accredited representatives.[15] He was a dreamer whose dreams were both practical and utopian, both selfish and humanitarian. Meditative, taciturn and melancholy by nature, he had remarkable patience and knew how to conceal his feelings and how to keep his own counsel. Yet, this brooding sphinx could act with reckless impulsiveness one moment and with iron determination the next. He could be decisive but he was often painfully vacillating, fearing to take any step which might compromise his future actions. His outlook was cosmopolitan rather than French. "Essentially he was an international figure: too good a citizen perhaps of Europe to be the ultimately successful ruler of any country in it." [16] Baron Hübner, the Austrian Minister at Paris, wrote that in the last analysis it was Louis Napoleon himself who would be the artisan of his political fortunes. "His mind is chimerical, his character impenetrable, dissimulating, false, vindictive, not even exempt from instincts of cruelty, and offering no guarantees; his antecedents, his fabulous career—push him naturally toward the marvelous and toward adventure." [17] Louis Napoleon was a fatalist; he believed in his star. In order to foresee the course he would follow, one would have to know the course of that star. "It is this fatalism, found at the basis of his character, nourished by a success and by a return to fortune unparalleled in history, which renders all calculations impossible." [18]

As the heir to the Napoleonic tradition, Louis Napoleon believed that it was his mission in life to realize the ideals which his famous uncle had expounded at St. Helena. The Emperor had posed as the champion of nationalities, as the Son of the Revolution, whose efforts to establish liberty in France had been frustrated by the wickedness of the allies. Louis Napoleon's all-consuming ambition was to complete the work of his uncle, for he never doubted the latter's sincerity. He had set forth his views in various treatises, while his years in prison had given him leisure to meditate upon his mission.

First and foremost in his program was the principle of nationalities.[19] Though he had only a vague understanding of this principle, he saw in its realization the establishment of a new order in Europe, culminating in a confederation of states. He planned to give liberty and unity to the Italians and the Germans, to bring about a personal union of Moldavia and Wallachia, and to set up an independent Poland. At times he even toyed with the idea of securing the freedom of Hungary from Austria and Finland from Russia, of uniting Spain and Portugal, and of constituting a single Scandinavian Kingdom.

The second of his guiding principles, upon which the first really depended, was the revision of the *status quo*. To Louis Napoleon, the *status quo* meant the Settlement of 1815, which had brought the downfall of his dynasty and the humiliation, isolation and mutilation of France. He was determined to restore the Bonaparte dynasty, to make France an equal among the great powers, and to win allies.[20] The other powers, he observed, had satellites among the smaller states—Austria in South Germany and Italy, Russia in the Balkans, England in Portugal—but France had none.[21] Above all, he wished to conclude an alliance with a great power and to smash the Holy Alliance of Austria, Prussia and Russia, which upheld the *status quo* and kept France isolated on the continent. There were other aims which influenced his foreign policy such, for example, of obtaining domination in the Mediterranean which he regarded as the natural sphere of French interests.[22]

In order to realize his program, Louis Napoleon did not intend to emulate his illustrious uncle and resume the policy of conquests. Rather he hoped to achieve his purpose by peaceful means. By offering his mediation or by proposing a congress of the great powers, he would prevent or settle international disputes as they occurred. His greatest dream was the convocation of a general European congress which would adjust all existing differences and create a new order to replace the one established at Vienna in 1815. Though he engaged in great wars for the fulfillment of his aims, Louis Napoleon remained at heart a man of peace.

Having before him such a program, Louis Napoleon was a challenge to the old order and especially to the influence and the power of the Hapsburgs. The international developments of the dozen years following the *coup d'état* left no doubt as to the seriousness of this challenge. In the first important issue of European diplomacy—the question of extending recognition to the Second Empire—the French ruler emerged triumphant although somewhat bruised by the cavalier treatment of the conservative powers. Determined to smash the Holy Alliance and to lift France out of her isolation, Napoleon found the opportunity at the close of the Crimean War. Not only did the war alienate Austria and Russia but it sharpened the rivalry in Germany between Austria and Prussia, while at the same time it led to an intimate *entente* of France and Russia. Paris became the diplomatic capital and Napoleon the virtual arbiter of European affairs.

With the end of the conservative bloc, Austria's position was badly shaken. As a *status quo* power, defending the Vienna Settlement of 1815, she was no longer able to withstand the assaults of rising nationalism and the revolutionary movement. Napoleon, the champion of oppressed nationalities, could count on the diplomatic and moral support of England and to a certain extent of Prussia and Russia in the Italian question, on Russia in the Balkans, and at times on Prussia in Germany. Austria alone could be considered a persistent defender of the treaties of 1815 and an uncompromising foe of the principle of nationalities. It was this principle which struck at her dominance in Italy, her leadership in Germany, and her influence in the Balkans, and which at all times threatened the integrity of her own dominions. She was vulnerable from all sides—an easy target for Napoleon. Alliances were practically ruled out for her except at the cost of heavy sacrifices. It was the unwillingness of Franz Joseph and his advisers to make such sacrifices that in the end proved disastrous for the Hapsburg Empire. By yielding her leadership in Germany to Prussia, Austria might have held on to her Italian possessions. Or she might have strengthened her position in Germany by abandoning Venetia. In the one case she would have had the support of Prussia, in the other the support of France.

Actually the greatest threat to Austria during the period came not from nationalism and the revolutionary movement as such, not from the ambitions of Prussia or the hatred of Russia or the liberal propensities of England, but from Napoleon himself. Without his interference the dispute between Russia and Turkey would not have developed into a long and costly war which proved so disastrous for Austria's position. Nor would there have been an Italian War in 1859 which put an end to Hapsburg dominance in the Peninsula. The same point can be made about Poland and the frequent squabbles in the Balkans. It was indeed through Napoleon's aid or encouragement that nationalists in Italy, Hungary, Poland, Montenegro, Rumania and Serbia organized for resistance to the established order. He was the leader of the forces—sometimes open, sometimes secret—that struggled against the Hapsburgs.

Perhaps no problem of foreign affairs offered more difficulties for the Austrian statesmen than the problem of dealing with Napoleon. Throughout the years from 1852 to 1864 a persistent effort was made to wean him from his nationalistic-revolutionary tendencies and to appeal to conservative-dynastic interests. It was thus in every question dividing the two powers. How far Napoleon would go in any given circumstance, was the point of immediate concern for Austria. The Austrian representatives at Paris endeavored to follow every move, study every mood, and even to analyze the thoughts of the French Emperor in the hope of understanding and explaining his intentions. To lift the veil of mystery with which Napoleon surrounded himself was no easy matter. It was well known that he held the reins of foreign policy in his own hands, that his ministers were mere servants, often not informed of the imperial plans or often misled by them.[23] Among his advisers were both friends and enemies of Austria—the Empress, Drouyn de Lhuys and Walewski among the former, Prince Napoleon, Fould, La Valette and Thouvenel among the latter. None of the ministers was outstanding. Thouvenel, considered the most capable, was mistaken about all the important questions which came up in his day.[24] Drouyn de Lhuys, a hold-over from the Orleanist Monarchy, knew more about agriculture than foreign affairs and, while regarded as an Austrophile, his sympathies were platonic and confined to well-turned phrases which cost nothing and brought little in return.[25] Walewski, a natural son of Napoleon I, though opposed to the Italian policy of the Emperor, was devoted to the Bonapartist cause. The Empress, a clerical sympathizer, was anti-Italian and conservative. Eager to have a hand in high politics, she dabbled in foreign affairs though she acted more on impulse than by reason. She was on excellent terms with Prince Richard Metternich and often informed him about the Emperor's plans. Of Austria's enemies, the most bitter was Prince Napoleon, cousin of the Emperor. He was strongly pro-Italian and anti-clerical, associated with foreign revolutionary leaders, and though he sometimes embarrassed the Emperor by his lack of tact, the latter was devoted to him.

As it was common knowledge that Napoleon formulated his own policies, so it was considered necessary by diplomats in Paris to humor him. Personal contact with the Emperor was therefore essential. The latter provided the opportunities by inviting the diplomats to balls and hunts and even private *soirées*. Both Hübner and Metternich, the Austrian representatives, enjoyed the Emperor's hospitality. Biarritz, Compiègne and Fontainebleau are frequently mentioned in their dispatches and private letters.

Not only did the principle of nationalities serve Napoleon as a weapon against the Hapsburgs: it was also a means by which he hoped to increase the power and dominions of France. In return for the encouragement he gave the various subject nationalities, Napoleon expected their support as allies as well as territorial compensations. Another weapon he employed against Austria was the principle of non-intervention. It was his insistence upon this principle that prevented Franz Joseph from intervening in Italy after Villafranca in order to restore the Hapsburg rulers or to reconquer Lombardy. Hardly less irritating to the Austrian statesmen were Napoleon's proposals for congresses and plebiscites and his penchant for acting as arbitrator or mediator of disputes. In addition, there was the general attitude of distrust against Napoleon which was so noticeable in Vienna after the death of Schwarzenberg. From bitter experience the Ballplatz learned that the French ruler could not be relied upon, that his pledges and promises were quite often empty phrases or concealed ulterior motives. This distrust was by no means confined to Austria and it increased considerably after the Italian War of 1859. On the other hand, it can be said that by the very principles he advocated, Napoleon was moving with his times while Austria was still anchored to the past. In opposition to eighteenth century dynastic and conservative principles, the French Emperor elevated the principle of national self-determination to a principle of international affairs. No other ruler of his age was more modern in spirit.

By contrast, Franz Joseph was averse to change in the existing order. His principles were diametrically opposed to those of Napoleon: *status quo* in place of revision, monarchical sovereignty instead of popular sovereignty, intervention versus non-intervention, and dynastic interests versus revolution. The dissimilarity in character was no less marked. Franz Joseph was a knight of the old school, a grand seigneur, always correct, punctual, tactful and self-controlled.[26] Though bureaucratic and methodical by nature and lacking imagination, he was highly conscious of his position and had a strict sense of duty and of truth.[27] Unlike Napoleon, he was not a dreamer and was impatient with vague, abstract ideas. After the death of Schwarzenberg, he took complete charge of Austria's foreign policy, kept in constant touch with affairs, and read much of the diplomatic correspondence.[28] He was influenced by certain intimates such as his mother, the Archduchess Sophie, Cardinal Rauscher and, above all, Colonel Count Charles Grünne, his aide-de-camp until 1859.[29] He was reserved toward his ministers, who seldom received his entire confidence. Buol and Rechberg, who administered the foreign office from 1852 to 1864, were disciples of Prince Clemens Metternich[30] and were not above average ability. Franz Joseph avoided "strong" men after Schwarzenberg. For such misfortunes as befell his Empire, the responsibility was largely his own. His youth (he was born in 1830), his inability or unwillingness to carry out a policy to its logical conclusion, his cautious and irresolute nature, were liabilities for the ruler of a state as heterogeneous as Austria in an age when swiftly moving forces were converging to destroy it.

CHAPTER TWO

The Establishment of the Second Empire and Its Recognition

THE *coup d'état* of December 2, 1851, by which the Prince-President, Louis Napoleon, seized power in France, was hailed with joy by the conservative rulers of Europe. Not only was this a victory for their cherished principles of law and order but it opened a breach between Louis Napoleon and the radicals of all countries and led to a serious tension between France and England. Although Lord Palmerston had approved the *coup d'état* for political reasons, English public opinion strongly condemned the destruction of the parliamentary system and before the end of the month, he was forced to resign.

But while they applauded Louis Napoleon's victory, the conservative rulers were not completely reassured about his future plans. If, in their eyes, he was the best guarantee of law and order in France, he was at the same time a Bonaparte. Would the *coup d'état,* they wondered, be merely the prelude to the reëstablishment of the imperial regime? Would Louis Napoleon resume the policy of conquests pursued by his famous uncle and attempt to revise the boundaries fixed by the treaties of 1815?

Tsar Nicholas of Russia considered it a point of honor to prevent the restoration of a throne which his brother, Alexander I, had helped to overthrow. Only if Louis Napoleon respected the treaties and remained content with his present position, could Russia maintain friendly relations with him.[1] In a conversation with the French envoy, General Castelbajac, on January 19, 1852, the Tsar repeated his approval of the *coup d'état* but declared that the restoration of the empire would threaten the general peace. He begged General Castelbajac to urge his government to renounce such a serious project.²

The Tsar's allies, Austria and Prussia, were likewise concerned over the future plans of Louis Napoleon. But Austria's attitude at first was influenced less by the principles involved than by the question of expediency. In a dispatch to Baron Hübner, which he wrote on December 5, 1851, Prince Schwarzenberg made it clear that Austria had no intention of interfering in the internal affairs of France and, in giving his approval to the *coup d'état,* he merely expressed the hope that Louis Napoleon would respect the treaties.³ "The pledges," he continued, "which Prince Louis has already offered concerning the firmness and moderation of his character, inspire in us the confidence that these eminent qualities will never cause him to fail in the accomplishment of the mission which appears to be reserved to him." So long as Louis Napoleon did not violate the boundaries established by the treaties or attempt to spread revolution outside France, he could rest assured that no coalition would be formed against him.⁴ "A France," he wrote in a private letter to Hübner on December 18th, "which concerned itself only with internal questions would find in us sympathy and support. A France pursuing conquests, whether Empire or Republic, would have to count on our enmity. An attack by France against any part of the territory of Austria or Prussia would be considered by both powers as a joint *casus belli.* In this respect there are positive understandings with Prussia, behind which Russia stands as a reserve." ⁵

Although insisting that Louis Napoleon accept the territorial *status quo,* Schwarzenberg was willing to concede him the title of Emperor. In a memorandum dated December 29, 1851, copies of which were sent to Berlin and St. Petersburg, he explained at some length his reasons for this attitude. One could consider the question of the empire, he wrote, either from the viewpoint of the treaties or from that of expediency. Article II of the treaty of November 20, 1815, had forever excluded the Bonaparte family from the sovereign power in France but the situation which had produced this treaty had since changed. Louis Napoleon was now the best guarantor of order in France. The rulers of Austria, Prussia and Russia should base their policy not upon the letter but upon the spirit of the treaty, whose aim was the establishment of peace in Europe. If they had adhered to the letter of the treaty, they would have refused to recognize Louis Napoleon as President of France. Could they now justify themselves in the eyes of their subjects and before humanity if they endangered the general peace merely for a question of a title? This had not been sufficient cause for war in the past. Schwarzenberg admitted that Austria and Russia had broken off diplomatic relations with Napoleon I but he pointed out that they had done so not because he assumed the title of Emperor but simply because he had invaded the rights and territories of other nations. In the case of Louis Napoleon even this motive was lacking as he had already declared his love of peace and denied any aggressive plans. Schwarzenberg professed to believe in the sincerity of these assurances since they were in accord with the interests of Louis Napoleon. While warning Prussia and Russia not to consider the question of the empire as a question of principles, which would lead to interminable wars, he reminded them that there was no other possible ruler for France. In recognizing Louis Napoleon as Emperor, the powers would be merely accepting a *fait accompli.* Furthermore, to delay recognition would enable England to reëstablish the *entente cordiale* with France —a prospect by no means pleasing to the conservative powers. In thus arguing in favor of recognizing Louis Napoleon as Emperor, Schwarzenberg urged that the three powers act in common accord. Recognition should not be given unconditionally: the three powers should demand assurances from Louis Napoleon that he would respect the treaties.

One of the questions that arises in connection with the memorandum is whether Schwarzenberg in recommending recognition of Louis Napoleon as Emperor hoped to win him as an ally. The possibility of concluding an alliance with France could be realized only if Louis Napoleon was willing to accept the territorial *status quo.* But it was precisely upon this point that doubts existed in the minds of the conservative rulers. Schwarzenberg was too shrewd a statesman not to calculate the obstacles confronting such an alliance—the traditional hostility between the two countries, the attitude of Louis Napoleon regarding the treaties of 1815, and the inevitable conflict between dynamic and static policies.[6] The principal proponent of an Austro-French *entente* was Hübner, who was inclined to take too rosy a view of its possibilities. Hübner was well aware of the defects in the character of the French ruler. "If Louis Napoleon," he wrote to Schwarzenberg on January 11, 1852, "were a statesman rather than an adventurer, if he did not appear to me condemned by his success to follow the most bizarre and adventurous routes, I would say that as long as he is found at the head of France, the policy of peace will be maintained. But being what he is, he defies all calculations and it would be rash to predict the course he will follow."[7] Yet, while he saw a restless, hesitating, contradictory mind, full of imperialistic and revolutionary projects worked out during years of imprisonment and exile, though tempered by conservative instincts—a mind which at one moment centered on wars and conquests and the next contemplated the pleasures of peaceful, orderly government— Hübner was firmly convinced that Louis Napoleon could be guided into correct channels and become a strong supporter of conservative principles if given sufficient encouragement.[8] This was an opinion he repeated over and over again in his dispatches. While there is no conclusive evidence to prove that Schwarzenberg accepted Hübner's point of view, it is undoubtedly true that he would have welcomed France to the circle of conservative powers. More than this, from what is known of his policies, he would have concluded an alliance with Louis Napoleon if no other means existed of defending Austria's vital interests. But the position of Austria at this time was not unfavorable. It is an exaggeration to stress her weakness, particularly the dangers in Italy, Germany and the east. In taking this viewpoint, one evidently thinks of the future rather than the conditions as they were in 1851-52. There was then no real Italian question and no particular reason to fear either Prussia or Russia. France was not strong at the moment, nor did England present any real threat to Austria's vital interests. Allied with Prussia

and Russia, facing no serious dangers from any side, there was no
compelling reason why Schwarzenberg should conclude such an
alliance.

Concerning England, Schwarzenberg left no doubt as to his attitude. He regarded her as a troublemaker. Her policy of encouraging
liberalism in Europe might one day prove dangerous to Austria's
position in Italy. Schwarzenberg therefore sought to isolate England
and hoped that this might be realized through the destruction
of the Anglo-French *entente*. By playing off the two maritime powers
against each other, he would prevent either or both from interfering with Austria's vital interests. In any case, he regarded England
as the more dangerous of the two. A practitioner of *realpolitik,*
Schwarzenberg's aim in advocating the recognition of Louis Napoleon
was not to conclude an alliance with France but rather to draw
the latter away from England.

The memorandum produced a rather disagreeable impression in
Berlin and St. Petersberg.[9] Nesselrode, the Russian Chancellor,
attributed Schwarzenberg's attitude to the reports of Hübner and
was inclined to discount the prospect of reëstablishing the empire
in France. There were too many difficulties in the way. "So long
as Louis Napoleon," he said to the Austrian representative, "has
the conviction that we are in accord *à trois,* he will do nothing
and perhaps (referring to England) we will even be *à quatre,* for
fortunately there is a Belgium."[10] Although Lord Malmesbury,
an old friend of Louis Napoleon, was Foreign Secretary in the
new Tory Cabinet, Nesselrode evidently believed that England's
concern over a possible French invasion of Belgium as well as
the close relations existing between Queen Victoria and King
Leopold,[11] would bring about an English *rapprochement* with the
conservative courts.[12] The chief danger, he believed, would come
not from England's liberalism but from the possibility that Louis
Napoleon would inaugurate a policy of expansion.[13] He agreed
with Schwarzenberg that the powers should not adhere strictly
to the letter of the treaty of November 20, 1815. Louis Napoleon
should be recognized as Emperor provided he promised to respect
the territorial *status quo* and provided it were clearly understood
that the exception in this case was temporary and transitory.[14] In

other words, Nesselrode insisted that the reëstablishment of the empire in France must not include the restoration of the Bonaparte dynasty. As the Prussian attitude did not differ in any important respect from that of her allies, the three conservative courts were in substantial agreement concerning the question.

This was the situation when, on April 5, 1852, death carried Schwarzenberg from the scene. It was a hard blow to the young Emperor, Franz Joseph. "The man," he wrote to his mother, the Archduchess Sophie, "who since the beginning of my reign has stood by my side with such devoted loyalty and blind affection, with an iron consistency and unshakable energy, has passed away and such a one will never come again." [15] Schwarzenberg was undoubtedly the greatest statesman of his day. Under his guidance the close ties with Russia were maintained, relations with France were improved,[16] the ambitious designs of Prussia were checked, and England was more or less isolated. Never again was the prestige of the Hapsburgs to be so high nor the influence of Vienna so important in European politics.

Immediately upon the death of Schwarzenberg, the Emperor summoned to the Ballplatz Count Ferdinand von Buol-Schauenstein, Austrian Ambassador at London. The choice of Buol was advised by Schwarzenberg, who had recommended him as Ambassador to St. Petersburg in 1848 and had later employed him at the Dresden Conference. Buol was not given the position of Minister-President because the young ruler took over the burden of the administration and kept the threads of foreign policy in his own hands. It is perhaps unfortunate for his reputation that Buol was the successor to such great ministers as Metternich and Schwarzenberg and that during his years in the Ballplatz Austrian power and prestige underwent a sharp decline. It is unfortunate because Buol was not as weak as he is frequently portrayed. That he was not a great statesman is undoubtedly true but neither was he simply "a weak copy of the original Schwarzenberg." [17] He had his faults—vain to a considerable degree, unbending in his ways, frequently irritable, and lacking in boldness and tenacity.

Friedjung, Srbik, Redlich and other Austrian historians have been unusually severe in their criticisms of Buol but it is difficult to see how he can be entirely blamed when the broad lines of Austria's policy were actually determined by the Emperor himself. Not having a free hand and not enjoying the dominant position and prestige which had been Schwarzenberg's, Buol labored under a handicap from the start.

No change of policy took place in Austria following the death of Schwarzenberg. The latter's principles were carefully adhered to, while the course of action to be followed in the question of the empire had already been determined when Buol took office. The three conservative powers were agreed on the importance of obtaining guarantees from France but it was difficult to decide as to the nature of these guarantees. They found their role as guardians of the treaties of 1815 none too comfortable since these treaties had been disregarded in allowing the downfall of the Bourbons in France in 1830, in the creation of the Belgian Kingdom, and in the suppression of the Republic of Cracow. Prussia and Austria were in particularly weak positions in insisting too much on the treaties. In 1848 Prussia had violated the Federal Pact and had invoked revolutionary law; while Austria, in seeking to introduce all her provinces into the German Confederation had threatened not only the balance of power in Germany but the entire system set up in 1815. Moreover, to impose humiliating conditions upon a new government which had need of consolidating itself, might prove a dangerous expedient and provoke the very complications they wanted to avoid.

That the imperial restoration was only a question of time, however, became clear as the propaganda in its favor increased from day to day. In May 1852, Tsar Nicholas and Nesselrode visited Vienna and discussed the question with Franz Joseph and his minister. On the 13th a secret protocol was concluded which the two courts submitted to Prussia for approval.[18] It was agreed that the mere proclamation of the empire would not in itself be a sufficient motive for severing diplomatic relations with France but that recognition should be accorded only after they had received from Louis Napoleon "sufficient guarantees concerning his peaceful policy, as well as positive assurances that he does not intend to alter the territorial limits established by the treaties."[19] Such recognition was to be *de facto* and not *de jure* in order not to change the provision of the Second Treaty of Paris, which excluded the Bonaparte dynasty forever from ruling in France. Moreover, recognition of Louis Napoleon was not to imply recognition of his successor. The protocol did not specify the form in which the guarantees should be given. Should the three powers demand a formal statement from Louis Napoleon as a condition of recognition or should they be content with such public pronouncements as he had already made?

Although Louis Napoleon was pleased to see the French public express itself in favor of the empire, he hesitated to proclaim it because of the attitude of the conservative powers. In the aim of learning the intentions of these powers, he sent his personal emissary, Baron de Heeckeren, to Vienna and Berlin. Heeckeren arrived in Vienna on the very day the secret protocol was concluded. He was received in private audience by Franz Joseph and had a lengthy discussion with Buol. He assured the latter that Louis Napoleon would respect the treaties and that while he did not desire the imperial dignity, he could not resist the popular will. Buol replied that since Louis Napoleon did not wish the honor, the question need not be discussed but "that the eventuality where the President will be forced to accept the empire will be a cause of anxiety to all friends of peace and order." [20]

From Vienna Heeckeren proceeded to Berlin where he obtained an interview with the Tsar, who was visiting Frederick William IV. The principal concern of Louis Napoleon, he assured Nicholas, was to promote the welfare of France by maintaining peace at home and abroad.[21] But in view of the desires of the French people, it was necessary to take into account the reëstablishment of the empire and in this eventuality the Prince-President offered assurances that it would involve no change in his foreign policy, no violation of the treaties or the boundaries, and that he would even go so far as to disarm if the powers would extend recognition, show him confidence and good will and support him in the struggle against the revolutionary party. Nicholas replied that while he recognized the services which Louis Napoleon had rendered to the cause of law and order in France, he strongly advised against any attempt to reëstablish the empire. He reminded Heeckeren that the position of the Prince-President was so strong that no possible advantage could be gained by a change of government.

Regarding the results of Heeckeren's mission as a setback to the imperialist movement in France, Louis Napoleon decided to postpone the execution of his plans until a more favorable moment. Meanwhile, the conservative courts directed their attention to England.[22] During the negotiations which led to the secret protocol, Prussia had proposed that England be invited to join but nothing came of this. Count Nesselrode could see no advantage in extending the protocol, while the Tsar held that in any case the initiative should come from London.[23] The three powers, however, were none the less anxious to establish a common front with England in order to resist the pretensions of Louis Napoleon. Thus, in May 1852, notes were exchanged between London and St. Petersburg and between London and Vienna concerning a possible French invasion of Belgium and it was agreed that if such an invasion took place, England would employ her fleet while the three continental powers would give military aid.[24] As to the reëstablishment of the empire in France, Lord Malmesbury expressed himself as favorable to the course of action planned by the conservative courts but was unwilling to identify himself with it.[25] He suggested, however, that recognition of the empire might be preceded by a preliminary agreement reached with Louis Napoleon, who should be urged to sign a convention as a solemn pledge of his intentions to respect the treaties and territorial arrangements. England, for her part, would exert pressure at Paris to obtain such a convention. In making this suggestion, Malmesbury announced that England would not depart from her usual custom of extending recognition to any *de facto* government without long delay and without conditions. Thus, England was willing to join the conservative powers in obtaining guarantees from Louis Napoleon but would not refuse recognition in case such guarantees were not forthcoming. To Buol such an attitude was contradictory. Convinced that there was no chance of getting Louis Napoleon to agree to a convention, he rejected the suggestion.[26] He saw clearly that any attempt in this direction would merely serve to arouse the national *amour propre* of the French. Furthermore, to conclude such a convention would be to annul the treaty relative to the exclusion of the Bonapartes and would deprive the powers of their freedom of action.[27]

Meanwhile, in France, demonstrations in favor of the empire continued. Persigny, the loyal friend and adviser of Louis Napoleon, made arrangements for the latter to visit the provinces in September 1852, and large crowds were at hand with instructions to shout "Vive l'Empéreur." At Bordeaux on October 9th Louis Napoleon accepted the empire and sought to reassure the conservative rulers. "There is," he declared, "one apprehension and that I shall set at rest. A spirit of distrust leads certain persons to say that the empire means war. I say the empire means peace. It means peace because France desires it: and when France is satisfied the world has rest."

The conservative rulers, however, were not convinced by this assertion and Nicholas, in order to show his disapproval of the events taking place in France, temporarily recalled Kisseleff from his post in Paris.[28] Yet, there could be no doubt that the proclamation of the empire was imminent. Hübner, who was following the situation closely, regarded opposition to the restoration as not only futile but childish, for he realized that it could not be prevented without inflaming French nationalism and without provoking war.

On November 4th, the French Senate was convoked to listen to a message from Louis Napoleon. Three days later it presented a *Senatus Consultum* reëstablishing the empire in the person of Louis Napoleon and conferring upon him the right to nominate his successor in default of a direct heir. The French nation was called upon to ratify this action in a plebiscite which it did by an overwhelming majority. Drouyn de Lhuys, the French Minister of Foreign Affairs,[29] declared in a dispatch to his representative at Vienna, that there was no intention of vindicating the legitimacy of the Bonaparte dynasty, or of negating the acts of the French rulers from 1815 to 1848.[30] If Louis Napoleon, he continued, had desired to base his claim to the throne on the principle of legitimacy, he would have taken the title of Napoleon V, for both Joseph and Louis, the brothers of Napoleon I, would have to be counted. Moreover, he would simply take the crown without waiting for popular sanction and would date his reign from the death of his father. "He calls himself Napoleon III because for us in France Napoleon II had been Emperor in fact as well as in law: he was called to the Empire by the abdication of Napoleon I, was proclaimed by the two chambers, and public acts were issued in his name. His reign was brief (it lasted only eight days) but it is inscribed in our history and no one can efface it, Louis Napoleon no more than another." [31] Could Louis Napoleon, he asked, ignore the wishes of the French people? Had he not earned the gratitude of Europe by establishing a strong government, suppressing anarchy, and checking the subversive movements? In objecting to the empire were the conservative rulers not losing sight of the fact that it would mean a return to dynastic principles, the very principles they were so determined to uphold? Had the Prince-President not renounced warlike intentions when he said that the empire meant peace? As for the title, why not call a thing by its name?

Such arguments failed to impress the conservative powers, who saw in the figure III a dangerous threat to the peace of Europe. While the Tsar had no strong objections to an elective empire, he was unalterably opposed to the reëstablishment of the Bonaparte dynasty and was particularly offended by the figure III. Before the *Senatus Consultum* he had appealed to Berlin and Vienna not to recognize the hereditary empire in France should it be proclaimed, and both cabinets had agreed. In the opinion of Buol the figure III involved not only a recognition of the First and Second Napoleons but a disavowal of past history. "It will be the virtual abandonment of all the engagements contracted between the powers at the time of the fall of Napoleon and the destruction of the order of things we established and maintained with so much effort up to the present." [32]

Hübner and his colleagues of Prussia and Russia found their positions exceedingly difficult. They were overwhelmed with instructions calling on them to combat the reëstablishment of the empire and, above all, the title.[33] Hübner was ordered to take no part in the fête of August 15th commemorating the birthday of Napoleon I.[34] "Between private persons who respect each other," wrote Buol, "there are sometimes delicate questions which one avoids if one wishes to live in good understanding. This is even more so the case among governments. Why should they (the French) force Europe to celebrate a fête odious to it?" [35] Buol also protested against the image of Napoleon I on the cross of the Legion of Honor.[36] Hübner, who regarded the question of the empire as a simple matter of etiquette, was severely critical of Buol's attitude. There are frequent complaints in his journal of the tone employed by Buol in his private letters. In writing to his chief, Hübner always had in mind the thought of reaching Franz Joseph. "Therefore, I have to tell the very truth in my letters; I have to tell it with forbearance and with rhetorical prudence. I have to make Count Buol understand without creating the impression that I am in opposition to my chief." [37] This was not an easy task as Hübner's position *vis-à-vis* his government was not as strong as it had been in the days of Schwarzenberg. "The Prince had great confidence in me. I was able to write to him and to speak to him from my heart and I knew beforehand that he would enter upon my ideas. Count Buol knows me very little. . . ." [38]

The conservative powers were still hopeful of persuading England to join them in a common front. On November 8th Lord Malmesbury addressed a memorandum to the governments of Austria, Prussia and Russia.[39] In this he declared that the reëstablishment of the empire was not a return to the past and that it was necessary to distinguish between the First and Second Empires. He maintained that the time to ask for explanations was when the credentials were presented and that they should accompany the recognition and not precede it. Finally, he suggested that the four powers should attempt to work out an agreement among themselves. Acting upon this suggestion, instructions were sent to the representatives of Austria, Prussia and Russia at London directing them to make every effort to bring England into an accord involving the non-recognition of the dynastic title, "Napoleon III," and the simultaneous recognition of Louis Napoleon as Emperor.[40] Malmesbury, however, was not prepared to go that far. While opposed to the figure III,[41] he informed the Russian Minister, Brunnow, that his government would accept Louis Napoleon "as Emperor *de facto in presente* and would not allude to hereditary chances, retrospective or future, but leave those to the French people." [42] Drouyn de Lhuys had already given

Lord Cowley, British Ambassador to Paris, verbal assurances that Louis Napoleon acknowledged all the acts which had taken place since 1815 and laid no hereditary claim to the French throne.[43] Malmesbury insisted that these assurances be put into writing and to this Drouyn de Lhuys agreed. After receiving the written assurances, the English Cabinet, on December 2nd, decided to recognize Napoleon III "without further reserve." [44]

There were, of course, several reasons for England's attitude. The French threat to Belgium did not greatly disturb the English statesmen who, moreover, saw the advantage of retaining the good will of Louis Napoleon as a possible ally against Russian pretensions in the east. At the same time, the tension in Anglo-French relations had become less acute. On the eve of his departure for London to attend the funeral of the Duke of Wellington, Lord Cowley had an interview with Louis Napoleon, who assured him that his claim to the throne was based not upon the principle of legitimacy but upon "the unanimous vote of the French people," and that he had every intention of observing the treaties though he could not make a public and solemn declaration to this effect without offending the susceptibility of the French nation.[45] The fact that France was represented at the funeral of the Iron Duke, who had been an irreconcilable enemy of the First Empire, made a deep impression upon the English people.

Though England was no longer to be counted upon, the Tsar did not abandon hope of preventing the reëstablishment of the dynastic empire in France. Ignoring the *Senatus Consultum* and the plebiscite, he appealed directly to Louis Napoleon by means of an autograph letter. In this he acknowledged the great services which the Prince-President had rendered to the cause of order and urged him not to take a title which would offend the dignity of the powers and cause a rift in their relations with him. The letter was accompanied by a lengthy memorandum from Nesselrode, which developed the reasons why Russia could not recognize Louis Napoleon as Napoleon III.[46] Nesselrode declared that the title was an abnegation of the past, rendering null and void everything which had been done in 1814-1815, and making the period of thirty-eight years since then appear as a dream, Louis XVIII, Charles X and Louis Philippe as mere phantoms, and those princes who were confirmed in their powers in 1815 as usurpers. The acceptance of the title would be a rude blow to the prestige of the powers and a humiliation for Europe. The memorandum produced a bad impression in Paris and did much to offset the appeal in the Tsar's letter. In any case, that letter arrived too late. It was delivered to Louis Napoleon at St. Cloud by Kisseleff on November 28th and as it was addressed to the President of the French Republic rather than to the Emperor of the French, Drouyn de Lhuys persuaded his master not to reply. Nicholas, of course, was deeply offended.

On December 1st, Drouyn de Lhuys issued a circular officially notifying the powers concerning the reëstablishment of the empire. The members of the diplomatic corps were requested to ask their governments for letters of credit. The first state to extend recognition was the Kingdom of the Two Sicilies, whose credentials were presented on the third, the day following the coronation ceremonies at Notre Dame. Switzerland, Piedmont, Belgium and other secondary states extended recognition within ten days, while England was the first great power to take this step.

Realizing that they no longer could prevent the reëstablishment of the empire, the conservative rulers decided to delay recognition. Their representatives at Paris had merely acknowledged the circular of Drouyn de Lhuys while letting it be known that a joint reply would be given later. For the Tsar, postponement was unavoidable as he had received no reply to his autograph letter.

Just what form the joint reply should take had not been determined when the empire was proclaimed. The secret protocol of May stipulated that recognition should be extended only after the three powers had received from Louis Napoleon guarantees concerning his peaceful intentions and concerning the treaties and existing territorial arrangements. It was also stated that the recognition of Louis Napoleon would not imply the recognition of his successor. In other words, the three powers were firmly opposed to the return of the dynastic empire in France. Despite the categorical nature of these provisions, however, the Russian Government seemed disposed to alter them somewhat. Thus, in his autograph letter to Louis Napoleon, the Tsar made no mention of guarantees and his only reservation concerned the title. In the eyes of Buol this was hardly consistent with the May protocol. On December 2, 1852, he sent an important dispatch to Mensdorff, a copy of which was submitted to the Russian Cabinet.[47] Maintaining that the reservation concerning the title was important though incidental, he proposed that recognition be made simultaneously by the three courts; that if guarantees could not be obtained, at least they should be mentioned in the credentials; that it should be explicitly stated that the figure III could not be recognized, and that if the question of succession were raised by the French Government, the three courts would delay a reply; and, finally, as to the salutation to be employed toward the new Emperor, Buol suggested "Sire" instead of "Mon Frère." He added that Franz Joseph did not feel that he could give the address "Mon Frère" to a ruler elected by the people.

This last proposal has become the subject of much discussion. Why, it is asked, did Buol suggest "Sire" when Austria, as will be seen later, employed the customary salutation in her credentials? One explanation given is that Buol suspected England of trying to persuade Russia to recognize the title without demanding guarantees.[48] The Tsar, it is well known, laid great emphasis upon an agreement with England and Buol evidently feared that he might make common cause with Louis Napoleon in return for concessions in the east. As this would mean the isolation of Austria and probably threaten her position in Germany, Italy and the Balkans, Buol in his dispatch urged Russia at least to remain loyal to the spirit of the May protocol. He made it clear that Austria would not set aside principles simply to reach an understanding with England. Whether his proposal was a blunder as is sometimes held or a shrewdly calculated step to prevent a *rapprochement* between Nicholas and Louis Napoleon,[49] it nevertheless exposed him to the criticism of being niggardly and lacking in loyalty.

In any case, Nicholas fell for the bait and agreed that the customary address should not be employed. On the other hand, no mention of guarantees was made in the official credentials sent to Kisseleff. Instead, it was stated that Russia was reassured by the terms of the French notification and by the speech of Louis Napoleon to the legislative body that he recognized the governments which had preceded him and that he intended to uphold the treaties and existing territorial arrangements. Nor was any mention made of the title "Napoleon III." Louis Napoleon was simply "S. M. Empéreur des Français," and the salutation employed in the credentials was "Sire et bon ami." [50]

As for Prussia, her policy was dictated solely by self-interest. While the cautious and vacillating Frederick William IV entertained a feeling of great aversion for Louis Napoleon, he was at the same time very much afraid of a French invasion of the Rhine. Yet, he had no intention of challenging France alone and, indeed, was most anxious to avoid giving offense. On December 18th he received a visit from his nephew, Franz Joseph of Austria, who came to Berlin in order to discuss the situation in France. The two rulers decided to employ the customary salutation of "Mon Frère" in their letters recognizing the new empire. Back of this decision lay strategic considerations. As neighboring states of France and having the Rhine and Lombardy-Venetia to defend, the two German powers were naturally more exposed to attack from Napoleon than was Russia. Besides, in spite of his aversion for the Bonapartes and his horror of the principle of national sovereignty, Franz Joseph dared not surrender too completely to the Tsar.

This action on the part of his two allies greatly offended Nicholas, who was now left alone to employ the obnoxious salutation.[51] At a parade on Christmas day he reproached Mensdorff and Rochow, the Prussian Minister, because of the sudden change of attitude which, he declared, he had not expected after Buol's dispatch of December 2nd.[52] He was particularly peeved because no warning of this change had been given him beforehand and for this he blamed Buol. Prussia alone, he insisted, would not have dared to use the customary salutation had Vienna remained firm. As it was, the lack of agreement would give Louis Napoleon the impression that the alliance of the three powers was weak.

There seems to be little doubt, however, that Austria would have adhered to her original plan regarding the salutation had Prussia done likewise. In a dispatch to Hübner, Buol wrote: "If our two allies had expressed themselves in favor of the application of the formula, 'Sire and good friend,' then we also would have accepted it. But from the moment we were convinced that Prussia resisted, it would have been difficult to separate from her. If the two great (German) powers are not united, confusion immediately results among the German states. As it is, only Russia remains consistent with herself, for we would have refused Louis Napoleon that which we believed possible to grant to Louis Philippe." [53]

Meanwhile, the delay of the conservative courts in extending recognition caused considerable irritation at the Tuileries. There was some talk of reprisals, while England seized the occasion to urge a close *entente* between the two maritime powers.[54] Drouyn de Lhuys regarded the concert of the three courts as a threat to France and declared that he could not comprehend the use of the word "allies" since there was no reason for reviving coalitions. "The three courts are allies," Hübner reminded him, "because they are bound by a treaty. The Emperor of France is not their ally because he does not as yet exist for them. He can only become such when he is welcomed to the European family and if he observes the treaties and follows a policy similar to theirs." [55]

The representatives of the three courts held a "council of war" in the boudoir of Princess Liewen where they compared their instructions.[56] Two days were spent in planning a course of action. It was finally decided that Hübner and Hatzfeldt, the Prussian Minister, should withhold their credentials until Kisseleff had presented his. On January 3, 1853, Kisseleff had an interview with Drouyn de Lhuys to whom he submitted the letters of credit and carefully explained that the Tsar, while desiring to be on good terms with Napoleon, could not recognize as brothers those rulers holding their thrones by virtue of the principle of national sovereignty. The two governments, argued Kisseleff, had different principles.[57] The French Minister replied caustically. He reminded Kisseleff that the Russian dynasty was still a young one and had no right to make such pretensions and he asked why Nicholas should adopt an attitude different from that of Alexander I, who had addressed Napoleon I as "Mon Frère." He promised to submit the letters to the Emperor but warned Kisseleff that he would advise against their acceptance since the customary salutation was not employed.

The affair had now reached a crisis, for unless Napoleon were willing to swallow his pride, a break between France and the conservative courts appeared inevitable. The Emperor convened a meeting of the Council of Ministers. Fould, Minister of Finance, advised him to disregard the insult but Drouyn de Lhuys and Persigny strenuously opposed acceptance of the Russian letters on the ground that the salutation placed Napoleon outside the family of European rulers and implied that the empire was only transitory.[58] This argument impressed Napoleon but he decided to reserve a decision until the views of the Austrian and Prussian representatives could be ascertained. On January 4th Drouyn de Lhuys had interviews with Hübner and Hatzfeldt and explained to them the French attitude. Hübner warned him against making a political affair out of a mere question of etiquette and declared that if the Russian credentials were refused, it would be necessary for him to withhold his own.[59] Essentially the same language was employed by Hatzfeldt and the solidarity of the three courts was clearly demonstrated.

Persuaded by his Foreign Minister, the Emperor agreed to announce to the Council of Ministers, which was to meet on the following day, his refusal to accept the Russian letters. But before this action was taken, Morny, who was in favor of good relations with Russia, prevailed upon him to change his mind. When the Council of Ministers convened on the fifth, therefore, Napoleon announced that he had decided to accept the Russian credentials.[60] Later in the day Kisseleff was received in the Tuileries by the Emperor who, setting aside the usual practice of handing the credentials to the Foreign Minister, read them himself.[61] Then, turning to Kisseleff, he said: "You will thank His Imperial Majesty warmly for his kindness and, above all, for the expression 'Good Friend' of which he has made use, for one has to endure one's brothers but chooses one's friends." This marked the end of the crisis although Napoleon postponed audiences with Hübner and Hatzfeldt a whole week in order to show his displeasure.[62]

Viewed from a century later the affair appears somewhat inconsequential. Yet, there are certain factors in the situation which must be considered. The settlement of 1815 was still the public law of Europe despite the breaches which had been made in its façade. That settlement was directed against the France of Napoleon I and was designed to prevent a recurrence of the policies he had pursued. The exclusion of the Bonapartes from the throne of France was not a mere act of revenge on the part of those who had suffered at the hands of the Corsican Conquerer but was considered a necessary safeguard to peace. Surely those whose interest it was to maintain the treaties could not regard with indifference the reëstablishment of the French Empire, particularly by one whose express aim was to destroy those treaties. Yet, as we have seen, it was not the question of the empire as such which aroused the greatest fear, for the conservative courts were prepared to accept that, but the title. Not only was the title a violation of the treaties but in the eyes of the conservative rulers it was a direct challenge to the very principles they were pledged to defend. To recognize the title was to admit that these principles were no longer applicable. On the other hand, one cannot deny that in their strict adherence to legalism, the conservative courts were blind to the realities of the situation. Recent history amply and clearly demonstrates the futility of attempting to perpetuate a settlement which imposes humiliating conditions upon a great nation. If Louis Napoleon was regarded by the conservative rulers as a threat to the established order, by the French he was hailed as a symbol of freedom from its restrictions. In treating him as an intruder into their charmed circle, as an adventurer and a *parvenu,* these rulers revealed a singular lack of perspicacity, for such satisfactions as may have come to them momentarily, were to be paid for in later years. How much their disdainful attitude contributed to the bringing on of the Crimean War and the hostility to Austria which culminated in the Italian War of 1859 is not easy to determine, but Louis Napoleon did not forget the affront.

CHAPTER THREE

Beginnings of the Crimean War

FOLLOWING THE DIPLOMATIC crisis over the recognition of the Second Empire, Austria showed remarkable agility in adjusting herself to the situation. More than that she tried to persuade Napoleon to pursue a policy based upon the principles of law and order. Facing financial difficulties, embarrassed by disorders in Switzerland, and by threats of revolution in Italy and Turkey, Austria had need of Napoleon's good will. Numerous marks of favor were bestowed in an effort to overcome the Emperor's resentment and to wean him from his revolutionary tendencies. These efforts, however, met with little success for Napoleon had no thought of adopting a conservative foreign policy. "I am very absolutistic at home," he said to one of his intimates, "unfortunately, I am compelled to be and always will be. I will even be despotic. But outside, I will be liberal, and very liberal." [1]

Both Schwarzenberg and Buol made attempts to persuade Napoleon to join Austria in taking common measures in Italy and Switzerland but to no avail. Indeed, he threatened to invade Belgium if Austria sent an army into Switzerland.[2] Many French political refugees—Orleanists, Republicans and Socialists—had flocked to Belgium where they conducted a violent press campaign against Napoleon. What especially ruffled him, however, was not so much the actions of these refugees as the announcement that the Archduchess Marie of Austria was to marry the Duke of Brabant, heir to the Belgian throne. This aroused his suspicion that Austria was in league with his enemies, a suspicion which was strengthened by the cordial reception tendered to King Leopold in Vienna. Napoleon at this time hated Leopold because of his connection with the Orleanists. There was widespread apprehension of a sudden French invasion of Belgium.[3] Indeed, in the spring of 1853 Napoleon seemed entirely preoccupied with Belgium. "For him the eastern question does not exist. He speaks only of Belgium and Switzerland, offense and vengeance." [4] The marriage announcement had let loose a resentment against Austria that had been smoldering since the Second Empire was proclaimed.

Of much greater significance in the relations between Austria and France was the reopening of the eastern question by Tsar Nicholas of Russia in February 1853. Beginning with a rather minor dispute between Roman Catholic and Greek Orthodox pilgrims concerning rights to certain buildings in the Holy Land, it led to demands by Russia on Turkey, which culminated in war and the intervention of England and France. Although the entrance of Russian troops into the Principalities of Moldavia and Wallachia early in July provoked great excitement in the European cabinets, Tsar Nicholas apparently believed that a war with Turkey could be localized. In any event, he counted on the benevolent neutrality, if not the active aid of his allies, Austria and Prussia.

It was not long before the Tsar realized that he had misjudged the situation. England's opposition became a foregone conclusion once it was clear that the Russian plans threatened the Ottoman Empire and her own interests in the east. In the case of France, the decision depended as much on the question of interests as on the personal desires of Napoleon. Not only did he want to prevent Russia from establishing a preponderant position in the Mediterranean, but he was determined to smash the Holy Alliance, which he considered the principal obstacle to the triumph of the principle of nationalities. The preservation of the Ottoman Empire was of secondary importance.

The Tsar experienced his greatest disappointment, however, in the hopes he placed on his allies, particularly Austria. More than any other power, Austria was interested in preventing the outbreak of war in the east, above all, a war in which England and France would be lined up against Russia. In view of her geographic position, her internal conditions, still unsettled after the upheaval of 1848-49, and her ethnic problems, the ambitious plans of the Tsar were decidedly dangerous. Yet, Franz Joseph had no desire to oppose Nicholas. Not only did he remember the aid which the latter had given in the dark days of 1849, but he felt bound by the principles of the Holy Alliance, and he knew it would be easy for Russia to excite Pan Slav agitation in his heterogeneous territories. On the other hand, he realized that Austria could not remain a passive spectator while Russia proceeded to destroy the Ottoman Empire. That his own interests conflicted with those of the Tsar was clear enough. Whereas the maintenance of the Ottoman Empire was considered to be vital to Austria, Russia favored the establishment of independent Christian states in the Balkans subject to her influence. For the time being, Franz Joseph decided to resist the Russian designs as far as possible without actually drawing the sword. The appeals which Nicholas addressed to him throughout the spring and summer of 1853 fell on deaf ears.[5]

While Franz Joseph resisted the appeals of the Tsar, his Foreign Minister sought to prevent the outbreak of war by means of diplomacy. Buol assured Westmorland, the British Ambassador to Vienna, that Austria regarded the maintenance of the independence and territorial integrity of Turkey as essential to her interests and would conclude no engagement with Russia barring the employment of arms against that power.[6] Since, however, Russia had asked Austria to intercede with the Porte, Buol urged England and France to have confidence in the assurances of the Tsar that the occupation of the Principalities did not mean war. Turning aside a suggestion of England and France for a conference of the signatory powers of the Treaty of 1841 to consider ways and means of maintaining Turkish integrity, Buol proposed direct negotiations between Russia and Turkey.[7] This was rejected by France on the ground that Turkey would refuse and that it would convert the eastern question from one of European interest into one of a private understanding between Russia and Turkey.[8] On October 4, 1853, Turkey sent an ultimatum to St. Petersburg declaring that war would follow within fifteen days if Russia refused to evacuate the Principalities. Despite the outbreak of hostilities (October 29th) Buol did not abandon hope of a peaceful settlement and proposed that a joint note be drawn up by the conference of the four powers, Austria, England, France and Prussia, which had meanwhile convened in Vienna.[9] The joint note, dated December 5th, requested Turkey to make known the conditions under which she was willing to conclude peace.[10] Unfortunately for Buol's efforts, the destruction of a Turkish squadron by the Russians in the harbor of Sinope (November 30th) delayed presentation of the note to the Porte, while it led England and France to inform St. Petersburg that their fleets would take control of the Black Sea. Near the end of December the joint note was presented to the Porte and elicited a favorable reply.[11] On January 12, 1854, the Vienna Conference reconvened and on the following day signed a protocol stating that the terms set forth by Turkey conformed to the ideas of the conference and should be communicated to St. Petersburg.[12]

Still confident that he could persuade Austria to take his side, Nicholas continued his efforts in this direction. But realizing that Franz Joseph was unmoved by his personal appeals, the Tsar sent Count Orloff to Vienna with instructions to make known the conditions upon which Russia would conclude peace and to obtain Austria's neutrality.[13] In return, the Tsar promised to reach an understanding with Austria and Prussia concerning the reëstablishment of the political equilibrium in the east. Baron Budberg, the Russian Minister at Berlin, was charged with a similar mission to the Prussian Government. Orloff's instructions employed the ideology of the Holy Alliance.[14] They pointed out that England wanted revenge for the defeats which Russia had inflicted upon her policy and after the war would be Austria's worst enemy in Hungary, Italy and the east. How could Austria think of aiding England to defeat the Russians? There were three possible courses which the two German powers could follow. First, they could join Russia and bring on a general war. Secondly, they could join the western powers. This would not ruin Russia but in the end the dominating influence of France would be very threatening to the German states. Finally, they could remain neutral and to insure their neutrality against aggression by England and France, the Tsar was prepared to promise military assistance.[15]

To Orloff's request for a declaration of strict neutrality, Buol replied that this would be possible only if Russia agreed to respect the independence and territorial integrity of the Ottoman Empire, evacuate the Principalities, and not bring about changes there which would alter the relations of the Sultan to his subjects, and not cross the Danube.[16] When asked point-blank by Franz Joseph if Russia would promise to maintain the *status quo* in Turkey and not cross the Danube, Orloff was unable to give a definite answer but showed him an autograph letter from the Tsar.[17] In this, Nicholas declared that Russia would not cross the Danube so long as the attitude of the western powers or the stubbornness of Turkey did not necessitate a change.[18] As for the *status quo,* it could no longer be spoken of since Turkey was completely under the influence of England and France. While declaring that he would never permit the liberated Slav subjects of the Sultan to come again under the Turkish yoke, Nicholas promised to see to it that they exercised no harmful influence over the Slavs of the Austrian Monarchy. Finally, he urged Franz Joseph to maintain the old alliance of the three courts.[19] No longer deceived as to the real aims of the Tsar and fully conscious of their threat to Austria's position in the Balkans, Franz Joseph refused to bind himself by a written engagement. The Russian proposal was definitely rejected.[20]

At Berlin the mission of Baron Budberg also ended in failure. While Frederick William IV was prevented by religious scruples from siding with Turkey, the aggressive designs of the Tsar precluded an understanding with Russia. In a letter to Nicholas, the King explained that it was morally impossible for him to contract a written engagement.[21] He had been asked by London, Paris and Vienna what side he intended to take in case of a rupture between Russia and the western powers, and had replied that Prussia's attitude was one of impartiality. "I am honor-bound not to sign anything after that." Believing that an agreement with Russia would be the signal for war with England and France, Frederick William advised Nicholas to accept the proposals of the Vienna Conference.[22]

The refusal of Austria and Prussia to accept the Russian offer paralyzed the Holy Alliance although technically it did not end until the conclusion of the tripartite treaty of December 2, 1854. The failure of Orloff's mission signified that the bonds between Austria and Russia were loosened. Thereafter Austria drifted farther away from her ally and nearer to the western powers.

For the moment, however, Vienna was determined to retain freedom of action and followed a policy which can be described as "watchful waiting." It was a logical position to take particularly since England and France had not yet entered the war. By delaying her decision and by seeking to avoid the danger of being drawn into a situation where she would become the principal target for Russia, Austria had much to gain and very little to lose. But admitting that such a course was dictated by her own interests, it was a difficult one to maintain. From the beginning of the eastern crisis there had been pressure from France as well as from Russia. "The circle in which we now move is rather thankless," wrote Buol in June 1853; "pressed from both sides we fail to satisfy either one. One charges us with ingratitude, the other reproaches us with subserviency and offers us support in order to regain our independence." [23]

At Paris, Hübner resisted as best he could the pressure of the French. He refuted the charge of Austrian subserviency to Russia by explaining to Drouyn de Lhuys that the reason for the Tsar's intervention in Hungary in 1849 was simply to prevent the spread of revolution to Poland, "like a neighbor who hastens to extinguish a fire which threatens his own house." [24] This assistance, he added, did not prevent Franz Joseph from combining the duties of friendship with the desire to preserve peace and the Ottoman Empire.

With the outbreak of the Russo-Turkish War, the French pressure increased. Napoleon refused to entertain a suggestion made by the representatives of Austria, Prussia and Russia at Paris that he employ his influence with England in order to keep the war localized. To the Duc de Morny, who acted as intermediary for Hübner, he said: "I cannot separate myself from England merely because the northern courts desire it. Without England I will be isolated in Europe. Alliance with revolution repels me and is dangerous but I have no choice. Moreover, in the eyes of the continental courts I am a revolutionary. They do not care for me." [25] All sorts of arguments were employed in order to persuade Austria to take sides against the Tsar. Drouyn de Lhuys hinted that she might annex the Principalities even without compensation for the other powers.[26] But he also resorted to threats and declared to Hübner that Austria could not remain neutral without committing suicide and that if she joined Russia, France would stir up revolutions in Hungary, Italy and Poland.[27] In the end Austria would lose her rank as a great power since a victory for Russia would make her a tributary of that state, while a Russian defeat would leave her at the mercy of the western powers and revolution. Napoleon was equally emphatic. On the one hand, he proposed the conclusion of a secret *entente* between Austria and France for the purpose of preventing both Russian aggression against Turkey and the spread of revolution in Europe. At the same time he uttered a warning:[28]

You must declare yourself either for or against. If you are for me, that is, for Europe, I will be for you with all my forces and will support you where you are weakest. I will see to it that they do not stir in Italy and will conclude an agreement concerning the means of reëstablishing order in a definitive manner in Italy, Switzerland and everywhere on the continent.

On the other hand, if you are for Russia—since neutrality is impossible for Austria in a war between Russia and England and France in the east—if you declare yourself for Russia then, naturally, in spite of myself, I will attack you where you are most vulnerable. I will stir up Italy.

Although Buol was not intimidated by the French threats, he was nevertheless annoyed. "The idea of wishing to engage us by means of threats in a war which is not agreeable to us seems so monstrous to me that I refuse to attach credence to it. It certainly cannot change our attitude. No doubt we can be forced into war but to compel us to make it, never!" [29] He was aware that the attempt of the western powers to force Russia to yield was certain to enlarge the conflict and thus increase the difficulties facing the Austrian Government. Since the Tsar had already announced his intention of remaining on the defensive and had assured Franz Joseph that he contemplated neither conquests nor an extension of power, Buol felt that this was all that one could reasonably expect. "The confidence of the Emperor in the words of his august friend is complete and he experiences a real repugnance about associating himself in any act which implies a confession of doubt." [30] Hence, any suspicion concerning the Tsar's motives would only cause the latter to abandon his moderate attitude and would destroy hope of a peaceful settlement. Buol rejected Napoleon's suggestion for a secret Austro-French *entente* and in its place proposed a general agreement which would include Russia. Only if the latter refused to participate or adopted aggressive tactics, would Austria be prepared to reach an agreement with France. He made it clear that the western powers must not count on Austria to drive the Russians from the Principalities or attempt to force her into a war she did not want.

We do not wish to fight either for the Crescent or for the Greek Cross; we can be drawn into the struggle only by questions of European significance connected with it. But even then we do not permit others to impose upon us either the time or the field of operations. It is not from Paris that the word will come if we decide to enter Wallachia or Serbia. Let them rest assured that we shall not take up the challenge. They should stop dreading or hoping at Paris. No doubt Austria will have an important word to say in this question; perhaps she will have the last word, but she will not be fool enough to fire the first shot of the cannon.[31]

In view of her geographic position and her interests in the Balkans, Austria could not expect to evade the issue indefinitely. At its best, a neutral position would afford only a temporary escape. "Do you seriously believe," Buol was asked by Bourqueney, French Minister at Vienna, "that it is possible to maintain a real neutrality, that is, a perfect balance between the good and the bad, the just and the unjust? Will you remain equally the friend of those who violate the public law of Europe and those who defend it, of those who attack the Ottoman Empire and those who protect it?" [32] Such a policy seemed to the French Minister a dangerous illusion. Buol was aware of its weakness and of the ease with which Napoleon could precipitate matters by stirring up revolutions in Italy and Hungary. He tried to reassure Bourqueney that Austria had not abandoned the principles which she held in common with the western powers though she preferred to proceed more cautiously. "We found you a bit too hasty during the past three weeks; you, in turn, found us a bit slow. However, we draw nearer and nearer to each other and with an identical policy, God willing, we shall never separate." [33] From his side Franz Joseph declared to Bourqueney: "I will not abandon any of the principles we uphold together; nothing will make me deviate from the common aim we follow." [34]

Though inclined to the side of Turkey and the western powers by the Russian attitude, Austria preferred to keep her hands free. To Hübner this policy seemed too cautious and he urged Buol to conclude an alliance with the western powers.[35] He had apparently expected that the rejection of the Tsar's proposal concerning neutrality would be followed immediately by a positive orientation toward the west.[36] "For a great power," he wrote to Buol on January 30, 1854, "neutrality is possible only so long as its special interests and the European equilibrium are not in danger. Beyond that, neutrality becomes impossible." [37] Even if it were possible, argued Hübner, it would not be a wise course as it offered no assurance for the security of Austria and would frighten rather than calm European public opinion inasmuch as it would enable Russia to defeat the western powers. Neutrality was not a pledge of peace but a means of provoking a general war; whereas intervention on the side of England and France would quickly convince Russia of the wisdom of coming to terms. Moreover, a policy of neutrality would encourage Russia to take steps which would end by making her the enemy of Austria. Predicting that Austria would disappear from the map of Europe as an independent state and would become the first vassal of the Tsar if the latter were permitted to increase his influence in the east, Hübner urged Buol to take decisive measures to check the Russian advance. "Russia wants to advance. Austria ought to warn her to halt and to stop her even at the cost of her last soldier and her last florin. That is the eastern question. Everyone knows it. Let us have the courage to see it and, if necessary, to say it to Russia." [38]

Hübner saw three factors which were holding back Austria from taking the side of the western powers: the Holy Alliance, the fear of exchanging this for an alliance with England and France which might prove less durable, and the obligation of recognizing the services rendered by the Tsar in 1849. None of these, in his opinion, was of sufficient importance to warrant a policy of neutrality. The Holy Alliance was strong when directed against a common danger but weak whenever it was a question of Turkey, for in the eastern question revolution was the natural ally of Russia. As for an alliance with the western powers, did not Austria and France have common interests in combatting liberalism in the west and the designs of Russia in the east? And was not the only possible basis for an alliance between independent states a community of interests? "So long as Russia makes war on Turkey, she cannot be an ally of Austria; and an alliance must be with those powers which aid Austria by stopping Russia." [39] To those who urged the necessity of recognizing the services of 1849, Hübner replied:

This is not serious since no obligation can go so far as suicide. Moreover, in 1849 the august friend of the Emperor, while performing a magnanimous act, at the same time discharged a duty toward his own states. I throw out once and for all this argument which in reality is not one. Meanwhile, it perhaps will be useful to inform the Russian Cabinet that the forbearance and the abnegation with which Austria has carried on negotiations for nearly a year is proof in our eyes of gratitude. This is not all. The *status quo* existing between Russia and Turkey is hardly tolerable for Austria. A splendid occasion is presented to deprive Russia of part of the exorbitant advantages she is assured by her treaties with Turkey. France and England have united against Russia and are disposed to go to the limit; they implore the aid of Austria in order to reduce Russian preponderance. Well, Austria has not yielded. Up till now, she has insisted upon the maintenance of the *status quo ante bellum*. That is our recognition of the debt. It seems to me that it has been largely discharged.

Having in this manner disposed of the factors which were restraining Austria, Hübner pointed out that she alone could decide the eastern question, and that only by taking decisive action could she hope to win Russia's respect or the good will of the western powers. "Do not fear, then, to get involved with Russia. That is already done. Do not hope to coax her to the limit by methods that will be taken for weakness and will only encourage her resistance. Let us say to her amicably and without boasting but at the same time clearly: 'You are where you should not be, leave!' From this language Russia will understand that the complacent ally of whom she dreamt can well become a fearful adversary whom it is better to conciliate, with whom it is henceforth necessary to reckon." [40] Not only did Hübner emphasize the need for a reorientation of Austria's policy but, in addition, he suggested certain measures which she could take at the present stage of the crisis. These included the concentration of troops along the frontiers of Serbia and Wallachia; the conclusion of an engagement with France concerning Italy; the arrangement of a loan at Paris and London; and a demand that the Principalities be evacuated by Russia within a fixed period.[41]

One reason for Hübner's strong advocacy of a western orientation was his belief that through an alliance with Austria, Napoleon could be weaned from revolutionary and nationalistic tendencies to a frankly conservative policy. In this belief he was encouraged by Drouyn de Lhuys, who never missed a chance to express his hope of reaching an understanding with Austria as the strongest guarantee against subversive agitation in Europe. An argument which the French Minister employed at this time was that without Austrian support, the war against Russia would be fought in the Crimea and as the burden in this case would fall on England, the latter would reap the advantages—a prospect neither Paris nor Vienna could desire.[42] Besides, in seeking a solution with the exclusive support of England, Napoleon would not be able to prevent the Poles, Hungarians and Italians from participating in the war.[43] Drouyn de Lhuys declared that he simply could not understand why Austria should wish to be neutral. Hübner explained to him, however, that the word "neutrality" had not been mentioned in Buol's dispatches nor, so far as he knew, in the explanations which the Austrian Foreign Minister had given to Bourqueney. "Neutrality in the mouth of a great power can have no other meaning than that of abstention so long as the interests of that power, special as well as European, do not permit it to take part in the struggle." [44]

In the meantime, the hope of localizing the Russo-Turkish conflict was rapidly vanishing. On February 6, 1854, Russia broke off diplomatic relations with England and France. Negotiations now began for a united front of the four powers, Austria, England, France and Prussia. Late in February a draft convention was drawn up which called for the integrity of the Ottoman Empire, the evacuation of the Principalities, the revision of the Treaty of 1841, and continued efforts to bring about peace on the basis of the protocol of January 13, 1854.[45] This protocol, which had set forth conditions of peace acceptable to Turkey and the Vienna Conference, had been rejected by Russia. On February 27th England and France sent ultimatums to St. Petersburg demanding the evacuation of the Principalities by April 30th or war would follow.[46] Actually war was declared on March 27th and on April 10th England and France signed an alliance and invited all states of Europe to join.

The plan for a united four-power front failed to materialize owing to the refusal of the Prussian King to sign the convention.[47] Austria, on the other hand, adhered to its principles though Buol insisted that its terms remain secret until hostilities between Russia and the western powers had actually started.[48] In approving the ultimatums and in supporting them at St. Petersburg, was it Austria's intention to give more than diplomatic assistance? This appears to have been the impression of England and France.[49] On March 2nd Napoleon informed the *Corps Législatif* that while Austria had not yet entered an alliance with France, she "will enter." These words caused a slight panic in the Paris Bourse, which had expected no delay. "In fact," wrote Hübner, "nothing could better reveal than this incident the immense value which the most peaceful section of the populace of France and all countries, namely, the men of finance, attach to the close union of Austria and France." [50] The thought that his government was considering the advisability of concluding an alliance with the western powers was quite enough to send Hübner's hopes soaring. Austria's future, he declared, was at stake and it was now a question of safeguarding her vital interests: the majesty of the throne, the independence of the state, the universality of the Church, and the freedom of her great commercial artery.[51] Never, in his opinion, did a war offer greater chances of success and never was there a more sacred cause to defend. But Austria should have the courage to continue the struggle and not be held back by secondary considerations, "not wish to spare the enemy by a generous but fatal sentiment and, above all, not choose half-measures which would be our certain ruin." [52]

Despite the impressions of England and France, and despite the hopes of Hübner, it is clear from an examination of the Austrian documents that no military support was contemplated at this time. Indeed, Buol left absolutely no doubt that while associating herself with the policy of the western powers, Austria was determined to retain her freedom of action until such a moment as her interests compelled her to give material aid. [53] An attempt made by Bourqueney to obtain a written engagement regarding Austrian military cooperation against Russia ended in failure. All that he succeeded in getting was an oral promise from Franz Joseph to the effect that the western powers could be assured of the support of the Austrian army from the day when their troops appeared on the banks of the Danube. [54] In no case would Austria take the first step.

That Vienna did not attend to go beyond diplomatic support at this stage of the crisis is also evident from the fact that Buol considered it necessary to curb Hübner's enthusiasm and to warn him to avoid any commitments. "There should be no haste in declaring war. We prefer to prepare for war and to talk peace." [55] The western powers, he stated, should not expect Austria to enter into military arrangements so long as they were not in agreement as to their plans of campaign. Austria would not follow them to Asia nor would she compromise herself if they scattered their forces. Only if they sent their armies to the Danube would she be ready to join them but even then only after they had made peace proposals acceptable to all Europe. "Do you not find," he asked, "that there is too much affectation in proclaiming an alliance which is only in the process of being made? The persistence also which is shown in congratulating us on the recovery of our independence, is it not put on too much? In alliances there should be mutual respect and even mutual concessions; that is what we have observed toward Russia and we deny that state of servitude of which we are accused. But if we have escaped from one dependence, we have no desire to embrace another. . . . It seems to me that they are

trying to make us pull the chestnuts out of the fire and to declare
war and fight battles for others. Turkey already finds herself in
that position. I depend upon your prudence to the end that we do
not find ourselves in the position of defending a role we most certainly would not accept. The Emperor Franz Joseph does not like
the manner in which France and England have embarked upon
this great affair and he recommends to you to safeguard particularly
the freedom of action we desire to preserve." [56]

Negotiations designed to draw Austria and Prussia into an alliance with the western powers continued after the collapse of the
four-power convention. Austria's active participation in the war depended, however, on several factors. In the first place, it would
be necessary for the allies to send their troops to the Danube, for
at no time did Franz Joseph consider a campaign in the Crimea.
The concentration of Russian troops in the Principalities and in
Poland was a direct threat to the Austrian Monarchy. Secondly, the
support of Prussia and the German states was deemed necessary
before Austria could run the risk of challenging the Tsar. Without
such support, Prussia might take advantage of Austria's involvement
in order to acquire leadership in the Bund. Finally, Vienna desired
a guarantee from Napoleon that the *status quo* in Italy would be
maintained while the war in the east was in progress.

With regard to Italy, Napoleon had already sought to reassure
Austria. An article which appeared in the *Moniteur* on February 21,
1854, and which was written under the direct inspiration of the
Emperor, disclaimed any revolutionary aims and warned revolutionary elements that they could expect no support from France.
Buol wanted something more binding than this and instructed
Hübner to enter negotiations with the French Government for a
treaty which would guarantee the *status quo* in the Peninsula. [57]
France was willing to give such a guarantee in return for support
against Russia. Although Buol preferred that the treaty be limited
to Italy and that the question of Austria's participation in the
eastern conflict be regulated by a general agreement to be signed
by the four powers, he yielded in the face of Napoleon's insistence
for mutual concessions. [58] Moreover, the French ruler stipulated that
the treaty must be kept secret until such time as disturbances oc-

curred in Italy, whereas Buol desired to inform the Italian princes immediately in order to give a salutary warning to all agitators.[59] The convention as finally agreed upon provided that the two powers would use their influence both in order to prevent aggression in Italy against the *status quo* and to settle the eastern crisis; and that eventually they would cooperate militarily in Italy and the east.[60] This was left unsigned, awaiting Austria's intervention against Russia. Drouyn de Lhuys explained to Hübner that were its terms made known, it would be very unpopular in France. "I believe, therefore, that it will be better to wait until a great act has regulated the military cooperation of the powers in the east; then the moment will come when we can very easily reach an agreement concerning the convention on Italy and when the French Government would no longer object that it immediately be made public and thus produce in Italy the moral effect which you have in view." [61] The convention was simply a future program which would become effective if and when Austria entered the war against Russia.

The problem of obtaining the support of Prussia and the German Confederation was more difficult. From the very beginning of the eastern crisis the Prussian attitude, and especially the actions of the King, had aroused suspicion in Vienna. Not only had Frederick William IV divulged confidential information to the Tsar concerning the Vienna Conference which weakened its effectiveness, but he had strongly hinted that Prussia's participation therein was only "an unavoidable consequence" of Austria's attitude.[62] In December 1853, the King had sent Count Pourtalès to London in order to convince the English Government that Prussia could render important services to the common cause as a mediator providing the western powers would guarantee the integrity and the inviolability of the Prussian and German frontiers and would agree to refrain from interfering in German affairs and not oppose such steps as Prussia might take in securing leadership in the Bund.[63] Though England rejected the King's proposal, the affair was regarded suspiciously in Vienna as an attempt on the part of Prussia to cut loose from her obligations to support Austria's interests in Italy. After rejecting the four-power convention, Frederick William sent General Groeben and Prince Hohenzollern to London and Paris in order to explain why Prussia could not sign, while General Lindheim went to St. Petersburg with a proposal that Russia evacuate the Principalities if the western powers agreed to evacuate the Black Sea.[64] None of these missions succeeded.

Having failed in his attempts at mediation and seeing the shadow of war drawing closer and closer, Frederick William was now filled with anxieties for his country's future. Geographic conditions would compel the western powers, if they wished to strike a decisive blow against Russia, to bring pressure upon central Europe. Would Prussia be able to resist such pressure? Would Napoleon seek to take advantage of the war in order to gain the Rhine frontier and to reëstablish the Polish Kingdom? And was it not possible for England to destroy Prussia's commerce? Such thoughts caused the King to look with more favor toward Vienna. The secret treaty of alliance concluded by the two great German powers in May 1851, according to which each promised aid in case of any attack on the other's territories, within or without the Confederation, was about to expire. Early in March 1854, Frederick William sent Colonel Edwin Manteuffel to Vienna with an autograph letter for Franz Joseph proposing a treaty of alliance.[65] According to the King's proposal, if Austria were compelled to occupy Serbia or Bosnia in order to force the evacuation of the Principalities and if this should bring on a Russian attack against Hapsburg territory, Prussia and the German Bund would give support.

On March 22, 1854, Franz Joseph convened a Crown Council to consider the Prussian proposal and to determine the course to be followed in the event of war between Russia and the western powers.[66] At this meeting Buol pleaded eloquently for an alliance with the western powers. He declared that once more as in 1813 an opportunity was presented for Austria to throw her weight into the scales, that England and France counted upon her support, and that if she refused, they would accuse her of preventing a quick defeat of Russia. Were Napoleon denied a military success in the east, he would seek it elsewhere, perhaps in Italy. Buol was in favor of proceeding immediately to the conclusion of an alliance with the western powers without waiting for the support of Prussia. To those who insisted upon making this alliance dependent upon one with Prussia, he warned that it would mean the loss of Austria's leadership in Germany. Let Austria, he urged, join the western powers and all the German states would follow her lead as they did in 1813. The majority of the Council, with whom the Emperor sided, vetoed Buol's proposal and it was decided that the alliance with Prussia should come first and that General Hess, the Chief of Staff, should be sent to Berlin. Upon command of the Emperor, Hess expounded the arguments for the Prussian alliance.[67] He contended that Austria could only with great reluctance make common cause with the western powers against Russia since the latter's aid might one day be needed against revolution. After all, were not England and France the protectors of revolution? Hess also pointed out that the war in the east would probably last for several years during which Austria's finances would be ruined, Poland would grow into a second revolutionary France, while Austria would be pushed eastward and estranged from Germany. Only the Prussian alliance could give the aid Austria required, protecting her position in Germany, while enabling her to pursue an energetic policy in the east. Besides, such an alliance would curb the ambitious designs of Frederick William.

In the instructions which Buol drew up for Hess and which were read to the Council on March 25th, a more detailed reference was made to these designs.[68] Buol asserted that the fundamental principle of Prussia's policy was to win dominance over Germany and that not even the well-known respect of Frederick William for the Austrian Emperor had modified this desire for German leadership. This policy was no less dangerous than the Russian encroachments in the east. The aim of Prussia seemed to be directed toward limiting Austria's action against the Tsar and toward keeping her in a position of compromising neutrality toward England and France. From this, Prussia expected to derive three advantages: furthering her position in Germany through Russia, placing all the responsibility on Austria as far as the western powers were concerned, and winning German public opinion to her side. Hess was instructed to learn if Austria could count on Prussian support in forcing Russia to evacuate the Principalities. In case of a favorable reply, he was to proceed to the conclusion of a military con-

vention which was not, however, to be limited to the duration
of the war.

When these instructions were submitted to the Council for
approval, Buol renewed his plea for intervention on the ground
that Russia, despite the assurances of the Tsar, treated the Principalities as incorporated provinces.[69] He also raised the spectre
of revolution but declared that it would be greatly discouraged by
an alliance of Austria with the western powers. Franz Joseph replied
that Austria would remain loyal to the principles agreed upon
with England and France but that not being prepared for war,
she must reserve to herself the liberty of deciding when to intervene. Moreover, there could be no question of armed intervention
until she had made certain of Prussia. The alliance with Prussia
would be followed by one with the western powers. Hess was to
inform Berlin that at the moment Austria did not intend to take
effective measures against Russia but would do so only in case of
necessity and only after completely exhausting peaceful means.
According to the Emperor, this involved no change in the policy
as outlined by Buol but merely postponed action. The Council
approved these views. Before the close of the meeting, Buol made
a final but futile plea for an immediate alliance with the western
powers, asserting that further postponement would only serve to
increase Austria's difficulties as Berlin was certain to report matters
to St. Petersburg. This, of course, would give Russia a feeling of
security, while increasing the suspicions of the western powers against
Austria.

The difference of opinion revealed in the meetings of the
Council was even more evident in the higher circles of Austrian
society. The greater nobility and many of the generals were decidedly Russophile in sentiment and looked upon the Tsar as the
guardian of law and order without whose support Austria would
be unable to defend her Italian possessions.[70] On the opposite side
were those who wanted cooperation with the western powers against
Russia. Buol, Hübner, and Bach, Minister of Internal Affairs, were
the leading members of this group and they had the support of
the Archduchess Sophie, mother of the Emperor, who at this
period exercised a strong influence over her son. Clerical circles

with which she identified herself were active in promoting an alliance between Paris and Vienna. Leaning neither toward Russia nor the western powers were Baron Bruck, Internuncio at Constantinople, and General Hess.[71] They advocated an independent, neutral, but above all German policy and wanted Austria to ally with Prussia and the German states in order to resist both Russia and the western powers. There were others, like the former Chancellor, Prince Clemens Metternich, whose main concern was to get control over the lower Danube and to force the Tsar to renounce his designs over the Principalities. So long as Buol concerned himself with this task he could count on Metternich's support and it was only when he advocated an alliance directed against Russia that he found the former Chancellor against him.[72] Count Franz Colloredo, Austrian Ambassador at London and close friend and disciple of Metternich, also saw the danger of Russian control over the lower Danube but once the Tsar had withdrawn from the Principalities, he urged caution in order to avoid a break with St. Petersburg.[73] That such a division of opinion increased the difficulty of formulating a clear, decisive policy, is undoubtedly true. While Franz Joseph listened attentively to the various opinions, he never completely identified himself with any one group.

In Prussia also there existed a sharp difference of viewpoint concerning policy.[74] On one side was the Liberal Party which denounced Russia as the arch-enemy and regarded England as Prussia's natural ally, while strongly advocating cooperation with the western powers. Although its influence over Prussian policy was rather slight, its views were widely disseminated through its journal, the *Preussische Wochenblatt*. Prince William, the King's brother, who was later to succeed to the throne as William I, supported the Liberals and, while he favored an alliance with the western powers, entertained a deep distrust of Austria and was severely critical of her Italian policy. On the other side, were the members of the Conservative Party, supported by the Queen and the King's second brother, Prince Karl. They were definitely in favor of Russia and regarded the Tsar as the great bulwark of conservatism in Europe and the western powers as allies of revolution. According to them, there was little advantage and much danger in joint action with

England and France, and they sought to save the old alliance with Russia and to form a close union with Austria in order to prevent the latter from joining the other camp. It was their influence which held the King to a policy of neutrality. The Prime Minister, Otto von Manteuffel, tried to hold a position between the opposing groups and desired at all cost to save Prussia from engaging in a test of her military strength.[75] Though frequently thwarted by the King, who carried on a direct correspondence with the Prussian ambassadors and special emissaries, as well as with foreign rulers, Manteuffel leaned to the side of the western powers. The King himself was torn by conflicting emotions. Devoted to his dynastic ties, he had a horror of revolution which amounted almost to a mania. While moral scruples prevented him from joining the Tsar, he dreaded the thought of breaking with Russia and hoped somehow that it would be possible to maintain the Holy Alliance as a check against Napoleon. On the other hand, religious considerations impelled him toward England, the other great Protestant power, though he regretted her support of the Turks against the Christians.

While the alliance negotiations were underway at Berlin,[76] Russian troops crossed the Danube, thereby increasing the threat to Austria's security. The Vienna Conference was reconvened and on April 9th a protocol was signed which called for the integrity of the Ottoman Empire, the evacuation of the Principalities, the independence of the Sultan, and guarantees to regulate political relations with Turkey in order to safeguard the European equilibrium.[77] The protocol was transmitted to St. Petersburg.

On April 20th the Austro-Prussian treaty of alliance was signed at Berlin. By its terms the two powers guaranteed each other's possessions and agreed that an attack made against the territory of one would be considered an attack against the other. They promised to protect the rights and interests of the German states from any attack whatever, to keep their armies on a war-footing, to invite the members of the Confederation to adhere to the treaty, and not to conclude alliances with other powers not in accord with the terms of the treaty.[78] Frederick William believed that Prussia's interests would be safeguarded by a clause which stipulated that she was not to be called upon to defend Austrian territory unless Austria had previously obtained Prussia's consent to her plans. General Hess, however, declared that on the basis of the protocol of April 9th, Austria was about to demand the evacuation of the Principalities and, if necessary, to use force in case Russia refused. He, therefore, requested Prussia's consent to this plan and her promise to defend Austrian territory. The King agreed and an additional clause was incorporated into the treaty providing that Prussia was to support Austria in demanding Russian withdrawal from the Principalities. A joint military action would follow only if Russia attempted to annex the Principalities or in case of an attack on, or of the crossing, of the Balkans by Russian troops.[79]

In signing the treaty the two powers had different aims in view. Austria hoped through the alliance to prevent any decrease of her influence in Germany while she pursued an energetic policy in the east.[80] It was her intention to employ the military resources of Prussia and the German states in order to oppose the Russian threat. The alliance with Prussia was of secondary importance to an alliance with the western powers. For Prussia, on the other hand, the alliance was regarded as a means whereby Austria could be kept from joining the western powers and would enable all the German states to adopt an independent policy in the eastern struggle. These conflicting aims were to be the source of considerable misunderstanding later.

At the moment Frederick William hoped to avoid the stipulation of the additional clause by persuading the Tsar to make concessions. With this thought in mind, he wrote to Nicholas apologizing for having signed the treaty, and urged the Tsar to check his march toward the Balkans and to evacuate the Principalities.[81] Nicholas, however, declined to make any concessions and hinted that the King would serve better the cause of peace if he took a strong and independent position toward the western powers, instead of making himself the advocate of their unjust claims.[82] It was not only in his correspondence with the Tsar that Frederick William revealed his intention of evading the alliance stipulation. He gave further proof of it by recalling Bunsen from his post in London and by dismissing General von Bonin, the Minister of War, and replacing both with men more favorable to Russia. To Nicholas such actions could only mean that Prussia did not intend to go to the limit against Russia. On May 7th the King appealed to Franz Joseph not to do anything which would involve Austria and Prussia in the war.[83] To fight against Russia, he warned the Austrian ruler, would simply promote the interests of Napoleon, who would then be able later to strike with ease against the German powers.[84]

In requesting the adherence of the German states to their alliance, Austria and Prussia reminded them that "the continuance of Russia's warlike attitude on the lower Danube was incompatible not only with the most important interests of Austria as a neighboring state but with those of Germany as well." [85] This reminder, however, made little impression. A number of the German courts, including Bavaria, Würtemberg and Electoral Hesse, were related to the royal family of Russia and their sympathies were decidedly with the Tsar. On the other hand, their fear of France persuaded them to stay out of the war unless German interests became involved; while at the same time they saw a chance to increase their influence in the Confederation at the expense of both Austria and Prussia. On May 25th the ministers of the German secondary states met at Bamberg and drew up a note addressed to Austria and Prussia. In this they demanded that their adherence to the Austro-Prussian Alliance should be given collectively and not individually, that the Confederation should be admitted to the peace congress as a European power and should approve of any arrangements designed to regulate the Danube and the rights of the Christians in Turkey.[86]

While the independent attitude displayed by the German states irritated Buol, he proceeded on the theory that Prussia and the Confederation must follow Austria's lead and on June 3rd sent an ultimatum to Russia demanding the evacuation of the Principalities. Buol had shown the text of the ultimatum to Alvensleben, the personal emissary of Frederick William, on May 31st.[87] A week later, on June 8th, the two German rulers and their Foreign Ministers met at Tetschen, Bohemia. Here the Prussian King approved the ultimatum and promised to support it at St. Petersburg, though he was somewhat disappointed because Austria had not demanded the withdrawal of the Anglo-French fleet from the Black Sea, which he regarded as a necessary condition of peace.[88] He had already urged Nicholas to reply amicably to the Austrian demand, arguing that it would be a good way of striking back at Buol and of removing the pretext for war.[89]

The situation had now taken a critical turn. While rejection of the ultimatum did not necessarily mean immediate war between Austria and Russia, it would have undoubtedly prepared the way for such a struggle. The occupation of the Principalities and the crossing of the Danube by Russian troops constituted a serious threat to Austria's security in the east. It was Buol's opinion, however, that Russia would agree to evacuate rather than run the risk of extending the theater of war and in this he proved to be correct.[90] On June 14th Austria and Turkey concluded a treaty which provided that every means be employed to obtain the evacuation of the Principalities by Russia.[91]

Count Valentin Esterhazy, the Austrian Minister at St. Petersburg, presented the ultimatum to the Tsar in a private audience. He was coldly received and severely upbraided because of the hostile attitude which Franz Joseph had adopted toward Russia.[92] Nicholas declared that this attitude was all the more difficult to understand since the two states had common interests in the east. He complained bitterly that Franz Joseph had evidently forgotten what Russia had done for him and asserted that the confidence which had existed between the two empires was destroyed and that the former intimate relations would never again exist.

The Tsar replied to the ultimatum on June 29th. He agreed to withdraw from the Principalities provided Austria would not join his enemies and would prevent them from engaging in further hostilities against Russian territories.[93] After an armistice had been arranged, Russia would enter into peace negotiations on the basis of the protocol of April 9th, with the exception of the last point.[94] Despite the conditional nature of the Tsar's reply, Russian troops were recalled and on August 20th Austrian and Turkish troops entered the Principalities in accordance with the Treaty of June 14th.

In making her demand on Russia, Austria had counted on Prussian support in case military action became necessary. Prussia, however, did nothing to justify this expectation. On the contrary, no steps were taken to place the army on a war-footing.[95] Frederick William was satisfied that in giving diplomatic support he had gone far enough. In a letter to the Russian Empress he strongly advised that no objections be raised against the Austrian occupation of the Principalities. "Because I know positively and believe that I can vouch for it with my word of honor that Franz Joseph is as far removed as heaven from earth in undertaking this occupation against Russia with any trace of enmity. . . . I have the word of Franz Joseph that it is so and that if he marches in case of an unfavorable Russian reply, he will stop at the Russian frontier. . . . God knows that should Franz Joseph march, he comes as a friend and not as an enemy." [96] According to Frederick William, the Austrian ruler had no thought of war unless he were attacked but it was otherwise with Buol, who hoped that Nicholas would do something drastic. "Franz Joseph wants peace, Buol (dancing on Bourqueney's rope) wants war." [97] The King regarded the conditions set forth in the Tsar's reply as entirely just and directed Alvensleben, his special emissary, to explain this to Franz Joseph.[98] It should be Austria's duty, he declared, to act as mediator between Russia and the western powers. If she failed in this, "then my beloved nephew will not stand well in the annals of history and Buol very badly—among the wicked ministers." [99] In a letter to Franz Joseph, he wrote: "Turn your heart again to the noble Emperor and to Russia! By God, he deserves it. Speak to him once more friendly and confidentially. I do not doubt that it will be easy for Your Majesty to dispel his unfortunate suspicions and to influence him favorably for the aims you have in view and against which I must guard myself so long as imminent danger of war with Russia can result from them. Otherwise, I am agreed because I find in the same a worthy political wisdom." [100]

Although the Tsar had placed conditions to his acceptance of the Austrian demand, Buol had won a diplomatic success. Without drawing the sword, he had obtained Russia's consent to the withdrawal of her troops from the Principalities. At the same time, this had removed the chief pretext for war and rendered unnecessary Prussian mobilization for the defense of Austria's territories. The Austro-Prussian

Alliance now became more palatable to the German states and on July 24th, they announced their adherence to it.

Encouraged by these marks of success, Buol drew closer to the western powers. Negotiations concerning a tripartite alliance and the bases of peace had been going on for some time.[101] On August 8th notes were exchanged by the three powers, Austria, England and France, as a pledge of their perfect *entente*. These notes declared that the relations between Russia and Turkey could be established on a solid and durable basis providing, first, that the protectorate which Russia had exercised over the Principalities and Serbia were terminated and the privileges accorded by the Sultan to these territories were placed under the collective guarantee of the powers through a treaty concluded with the Porte; second, that the navigation of the Danube to its mouth were not fettered by any obstacles and were regulated according to the principles determined by the Congress of Vienna; third, that the treaty of July 13, 1841, be revised in the interests of the European equilibrium; and, fourth, that Russia abandon any pretensions she might have of exercising a protectorate over Turkish subjects, that she join with Austria, England and France in obtaining the confirmation and observation of the religious privileges of the various Christian communions, and avoid any attack upon the dignity and independence of the Sultan. In addition, England and France announced that they reserved the right to make known later the special conditions upon which peace should be granted to Russia, and that they would not consider any Russian proposal which did not imply acceptance of the four points.[102]

On August 10th Buol enclosed these demands in a dispatch to Count Esterhazy, with instructions to present them to the Russian Chancellor. He declared that if Russia accepted the four points, Austria would bring pressure to bear on the western powers to enter into negotiations for peace and the arrangement of an armistice.[103] As an indication of her good will, Austria had already suspended a part of her military operations and was prepared to take further measures along the same line. Should England and France make exaggerated demands or place any obstacles to the conclusion of peace, they would bear the responsibility and Austria's relations with them would necessarily undergo a change.[104] While taking this conciliatory tone, Buol was not too optimistic concerning Russia's intentions. Indeed, he seems to have expected Russia to reply to the four points by breaking off diplomatic relations with Austria, for he expressed doubt that Esterhazy would remain much longer at his post.[105]

In presenting the four points to Russia, Buol had taken care to inform the Prussian Government and had requested its cooperation. Prussian support now seemed as necessary as ever, since the presence of a large force of Russian troops in Poland constituted a serious threat to the Austrian Monarchy. It was still possible that Austria might be compelled to fight against her mighty neighbor and the support of Prussia and the German states would then become of vital importance. Buol was confident that he could count on his German allies in case of a Russian refusal to accept the four points.

Prussia, however, had been informed only after the exchange of notes had taken place. This angered Frederick William who, in any event, was in no mood to run the risk of war. Although he could see no advantages in the four points for Prussia, he announced on August 13th that he would support them and recommend them to the Tsar as the basis for peace negotiations.[106] At the same time, he informed Vienna that Prussia would not promise to take up arms against Russia if the latter rejected the four points. A few days later, Franz Joseph assured the King that his troops would not advance beyond the Pruth and would not attack Russian territory, but if Russia rejected the four points, complications might arise, in which case he counted on Prussia and the Confederation.[107]

In her dealings with the Confederation, Austria met with no greater success. Thanks to the ceaseless intrigues of Bismarck, Buol's attempt to bring the military forces of the Confederation under Austrian leadership was doomed to failure.[108] When the Tsar's note of June 29th together with the four points were presented to the Diet, Buol was severely criticized for the methods he had employed. Satisfied with the Tsar's note as far as German interests were concerned, the Diet flatly refused to mobilize in defense of the four points, of which only the first two seemed to be of any importance to Germany. Austria, according to the German states, had no right to invoke the Treaty of April 20th, and they would defend her only if she were attacked in her own territories, not in the Principalities. Moreover, they insisted that Austria maintain the Principalities in a state of strict neutrality and that she promise not to attack Russia.

Aware that Austria's influence in the Confederation had fallen to a low point, Buol had considered the advisability of not asking for support in order to avoid a defeat. But now in the face of such a defeat, he sought to direct the wrath of the western powers against Prussia, while warning the latter against hiding her cowardice behind the cloak of German nationalism. As for the German princes, their "cowardly attitude in this crisis will not be forgotten or forgiven by their own subjects, and if they failed Austria at this time they would look in vain for her aid in the hour of danger."[109]

Once more it was Prussia's negative policy and her influence over the German states which had frustrated Buol's plans. The Alliance of April 20th was emasculated through the actions of Frederick William, whose purpose in concluding it, as we have seen, was to prevent Austria from joining the western powers. In the struggle which took place in the Diet Prussia held the advantage because her determination to avoid war with Russia was favored by the German states. So long as Franz Joseph regarded the support of his German allies as necessary, Austria could not openly take the side of England and France. It was obviously impossible in the circumstances to maintain his leadership in Germany while pursuing an energetic policy in the east.

CHAPTER FOUR

The Alliance of December 2, 1854

IF THE ATTITUDE OF Prussia was disappointing to Austria, the latter's cautious policy was no less disappointing to the western powers. From his post in Paris, Hübner continued to urge intervention against Russia. He regarded the crossing of the Danube by Russian troops late in March 1854 as an attack on Austria's vital interests and reported that it had created a small panic in French political and financial circles which Drouyn de Lhuys attributed to the lack of clarity in Austria's policy.[1] Insisting that Austria must join the western powers, the French Minister predicted the formation of a new alignment at the end of the war consisting of Austria, France and Prussia to which Russia might be invited.[2] England would be excluded from this alignment because her insular position and maritime interests absorbed her attention in a direction Europe could not follow.

With the conclusion of the Austro-Prussian Alliance and the stiffening of Austria's attitude toward Russia, French expectations increased momentarily. Asked by Napoleon if his government now intended to break off diplomatic relations with the Tsar and draw the sword, Hübner was forced to admit that Franz Joseph desired to remain out of the war and to bring about peace, and that only if Nicholas refused to evacuate the Principalities, would he consider what methods to employ in order to achieve this end.[3] This attitude seemed too narrow to Napoleon, who held that it was not merely a question of the Principalities but whether or not Russia was to become the dominant power in Europe. As a veiled threat to Austria and Prussia he intimated that one result of the war should be the reëstablishment of an independent Poland or at least of the Grand Duchy of Warsaw as a buffer between Germany and Russia but excluding Galicia and Posen.[4] Drouyn de Lhuys also pointed out that the war was not confined to the question of the Principalities but that a satisfactory peace should include a protectorate by Austria over the Principalities and Bessarabia and her control over the Danube, and the acquisition of the Transcaucasian provinces by Turkey and the Baltic provinces by Sweden.[5]

Hübner was far from happy in being compelled to defend a policy with which he was not in agreement. In his journal he complained about the difficulties of his position and the lack of clarity in Buol's dispatches and private letters.[6] He realized that Buol was in favor of an alliance with the western powers but held that he was too weak to overcome attacks against his policy. In his opinion there were only three factors which concerned Austria in the eastern question. The first was whether the aggrandizement of Russia in the east would constitute a fatal blow to Austria's position as an independent state and a great power. The second was whether the *status quo ante bellum* did not contain the possibility of an increase of Russian power which was incompatible with Austria's vital interests. Finally, it was necessary to know if Napoleon merited Austria's confidence. "Has he broken seriously with revolution? Is there not a risk of exchanging the Russian alliance for one with the western powers? I answer 'no.' Napoleon will remain conservative so long as he is the ally of Austria; however, the day Austria assumes a hostile attitude toward him, he will, under the influence of certain circumstances, again become revolutionary."[7]

By "hostile attitude" Hübner meant not only action taken against France but the adoption of a neutral position in the war. What, he asked, would be done in case Russia refused to evacuate the Principalities? It was his opinion that Vienna would follow one of two courses: either attempt to weaken Russia and prevent her from taking revenge, or show moderation in order not to exasperate her and to keep the door open to a future alliance.[8] The first course was hardly logical because it would be a question of weakening Russia only if the four powers were united. Such a coalition, moreover, must be defensive, for once it became a question of dismembering Russia, it would fall apart.[9] "I conclude, for the moment at least, that it will not only be premature but logically impossible to form a plan of aggression and conquest against Russia tending to weaken her materially." The second course was inspired by fear rather than wisdom. "Can one reasonably hope to coax Russia by moderation at the very moment one obliges her to renounce projects whose accomplishment has been for eighty years the principal motive and almost the exclusive aim of her policy?" There could be no reconciliation between Austria and Russia, according to Hübner, until the eastern question was settled in a definitive manner, and this could be done only by maintaining the integrity of the Ottoman Empire and by providing better government for the Balkan Christians by placing them under European protection and thus depriving Russia of the excuse to intervene in Turkish affairs. Under such an arrangement, the Christians would cease to look to Russia for support, and the latter, in turn, would be compelled to renounce her designs on Turkey. Then, and only then, would a reconciliation between Austria and Russia become possible. "Once the poisoned arrow which she (Russia) has carried in her flank for almost a century is extracted, the wound will heal sooner or later and the return of good relations with Russia is as certain as it will be impossible if we content ourselves with a solution which in reality is not one."[10]

If Hübner found cause to complain about the difficulties of his position, the fault did not lie entirely with Buol. Had the latter been given a free hand, he would have concluded an alliance with the western powers, but lacking the full support of the Emperor and facing criticism from all sides, he was seldom able to act decisively. Unfortunately, he was held responsible for policies which he did not always desire. Hübner charged him with lack of strength to overcome opposition to his policy. This may be true but in fairness one might ask if any other Austrian statesman of the time could have produced different results. Granted the defects in Buol's character, it is necessary to remember that the actual control of Austria's policy was in the hands of the young Emperor and that the choice which faced the country was a most difficult one. Austria could hardly have avoided the consequences no matter what course she had followed. To have sided with Russia would have brought on the enmity of England and France, which were in a position to stir up revolutions in Hungary, Italy and Poland. An alliance with the western powers seemed no less dangerous. While it is true that in this case Austria would have had the support of her allies, it is no less true that she would have borne the brunt of the Russian wrath. There is no reason to suppose that Russia would not have carried the war to the Balkans and attacked Austria through the Principalities, while she stirred up revolts among the Slavs. When one considers these factors, as well as the financial plight of Austria, it is understandable that Franz Joseph wished to avoid such a choice which, indeed, was a choice between two evils. It is also clear that his main concern was to safeguard Austria's interests. Buol, on the other hand, favored an alliance with the western powers and sought by every means to overcome opposition to it. Hübner, not being fully informed about the situation in Vienna, was inclined to minimize the difficulties and was probably too optimistic about Napoleon's good will toward Austria. Under the circumstances, Buol was justified in curbing the envoy's enthusiasm for the western alliance and in preventing him from committing his government too far.

Yet, the fact remains that in the eyes of the French Austria's policy was ambiguous, hesitant and vacillating. The proposed four-power convention of February, followed by the protocol of April 9th, the conclusion of the Austro-Prussian Alliance, and the Austrian ultimatum to Russia of June 3rd, demanding the evacuation of the Principalities, certainly gave France sufficient grounds to expect the active cooperation of Vienna. Furthermore, Franz Joseph and his Minister repeated over and over again their loyalty to the principles set forth in the various protocols of the Vienna Conference. They insisted not less than the western powers upon the preservation of the political independence and the territorial integrity of the Ottoman Empire. But, as we have seen, Austria sought to check not only Russia in the east but the influence of Prussia in Germany. Without Prussian support against the Tsar, she refused to throw herself completely into the arms of the western powers. It was perhaps a mistake to make her policy dependent upon the aid of Prussia, for in doing so she gave Berlin the upper hand. Whenever Austria took a step nearer to the western powers or displayed a firm attitude toward the Tsar, it was Prussia which held her back. Neither Hübner nor the French would agree that the collaboration of Prussia and the German states was necessary. They believed that such collaboration would follow once Austria joined England and France in the struggle against the Tsar.

In a letter to Hübner on July 2nd, Buol explained the policy he had adopted toward Russia.[11] He declared that Austria would not conclude a separate peace with the Tsar and would continue to insist upon guarantees for the integrity of the Ottoman Empire. Should Russia refuse to evacuate the Principalities, Austria would seek to obtain this either by means of strategy or by force, counting on Prussia's assistance. In case Russia's reply was evasive, he suggested that the western powers propose an armistice and submit peace proposals to St. Petersburg, which Austria would support. A refusal by Russia to accept these proposals would be the signal for Austrian troops to enter the Principalities. In a second dispatch of the same date, he gave his approval to the bases of peace suggested by Drouyn de Lhuys, which called for the freedom of the Danube, guarantees for the Principalities, the abolition of Russia's protectorate over her coreligionists in Turkey, and the opening of the Black Sea.[12]

Austria's chief concern, as indicated in Buol's dispatches, was the liberation of the Principalities from Russian control. France, on the other hand, wanted Austria to take a broader view of the struggle and to conclude an alliance with the western powers. On July 9th Hübner urged Buol to agree to a tripartite alliance on the basis of Drouyn de Lhuys' peace program and expressed confidence that Prussia would follow sooner or later.[13] Any further delay, he warned Buol on July 22nd, would lead to a rupture with England and France and this, in turn, would increase the influence of the Russian party at Berlin and resurrect the revolutionary groups throughout Europe.[14] Only by throwing her weight into the scales on the side of France, could Austria prevent England from making the Crimea the theater of war but "it is necessary to strike while the iron is hot."[15]

Buol replied to these urgent pleas by instructing Hübner to discuss the subject of an alliance without however making any binding engagements.[16] A draft treaty of a tripartite alliance was drawn up by Drouyn de Lhuys which provided that negotiations with Russia should be upon the basis of the four items mentioned in his peace program, that Austria should occupy the Principalities and would receive the support of the western powers in the event of war with Russia.[17] At the same time, Drouyn de Lhuys proposed that the four points of August 8th be accepted by the three powers through an exchange of notes rather than in a formal protocol. By the end of July both Austria and England had agreed to the draft treaty and the proposal for an exchange of notes.[18]

The scheme for the tripartite alliance failed to materialize because Austria learned that the Russians were in the process of evacuating the Principalities.[19] Since this removed the immediate danger of war with Russia, Austria could see no advantage in concluding the alliance. Buol, however, proceeded with the exchange of notes regarding the four points, which were transmitted to St. Petersburg.[20] On August 20th Austrian and Turkish troops entered the Principalities in accordance with the terms of their treaty of June and six days later Russia flatly rejected the four points.[21]

Having attained her immediate objective, Austria was content to let matters rest for the moment. Although the western powers held that she was morally bound to enter the war, this was not the view of Franz Joseph and Buol.[22] Indeed, the latter argued that there was no need to push affairs too far since what Russia had not yielded in principle, had already been obtained in fact.[23] Had not the Russian troops been withdrawn from the Principalities? Was not the mouth of the Danube free and Russia's naval power in the Black Sea practically destroyed? Did Russia now protect a single one of her coreligionists in Turkey? To enter the war at the very moment Russia had taken her first step backwards, would destroy any hope of bringing the Tsar to terms and would be misconstrued in Germany. "We cannot rid ourselves of the fear," Buol wrote to Hübner, "that it would offer Prussia a pretext for rallying around the flag of passive neutrality those German governments already leaning too much to the opinion that the evacuation of the Principalities satisfies German interests while they only seek a motive in order to withdraw their moral support from us."[24]

It was the refusal of Prussia and the German states to back up their ally that restrained Austria from going forward with the alliance project.[25] In arguing that there was no longer any reason to fight Russia, Buol was merely trying to justify the inaction of his government. On the other hand, it is true that the Russian withdrawal from the Principalities removed the chief pretext for war between the two eastern powers. Concerning this point Buol wrote to General Hess: "With the consent of Europe and against the will of Russia, and without actually being at war with her, we have the predominant influence in the Principalities. It would be foolish to undertake more than this. Russia did not accept our challenge."[26] Furthermore, Austria had not promised the western powers military assistance in connection with the four points. At no time since the beginning of the crisis had she failed to insist upon her freedom of action. In every instance Buol carefully left open the way for a retreat. The draft treaty having been rejected, Vienna was not willing to go beyond diplomatic support to the western powers.

Drouyn de Lhuys, the architect of the proposed tripartite alliance, was unable to hide his disappointment and reminded Hübner that more than a passive attitude was expected of Austria.[27] He criticized the attempt of Buol to justify Austria's lack of cooperation on the ground that the western powers had decided to fight in the Crimea. Not only had Austria refused to concert a plan of campaign for the Danube sector but despite the rejection of the four points, she still temporized and thus permitted the Russians to concentrate their forces in Asia.[28] Hübner tried to calm the angry Minister by arguing that it was Austria's occupation of the Principalities which made it possible for the allies to undertake the Crimean expedition. "Without us, the Russians would be on the Danube and you in the Balkans. We have thus loyally and effectively contributed to the success of the enterprise in which the four powers find themselves engaged in varying degrees."[29] He pointed out to Drouyn de Lhuys that Austria had never promised to fight if Russia rejected the four points, that having retained her freedom of action, she could still enter the war but that Franz Joseph resented the attempt of the western powers to force him to break with the Tsar. "These powers should remember that a declaration of war by Austria would only serve to strengthen Russian influence in Prussia and the German states."[30]

Buol, who realized that no further action could be taken at the moment, was offended by the French attitude. "What more can the allies expect?" he asked. "What is the urgent motive and justification for a declaration of war against Russia at this time? Our task was to obtain, by force if necessary, the evacuation of the Principalities. Russia preferred to yield this region. It is permissible to state that our attitude has contributed to a result for the allies which would have cost them an immense amount of effort and a bitter struggle to obtain. And just because this result has been achieved without bloodshed, is it any less important?"[31] At the same time Buol knew that such arguments could not hide the fact that Austria had been placed in an intolerable position by the desertion of Prussia and the German states. He saw that unless a more decisive policy was inaugurated, Austria would soon find herself isolated and a target from all sides. Already estranged from Russia and having temporarily lost her leadership in Germany, there was grave danger of losing the good will of the western powers as well. There seemed to be only one way out of the dilemma and that was to ignore Prussia and the German states and to join the western powers. On September 26, 1854 Buol submitted a report to the Emperor.[32] In this he pointed out that Prussia's aid could not be counted upon, that Austria's position in European affairs had not been achieved without effort and could easily be lost to please "our German friends and allies," who were jealous of this position and who "play a contemptible role with Your Majesty." As it was now too late to retreat in view of the heavy sacrifices already incurred, Austria should conclude an alliance with the western powers. He warned Franz Joseph that any other course would lead to isolation and that those who believed that the Holy Alliance could be reëstablished were indulging in wishful thinking.

In making his appeal to the Emperor, Buol was aided by several factors.[33] In the first place, General Hess, who had opposed the alliance with the western powers, was now in the Principalities, too far away to influence the decision. Secondly, the success of Buol's diplomatic campaign, which had enabled Austria to occupy the

Principalities, apparently convinced Franz Joseph that the Tsar could be prevailed upon to accept the four points without the necessity of drawing the sword. Finally, the Minister had the support of the Archduchess Sophie, whose influence over her son by no means diminished after his marriage.[34] The Emperor was in the mood to heed the advice of Buol and agreed that negotiations for a treaty of alliance should be undertaken.[35]

Having at last obtained a free hand to carry out his ideas, Buol instructed Hübner to propose to Drouyn de Lhuys the conclusion of a tripartite alliance and the reconvening of the Vienna Conference in order to discuss the four points.[36] A draft treaty had already been drawn up by Bourqueney and Westmorland, the British Ambassador to Vienna, and was forwarded to Paris and London on October 2nd.[37] But now the French Minister, who had made such strenuous efforts to draw in Austria, appeared curiously indifferent. He expressed doubt about the sincerity behind the proposals and said to Hübner that Buol attached too much importance to the Conference, which could accomplish nothing.[38] It would be otherwise if Austria would state when she intended to enter the war in case peace was not concluded within a certain period. Unless this was done, Drouyn de Lhuys could see no value in the proposed tripartite alliance.[39] But the Minister really had no intention of closing the door to such an alliance and a few days later agreed to the proposal to reconvene the Conference. The British Cabinet, however, rejected this plan though it was in favor of the tripartite alliance.[40] It thus became necessary to find a formula acceptable to the three powers.

The slowness with which negotiations proceeded exasperated Hübner, who kept urging Buol to greater speed. Unable to comprehend why there should be any delay, he assumed that it was owing to Austria's fear of Prussia—a fear which he considered unnecessary. "Placed in the alternative of acceding to the treaty of the triple alliance which Your Excellency proposes or of isolating herself, Prussia will yield immediately or after a brief fluctuation which can only be to Austria's advantage."[41] He predicted that the other German states would join within forty-eight hours when called upon by the three powers.[42] Moreover, he mentioned that the Polish question had been recently brought up by Napoleon, who again expressed a desire to reëstablish the Grand Duchy of Warsaw. "Why," the Emperor asked Hübner, "have the governments such a great repugnance of seeing a part of the old Poland reconstructed? Because Poland and revolution, Poles and revolutionaries have become, so to say, synonymous. . . . Wherever there was a revolution . . . one was sure to meet Poles, if not Poland. But will it not be possible to change this state of affairs precisely by reconstituting the Grand Duchy of Warsaw?"[43] Drouyn de Lhuys had also alluded to the subject and had declared that the Polish question would be decided for or against, with or without Austria, depending upon whether or not she joined the allies.[44]

Hübner was aware that the Polish question would arouse concern in Vienna and he made the most of it as an argument for speeding up the negotiations for the alliance. He warned Buol that the question could be avoided if Russia made peace during the winter, but if she refused, Poland would become a battleground. "In what concerns Poland, I do not hesitate to say that the only way for Austria to avoid this thorny question is the conclusion of peace during the winter. The day the first cannon ball is fired on the banks of the Vistula, the Polish question will become inevitable."[45] Meanwhile, he urged Buol not to be deceived by such concessions as the Tsar might be induced to make in order to prevent Austria from joining the western powers, for they would be illusory. Nicholas might agree to accept the four points; he might promise not to cross the Danube or the Pruth and to withdraw his troops from Poland, but he would not be sincere.[46] The allies were counting on Austria's support and had inscribed on their banners the slogan: "no revolution, no conquests." To desert them now would be disastrous, for they would seek supporters in Poland, who would rise under the national flag. "This will permit Italy to stir. The ambitions of Sardinia will be encouraged, at first secretly, then openly. England will fight Russia in Asia, while France resumes her military traditions along the Rhine and on the Po. The secondary states will transfer their sympathies from Russia to France while Austria, embroiled in the east and the west, will come face to face with England, France and revolution, and will find herself alone in the midst of chaos."[47] Any further delay in concluding the alliance would create distrust, doubts and suspicions of all kinds at Paris and would strengthen the influence of England, which was only lukewarm to it. "Let us sign, then, let us sign! Time passes and events march. Unless I am mistaken, we have arrived at the decisive moment."[48]

It was indeed the march of events which hastened the conclusion of the alliance. On October 22nd Austria's army was placed on a war-footing and by the end of the month she had nearly a million men stationed in Galicia, Bukowina and Transylvania, facing the Tsar's troops. The Russian defeats at Balaclava (October 24th) and at Inkerman (November 5th) led all Europe to expect Austria's entrance into the war. Furthermore, the situation in Germany had begun to look more hopeful from the Austrian viewpoint. The knowledge that Buol was negotiating with the western powers for an alliance and that he planned to draw in the German states, created uneasiness in Prussia. Frederick William knew that it would be difficult to resist the combined pressure of Austria, England and France but he hoped to forestall this pressure by persuading the Tsar to accept the four points. The plea of the Prussian King, which was supported by Nesselrode, coupled with the threatening attitude of Austria and the Russian reverses in the Crimea, convinced Nicholas that the time had come to yield. On November 17th he accepted the four points.[49] A week later, on the 26th, Prussia contracted a new engagement with Austria, to which the German Confederation acceded on December 9th. Prussia guaranteed the Austrian troops in the Principalities against attack and agreed to support the four points in the Frankfurt Diet.[50] This engagement, the King hoped, would enable him to gain time and, if possible, to bring about a rift between Austria and the western powers.

Neither the acceptance of the four points nor the Prussian engagement deterred Buol from going ahead with the negotiations for a tripartite alliance. The necessity of keeping a large army on a war-footing had practically exhausted Austria's finances and this unsatisfactory situation could not be prolonged. Either the army must be reduced to a peace-footing or Austria must enter the war. But in order to enter the war she required support and since this was not forthcoming from Prussia and the Confederation, the only alternative left was to turn to England and France. The latter powers having suffered enormous losses in the siege of Sebastopol and being more or less disheartened by the general military situation, had increased their pressure on Vienna. Following the British rejection of the first draft of the alliance treaty, largely because of its proposal for reconvening the Vienna Conference, the French drew up another draft in October. This was accepted by the British Cabinet and was then forwarded to Vienna. Buol suggested several amendments which caused a further delay.[51] With the acceptance of these amendments by England and France, the treaty awaited the final approval of Franz Joseph. This was given after a brief hesitation and on December 2nd the treaty was signed.

The three powers agreed not to depart from the principles set forth in the protocols of the Vienna Conference and in the four points and not to negotiate a separate peace with Russia. They reserved the right to propose "such conditions as they deemed necessary" in the interests of Europe. Austria promised to defend the Principalities and in the event that she became involved in war with Russia, the western powers would support her through an offensive-defensive alliance. Finally, the treaty stipulated that if peace was not established on the basis of the four points by January 1, 1855, the three powers would deliberate regarding the means of attaining their object, that is, the reëstablishment of general peace.[52] On December 22nd Austria and France signed the convention relative to Italy, which provided that the two powers would cooperate to prevent any aggression against the *status quo* in the Peninsula while they were engaged in the east. It was agreed that Austria should notify the Italian courts of this convention.[53]

There are two important questions that arise in connection with the treaty of December 2nd. First, did it mean that Austria was to enter the war if peace was not concluded by January 1, 1855? Article V merely provided that the signatories would deliberate concerning the best means of attaining general peace. When this article was drafted by the French the only possible means were warlike measures but after Russia's acceptance of the four points the situation changed and negotiations rather than war offered the best means of reëstablishing general peace.[54] In any case, Article V was capable of various interpretations and could easily be circumvented. The second question is whether Austria signed the treaty because of threats by the western powers. Most writers on the subject leave the impression that Franz Joseph agreed to it only after England and France threatened to withdraw their ambassadors from Vienna and after Buol submitted his resignation. Eckhart, who made a careful study of the evidence, refers to this as "the legend of Austria's resistance" and declares that she signed the treaty of her own free will.[55] The source of the legend was a report of Count von Arnim, the Prussian Ambassador at Vienna, dated December 4th. No one was more surprised by the conclusion of the treaty than von Arnim and his Russian colleague, Prince Gortchakoff. In his report von Arnim stated that when Gortchakoff was informed of what had taken place, he begged Buol to mitigate the effects at St. Petersburg. Buol thereupon related that during the evening of December 1st, the ambassadors of England and France had called upon him demanding that the treaty be signed immediately; in case of a refusal, they threatened to request their passports. According to von Arnim's story, Buol informed Franz Joseph of what the English and French ambassadors had said and declared that his position was such that he must submit his resignation if the treaty was not signed.[56] Von Arnim added that the Emperor, who was ordinarily so busy, no longer concerned himself with affairs, even those of the greatest importance. "He lacks, I regret to say, energy and action; he follows the advice one offers without examining its scope and what is worse is that in his ill-chosen surroundings there is no one . . . competent to give him advice." Eckhart suggests that the legend that Austria signed under duress was invented by Buol himself, who had a bad conscience so far as Prussia was concerned, for despite Manteuffel's request for postponement and despite Russia's acceptance of the four points, the treaty was signed. Buol knew of von Arnim's report and though it was hardly flattering to his ability, he made no attempt to contradict it, which would seem to indicate that he found it to his advantage to allow the erroneous information to remain. Moreover, in his dispatch to the Austrian representative in Berlin concerning the treaty negotiations, he did not mention the dramatic events of December 1st.[57] As a matter of fact, Buol found von Arnim to be a very agreeable representative of Prussian interests. At home, however, the Ambassador was severely criticized and Bismarck went so far as to demand his immediate retirement. But though the King was surprised "how unbelievably bad" von Arnim had filled his post, he permitted him to remain and even Manteuffel merely inquired politely if he felt physically able to participate in future conferences.[58]

Not only is the story of the Anglo-French ultimatum a myth. Von Arnim's account of the Emperor's political inactivity is also incorrect. Here again the Ambassador followed the Russian version. At St. Petersburg the opinion prevailed ever since the Austro-Russian tension set in that Franz Joseph had been led astray by Buol and had taken steps which he did not actually approve. Meyendorff, the Russian Ambassador in Vienna until July 1854 and Buol's brother-in-law, wrote in April of that year concerning the Emperor: "He thinks more of his marriage than of anything else. He frequently writes long letters to his bride and while Buol signs infamous protocols, His Majesty is hunting mountain cock and in the evenings one often sees him at the circus! One can hardly comprehend his conduct since it is his rule never to ask anyone's advice and never to listen to anyone. When Buol submits a diplomatic note to him, he merely asks: 'Is it consistent with what we did before?' If Buol answers 'Yes' the Emperor signs."[59]

This idea of the Emperor's political inactivity and of Buol's influence over him was generally accepted in Viennese court circles, where it was attributed to the shock following the attempt made on the Emperor's life at Milan and to his marital bliss.[60] It is true that Franz Joseph was less active at this time than he had been previously and that since Austria's occupation of the Principalities, he trusted Buol more and more and listened to his advice on foreign policy.[61] But as Eckhart justly observes, the main lines of foreign policy had already been determined and it was only necessary to follow them. "It would be misjudging the character of Franz Joseph," he writes, "if one asserts that he had no definite opinions about foreign policy and followed blindly the ideas of his Minister."[62] In the negotiations leading up to the treaty of December 2nd, the

Emperor took a personal part, reading the notes and dispatches attentively, calculating their effect, and giving his approval after being entirely convinced. There is no evidence that he wavered at the end and submitted under the pressure of threats from the western powers. Like Buol, he regarded the treaty as a means of reëstablishing peace, so sorely needed by his country.

Great was the Russian anger when news of the treaty reached St. Petersburg. Nicholas was deeply offended and ordered the removal from his workroom of two gifts which had been presented to him by Franz Joseph: a statue and a portrait of the Austrian ruler. The statue was given to a valet. Upon receiving the Austrian representative, the Tsar asked if he knew the names of the two stupidest kings of Poland and replied: "The first was King John Sobieski, who liberated Vienna from the siege laid by the Turks, the second am I. For both of us saved the House of Hapsburg."[63]

Among the French, on the other hand, the treaty was hailed with enthusiasm. "The jubilation in Paris is great and universal," wrote Hübner, who was himself the object of a "small ovation."[64] In general, the conservative groups were pleased, while the liberals and revolutionaries were strenuously opposed. All movements hostile to Austria: constitutionalism, parliamentarism, Italianism, socialism, and so forth, had been on the side of Russia ever since the beginning of the eastern crisis. "The continuation of the alliance of the north turned the scales in their favor, while the return of central Europe to that old policy, which at the time of the great and immortal Empress, Maria Theresa, had been so beneficial to Austria and to Europe, becomes fatal to them."[65] Napoleon was overjoyed when he received the news and embraced the Empress.[66] "As soon as it seems safe to do so," wrote Hübner, "he will be ready to make peace. It is different with England. She wishes the destruction of Sebastopol and the Russian fleet. For her the Austrian alliance has a real and important value only if Austria enters the war. For Napoleon this alliance is invaluable for peace. Unless I am mistaken, this is the difference which divides the French and English governments."[67]

Napoleon, of course, saw in the treaty the realization of one of his aims—the end of the Holy Alliance. In the opinion of Drouyn de Lhuys, there was still another advantage. The treaty would offset

England's preponderant role and make the war more continental and less maritime. "Placed between Austria and France, England will be obliged to measure her step according to that of her allies."[68] The Minister's hopes were based upon the assumption that Austria would enter the war but already there were suspicions that she would be satisfied with a bad peace rather than draw the sword. "The same fear," wrote Hübner, "having been expressed to me almost verbatim by Lord Palmerston a few days before the signing of the treaty and by other statesmen of the same nation . . . I am hardly mistaken concerning the origin of these apprehensions."[69] The treaty evoked little enthusiasm in England where the main concern at the moment was the siege of Sebastopol. Indeed, from the beginning of the negotiations, the English had been doubtful about Austria's intentions.

At Berlin there was deep resentment.[70] Frederick William was violently angry, feeling that he had been betrayed by Austria, and he decided to have nothing to do with the treaty. A copy was presented to Manteuffel on December 16th by representatives of Austria, England and France, who requested Prussia's adherence to it. Three days later Manteuffel replied through the Prussian legations in Vienna, London and Paris, calling attention to the services that Prussia had rendered in the war through diplomacy, and stating that before she could go further, it was necessary to know the interpretations which the three powers gave to the four points.[71]

The alliance of December 2nd was a triumph for Buol's diplomacy. For the moment at least the position of Austria was greatly improved. Already occupying the Principalities, she was assured of the support of Prussia and the German states in case of a Russian attempt to regain them. France and England were now allies whose aid could be counted upon in an Austro-Russian war. The alliance was a fulfillment of the aim Buol had pursued throughout the year 1854. It marked the *dénouement* of the Holy Alliance, which virtually ended with Austria's refusal to accept the Tsar's request for a pledge of benevolent neutrality. It was indeed, as Professor Henderson says, a diplomatic revolution. The crowned Carbonaro and the proud ruler of the Hapsburgs were now allies, reviving the policy of Kaunitz.

CHAPTER FIVE

The Close of the War and the Congress of Paris

THAT PEACE COULD not be concluded by the beginning of the new year and that further discussions between the signatories of the treaty of December 2nd would become necessary, was soon made evident. The crucial question concerned Austria's participation in the war should Russia reject the peace proposals. Buol appeared anxious to lose no time in taking up the execution of Article V which, from the Austrian viewpoint, meant the resumption of peace negotiations with Russia. The latter's acceptance of the four points and her willingness to see the Vienna Conference reopened, in which she agreed to be represented, seemed to offer the best means of ending the war.

England and France insisted, however, that before the Conference convened, Austria should join them in framing a collective explanation of the four points to serve as the basis for the negotiations. To this Buol agreed and on December 28th a memorandum was handed to Gortchakoff, the Russian Ambassador at Vienna.[1] The most important section of the memorandum concerned the third point which stated that the purpose of revising the treaty of July 13, 1841, was to "connect the existence of the Ottoman Empire more completely with the European equilibrium and to put an end to the preponderance of Russia in the Black Sea." Gortchakoff raised no objections to the statement relating to the Ottoman Empire but protested the demand terminating Russian preponderance in the Black Sea.[2] While awaiting instructions from St. Petersburg, he obtained an assurance from Franz Joseph that Austria would not approve any attempt to humiliate Russia by virtue of the demands of the third point.[3] On January 7, 1855, upon instructions from Nesselrode, Gortchakoff informed the three powers that Russia adhered to the four points as set forth in the memorandum of December 28th with the exception of the demand in the third point calling for the end of Russian preponderance in the Black Sea. Thus the way was cleared for the coming peace conference in Vienna.

The apparent reluctance of Austria to enter the conflict, however, served to increase the irritation of the western powers, particularly in view of the unfavorable reports from the Crimea. Sebastopol continued to hold out, cholera was decimating the allied forces, while the rigors of winter practically put an end to the fighting. Under the circumstances, England and France were favorably inclined to consider aid from Piedmont. Ever since the conclusion of the Anglo-French alliance, April 10, 1954, King Victor Emmanuel and Cavour had been anxious to have Piedmont join but were opposed by some of the ministers in the cabinet.[4] After several weeks of negotiations a treaty was concluded, January 1855, by which Piedmont adhered to the Anglo-French alliance and agreed to enter the war as an equal and to send 15,000 troops to the Crimea.[5] Though assured by France that the inclusion of Piedmont was for military purposes only, Buol could not conceal his distrust. He made no official protest but insisted that the new alliance should not serve as a point of departure for territorial aggrandizement or give Piedmont the right to be a contracting party to arrangements of a European character at the peace congress.[6]

Meanwhile, Buol tried to induce Berlin to adhere to the treaty of December 2nd. The reply from the Prussian Government was not encouraging, however. It stated that there was now less reason than ever to expect a Russian attack, that if Austria invaded Russia she could not count upon aid from her German allies, and that inasmuch as the additional clause of November 26, 1854 implied support of the four points by both powers, the exclusion of Prussia from the Vienna Conference released her from this obligation.[7] Thus rebuffed by Prussia, Buol decided to approach the members of the German Confederation. On January 14, 1855 he addressed a circular to the German governments in which he requested them to mobilize half of their federal contingents and place them under the leadership of Austria.[8] At the same time, the Austrian representatives at the German courts were secretly instructed to find out what would be the attitude of these courts in case they desired to join Austria and the Diet did not approve because of Prussian opposition.[9] Buol promised those states which agreed to cooperate in the efforts to obtain peace, a guarantee of their territorial possessions and a share in the advantages accruing from the war proportionate to the size of the forces they deployed. Unfortunately, his effort fell short of the mark and actually turned the sympathy of the German states more than ever toward Prussia. Buol then transferred the negotiations to the Diet where the influence of Bismarck had been increasing steadily since the beginning of the war. On January 30th the Diet rejected the request for mobilization and a week later adopted a resolution which provided that the federal contingents be placed on a war-footing in their respective cantonments, which meant that they would not leave German soil and would simply defend German interests.[10] Once more Buol's attempt to win the German states ended in failure.

As yet the treaty of December 2nd had produced no tangible results. From the first there existed a fundamental difference as to the means to be employed in order to bring the war to a close. Austria hoped to secure peace without fighting, while the western powers insisted that she become an active belligerent. Moreover, she had no desire to weaken Russia to any great extent, whereas England and France were determined to destroy Russian power in the east. Could one speak of an alliance when there was no common aim regarding the enemy? Far from satisfied with Austria's attitude, Drouyn de Lhuys declared that she must act as if military action appeared to her not only possible but probable.[11] In addition, he announced that the four points no longer sufficed to hold Russia in check and that other guarantees were needed.[12] Buol, on the other hand, stood squarely by the four points as the basis of peace and refused to accept whatever other conditions the western powers might suggest as a *casus foederis* for Austria should Russia reject the proposals. His mistake was in entertaining the belief that he could prevail upon London and Paris to accept a peace through negotiations rather than through a military victory. When in January 1855 he sent out feelers to St. Petersburg concerning peace negotiations, the French suspected that he was trying to make a separate bargain with Russia and that he was ignoring, if not actually condemning in advance, the demands of the allies.[13] On January 26th Napoleon appealed directly to Franz Joseph to enter the war and thus secure an honorable peace.[14] In his reply, the Austrian ruler emphasized his conviction that peace was still possible and that the Tsar would negotiate on the basis of the four points rather than carry the war *à outrance* against continental Europe.[15] He assured Napoleon, however, that if the peace negotiations failed, Austria would enter the war.

No one regretted more keenly than Hübner the rift which once more was beginning to appear in the relations between Paris and Vienna. Having hailed with enthusiasm the conclusion of the treaty of December 2nd, in which he detected the first real evidence of unity between the two courts, he now realized that he had built his hopes too high. Convinced, however, that an alliance with Napoleon was a necessity for Austria, he continued his efforts to make the alliance a reality. He addressed himself to both parties. To Napoleon he pointed out that Austria would be compelled to separate from the western powers if, in view of the Tsar's acceptance of the four points, they still insisted upon the destruction of Sebastopol and the Russian fleet in the Black Sea.[16] He reminded the Emperor that France had already obtained a great advantage from the war in leaving her isolation and in putting an end to the Holy Alliance. But Napoleon remained unconvinced of the wisdom of moderating the demands on Russia which, he well knew, would lead to serious difficulties with England. At the same time Hübner took it upon himself to warn Buol that if Austria failed to enter the war, she would find herself isolated, "placed between the rancor of the western powers and the vengeance of Russia, between Prussian ambitions and the revolutionary movement."[17] Since the western powers regarded the destruction of Sebastopol and the reduction of Russian naval power in the Black Sea to be of vital importance, Vienna should take this into consideration, for an alliance with France overshadowed all other questions.

In February 1855 Napoleon announced his intention of going to the Crimea to take personal command of the allied forces.[18] This plan encountered immediate opposition. England objected to it not only because she had little faith in the Emperor's military genius and hence had no desire to place her troops under his command, but also because she feared the outbreak of revolution in France after his departure and the possibility that he might be overthrown. All the French ministers opposed it,[19] while the announcement "caused considerable anxiety in the public and the Bourse, disturbed the friends and encouraged the enemies of the Emperor."[20] Hübner declared that the plan could not be justified in any sense, for it was dangerous, adventurous, inopportune and useless. "If the French army in the Crimea," he wrote, "should suffer a reverse while Napoleon is there, his prestige will be diminished and, moreover, there is the possibility that he might be killed. Because of the hesitations of Austria and the tergiversations of Prussia, Napoleon wants to go to Sebastopol in order to give new life to the army and to settle the eastern question himself."[21] The Austrian Government objected to the plan on the ground that Napoleon was under obligations to his allies and, in case of his death, no one knew who would succeed him. It is also likely that Buol saw the advantage of having the Emperor remain in France rather than visit the east where he might feel inclined to work out some fantastic schemes directed against Austrian interests. On March 11th Franz Joseph made a personal appeal to Napoleon to abandon the project.[22]

Despite the opposition, however, Napoleon was not easily persuaded to give up a plan which he had worked out in detail. Not even the death of Tsar Nicholas, which occurred on March 2nd and which raised hopes in France of an early peace, caused any noticeable hesitation on his part. During a visit to Windsor Castle in April every effort was made to dissuade the Emperor but he replied evasively and left England without committing himself.[23] Only gradually did he abandon the plan.[24]

The death of Tsar Nicholas brought no appreciable change in the general situation though it was thought that his successor, Alexander II, would prove more tractable. In Austria there appeared to be more hesitation than ever before and the sentiment for a closer *rapprochement* with Prussia was revived momentarily. It was suggested in a letter which Franz Joseph wrote to Frederick William in which he referred to the "noble memory of the Tsar Nicholas," "the generous friend and savior."[25] But the idea of a *rapprochement* turned out to be a delusion. The rivalry in Germany and complaints of indiscretions committed by Berlin, as well as the accusation that Prussia had deliberately tried to undermine confidence in the Austrian Government by depicting Franz Joseph as opposed to entering the war, caused it to vanish.[26] Count Georg Esterhazy reported from Berlin that Manteuffel had shown the English Ambassador a dispatch from von Arnim in which the latter described a visit of Gortchakoff to Franz Joseph following the death of the Tsar. The Emperor was said to have expressed regret about the treaty of December 2nd and to have declared his willingness to resume closer relations with Russia.[27] In telling the French Ambassador about von Arnim's report, Manteuffel had gone so far as to cast doubt upon the honesty of the Austrian Cabinet. Similar information reached Buol from London and Paris.[28] From all this it appeared that Prussia was not only trying to show that there was a difference between the policy of the Emperor and his minister but to drive a wedge between Austria and the western powers.[29] Buol attributed Prussia's intrigues to her disappointment in not being invited to the Vienna Conference, which reconvened on March 16th.[30] In a dispatch to Drouyn de Lhuys, Bourqueney referred to "energetic steps" which Austria had taken toward Prussia.[31]

Your Excellency will agree with me that this constitutes a real evidence of the sincerity of the Austrian alliance and a guarantee of its duration beyond the eastern complications which agitate Europe at the moment. Austria desires peace; she believes in its approaching reëstablishment and far from preparing in this case for the reconstruction of her old alliances by a *rapprochement* with Prussia, she is, in fact, alienating herself more than ever from this power. . . . Evidently, the Vienna Cabinet has broken irrevocably with the traditions of the past and whatever might be the result of the coming conference, Austria upon the reëstablishment of peace, will not seek support for her policy in the north.

Austro-Russian relations underwent no immediate improvement after the death of Nicholas. In a letter of condolence, which he addressed to Alexander II, Franz Joseph gave assurance that "the memory of the bonds which unite me to the one whom we mourn, is only equal in my heart with the desire to cultivate the same relations with the heir to his throne . . . and to do everything compatible with my duties in order to contribute toward facilitating the immense task whose accomplishment Providence has reserved to you."[32] In his reply of March 17th, Alexander II left no doubt as to his attitude. He complained bitterly that the conduct of Franz Joseph during the past year had broken his father's heart, "for instead of finding in you the friend and faithful ally upon whom he counted and whom he loved like his own son, he saw you follow a political course which drew you closer and closer toward our enemies and which will lead us inevitably, if it is not changed, to a fratricidal war and make you accountable to God!"[33] Alexander declared that he would continue the war even though all Europe was lined up against him rather than submit to a dishonorable peace. "Be convinced that this sentiment is shared by all Russia and God, who saved us in 1812, will not desert us."[34]

Thus any hope Franz Joseph might have entertained of effecting a *rapprochement* with his former allies, Prussia and Russia, vanished into thin air. Would he now be able to resist the pressure of the western powers to get Austria to enter the war? The answer to this question, it was thought, would be determined by the results of the Vienna Conference, whose reopening had been accepted by the new Tsar.[35] Called to consider the possibility of terminating the war on the basis of the four points, the Conference at first made rapid headway and within a few days an agreement was reached on the first two points, those relating to the Principalities and the Danube, in which Austria was primarily interested.[36] The real difficulty arose over point three. Russia was willing to respect the integrity of the Ottoman Empire but refused to join in a collective guarantee. Furthermore, and what was most important, she would not accept a reduction of her naval power in the Black Sea. Since this was the dominant thought of the western powers, particularly England, the Conference faced an impasse. The English and French delegates would not discuss the fourth point until the third was settled, while Gortchakoff announced that he had to get instructions from home.

Everything now depended on finding a solution for the third point. England, supported by France, was determined to limit the Russian naval strength in the Black Sea to four warships. The question was whether this could be done without impairing Russia's rights of sovereignty. Austria, while agreeing to a limitation of Russian naval power favored a counterpoise plan which would admit foreign warships through the Straits in sufficient number to guarantee the integrity of the Ottoman Empire.[37] Russia, of course, bitterly opposed the English demand but was quite willing to open the Straits to warships of all nations and even allow them in the Black Sea.

Lord John Russell, Minister of Colonies in Palmerston's Cabinet, was appointed First English Delegate to the Conference.[38] He had been instructed to insist upon a strict limitation of Russia's naval power in the Black Sea or failing this to break off negotiations and demand that Austria join the western powers on the basis of the treaty of December 2nd.[39] Buol, however, refused to accept the English demand limiting Russian naval power in the Black Sea to four warships and instead proposed his counterpoise plan which, in turn, was rejected by Clarendon.[40] The most that the Austrian minister would agree to was the limitation of the Russian fleet to its strength in 1853.

In view of the impasse which faced the Conference, Drouyn de Lhuys decided to take a hand. He saw that if the Conference was to be saved and, above all, if Austria was to be prevailed upon to enter the war, it was necessary to devise a more equitable solution of the third point than the one presented by England. He therefore proposed the neutralization of the Black Sea which would apply to all nations. This was approved by the British Cabinet.[41] When the neutralization plan was submitted to the Conference on March 26th it was rejected by Austria. Drouyn de Lhuys thereupon decided to attend the Conference in person.[42]

A conservative statesman and a devout Catholic, Drouyn de Lhuys regarded the system set up by the Congress of Vienna in 1815 as the best safeguard for France since it sanctioned the disunity of her neighbors, Germany and Italy. He was a convinced and ardent advocate of an Austro-French alliance, which he thought would end the war promptly and constitute the best guarantee against revolution. To ally with the oldest royal house in Europe would flatter the *amour propre* of his master, bind him to a policy of territorial preservation, and remove him from ambitious Prussia and especially from revolutionary Italy.[43] Concerned over the revolutionary tendencies of the Emperor and aware that in the struggle against Russia France was sacrificing her blood and treasures to serve the ends of England, whom he distrusted, Drouyn de Lhuys was determined to make the most of his stay in Vienna in order to establish a close union with Austria.

Before proceeding to the Conference, the French Minister visited London for a final understanding with Palmerston and Clarendon regarding his neutralization plan. In discussions with the British statesmen two alternatives were worked out which were to be submitted to Austria before they were presented to Russia. One of these was the neutralization plan, the other called for the limitation of the Russian fleet in the Black Sea to four vessels and the opening of the Straits to the warships of England and France.[44] Austria was to be asked to select one of these alternative proposals and to take part in the war if Russia rejected the one selected.[45] In case Austria should refuse to fight Russia if the latter rejected one of the proposals, the neutralization plan would be presented to the Conference. Russia's refusal to accept this would lead to a rupture of the negotiations.[46]

The French Minister arrived in Vienna on April 6th and had an interview with Buol. "I found in Count Buol," he wrote to Napoleon, "an attitude most favorable to us, sincerely favorable to our views in everything which does not imply the question of war but less decisive in all the *démarches* which can lead to drawing the sword."[47] Buol opposed the neutralization plan on the ground that Russia would not even consider reciprocity with Turkey, and while prepared to support the demand for the limitation of the Russian fleet in the Black Sea, he would not consider it a *casus belli* in case of a Russian rejection.[48] Moreover, he declared that he could not propose war to the Frankfurt Diet for two vessels more or less.[49] This attitude annoyed the French Minister, who replied that it was necessary to envisage the treaty of December 2nd in its entirety and not merely the separate clauses.[50]

During an audience with Franz Joseph on April 8th, Drouyn de Lhuys repeated the warning that the alliance intended by the treaty of December 2nd would be destroyed if the four points were not considered as inseparable. He also dwelt upon the advantages of an intimate alliance between Austria and France. Such an alliance, he declared, would enable Austria to maintain unity in her various domains, uphold her position in Germany, check the encroachment of Russia on the Danube, extinguish the germs of anarchy and socialism, and develop the prosperity of the Hapsburg Empire by capital and industry. "The great problem is to check the revolution without the aid of Russia and to check Russia without the aid of revolution. For thirty years this problem has remained unsolved and the result has been the simultaneous triumph of Russia and revolution. Today the solution is to be found in the alliance of Austria and France. . . . What brings me to Vienna is less the desire to conclude peace with Russia than to confirm and render fruitful the alliance with Austria. . . . In the eyes of true statesmanship, the eastern question, despite its significance, becomes in comparison with this other one a matter of secondary importance."[51] Franz Joseph replied that his mind was concerned with two duties: loyalty to his allies and solicitude for the interests of his people and he was resolved to fulfill both. As to the question of a closer alliance with France, he preferred to have it postponed until the end of the negotiations.

Despite the pleas of Drouyn de Lhuys and Russell, Buol remained firm in his opposition to the neutralization plan.[52] At the same time, however, he had no desire to see the Conference broken up and he therefore proposed that the Russian fleet in the Black Sea be limited to its strength in 1853. An ultimatum containing this proposal and providing for the closure of the Straits and a European guarantee of the territorial integrity of Turkey would be addressed to St. Petersburg.[53] Rejection of the ultimatum would bring Austria into the war.[54] Clarendon, who regarded peace on Buol's terms as "dishonourable," turned down the scheme and recalled Russell.[55] Before the latter's departure, he conferred at length with Buol and Drouyn de Lhuys and an agreement was reached which was to be presented to their governments for acceptance. This called for a graduated counterpoise plan whereby Russia would not exceed a set number of vessels, a guarantee of Turkish independence and territorial integrity, the closure of the Straits, permission for each of the allies to station two warships in the Black Sea after the signing of peace, and the conclusion of a treaty of guarantee between Austria, England and France.[56]

The new plan was flatly rejected by Clarendon, who held that it favored Russia more than Turkey.[57] Napoleon, who was visiting London during the middle of April, was induced to withhold his approval.[58] Upon his return to Paris, Drouyn de Lhuys sought to overcome Napoleon's objections to the plan, which had been drawn up in collaboration with Buol and Russell, but realizing that this could not be done, he submitted his resignation on May 5th and was succeeded as Foreign Minister by Count Walewski.

Hübner attributed the resignation of Drouyn de Lhuys to the influence of Cowley, who persuaded Napoleon that the minister was too pro-Austrian.[59] Drouyn de Lhuys gave his own version of the circumstances leading to his resignation in an interview with the Dutch Minister, M. de Lightenveld on June 2nd.[60] It was neither anger nor offended dignity that caused him to resign, he explained, but having ardently supported the idea of a double alliance, English and continental, he could not remain in the cabinet without sacrificing his convictions and without executing policies which he did not approve. When he returned to Paris, the Emperor had approved the plan after suggesting two amendments concerning the number of Russian vessels in the Black Sea. The amended plan was then sent to Vienna where it was accepted by Franz Joseph and Buol while Russell had also given his approval. After that it was submitted to the English cabinet which not only rejected it but threatened to resign if Napoleon insisted upon it. A conference was held in Paris attended by the Emperor, Drouyn de Lhuys and Cowley. The latter repeated the attitude of his government whereupon the Emperor drew up a dispatch for London rejecting the plan and instructed Drouyn de Lhuys to expedite it. This the minister refused to do and submitted his resignation, after explaining that he could not remain at his post while sacrificing his convictions and his authority. The Emperor wrote to him, urging him to keep his portfolio and suggesting an interview. Drouyn de Lhuys, however, insisted upon his immediate resignation and this time the Emperor agreed. Once freed from responsibility, the former minister explained his position in a memorandum which he submitted to the Emperor. In this he declared that it was a mistake to prefer an alliance with England to an alliance including Austria, which would lead to an honorable peace. As it was, France found herself alone with England and faced a possible armed neutrality of Germany. In order to substantiate his story, Drouyn de Lhuys showed Mr. de Lightenveld his correspondence with the Emperor.

In what concerns Austria, it is clear that she went much further than is generally supposed in seeking a *modus vivendi* with the western powers.[61] Responsibility for the failure of the Conference cannot be laid to her alone. Had Napoleon remained firm, it is quite likely that England would have been compelled to follow his lead. But seeing England's deep distrust of the Austrian Government, Napoleon preferred not to antagonize his ally. In explaining his position to Hübner, he said that while he recognized the value of Austria's support, he did not want an alliance which did not represent a free choice on the part of the allies—an alliance created by circumstances and disasters. "I would repent it; I could never forgive myself nor France either."[62] Rather than permit Russia to rebuild her naval power in the Black Sea, he was prepared to carry on the war with England alone.

Hübner was much disturbed by the Emperor's attitude and again warned Buol of the consequences of breaking with the western powers. Since Austria had accepted the principle of naval limitation, the difference was merely one of figures, which would not influence Russia's decision. What was of capital importance was Austria's relations with the western powers. "After all the sacrifices he has made, Napoleon does not consider himself able to conclude a peace which would give Russia the opportunity of reëstablishing her fleet on the old basis without losing the support of French public opinion and without abdicating morally. . . . To break the alliance with France will mean to compromise the tranquillity which now exists

in Italy, to deprive Austria of her position in Germany in favor
of Prussia, to change forcibly the conservative policy of Napoleon,
and to permit the triumph of English and liberal ideas in his cabinet,
finally, to isolate Austria and to place her at the mercy of Russia
and Prussia, who would become our implacable enemies."[63]

Not only had the tripartite alliance reached a critical stage.
Relations between Paris and Vienna had become worse than at any
time since the beginning of the war. France demanded that Austria
fulfill her obligations under the treaty of December 2nd; whereas
Austria maintained that she was now freed from those obligations.
Buol felt that his policy was not properly understood at Paris. "We
do not impose upon the belligerent powers a peace which is not
agreeable to them but we do not wish to impose upon ourselves a
war which is not dictated by our interests."[64] The western powers
contended, however, that the Austrian plan did not contain a solution corresponding to the sacrifices they had made inasmuch as it
would not put an end to Russian preponderance in the Black Sea.
The real difficulty was that the allies were not in agreement concerning the aim of the war. Austria would not admit that the aim was to
destroy Russian power in the Black Sea. This was a means rather
than an aim or end.

> In our opinion the common efforts of the allies should be directed
> toward the limitation of the political power of Russia to the point of ren-
> dering it most difficult, if not impossible, to abuse her material resources.
> The limitation, even the total destruction of the Russian fleet in the Black
> Sea will not alone suffice to deprive Russia of the advantages which her
> geographic position gives her toward Turkey. The dominating thought
> in our plan was to give the latter a collection of moral guarantees and
> counterweights.[65]

Austria, said Buol, wanted peace, even a mediocre one, rather than
embark upon a war whose aim was so uncertain; and neither seduc-
tion nor intimidation could persuade her to become a party to the
special designs of England and France.[66]

This attitude was resented by the western powers, particularly
by England, where the capture of Sebastopol and the destruction of
the Russian fleet had become questions of national honor and where
Buol's proposals were regarded almost as insults.[67] Palmerston gave

expression to this feeling in an ironic letter to Napoleon in which he declared that if the allies were successful in the Crimea, they might command the friendship and perhaps the sword of Austria, but if success failed them they would not even have her pen.[68] The French Emperor was more moderate in his attitude and, according to Hübner, seemed to realize that he had gone too far in yielding to English influence and was now anxious to extricate himself. "The retirement of Drouyn de Lhuys really did not bring about a change of policy, since France wishes to draw close to Austria. Napoleon realizes only too well the weight that Austria carries in the scale. Since his accession, he has acquired an accurate knowledge of the extent and the resources of the Austrian Monarchy. . . . I have neglected nothing in order to verify if, and to what extent, the assertions tending to make one believe that Napoleon has drawn close to revolutionary ideas, are authentic. I can assure you, Monsieur le Comte, that nothing has come to my attention to confirm them. On the contrary, it seems certain to me that no important change has taken place in the policy of Louis Napoleon. He will be a faithful and dependable ally so long as Austria and France march together, but the day the rupture occurs, he will have no scruples about employing revolution against us, which will serve him, as it always served the kings of France, in their struggles with the House of Austria."[69] But while no radical change had taken place in Napoleon's policy, he was nonetheless displeased with Austria's conduct and refused to believe Hübner's argument that a permanent alliance with her was "a thousand times more valuable than all the advantages, real or imaginary, which could result from a military success."[70]

Though the alliance of December 2nd still lingered, it was rapidly approaching its demise. According to Walewski, the signatories had regained complete freedom of action and Russia could now withdraw such concessions as she had already made.[71] The four points remained but the western powers no longer considered themselves bound to negotiate peace on this basis.[72] On the other hand, France was willing to continue the alliance providing Austria agreed to change her military and diplomatic attitude. In any case, it would be necessary to reach a complete understanding concerning the aim of the alliance, only vaguely indicated in Article I of the treaty, and concerning the conditions under which Austria was willing to enter the war. Walewski warned Hübner that if such an understanding was not reached, the treaty would become a dead letter and Austria could not then expect to participate in future peace negotiations.[73] Napoleon was no less outspoken and in a speech before the *Corps Législatif* on July 2nd, he reproached Austria for her inaction and said that he was still waiting for her to execute the engagements of December 2nd. He declared that France and England had agreed to negotiate on the basis of the four points merely to satisfy Austria, whose interests they were designed to safeguard. Later, in inaugurating the Universal Exposition in Paris, he said: "It is necessary that Europe pronounces: in the final analysis it is to public opinion that the last word belongs."[74] This was regarded as a warning to Austria.

Such warnings could not be ignored in Vienna considering the difficulties which faced the Hapsburg Monarchy. Being neither a belligerent nor a neutral, with her army on a semi-war footing, Austria suffered the disadvantages of war without hope of profiting from peace in case of an allied victory. In order to defray the cost of equipping an army against Russia, it had been necessary to levy a loan on the Austrian people, but when the money did not pour in rapidly enough, the Government sold the National Railway to a French syndicate for a trifle.[75] The political horizon was darkened by the estrangement from the western powers, the hatred of Russia, and the loss of influence in Germany. Yet, Franz Joseph was convinced that the course he had followed was both reasonable and honorable.[76] Buol, who had attached his name and political fortune to the treaty of December 2nd, complained that it was not Austria's policy which had changed but that of the western powers. "Paris and London," he wrote to Hübner, "should learn that they cannot dispose of our forces and make us march at their will. Rather than permit a sovereign, who is a tool of an English minister, to make the law for us, it will be better to return to dependence upon Russia. The idea that the interests of the continent should be deliberated upon and decided at London is antiquated. Today France and England want to carry on a war at any price, but they do not want the conditions which seemed good to them before the war. . . .

If Louis Napoleon returns to us, he will find us the same. If he allows himself to be dragged into the revolutionary current, and intimacy with Lord Palmerston could lead him into it, we would have to watch ourselves and thank Heaven that we did not engage ourselves more than we did."[77] Buol refused to admit that the sacrifices incurred by the western powers necessitated a change in the aim of the war and insisted that the four points serve as the basis of peace. "Let no one demand the impossible of Austria. Her active cooperation has been sacrificed by the rejection of her proposals. They ask us to enter the war without listening to our advice. Nevertheless, we agree to remain in our political position. The powers will find us there if they accept the price. The choice and the extent of the means to keep us, should be left to us"[78]

As the weeks went by and as the allies suffered a series of reverses in the Crimea, their relations with Austria tended to grow worse, while Napoleon appeared to become more dependent upon England. The gap which separated Austria from the allies was widened when Franz Joseph, in order to reassure Prussia and the German states, whose support he was still seeking to obtain, began recalling a number of regiments from Galicia. Though he tried to justify this action as required by economy and though Buol issued a statement to the press that it represented "merely a halt, not a change,"[79] the allies were not deceived. They could only see that it enabled Russia to withdraw troops from Poland and that it made the possibility of Austria's participation more remote than ever. Indeed, the latter gave every appearance of awaiting the outcome of the war in order to join the winning side and to impose peace. That such was not the real intention of Austria is made clear from an examination of the evidence. Despite the collapse of the Vienna Conference and the coolness which followed in Austria's relations with her allies, Franz Joseph and Buol wished to keep alive the tripartite alliance. They knew that the alternative was isolation. Fortunately, France had no desire to drop the alliance altogether. Although he was indignant because Austria failed to give military aid, Napoleon had not surrendered completely to the English. "His good sense enabled him to withstand the passionate and interested insinuations of the English diplomats."[80] There was no doubt that these diplomats had considerable influence over him. "He places great confidence in the friendship of Lord Palmerston. He also has a very high opinion of the capacity and the energy of Lord Clarendon; while Lord Cowley knows how to gain his favor and in critical moments exercises an unquestionable influence."[81] On the other hand, Napoleon had a certain amount of influence over English policy. According to Hübner, this influence rested upon the leading part France had taken in the military operations, the superiority of French diplomacy, and the personal popularity of Napoleon in England, where he was regarded, except by the bourgeoisie, as the representative of the democratic idea.[82] In August, Austria received positive assurances from Paris that the alliance of December 2nd was still in force.[83]

On September 8, 1855, the allies won an important victory which compelled the Russians to evacuate a part of the fortress of Sebastopol. Though the war was not yet over, this marked the beginning of the end. England still insisted that Russia must be beaten decisively but Napoleon had become tired of the costly venture and desired an early peace.[84] The Tsar also wanted peace and hoped that by detaching France from England he could obtain honorable terms. Numerous Russian agents, as well as representatives of the German secondary states in Paris, were attempting to bring about a Franco-Russian reconciliation. The most active was Baron Seebach, the Saxon Minister and a nephew of the Russian Chancellor. He had been charged with the protection of Russian subjects in France and did much to convince Napoleon of the advantages of an early peace with Russia.[85]

An incident arose in connection with the allied victory which, though of slight importance in itself, revealed how delicate Austro-French relations had become. Austria neglected to send the customary congratulations for this victory to Napoleon, who expressed astonishment to Hübner at this omission. Nearly a month elapsed before the latter received instructions to convey the felicitations of Franz Joseph.[86] Hübner immediately sought a private audience with Napoleon but it was not until October 18th, during a reception at St. Cloud, that he found the opportunity of carrying out his instructions. The belated manner in which Austria sought to retrieve her negligence did little to soften Napoleon's displeasure. The Empress was particularly outspoken and at a dinner on October 21st asked Hübner what his government had gained by its policy. "You did not conciliate Russia. You did not regain your influence in Germany, and you cannot count upon the gratitude of France and England."[87]

Though Buol was not greatly disturbed by the incident since he figured that he already had the Principalities in his pocket,[88] he was shrewd enough to realize that Austria's position would become worse if her passive policy continued.[89] He therefore devised a plan for ending the war which he hoped would not only win back the confidence of Napoleon but would enable Austria once more to act as mediator, a position she had forfeited after the failure of the last Conference.[90] According to his plan, the allies should propose peace terms to Russia, drawn up by England and France, but giving Austria the right to make observations before accepting them as her own. In case Russia rejected these terms, the war would continue on a restricted scale with Austria maintaining a defensive position on the Danube.[91] Buol made it clear that Austria would not engage herself beyond this point unless her own interests were threatened. "In a word," he said to the French Chargé d'Affaires, "Austria does not seek to gather the laurels; she will draw the sword only to defend her own interests or those of Europe in general. Finally, realizing that she can enter actively in the present war only by giving it an extension which would lead . . . to an alteration of the map of Europe, she will resort to force only when the absolute ineffectiveness of all other means has been demonstrated."[92] Convinced of Austria's loyalty to the alliance of December 2nd, the French Chargé d'Affaires believed that a complete victory over the Russians in the Crimea would lead to active cooperation of Franz Joseph, providing an agreement was reached regarding the profits of war. He characterized Austrian policy as a curious mixture of "hopes and fears, prudence and rashness, ambition and weakness," though at the moment it was based upon the assumption that the allies would succeed in driving the Russians from the Crimea before the winter.[93]

Early in October Bourqueney laid Buol's plan before Walewski, who welcomed it with great satisfaction. Upon his return to Vienna, Bourqueney entered into discussions with Buol. On November 14th a tentative agreement was reached which called for the renunciation by Russia of her protectorate over the Principalities, the establishment of an autonomous government for the Christians of Turkey under the collective protection of the great powers, rectification of the Bessarabian frontier, freedom of navigation on the Danube under the control of the contracting powers, the neutralization of the Black Sea, the conclusion of a treaty between Russia and Turkey, and the admission of the latter to the European Concert.[94] Finally, it was declared that the allies reserved the right to present additional conditions of a European interest. Acceptance of these terms by Russia would be followed by the signing of peace preliminaries, while their rejection would lead immediately to the complete rupture of diplomatic relations between Vienna and St. Petersburg and the conclusion of an agreement between the allies concerning the means to be employed in order to compel acceptance by Russia.[95]

In a private letter to Hübner, Buol stated that rejection of these terms by Russia did not mean that Austria would enter the war. "Without definitely excluding the chance of our active cooperation in the war, I would say that the energetic measures we support in these preliminaries do not imply the obligation of entering the campaign. I set forth to him (Bourqueney) the serious reasons why we cannot cooperate actively. . . . I said to him that our participation in the war cannot change its character and that we would merely produce new complications whose significance would be incalculable. Not only would it divert us from the aim we have set before us, but it would offer the enemy favorable chances to escape from the embarrassment of its present position. I insisted upon the principles that we have constantly placed before ourselves, namely, that Austria can take so grave a decision only from motives which directly touch her interests or which would be imposed upon us by the general interests of Europe. . . . It should be realized that Austria can take up arms only when all other means have failed. We do not intend to condemn ourselves to permanent inaction."[96] Buol attached one condition to the acceptance of the proposed terms by Austria: that England and France conclude with her a special treaty guaranteeing the independence and the territorial integrity of the Ottoman Empire.

Buol's draft was accepted by the French Cabinet.[97] England, however, did not intend to give up so easily. She was indignant because Austria, after having protected her own interests by the adoption of the first two of the four points and after having rendered them more humiliating for Russia by the demand that the Tsar give up the mouth of the Danube and even cede a part of Bessarabia to Moldavia, had weakened the third point concerning the Black Sea.[98] The English were determined to crush Russian naval power in the Black Sea and the Baltic.[99] But while Napoleon sought to pacify his English ally, he let it be known that he desired peace and threatened, if the war continued, to stir up revolutions in Hungary, Italy and Poland. England knew that if this happened, Prussia would probably join Russia and Napoleon would take Belgium and the left bank of the Rhine. In any case, there could be no doubt that Napoleon was determined to end the war. He sent an autograph letter to Queen Victoria urging the acceptance of Buol's draft and after a delay of several weeks, the English Cabinet yielded.[100] On December 16th, Buol instructed Count Valentin Esterhazy to submit an ultimatum containing the proposals to the Russian Cabinet and requesting that a reply be made by January 17, 1856.

Confronted by the reëstablished front of the three powers, Alexander II decided to play for time, still hoping to detach Napoleon and thus obtain better terms. Baron Seebach redoubled his efforts to arrange a reconciliation between France and Russia but he was unable to bring about a rift in the alliance. Napoleon admitted to Hübner that Russia had made advances but added "she is mistaken if she believes that I will be unfaithful to my allies, the Emperor Francis Joseph and Queen Victoria."[101] On January 5, 1856, Nesselrode replied to the Austrian ultimatum, accepting all proposals except the one in which the allies reserved to themselves the right to present additional demands of a European interest. Russia, he declared, could not accept conditions which were not made known. Exasperated by this attempt to stall for time, Buol warned Gortchakoff on January 12, 1856 that Austria would proceed to break off diplomatic relations if Russia did not give a complete acceptance without further delay.[102] On January 16th Nesselrode informed Esterhazy that the Russian Cabinet accepted without reservations.[103]

Although the war was now at an end, the allies were not in complete agreement concerning the special conditions of the peace terms. England still insisted that Russian power in the Baltic and the Near East must be reduced, whereas Austria having satisfied her own interests, did not wish to go that far. Napoleon tried to persuade Vienna that some concessions were necessary in view of England's attitude but meeting with no success in this direction he decided to bring pressure on England.[104] The admission of Prussia to the peace congress presented another difficulty. Lord Palmerston was severely critical of Prussia's role in the war and would not hear of her participation. Austria, however, intervened and it was decided to admit Prussia after the conditions of peace had been arranged.[105]

The peace congress was officially opened at Paris on February 25, 1856.[106] Walewski presided at its sessions while Bourqueney served as the second French delegate. Austria was represented by Buol and Hübner, England by Clarendon and Cowley, Russia by Orloff and Brunnow, Piedmont by Cavour and Villamarina, and Turkey by Aali Pasha and Djemal Effendi. The Prussian delegates, Otto von Manteuffel and Hatzfeldt, were not admitted until March 18th, and then only to ratify the decisions already taken. During the congress the Russians missed no opportunity of ingratiating themselves with the French or of showing their hatred for Austria.[107] A Franco-Russian reconciliation was taking place under the very eyes of the Austrian and English delegates, but though they viewed it with growing concern, they were unable to prevent it. On March 30th the Treaty of Paris was signed.

Napoleon hoped that the congress would give him a chance to raise certain questions not directly connected with the peace. In accordance with his views on nationalities, he desired to effect a settlement of the Italian and Polish questions and to bring about the union of the Principalities of Moldavia and Wallachia. He tried to convince Buol that something should be done for Poland and Italy and suggested that the liberal concessions given to the Poles in 1815 be restored, while Austria and France withdrew their troops from the Papal States.[108] In view of his growing friendship with Russia, it is likely that the Emperor made his reference to Poland in order that the problem of Italy should not stand out too prominently. At any rate, Buol replied that such matters were beyond the competence of the congress to discuss, that it was for the Tsar alone to decide on concessions for the Poles, and for Austria, France and the Papacy to arrange for the withdrawal of the troops.

There is no doubt that it was Italy rather than Poland that held the greater interest of Napoleon at this time. In a letter to King Victor Emmanuel, dated February 5, 1856, he promised to do everything possible at the congress to see that Italian interests were not forgotten.[109] On March 27th Cavour addressed a note to Walewski demanding reforms in the Papal States and the withdrawal of the Austrian and French troops. Walewski, with the approval of the Emperor, decided to bring Cavour's proposal, together with several others of European interest, before the congress.

At the session of April 8th, Walewski suggested an exchange of views regarding questions which might disturb European peace, such as those relating to Greece, the Papal States, Naples and Belgium.[110] Cavour had skillfully prepared the groundwork and had succeeded in making friends with most of the delegates, except the Austrian. Clarendon, who had been won over by the Piedmontese statesman, employed strong language in condemning the governments of Naples and the Papal States as well as the presence of Austrian and French troops in the Peninsula. He declared that while aware of the principle that ·a government should not interfere in the affairs of another state, there are "cases in which the exception to this becomes equally a right and a duty. The Neapolitan Government seems . . . to have conferred this right, and to have imposed this duty upon Europe."[111] The Austrian delegates bitterly protested the introduction of the questions and categorically refused to recognize any discussions concerning the internal affairs of sovereign states in the absence of their rulers—a principle which had been set forth in the protocol of Aix-la-Chapelle of November 15, 1818.[112] Though Buol argued that since the congress had completed its work, there was nothing more to do than to bring the sessions to a close, he was unable to prevent a discussion. Cavour seized the opportunity to indict the Austrian occupation of the Papal States as an anomaly, as a menace to peace, and as useless in view of the restoration of order in Italy. Although the congress took no action, he won a moral victory in thus denouncing before Europe the Austrian position in Italy. On April 16th Cavour addressed notes to England and France in which he elaborated upon the Italian question and declared that Europe could not continue to neglect it without endangering the peace.

Cavour's appeal alarmed Buol, who had just concluded (April 15th) a treaty with England and France guaranteeing the independence and territorial integrity of the Ottoman Empire. From the discussions which had taken place during the congress, he knew that the Italian question was the one thing that could wreck the *entente* of the three powers. Napoleon had not concealed from him that this was the most delicate of all questions standing between Austria and France and he, in turn, had assured the Emperor that he would do everything that was humanly possible for Italy. "Nevertheless," wrote Napoleon to Victor Emmanuel, "I have no illusions. Even with good intentions, is Austria placed in the position to do good?"[113]

For Austria the Crimean War proved to be a great misfortune. To begin with, she had incurred the hatred of Russia—a hatred which was increased by the humiliating terms of the ultimatum. Russia considered herself betrayed by the power with which she had been allied for over thirty years. Likewise, the war paved the way for a *rapprochement* between France and Russia which enabled Napoleon to carry out his plans in Italy and in the Principalities. The effects on Austro-French relations were even more important for the future. Napoleon did not forget Austria's refusal to take an active part in the war and he showed his enmity by the encouragement he gave to Cavour. In England also the vacillating tactics of the Vienna Cabinet created considerable ill-feeling. Even worse was the effect on the German question, which had been pushed into the foreground by the diplomatic duel at Frankfurt. Austria's influence among the German states had grown weaker, though to what extent was not apparent until 1859.

The reasons which prevented Franz Joseph from taking an active part in the war seemed sound enough at the time. Considering the ethnographic composition of his empire, he could not join the Tsar in effecting the liberation of the Balkan Slavs without endangering his own dominions. Furthermore, cooperation with Russia was prevented by anxiety for the Italian possessions and by fear of Napoleon's support of the revolutionary movement. On the other hand, the risk of losing his influence in Germany did not permit Franz Joseph to fight Russia on the side of the western powers. Finally, the lack of agreement among his advisers, the division of his court into Russophiles, Russophobes and neutralists, rendered a more decisive policy difficult of attainment.

In placing responsibility for Austria's conduct during the eastern crisis Buol has been usually singled out as the chief culprit. He has been accused of widening the breach with Russia, of entertaining too deep a distrust of Napoleon, of adopting a disdainful attitude toward Prussia, and of arousing resentment among the German states. No doubt there is some truth in these accusations. Buol was not a first-rate statesman. He possessed neither the skill of Metternich nor the firm leadership of Schwarzenberg. In fairness, however, it should be stated that the final decisions were made by Franz Joseph, who had too much confidence in his own abilities. It is not unreasonable to point out that if Buol had been given a free hand, Austria's policy during the Crimean War would have been less vacillating. From the start he wanted to conclude an alliance with the western powers independent of Prussia's actions. As we have seen, it was the subserviency of Franz Joseph to Prussia and the German states which weakened Buol's policy. Once it became clear that the Emperor drew back from active participation in the war, his minister had no alternative than to resort to diplomatic stratagems, conferences and protocols.

CHAPTER SIX

Near Eastern Affairs, 1856-1859

THE RELATIONS BETWEEN Austria and France underwent significant alterations in the period which followed the conclusion of the
Treaty of Paris, March 30, 1856. Ideas which Napoleon had in-
herited from his youth, but which he had hidden from view
during the Crimean War, emerged into the light of day and became
basic principles of his foreign policy. These ideas—the revision of
the treaties of 1815 and the furtherance of the cause of nationalities—came into direct conflict with the interests of Austria. The
latter because of the presence of many nationalities within her
borders, as well as those subject to the Sultan in the neighboring
states, and likewise because of her position in Germany and Italy,
defended the settlement of 1815 and the independence and territorial integrity of the Ottoman Empire. In both the Near East and
Italy Napoleon saw Austria standing squarely in his way, contesting
every effort on his part to change the *status quo*.

In this contest Austria was at a disadvantage. Not only did
she have more to lose, but her position in Europe was seriously
undermined by the Crimean War. Whereas in 1853 her prestige
had still shone with much of the brilliancy which had been given
to it by Metternich and Schwarzenberg, and whereas her influence
in Germany, Italy and the Near East had appeared to be firmly
established, the end of the war found Austria internally weak,
facing isolation, and deeply concerned as to the future. By contrast,
the position of France was strengthened. Before the Crimean War,
Napoleon had been looked upon as a *parvenu* among the crowned

heads, an object of suspicion in the European cabinets, an adventurer whose actions had to be carefully watched. The conservative powers had revealed their attitude in an unmistakable manner by delaying recognition of the Second Empire. Even England had hesitated to draw too close to the nephew of the Corsican Conqueror. Only in such small states as Piedmont and Switzerland had the Emperor seen possibilities of support. But the war had changed this situation. France was now the leading power on the continent, Paris the center of diplomacy, and Napoleon the virtual arbiter of European affairs. The hated coalition of the north had disappeared, apparently forever. No longer was France isolated, for in addition to the alliances concluded during the war with Austria, England and Piedmont, Russia was drawn to her side. Indeed, the Franco-Russian *rapprochement*, which began at the Congress, was one of the most astonishing results of the war. It did not mean, however, that Napoleon was cutting loose from England. On the contrary, as he explained to Hübner, the English alliance remained the cornerstone of his policy.[1] The Russian *entente* was merely superimposed upon it.[2] For the success of his Italian policy, he needed the friendship of both England and Russia.

The *rapprochement* between Paris and St. Petersburg was made possible by the transformation which had taken place in Russian policy since the beginning of the war. Not only was Russia at odds with one of the partners of the Holy Alliance, but her attachment to the treaties of 1815 and her defense of conservative principles, which had characterized the reign of Nicholas I, were less emphasized in the program of his successor. Both France and Russia desired to alter the *status quo*. While France was determined to revise the treaties of 1815 in her favor, Russia was equally determined to revise the Treaty of Paris, particularly the clauses relative to the Black Sea.[3]

In April 1856, Count Nesselrode, who had conducted Russia's foreign policy for nearly forty years, was succeeded by Prince Gortchakoff. Before his retirement, the aged Chancellor addressed a memorandum to the Tsar in which he stressed the absolute necessity of concentrating on internal affairs and of avoiding any foreign ventures which might interfere with them.[4] Urging Alexander II to retain as far as possible the policies of his predecessors, Nesselrode opposed the *rapprochement* with France, arguing that Napoleon was revolutionary and followed a policy of nationalities, whereas Russian policy must remain monarchical and anti-Polish.

Prince Gortchakoff held a different point of view. As the Russian representative in Vienna during the latter part of the war, he had acquired a deep-rooted hatred for Austria. His bitter words, "Austria is not state, it is only a regime," had circulated throughout Europe.[5] Intent upon breaking up the Anglo-French alliance and of substituting Russia for England in an alliance with France, Gortchakoff viewed with pleasure every dissension which arose between the two maritime powers. The absorption of the Tsar in internal affairs during the early years of the reign gave Gortchakoff virtually a free hand in the conduct of foreign policy. The Duc de Morny, the French Ambassador at St. Petersburg, who had received instructions to work for a *rapprochement,* was overwhelmed with attention.[6] Morny was quick to see the advantages of Russian friendship. Not only would it enable French financiers and traders to compete on more favorable terms with the English in the Russian markets, but if Napoleon desired to redraw the map of Europe peacefully, he would need the support of Russia.[7] From his side Gortchakoff realized that he must show an accommodating spirit toward Napoleon's ideas. In Italy, Russia would maintain an attitude of benevolent neutrality toward France. Should Napoleon attempt to acquire the Rhine frontier, Russia would not go beyond the employment of her "good offices" in aiding Berlin.[8] As to Poland, Gortchakoff intended to continue the policy followed by Orloff at the Paris Congress of assuring France that the Tsar had the welfare of Poland at heart. He was willing to make these concessions in order to win the friendship of Napoleon and to destroy the Anglo-French alliance. With the collaboration of Morny, he drew up a convention whereby France and Russia would cooperate to prevent infractions of the Treaty of Paris by Austria and England.[9] Morny forwarded the convention to Paris with a strong plea for its acceptance. It was rejected by Napoleon, who had no wish to abandon England altogether.[10] This attempt by Gortchakoff to undermine the Anglo-French alliance was premature, to say the least. Napoleon was not yet ready to redraw the map of Europe and therefore in no urgent need of a Russian alliance. The internal situation in France was such that a certain measure of reserve in foreign policy was necessary. The budget was unbalanced, the harvests were not up to expectations, discontent prevailed among the lower classes, while the army required rest and reorganization.[11] Besides, Napoleon was still the ally of Austria and England.

The treaty of April 15, 1856, which was signed at Paris, guaranteed the territorial integrity of the Ottoman Empire and declared that any infractions of the peace would be considered a *casus belli,* in which case the three powers in conjunction with Turkey would determine how their military and naval forces would be employed.[12] Though obviously directed against Russia, that power was not mentioned in the treaty. Napoleon had consented to this renewal of the tripartite alliance with tongue in cheek. He had yielded to the pressure of Austria and England, who hoped that it would offset the growing intimacy between France and Russia.[13] In a letter which they sent to Franz Joseph on April 16th, Buol and Hübner showed that they expected much from the treaty. "We like to flatter ourselves, Sire," they wrote, "that this treaty fulfills the aims you had in view in authorizing us to sign it. It is the necessary, the indispensable complement of the new policy that Your Majesty inaugurated by the treaty of December 2nd; that you have invariably followed since, and that has so essentially contributed to render peace to Europe and to safeguard the independence of Austria, indirectly compromised, the one and the other, by the encroachments of Russia in the east. Free from any recriminatory character, not naming anyone, but giving a salutary advice to the power which for so long a time has endangered the European equilibrium, this act . . . we dare hope, opposes a solid bulwark to the adversaries of the new European system, cuts short the intrigues of some, the illusions of others, and preserves Austria from the inconveniences of isolation."[14]

Austria soon realized, however, that she had built her hopes too high. How close relations between Paris and St. Petersburg had become was seen when the powers proceeded to carry out the terms of the Treaty of Paris. Several minor difficulties arose. Article 20 of the Treaty provided that the frontier between Russia and Moldavia should follow a line to the south of Bolgrad.[15] A delimitation commission was sent to establish the new boundary but upon its arrival discovered that there were two localities bearing the name of Bolgrad, one a little to the south of Yolpuk Lake, the other on the banks of this lake. Which was the Bolgrad referred to in the Treaty? The Russians upheld the former, the Turks the latter. Another point in dispute was Serpent's Island, situated some miles east of the Danube, claimed by both the Russians and the Turks.[16] Though of slight importance in themselves, the disputed territories led to a bitter controversy, with Austria and England backing the claims of Turkey, and France supporting Russia.[17] In January 1857 a settlement in favor of Turkey was finally reached.[18]

Regarded from the viewpoint of Austro-French relations, these questions are significant, for they reveal the ineffectiveness of the treaty of April 15th. Vienna was much puzzled by Napoleon's intentions and wondered how he could possibly reconcile the obligations he had incurred in this treaty with his support of Russia. While the Emperor was conscious of the apparent contradiction in his policy, he tried to minimize it by pretending to Hübner that he regretted having gone so far in supporting Russia and by stating that he had no intention of breaking his alliance with Austria and England.[19] When Hübner politely reminded him that there was a difference between his words and the actions of Walewski, "who spared no effort in making himself the zealous advocate of Russia at Constantinople, Turin, Berlin and the secondary German courts," the Emperor simply disavowed his minister. What was one to believe in the face of such conduct? Buol declared that if Napoleon persisted in supporting the Russians, this would be considered in Vienna as an indication that he no longer cared for the treaty of April 15th and had plans which ran counter to it. "There are contradictions in his language. He wishes to come to an understanding with his allies without neglecting his engagements with Russia. But how can he combine this? He disavows his minister and yet retains him."[20] Was one really expected to believe, he asked, that Walewski had acted against the wishes of his master? Hübner was unable to throw much light on the mystery. After considering the situation, he informed Buol that although Napoleon intended to maintain the treaty of April 15th, he did not seem to appreciate the importance of friendly relations with Austria. "In this respect he still has much to learn and a great deal will depend upon the convictions, intentions and conduct of his Minister of Foreign Affairs. But Your Excellency saw during the Congress that Monsieur le Comte Walewski had sympathy and consideration only for Russia and the facts prove that he had not changed his attitude since then."[21]

While the dispute over Bolgrad and Serpent's Island indicated the direction Napoleon's policy was taking, this was revealed more clearly in the question concerning the Principalities.[22] During the Vienna Conferences of 1855 and later at the Congress of Paris, France had advocated the union of Moldavia and Wallachia. Indeed, Napoleon had tried to connect this question with the liberation of Italy. At the Paris Congress he assured Cavour of his desire to do something for Piedmont and, if possible, to increase its territory.[23] Since there could be no interference with the Papal States nor any reduction of Austrian territory, he suggested that the Duke of Modena and the Duchess of Parma be sent to Wallachia and Moldavia respectively and that Modena and Parma go to Piedmont.[24] Clarendon, who had been informed of this scheme, hesitated to give his approval, preferring that Piedmont be increased at the expense of the Pope.[25] Nothing came of the Emperor's plan. The Treaty of Paris did not approve of the union but merely provided that the inhabitants of the Principalities should be permitted to express their wishes concerning it.[26]

The question of the Principalities sharpened the growing antagonism between Austria and France. Napoleon evidently thought that he could persuade the former to surrender her Italian possessions in return for placing an archduke over Moldavia and Wallachia, but finding no encouragement for this scheme in Vienna, he pushed his demand for the political and administrative union of the Principalities under a foreign prince.[27] Though Gortchakoff hesitated to take a definite stand on the union, he nevertheless supported the French, for he saw in this question a means of strengthening the *entente* with Paris.[28] Besides, he believed it would be a way of weakening Turkey and of disturbing Austria. England, at first favorable to the union, joined Austria and Turkey in opposing it.[29] Thus, the alignment was the same as in the dispute over Bolgrad and Serpent's Island.

Of all the powers, Austria was the one most bitterly opposed to the union.[30] In her provinces of Bukowina and Transylvania were many Rumanians, whose desire to join their fellow-nationals in Moldavia and Wallachia would undoubtedly be aroused by such a step. Moreover, Austria had important economic interests in the Principalities, having invested much capital and undertaken the construction of roads and telegraphic communications.[31] In the opinion of Franz Joseph, the union would lead to the separation of the Principalities from Turkey and to their control by Russia.[32] England also feared that the union would be a danger to the Ottoman Empire.[33]

To Baron Heeckeren, who at times acted as a special emissary for Napoleon, Buol complained bitterly about the intimacy of France with her former enemy. "How can France do such a thing," he asked, "considering all the financial sacrifices Austria made in abandoning her traditional policy?"[34] If Austria consented to the union, added Buol, she would run the risk of losing her own Slav subjects. France had less to lose, for unlike Austria and Russia, she did not border on Turkey and could find compensation only by altering the map of Europe. He warned Heeckeren that Austria would oppose any attempt to violate the territorial integrity of the Ottoman Empire and would never consent to exchange a single Italian village for a Turkish province. "I admit," he said, "that she (Russia) has been served marvellously by the chivalrous character of your Emperor, whom she persuaded, after a glorious war, that the finest role for France is to pose as the protector of nationalities in the east. This policy, in which she has so cleverly engaged your Sovereign, means the destruction of the Turkish Empire."[35] Napoleon, he continued, should repulse the caresses of Russia, abandon his role as champion of nationalities, draw closer to Austria, and follow a dynastic policy. "There are two policies for the French Government: the policy of the First Empire for whose services it is always necessary to have 600,000 men in order to impose its will everywhere—a difficult task which was accomplished only by the greatest genius of the century—; the other, according to what we know to be uppermost in the character of your ruler, is a dynastic policy, founded on conviction, good behavior and mutual concessions, a policy which has nothing unforeseen and which guarantees the tomorrow of each nation. This is the policy we wish to see Napoleon III follow and I can assure you that, far from finding us an obstacle in his way, we shall be only too happy to render a service to France whenever the occasion presents itself, without even showing ourselves jealous of her *rapprochement* with Russia."[36]

So embarrassing did the question of the union become in Franco-Austrian relations that for several weeks it was not mentioned in the conversations between Hübner and Walewski. When the ice was finally broken, the French minister declared that since it was his desire to establish an *entente* with Austria on all questions, he had selected this as the one which caused the greatest difficulty. "Austria," he said to Hübner, "maintains that the union will compromise her vital interests, while we are convinced that these interests will in no way be threatened."[37] If Austria would merely concede the principle of union, France would be most accommodating in putting it into operation. Indeed, the Emperor was prepared to give up the idea of placing a foreign prince over the Principalities and might make other concessions as well. Hübner did not inquire what these concessions were, for he did not wish to give the appearance of entertaining the thought or even suggesting that Austria might abandon her opposition.

In the elections which were held to ascertain the wishes of inhabitants, the returns from Moldavia were falsified so as to show a majority opposed to the union.[38] France and Russia, supported by Prussia, immediately demanded the annulment of the Moldavian elections; but Turkey, backed by Austria and England, refused. Buol was determined not to yield, for he regarded the unionist party as already lost, and believed that Napoleon was merely trying to extricate himself from an embarrassing position. "The empire of peace," he said to Bourqueney, "cannot give itself the airs of the empire of conquest."[39] France should realize, he added, that Austria would not sacrifice her interests to satisfy the *amour propre* of Napoleon.

It is unnecessary to enter into the details of the Moldavian crisis.[40] Suffice it to say that Napoleon turned to England and in August 1857 accompanied by the Empress Eugénie and Walewski, visited Queen Victoria and the Prince Consort at Osborne. Palmerston and Clarendon were also present. An agreement was reached by which the Emperor promised not to insist upon a complete union, while England dropped her opposition to the annulment of the Moldavian elections.[41] Speaking to Hübner about the Osborne conference, Walewski said: "There was much dirty linen between us and we washed it together."[42]

Vienna was now faced with a virtual *fait accompli*. Apponyi, the Austrian Ambassador at London, urged Buol to accept the agreement, pointing out that the English Cabinet had acted in good faith and was convinced that Napoleon would keep his promise.[43] To refuse would mean isolation. Austria would lose her only ally in the Near East, while her relations with France and Russia would grow worse. Apponyi reported that the conversations which Clarendon had at Osborne with Napoleon and Walewski were concerned with the relations of Austria to England and France. The intimacy between Austria and England had aroused the suspicions of the Emperor, who believed that it was England's desire to replace the Anglo-French alliance with an Anglo-Austrian alliance.[44] "I did everything possible," said Lord Clarendon to Apponyi, "to destroy this unjust suspicion. I proved to the Emperor and Walewski that our intimacy had no other motive than the complete identity of views which exist between our two cabinets concerning all questions which refer to the application of the Treaty of Paris and the treaty of April 15th. . . . "[45] At the same time Clarendon urged the French to establish better relations with Vienna. "Your relations with Austria," he said to them, "have cooled without the slightest reason. For eighteen months you reproached us for not rendering justice to Austria; you desired that we should blindly accept everything which came from her. Now you do the opposite. Austria has not changed; she wishes today what she wished then. What are your complaints against her? I can discover only one reason for your coolness; it is that Russia thinks she has cause to complain of Austria, that you have drawn close to Russia, and to please her you espouse her quarrels."[46] He reminded the Emperor and Walewski that Austria had been the first to break away from the Holy Alliance and had ranged herself on the side of France.

The Osborne agreement was approved by Austria and the crisis over Moldavia was settled. The elections were annulled and the representatives of France, Prussia, Russia and Piedmont, who had left their posts at Constantinople, now returned. But it was not a complete victory for Napoleon since he had failed to obtain the union of the Principalities. And despite the efforts of Clarendon, the relations between Paris and Vienna remained unchanged. Hübner reported that Napoleon did not conceal his disappointment, while the Empress said more than once that Austria had drawn the advantages from the war without having done anything.[47] "Meanwhile," continued Hübner, "they make the mistake of revealing this spite, which they should be most careful to hide from the world. The greater one is, the less one has the right to sulk." He was not invited to the hunts at Compiègne, though invitations were extended to the ambassadors of England and Russia and the Prussian Minister. "The Austrian Ambassador," he wrote, "can have the weakness of being secretly annoyed regarding an invitation he has received but cannot accept. He would never show his annoyance, still less complain, about an invitation he does not receive."[48]

The Osborne visit was followed a few weeks later by a meeting of the Tsar and Napoleon at Stuttgart, whither the two rulers had been invited by King William of Würtemberg to participate in the celebration of the latter's sixty-seventh birthday.[49] As the King's sister, Princess Catherine, had married Prince Jerome, brother of Napoleon I, and his son had married the Grand Duchess Olga, sister of Alexander II, he was related to both the French and Russian courts. The two Emperors and their Foreign Ministers arrived at Stuttgart on September 25, 1857, and remained three days. An agreement was concluded by which the two rulers promised to come to an understanding on all questions of a European interest, not to participate in any coalitions directed against the other, and to cooperate in the east and to reach an agreement in case of the dismemberment of Turkey.[50] The Tsar made no promises concerning his position in the event of an Austro-French war over Italy. In this respect there were only certain allusions made by Napoleon and Walewski, and the assurance given by the Tsar that he had no desire to "recommence the year 1849," that is, to give aid to Austria.[51] It was not possible to reach a closer *entente* at this time because of certain differences over Naples, Poland and the Balkans.[52]

Though she tried to conceal her disappointment, Austria's apprehensions were aroused by the Franco-Russian demonstration of friendship.[53] It accentuated her isolation and reminded her that such community of views as she had with England in the questions of Bolgrad and the Principalities, had not possessed the character of a definite alliance to take the place of those ties she had lost. In order that Austria's isolation should not appear too noticeable, however, Buol was able to arrange that Franz Joseph should meet Alexander II at Weimar, upon the latter's departure from Stuttgart.[54] The Tsar was careful to assure Napoleon in advance that he had nothing to fear from the Weimar meeting which, indeed, turned out to be a simple exchange of courtesies.

Unimportant in itself, the Weimar meeting was nevertheless an indication that relations between Austria and Russia were becoming more normal. In the months which followed the Congress of Paris, Russia's anger had gradually subsided. Franz Joseph had taken advantage of this to send one of his great nobles, Prince Esterhazy, to Moscow with instructions to study the possibility of improving the relations between the two countries. This maneuver pleased the Tsar, who received Prince Esterhazy with much friendliness and discussed Austria's conduct during the Crimean War without the slightest trace of bitterness.[55] Upon his return to Vienna, Prince Esterhazy submitted a report to Buol in which he pointed out that an Austro-Russian *rapprochement* could be attained within certain limits; that the advantage to Austria would be negative rather than positive and would consist simply in preventing Russia from following a policy conflicting with Austrian interests.[56] In order to offset the influence of Gortchakoff, whose attitude was distinctly anti-Austrian, he urged that every effort be made to win over the Tsar.[57] The Austrian Ambassador reported an audience with Alexander II who said: "I have always believed and I still believe that it can only be to Austria's advantage to come to an understanding with us and I beg you to say to the Emperor that he will find me fully disposed to facilitate the reëstablishment of our old relations."[58] Yet, while there was a slight improvement in these relations, Austria and Russia remained hostile to each other at least until the end of the Italian War of 1859. For the time being, the Russian policy was clearly oriented toward an *entente* with France. Napoleon, of course, made every effort to prevent an Austro-Russian *rapprochement.*

Regarded from the viewpoint of Vienna, the European situation in 1857 did not appear very hopeful. While relations between France and Russia tended to become more and more intimate, the gulf which separated Austria from France had been widened by differences in Italy and the Near East. The treaty of April 15, 1856, had turned out to be of little value. In Near Eastern affairs Austria and England had opposed France and Russia, but so far as Italy was concerned, Vienna could not count on English support.[59] Since Napoleon had apparently made up his mind to do something for the Italians, a conflict was bound to occur sooner or later. But he was in no hurry to act, for he knew that he could count on the Tsar's benevolent neutrality, while England's sympathy for Italy was too strong to admit of real opposition from her part. Franz Joseph and his Foreign Minister saw clearly that Napoleon held the balance, that if he so desired, he could threaten the very existence of the Austrian Monarchy. Not only Russia and England, but the revolutionary movement was on his side. The nightmare of an alliance between the French Emperor and revolution haunted the statesmen in Vienna. How could they ward off the disaster which threatened them without at the same time sacrificing the dignity or the principles of the Monarchy?

At first Buol thought that this might be done by gaining the friendship of Napoleon and his recognition of Austria's vital interests, or by convincing him of the dangers to France in pursuing a revolutionary policy. But the Emperor's conduct had not been reassuring. In the questions of Bolgrad and the Principalities, in which he had no direct interest, he had definitely preferred Russia to Austria. What reason lay behind this preference? Was it resentment because of the policy pursued by Austria during the Crimean War, or was it related to some political plan which the Emperor contemplated? What did he expect to gain by his equivocal policy in Italy and by his tactics in the Principalities? And why did Austria, who had not departed from the principles which had led her into the alliance of December 2nd have so much difficulty in reaching an understanding with France?

These questions occurred to Buol as he analyzed the policy of Napoleon. He explained to himself that the Emperor had need of external action in order to divert the attention of the French people from internal difficulties.[60] Buol could understand such a need but he wondered if Napoleon was not exposing himself to danger in finding Austria so frequently in his way. A struggle with Austria would throw him into the arms of revolution. Besides, he could hardly entertain the illusion that Austria could be induced by threats to abandon her principles. "We are and will remain the same," wrote Buol; "one will find us when one seeks us but we cannot enter into a competition of flatteries etc., with the common enemy of yesterday. We submit to the bad graces of France and the rancor of Russia, but we will remain faithful to our principles. Strong in a policy of right and honesty, we do not fear future complications. Austria wants nothing but what exists; she desires the integrity of the Porte and the maintenance of the present boundaries of Italy. We have placed our flag on . . . order and respect for the treaties. Does France wish to place hers besides ours? If not, there is no place for it."[61] What concerned Buol most of all was how far Napoleon would carry his resentment, whether it was merely a passing mood nourished by Russian intrigues or an indication of a serious political plan which might end in the complete estrangement of Austria and France. He instructed Hübner to watch for anything which might throw light on the matter.

Hübner was inclined to take a more hopeful view of the situation, and in his reply to Buol set forth what he considered to be the good and the bad sides of the Emperor's character.[62] On the good side, he mentioned Napoleon's commonsense and his shrewd instinct of gauging the wishes of the French people. "I have concluded that Louis Napoleon will always permit himself to be guided by what he believes to be the opinion, the interests, and the will of the country." So long as France desired peace, this would be the policy of the Emperor. At the moment, the French wanted peace seasoned with a little glory. Napoleon did not intend to fall into the error of Louis Philippe who had insisted upon "peace at any price" and had thus trifled with the honor of France. If the Emperor had so desired, he could have continued the war against Russia, as England had urged him to do, and embarked upon an adventurous policy. He could have sent his troops into Galicia and stirred up revolutions. But he had not done this because he knew that France wanted peace. Another point in his favor was that since the birth of the Prince Imperial,[63] he had given more thought to dynastic interests, which would tend to keep him within reasonable bounds. All this represented the good side of the Emperor's character. On the reverse side, Hübner mentioned the political ideas which Napoleon had derived from his youth, and his desire that Austria should cooperate in redrawing the map of Europe and voluntarily abandon her interests in Italy. Moreover, "this man who has done such great things, and who possesses such great qualities, has the weakness of attaching an exaggerated importance to small things." His resentment against Austria was not due to any deep-laid plans but rather to the pin-pricks which she had administered to him. Hence, it would be good policy to flatter the Emperor occasionally. "Russia exploits this weakness grossly, Prussia obsequiously, England decently and adroitly." Hübner concluded that Napoleon had no intention of threatening Austria and had no plans of a nature to disturb Europe. "But," he continued, "I also think, considering his lack of principles, his character which is inclined toward great resolutions and favored by fortune, certain traditions of his youth from which he has not completely rid himself, that one cannot surrender to a feeling of absolute security. On the other hand, with vigilance and care, and profiting from given situations, one has a good chance of keeping the chief of France in the tracks of a healthy policy."

Some of the apprehension at Vienna was dissipated by Hübner's character analysis. Buol agreed that Napoleon was too sensible at the moment to embark on a revolutionary policy but he considered it unfortunate that it was always necessary for him to have "a little glory at a bargain," which Walewski was not clever enough to procure for him.[64] He did not begrudge the Emperor the glory so long as it was not at Austria's expense.

In September 1857, Buol prepared a memorandum entitled: "Mes Idées sur la politique du Second Empire Française."[65] This declared that the key to Napoleon's policy was his tendency of watching for the favorable moment in order to redraw the map of Europe. From the beginning of his reign, Louis Napoleon realized that this could not be done by imitating the methods of his illustrious uncle. His ignorance of military tactics, the attitude of the French people, and the European situation, convinced him that he could not pursue a policy of conquests but must wait for time and circumstance to bring about a revision of the treaties in the interests of France. "Never advancing so far as not to be able to turn back when he encounters an insurmountable obstacle, retreating only so far as necessary in order to await an opportune moment, we have never seen him abandon this thought completely." Napoleon had hoped that Russia would reject the peace proposals and thus impose upon Austria the chief burden of the war, which would have led in the end to a revision of the map according to his ideas. At the Peace Congress he had endeavored to turn the negotiations in the same direction. In the question of the Principalities he had removed the mask which concealed this secret thought and had tried to strike a bargain with Austria by proposing to place them under an archduke, which would have made Austria an accomplice in destroying Turkey. "A clear refusal should have proved to him that I understood perfectly that it was not a matter of a free gift." Napoleon had become the crony of Russia in order to soften her opposition to the territorial sacrifices she was asked to make and, resenting the consolidation of Austria's influence in the Balkans, he had aroused suspicions concerning her good faith. Unable to obtain recognition in the Peace Treaty for the union of the Principalities, he succeeded in getting the insertion of vague articles relating to their organization, which anyone could interpret to suit himself and which seemed to imply that the wishes of the inhabitants should be consulted. "Louis Napoleon does nothing bluntly or hurriedly but will never abandon this good chance to redraw the map of Europe." He pursued the same policy in Italy where he hoped to involve England.

"Thus it is that Louis Napoleon tends to keep Europe in a continual turmoil so as not to miss the moment when he can strike a blow at the social system without betraying his program. He awaits anything: a revolution in the Seraglio, troubles in the Principalities, or an uprising in some part of Italy in order to set himself up as mediator. Meanwhile, he satisfies himself with these half-successes which throw dust in the eyes of the French, which keep the revolutionary spirit in a state of anxiety, and which are so many pinpricks to the conversative system. Complacent allies will not fail him; he will profit from the liberal propensities of England, from ambition, envy, from all those evil passions which are found at hand and which, moreover, are so easy to arouse."

In view of these dangerous tendencies, what policy should Austria follow? Buol concluded that nothing should be done which would discourage Napoleon from remaining faithful to his declaration that the empire meant peace but that every effort should be made to point out to him the advantages of peace and the dangers involved in threatening it. On the other hand, he did not believe that a real and lasting *entente* with France was possible. Napoleon would never join frankly with Austria in working for the maintenance of law and order and respect for the treaties, nor could Austria sacrifice her principles for the sake of obtaining his cooperation. Austria's policy, therefore, must be to combat subversive tendencies in whatever form they might appear. To suppose that an *entente* could be established merely by displaying more attention to Napoleon was a delusion, for the latter was not content to be treated as an equal by other rulers, but wanted to overshadow them. "Any unusual attention will be interpreted merely as an indication of fear and will provoke new demands." If Napoleon persisted in his secret designs, he must accustom himself to Austria's opposition, which thus far had caused them to fail for the most part.

Having indicated the broad lines of Austria's policy, Buol next considered the results such a policy might produce. Would Napoleon, exasperated by Austria's opposition, go so far as to decide on an open struggle against her? Would he, perhaps, try to form an anti-Austrian coalition? The first possibility appeared to Buol very doubtful, the second almost impossible. The financial condition of France was such as to make it exceedingly difficult to wage a struggle on a large scale, while Napoleon lacked an aim for war which could capture the imagination of the French people. Hence, the idea of war between Austria and France could be dismissed at the moment. But suppose that Napoleon should find a great power willing to associate itself in his schemes? Buol admitted that this would be dangerous for Austria but asked which of the great powers was likely to do this? It was foolish to suppose merely because Napoleon had obtained diplomatic support for some of his schemes that he would find it just as easy to form an offensive coalition. It was true that Russia had ambitious designs regarding the Balkans, but she was in no position to fight. And while England and Prussia might flatter the Emperor, they would think twice before actively co-operating in order to hand over Germany and Italy to him. "These considerations, coupled with the need for peace which all countries of Europe desire, render a general war very improbable for the moment, but if by chance it should occur, I believe, without wishing to indicate how the groups will line up, that Austria and France will never be found in the same camp. Whatever the future might be . . . it seems to me that Austria should constantly contest with France that moral ascendancy she tries to impose on all countries by employing in turn flattery and intimidation, and that she (Austria) should not cease in denouncing to Europe the illicit influence which France exercises externally for the benefit of revolution and should combat it even when the move threatens her directly. Any half-measure in this course will only strengthen the position of France to the detriment of ours and pave the way for a second French domination. Austria, in less favorable circumstances, has combatted the same principle; she ought not to draw back before it today. A calm and impassive behavior will be the most effective means perhaps of making Louis Napoleon forget a part of his dreams of Ham and lead him to more sober reflections in his palace of the Tuileries."

Buol's memorandum is important not only for its keen analysis of Napoleon's policy but also for its exposition of the difficulties confronting Austro-French relations. At the time it was written, September 1857, there were disturbing elements in the European situation.⁶⁶ In addition to the general unrest in Italy, the inhabitants of Albania, Bulgaria, Bosnia, Herzegovina and Montenegro had begun to stir. There was also the question of the Principalities which continued to separate Paris from Vienna. That Napoleon would seek to profit from such a situation appeared to be a foregone conclusion. Nationalism would be a mighty weapon in his hands, a weapon which could split asunder the Hapsburg Monarchy. Buol saw the danger as clearly as anyone. In a dispatch to Hübner,⁶⁷ he set forth his views concerning the principle of nationalties.

The social edifice of Europe rests essentially upon the territorial limits consecrated by the treaties. To desire to substitute for this principle one which will permit the so-called imprescriptable rights of nationality to co-exist with it, is evidently to open all the floodgates to the revolutionary torrent and to compromise in the gravest manner the peace and repose of the world. Would there be, we ask, a single monarchy in Europe which would have a chance to remain standing if the legitimacy of the constituent power of nationalities was once elevated to the height of a political axiom? Besides, Austria will always find herself among the adversaries of those who do not fear to provoke storms. . . . In taking this position, moreover, we have the consciousness of defending not only our vital interests but at the same time those of the social order and of all powers. Indeed, where is the power which has not been called upon to govern peoples of various races more or less assimilated by the action of time and circumstances? What all governments owe to their peoples, whatever be their origin, is a regime based on the eternal rules of justice and Christian civilization; what they cannot tolerate is the right of political emancipation supported by the sole title of nationality. To enter this course is equivalent to the inauguration of anarchy and general uprisings under the pretext of doing justice to the desires of rules and pretensions, badly defined, which nearly always conceal guilty projects and perverse tendencies. Do they not understand that the principle of nationalities, such as it is exploited today, serves as a mask for vulgar cupidities, unbounded ambitions, and all the evil revolutionary instincts? That postulated, nothing appears so dangerous to us as encouraging and caressing a principle of this nature.

For the moment, the chief danger was in the Balkans. The disturbances which occurred in Bosnia, Herzegovina and Montenegro were by no means unusual and were symptomatic of the unstable conditions existing in the Turkish Empire. Insufficiency of arable lands, Turkish misrule, Russian propaganda, as well as the nascent force of nationalism, were the basic causes. In Montenegro the land question had resulted in conflicts with Albanians and Herzegovinians.[68] With the consolidation of Turkish power over Bosnia, Herzegovina and Albania, these conflicts threatened to become serious. In 1853 war was averted by the intervention of Austria, whose ultimatum to the Porte compelled the Turks to refrain from pursuing a policy of extermination against the Montenegrins.[69] Thereafter Prince Danilo of Montenegro decided to abandon his claims to independence and to accept Turkish suzerainty in return for a rectification of the frontier which would give more land to his people, and he was encouraged in his decision by Austria, England and France.[70] The ambassadors of the three powers at Constantinople carried on negotiations with the Porte for the approval of this arrangement.[71]

With the end of the Crimean War and the subsequent *rapprochement* of France and Russia, the stiuation changed. Russia resented the fact that she had been excluded in regard to Montenegro, which she looked upon as her satellite. Gortchakoff, however, saw a way by which she could be heard. He offered to support France in the Principalities, if France would support Russia in Montenegro.[72] Napoleon accepted this proposal and when Prince Danilo arrived in Paris, March 6, 1857, he was received with reserve.[73] The two powers instructed their representatives at Constantinople to work together for a delimitation of the frontier between Montenegro and Turkey. The Franco-Russian accord was further strengthened at the Stuttgart meeting.

In the Montenegrin affair Austria championed the cause of Turkey and blamed outside agitators for the difficulties. Buol declared that France and Russia were too indulgent toward the agitators and too insistent on the duties of Turkey. "It is the unshakable policy of Austria," wrote Bourqueney to Walewski, "to defend the authority of the Porte where it is threatened and to maintain it where it has been compromised. This policy is dictated not only by the desire to uphold the Porte but by Austria's own interests in the provinces bordering on Turkey. Austria affirms her own sovereignty by working to consolidate that of the Sultan."[74] It was because of this twofold interest that Austria claimed, if not the right to impose a settlement, at least the right to a greater voice than those powers whose interests were not directly involved.

By the spring of 1858 the situation in Montenegro had become serious. The failure to delimit the frontier led to an armed uprising and Turkish troops were concentrated close to the disputed territories. The Montenegrins occupied Grahavo, while Prince Danilo effected a reconciliation with Russia and received the protection of the Tsar.[75] France joined Russia in protesting against the concentration of Turkish troops, while England proposed that commissioners be sent to arrange the delimitation of the frontier. Austria, however, suggested that the Montenegrins evacuate Grahavo and that Turkey halt her troops. While this suggestion was agreeable to the Porte, France and Russia accepted the English proposal as the lesser of two evils.[76] Taking advantage of this dissension among the powers, Turkish troops drove the insurgents from Grahavo and invaded Montenegrin territory.

The Montenegrin question was one more disturbing factor in Austro-French relations. When France proposed that it be referred to the conference which had been summoned to meet in Paris in order to consider the question of the future organization of the Principalities, Austria refused on the ground that it was outside the competence of the conference and could be brought up only with the consent of Turkey.[77] Buol did not intend to permit a repetition of what had taken place at the Paris Congress when the Italian question had been injected into the discussions. He felt that Austria could not alter her position in the Montenegrin affair without violating her faith in the treaties and without abandoning principles which had guided her in every eastern crisis.[78] To recognize the independence of Montenegro against the wishes of the Porte, which seemed to be what France and Russia wanted,[79] would constitute a flagrant violation of the territorial integrity of Turkey, guaranteed by the powers in the Treaty of Paris, and would give the signal for her dismemberment. Furthermore, it would be foolish to raise the question in the conference since Austria and Russia had diametrically opposite views. Even a French suggestion that the powers avoid the question of sovereignty and simply have the conference decide on the frontier between Montenegro and Turkey, was going too far to suit Buol. He believed that the best solution would be either a recognition of the territorial *status quo* of 1853, leaving the question of sovereignty in abeyance, or the territorial *status quo* of 1856, on condition that Montenegro recognize Turkish sovereignty.[80] The prolonged negotiations exasperated France and Russia, who decided to apply pressure. They threatened to recognize the independence of Montenegro unless Turkey withdrew her troops and accepted the *status quo* of 1856.[81] Turkey yielded and the Montenegrin affair came to an end.

Napoleon, of course, was far from pleased with Austria's conduct. Attending a dinner at the Tuileries in honor of the Queen of Holland and the Prince of Würtemberg, Hübner engaged the Emperor in a lengthy discussion regarding eastern affairs. By way of introduction he remarked that ever since the Congress of Paris the Emperor had maintained a certain reserve toward him and had avoided any mention of political affairs.[82] "I shall not speak to you," replied Napoleon, "in the idle language of diplomacy. I express my thoughts bluntly. I say what I think. . . . I made war in the east, Austria did not. If she had fired a single shot, I would find it quite natural that she should exercise in the east. . . a preponderant influence; but since I made greater sacrifices than she and all other powers, I believe that I also have a right to an influence proportionate to my sacrifices. Well, this does not please Austria. She blocks me in great and small affairs and that is what makes our relations unpleasant. Hübner replied that neither Austria nor any other power would permit France to exercise a preponderant influence in Turkey or elsewhere, and that it was precisely because Tsar Nicholas thought he could impose his will on Europe that a coalition was formed against him. The Emperor protested that he was not seeking preponderance but merely an influence that was due him. He repeated his favorite expression: that he had not made war for Turkey but against Russia. "It is said," he continued, "that the integrity of the Porte is a European necessity. Perhaps so, but it is a very sad necessity that permits in these beautiful countries, men as beastly as they are weak. What disturbs me is that my influence at Constantinople is nil while you, who have done less for Turkey, are all-powerful, yes, all-powerful." When

Hübner pointed out that this was quite natural in view of the fact that France had made demands which threatened the existence of the Ottoman Empire, while Austria had defended its independence and territorial integrity, Napoleon reverted to his complaints against the Vienna Cabinet: its attitude in the affairs of Bolgrad, the Principalities, Montenegro and the Danube. Everywhere Austria spoke against him, especially at Berlin and Constantinople, and everywhere and always she was in his way.

Hübner defended as best he could the Austrian point of view. He said that every state was guided by certain principles from which it could not deviate. "Austria has for her principles the respect due to the imprescriptible rights of rulers and the non-recognition of the pretensions of nationalities to establish themselves as political states." Ever since the Treaty of Paris, France had attacked these principles. But Napoleon was unimpressed and, indeed, refused to admit that Austria had principles. "The proof is your conduct in Montenegro. In 1853 you upheld the Montenegrins because the Turkish army was commanded by Hungarian refugees; today you uphold Turkey because I protect Prince Danilo." Hübner replied that Austria adhered to her principles tenaciously, that she had not departed from them in the questions which had arisen since the Congress, and that her opposition to Napoleon was due to his insistence on altering the Treaty of Paris. In the affair of the Principalities, in which France had no direct interest but which was of vital importance to Austria in view of the several million Rumanians residing in Transylvania, had France not sought to effect a settlement to the disadvantage of her ally? "This is not a small affair. It is a question of principles, a question of knowing if one should recognize—and Austria does not—the right of nationalities to constitute themselves as political states. Hence, nothing was more natural than Austria's opposition. And permit me to add, Sire, that it is not she who raised these questions: it is Your Majesty. I do not think, then, that Austria is everywhere found in the way of Your Majesty. On the contrary, I dare say that it is France who places herself in the way of Austria. And what is our course? It is the preservation of the public law, the thrones and the states, and the territorial limits such as they have been fixed by the treaties." The Emperor did not dispute this argument but merely remarked that the creation of a Rumanian state would not endanger the existence of Austria, since there were mountains between Transylvania and the Principalities.

The discussion turned next to the question of Montenegro. Hübner contended that although no French interests were involved, Napoleon had encouraged Prince Danilo to assume a position which violated the rights of Turkey. "I do not understand the conduct of the French Government, which together with the other two signatories of the treaty of April 15, 1856, recommended to Prince Danilo not so long ago the recognition of the suzerainty of the Porte and which today, in concert with Russia, threatens the Porte with the recognition of the independence of Montenegro. . . . What is it that has been able to modify so completely the attitude and the policy of the French Government?" Napoleon made no reply to this question but merely pointed out that while the Montenegrin affair was a small one it could lead to war. Had not the Crimean War started with the question of the Holy Places?

Hübner's lengthy discussion with the Emperor reveals the mutual distrust and suspicion which characterized Austro-French relations. It is obvious that the Napoleonic demand for treaty revision and the rights of nationalities could not be reconciled with Austria's insistence upon the maintenance of the *status quo*. Near Eastern affairs simply brought into sharp relief the nature of the conflict. According to Buol, the point of departure for any understanding with France concerning the Near East, was the execution of the Treaty of Paris. "It is not Austria," he wrote to Hübner, "who has changed colors and deserted the common flag. It is France who seems to regret the glorious efforts she made in the last war by being drawn today into the Russian orbit and by seconding the Russian projects which tend toward the dismemberment of the Ottoman Empire."[83] He was astonished that Napoleon should deny that Austria had principles and although he had no desire to begrudge the Emperor the influence that was due him, he would not agree to a partition of Turkey. However weak the Sick Man might be, he would most likely live a long time if he did not meet with a violent death. "It is not for us to apologize for the governmental system of Turkey; we know, as everyone does, its numerous vices. But while deploring them we believe that among all possible schemes in the present condition of Europe, the preservation of the Ottoman Empire is the least bad. . . . There are different ways of intervening in the affairs of Turkey—to help or to hinder her. France and Austria could join in helping Turkey by introducing civilization so as to prepare her for a better future. But to capitalize on the abuses of the Ottoman Empire in order to redraw the map of Europe will mean to plunge Europe into a violent crisis which might have incalculable consequences. Is this what Napoleon wants? Will he succeed in consolidating his throne if he permits himself to be carried away by the mirage of the unknown?"[84]

In the conference which met at Paris to arrange for the future organization of the Principalities, France demanded a common flag for Moldavia and Wallachia.[85] Although the Emperor no longer insisted upon a political union, he nevertheless desired to obtain the symbol of unity and the common flag would serve this purpose. Hübner, who represented Austria at the conference, tried to argue him out of it. "If Austria," he said, "agrees to a Rumanian flag how can she refuse the Galicians the Polish flag if they demand it? Belgium is in part inhabited by people of the Gallic race and speak the French language. If they are given the white flag, what would you say, Sire?"[86] The Emperor admitted that he would oppose this but declared that it was not the same thing since the white flag recalled the past. "And the Rumanian flag," rejoined Hübner, "will be a call to the future, to the future of those who dream of an independent Rumania and who can make it only as a result of the dismemberment of Turkey and the defection of several million Austrian subjects." He begged Napoleon to reflect on this danger and recalled to him the services rendered by Austria during the Crimean War.

So important did Austria regard the question of a common flag that she threatened to withdraw from the conference unless the demand was dropped.[87] France yielded and on August 9, 1858, a convention was concluded. While Moldavia and Wallachia were to retain their separate status, they were to have the same laws and the same army and would form a permanent alliance. A central commission composed of delegates from the two parliaments would discuss legislation common to both. Each province would freely elect its hospodar or prince, who must be a native. Thus, the union was almost achieved and to complete it, it was only necessary for the two provinces to elect the same prince, which was what France and Russia now sought to bring about. Colonel John Alexander Cuza, a great friend of France, was elected in Moldavia on January 17, 1859 and in Wallachia on February 5th. "You see," said the Empress to Hübner, commenting on the elections, "the Principalities desire union." "No, Madam," replied the Ambassador, "I merely see that there are boastful intrigues down there."[88] At this remark the Empress became impatient and repeated that the people wanted union. "Pardon Madam," said Hübner, "they wish independence and in order to get it they vote for union. But since Austria wants to maintain the Porte, she does not wish the independence of the Principalities and consequently opposes the union."

By her uncompromising attitude, Austria had forced Napoleon to withdraw his demand for a common flag. Yet, within six months after the end of the conference, the Principalities had set up a *de facto* union. What Austria had gained in form, she had lost in substance. And what was worse, France now began to speak the language of Nicholas I and insisted that the Sick Man could not survive much longer. In fact, said Walewski to Hübner, "he will succumb before you and I have white hair."[89] When the Ambassador asserted that this would mean war, Walewski replied: "Say rather an arrangement among the great powers by means of negotiations."

If Napoleon defended the cause of the Balkan Christians this was not only because it was the price for Russian support in the west, but also because he hoped in this way to compel Austria to make concessions in Italy. Vienna, however, refused to "make Italy the bargaining point for a solution of the eastern question."[90] Buol warned Bourqueney that Austria would oppose France or any other power that tried to upset the European equilibrium. "Austria can stand alone. She does not need the support or the alliance of anyone, neither that of France nor any other power. The only alliance to which we attach any value and which we seek is that with

Prussia." To this Bourqueney replied: "That alliance, I declare, you will never have."[91]

A further strain on Austro-French relations resulted from an uprising of the Serbs. The Governor of Serbia, Prince Alexander Karageorgevitch, who since 1842 had been more or less subservient to Austro-Turkish influence, had become very unpopular with his people, the majority of whom desired the return of Milosh Obreno-vitch, a protegé of Russia's. So strong did the agitation become that toward the end of 1858 Prince Alexander was forced to convoke the Skruptchina or national assembly, which had not met for a number of years. The Skruptchina demanded his abdication. On December 24th, the Prince complied with this demand, fled to Belgrade which was occupied by Turkish troops, and called upon Austria for aid. The latter announced immediately her intention of intervening on the ground that the agitation in Serbia might spread to her own provinces.[92] Walewski, however, warned Hübner that such intervention, without the preliminary approval of the great powers, would constitute a violation of the Treaty of Paris, and he hoped that Austria would desist.[93] Hübner contended that it was not a question of intervening in the internal affairs of Serbia but simply of protecting the Turkish garrison in Belgrade. "The fact that the Imperial Cabinet hastened to inform the great courts in advance, proves its loyalty. If we had the intention of making our-selves the masters of Belgrade, we would not have made you this overture; on the contrary, we would have plotted secretly and profited from the right moment to enter the fortress and give ex-planation after the event. . . . We would have acted by surprise."[94] Walewski held firm to his view that Austrian intervention would constitute a violation of the Treaty of Paris, which had set forth the principle that no intervention could take place without a pre-liminary agreement among the powers. He threatened to go to any length to maintain this principle, declaring that if Austria thought that she could violate it, there were those who would claim that the other treaties no longer existed.[95] The Ambassador employed all the arguments he could think of in order to convince Walewski that he was wrong. He pointed out that article 29 of the Treaty of Paris, which guaranteed Turkey the right to a garrison in Serbia, imposed upon the powers the obligation to maintain this right. Those who refused to take action—and the only action which could be of any use in the present situation was armed intervention—were themselves committing a breach of the Treaty. "Since Austria is disposed to safeguard a right which is guaranteed to the Sultan, one cannot deduce from this that she destroys the Treaty of Paris and that all other treaties are violated and cease to exist."[96]

In the Serbian question France would not yield an inch and as she was supported by England and Prussia, Austria had to draw back. Milosh was recalled by the Skruptchina and became Governor of Serbia. The Sultan gave his approval on January 12, 1859, although Milosh did not receive the hereditary title as the Skruptchina desired.

At the very moment when the situation in Italy was reaching a critical stage, Austria had received a setback in the Near East. The charge that she had contemplated a violation of the Treaty of Paris was repeated on a number of occasions by the French Government. If one treaty could be violated, why not another? In any event, the conflict between the interests and policies of Austria and France in the Near East since the Crimean War was but the prelude to a far greater conflict in Italy.

The Italian Question, 1856-1859. From the Congress of Paris to the Conclusion of the Franco-Piedmontese Alliance

NOWHERE WAS THE principle of nationalities more dangerous for the established order than in Italy. Its application in the Balkans served chiefly the aims of Russia and only indirectly could Napoleon hope to profit from it. His interest in the Principalities was based to a great extent on his desire to use them as bargaining points with Austria in exchange for Italian territory. It was in the Italian question that Napoleon openly pursued his aims of revising the treaties of 1815. The principle of nationalities was a powerful weapon which he employed not only to undermine the power and influence of Austria but to redraw the map of Europe. He saw that of all the great powers only France had nothing to fear from this principle. For aiding the Germans, Hungarians, Italians, Poles and Rumanians in their struggles for liberation, he expected to get compensation, either directly or indirectly. This policy was naturally suggested by the geographic position of France in Europe and by the weakness and division of her neighbors. Napoleon III was not the first French ruler to think of profiting from such a situation. In a sense, he was simply continuing the traditions of Henry IV, Richelieu, Louis XIV and Napoleon I.[1] Where he differed from his predecessors was in connecting the principle of nationalities with the policy of expansion.

Italy had an irresistible attraction for Louis Napoleon. Not only was his family of Italian origin but he had spent a part of his youth in the Peninsula and had shared the sentiments of the

Carbonari. Despite the opposition of influential groups in France, he had made up his mind to do something for Italy.[2] His plan at this stage was to establish an Italian confederation under the presidency of the Pope, with a diet like that at Frankfurt representing the various rulers, including Franz Joseph.[3] By such an arrangement, he hoped to obtain the needed reforms while decreasing Austrian influence and safeguarding the position of the Papacy.

At the moment, Austria's position in Italy was dominant. After the uprisings of 1848-1849, she had taken steps to consolidate her influence. Lombardy-Venetia was subject to her direct control, while treaties dating from 1847 gave her the right to occupy the Duchies of Parma and Modena, whose rulers were related to the House of Hapsburg. By various conventions she was allied to Tuscany, also governed by a member of the Hapsburg family, and the Two Sicilies, and her troops were garrisoned in the eastern part of the Papal States. Thus, only Piedmont remained outside her influence and it was Piedmont which had taken the lead in the struggles for liberation of Italy and which offered an asylum to political refugees from other Italian states. Moreover, Piedmont was the leading advocate of liberalism and constitutionalism on the continent.

Relations between Austria and Piedmont had grown steadily worse since 1853. Early in that year an uprising took place in Milan and an attempt was made on the life of the Austrian ruler. In retaliation, Franz Joseph issued an order, dated February 13, 1853, sequestering the estates of those who had participated in the uprising. Nearly a thousand estates were seized, including some which belonged to individuals who had become naturalized subjects of Piedmont. Cavour took up the cause of these subjects with Vienna but got nowhere. Austria defended her action on the ground that the greater part of Mazzini's loan, which had financed the uprising, had been subscribed to by the Lombard refugees. Piedmontese newspapers conducted a bitter campaign against the Hapsburg Monarchy and for a moment it seemed that a new struggle for Italian independence was about to take place. The recurrence of the eastern question and the outbreak of the Crimean War, however, thrust Italian affairs into the background. On December 2, 1854, Austria concluded her alliance with the western powers and three weeks later Paris and Vienna signed the convention designed to maintain the *status quo* in Italy during the war. As we have seen, Austria refused to draw the sword against Russia, whereas Piedmont joined the Anglo-French alliance and sent 15,000 men to the Crimea. In this way Cavour had established a claim to Napoleon's gratitude.

During the Congress of Paris, Napoleon displayed an avid interest in the fate of Italy and looked about for some way to compensate Piedmont for her services in the war. He warned Cavour, however, that there could be no interference with the Papal States and no thought of increasing Piedmont at Austria's expense.[4] His scheme to place the Duchess of Parma and the Duke of Modena as rulers over Moldavia and Wallachia respectively, while adding Parma and Modena to Piedmont, was rejected by Buol.[5] Cavour thereupon submitted a memorandum to the Emperor suggesting an alternate arrangement which would have given the Principalities to the Duke of Modena, Modena to the Duchess of Parma, and Parma to Piedmont but this was found to contain too many difficulties.[6] In the end, the only gain Cavour obtained at the Congress was the opportunity of discussing the Italian situation in the session of April 8th and thus bringing it before Europe.[7]

Napoleon's interest in Italy naturally aroused apprehension and suspicion in Vienna. The question uppermost in the minds of the directors of Austrian policy was how far the French Emperor planned to go in aiding the Italians in their struggle for liberation. Did he really contemplate a revision of the *status quo* in the Peninsula? It was Hübner's opinion that Napoleon's plans did not include more than the introduction of certain reforms. "I cannot believe," he wrote to Buol, "that he dreams of territorial changes, for he should realize that such projects will sever the ties he has considered so important to form with Austria."[8] The character of the French Emperor, the similarity of institutions in Austria and France, and their common antagonism to the parliamentary system were sufficient guarantees against any drastic changes. Napoleon had simply decided to cooperate in ameliorating conditions in central and southern Italy. "That, no doubt, is his thought; he will try to realize it with or without Austria. With her, it means external and

internal peace, not war and revolution. Without her, it will be a
period of troubles and difficulties; for nowhere more than in Italy
can Austria say: who is not with me is against me."⁹ Napoleon had
given Hübner positive assurances that he had no intention of bringing about, directly or indirectly, any territorial changes in Italy or
of favoring the establishment of constitutional and parliamentary
governments but would respect the independence of the rulers.¹⁰
At the same time, he recognized that no other question was as
likely to disturb Austro-French relations. "My will, my intentions,
and my interest," he said to Hübner, "are for a good understanding
with Austria on Italian affairs but you are well aware that men in
the highest positions are not masters of circumstances; they may be
able to direct them to some extent, but in the end it is the current
which carries them away. I fear that I myself may be carried away.
I am the ally of England, and the King of Sardinia, by his cooperation during the war, has earned my sympathy and gratitude."¹¹ He
urged Austria to seek an understanding with Piedmont which would
deprive the latter of any reason to complain.

Despite these assurances, Buol was unable to shake off his distrust of the French ruler, a distrust which had increased during
the Paris Congress. He insisted that the revolutionary agitation in
the Peninsula must be checked by positive action and wanted
Napoleon to join Austria in warning Piedmont. The revival of the
Austro-French *entente* would be the best means of keeping Cavour
within the bounds of moderation. "Austria," he informed the
French Chargé d'Affaires, "cannot remain silent regarding Italian
manifestations. The relative weakness of Sardinia cannot be a sufficient pretext for permitting her to attack a greater state with im-
punity, to hurl the most audacious defiance against Austria, to
compromise in this way the maintenance of general peace; in a
word, to play the role of *l'enfant terrible* of Europe."¹² Buol knew
that in view of the tension existing between Vienna and Turin, a
warning from Austria alone would assume a serious character and
might be followed by drastic measures if Piedmont did not mend
her ways. He declared that "a single Sardinian soldier passing the
frontier and entering the Duchy of Parma or any other part of the
present Italian territory occupied by a single Austrian soldier, will

mean immediate war between Austria and Sardinia."[13] However, nothing came of his suggestion that France join Austria in warning Piedmont. In view of his obligations to Cavour and his desire not to offend England, Napoleon refused to take such a strong stand.[14]

Nowhere throughout Italy were reforms more sorely needed than in the Kingdom of the Two Sicilies where Ferdinand II ruled with an iron hand. Following the denunciation of his administration at the Paris Congress, he was warned by England and France to treat his subjects more leniently. Austria was invited to participate in this warning but declined on the ground that she did not approve of outside interference in the affairs of a sovereign state which had not been requested by the ruler.[15] At the same time, Walewski's offer to aid Austria in Turin in return for her support in Naples, was turned down.[16] Russia also disapproved of the Anglo-French *démarche* because Ferdinand II had been one of her most faithful supporters during the Crimean War. Encouraged by this dissension among the powers, the King replied arrogantly to the remonstrances of London and Paris, claiming that interference in his government was unjustified and merely served to stir up revolutionary agitation. Although Napoleon was reluctant to engage himself further in the affair, not wishing to alienate Russia, he was offended by the King's attitude and joined England in warning him that the two maritime powers would recall their representatives from Naples and send their fleets to the Mediterranean.[17] The threat to send naval squadrons alarmed Gortchakoff who warned Morny that such action might force a break between France and Russia. He issued a circular proclaiming the principle of non-intervention and attempted to start direct negotiations between Ferdinand II and Napoleon. The King refused, however, and the two maritime powers thereupon recalled their representatives from Naples although the naval squadrons were not sent.

The Neapolitan affair was merely an interlude in the far larger question involving Austria's influence in Italy. While the maritime powers were engaged in the futile task of getting Ferdinand II to reform his administration, relations between Vienna and Turin became more dangerous for the maintenance of peace. Everything seemed to depend on Napoleon's intentions. Could he forget Austria's conduct in the Crimean War? Would he approve of strong measures against Piedmont, his former ally? And was it likely that he could be persuaded to abandon his policy based upon the principle of nationalities in favor of a dynastic policy? These questions were in the minds of the Austrian statesmen.

During a visit to Compiègne in October 1856, Hübner had an interesting conversation with Napoleon. The latter declared that he had no intention of effecting changes in Italy or of altering the map of Europe, though France had unprotected boundaries, and added that he regarded the alliance with England as the cornerstone of his policy and an alliance with Austria as a necessity.[18] Thus encouraged, Hübner related what Franz Joseph had said to him at Ischl: "Inform the Emperor Napoleon that I desire to have good relations with him. Let him found a dynasty, let him consolidate it and follow a truly dynastic policy; this will be a guarantee for Europe and I sincerely desire it." Napoleon was visibly affected by this expression of good will. "You find yourself," continued Hübner, "in the prime of life and in excellent health. May God preserve you for France and for Europe, but He can dispose otherwise, and I then see a cradle behind your throne. Where in Europe is the alliance which alone can benefit this imperial child if it is not with my august master, who extends his hand to you on condition that you follow a sovereign and dynastic policy and not a personal one? What other alliance could take its place?" This was a favorite approach with Hübner. A few days later the Emperor repeated his peaceful intentions and said: "I am good to Piedmont so long as the latter acts decently to everyone."[19] To this Hübner replied that all Austria wanted of France was that she cooperate in forcing Piedmont to act moderately and fulfill her international obligations.

While Napoleon sought to placate Vienna by assurances of his peaceful intentions, England set out to reconcile the differences between Austria and Piedmont. Acting upon English representations, the Austrian Government decided to try a policy of conciliation. On December 2, 1856, a decree was issued which raised the sequestrations imposed upon the property of former Lombards, who had become naturalized subjects of Piedmont. In January 1857, the

Emperor Franz Joseph and the Empress Elizabeth paid a state visit to Milan and a short time later it was announced that the Archduke Ferdinand Maximilian would assume the duties of Governor of Lombardy-Venetia.[20] By these acts Austria hoped to conciliate her Italian subjects and win the good will of Europe, but they came too late.

The new policy did not please Cavour, who saw that the raising of the sequestrations removed one of his chief complaints against the Hapsburgs.[21] Pressed by the English, however, he agreed to adopt a more conciliatory attitude and considered the advisability of sending a special envoy to compliment Franz Joseph upon his arrival at Milan. The envoy was not sent as Victor Emmanuel became infuriated when the Austrian police expelled from Milan a Piedmontese senator, who was visiting friends. This incident ended the attempts at reconciliation. On the day Franz Joseph entered Milan, the *Gazzetta Piemontese* announced that 7000 livres had arrived from Lombardy as a contribution to the national subscription for the purchase of 100 cannon for the fortifications at Alessandria, and that the people of Milan were raising money for the erection of a monument in Turin honoring the Piedmontese army.[22] In addition, there were reports that Mazzini was making a drive to raise money for the purchase of 10,000 rifles to be used against the "common enemy." Exasperated by attacks in the Piedmontese journals, Buol sent a sharp note to Count Paar, the Austrian Chargé d'Affaires at Turin, with instruction to present it to Cavour.[23] In it he enumerated his complaints against Piedmont and declared that the latter was not fulfilling her international duties nor her functions as a good neighbor, and demanded guarantees which would permit the two states to maintain desirable relations. Evidently, Buol hoped to intimidate Cavour.[24]

The latter replied to Buol's charges in a note to the Marquis Cantono, the Piedmontese Chargé d'Affaires at Vienna.[25] While expressing a desire to maintain friendly relations with Austria, he disclaimed any responsibility for the attacks in the Piedmontese press and pointed out that such attacks were not more violent than those of certain English or Belgian journals and had no influence beyond the Ticino. Besides, the Austrian journals, particularly those of Lombardy, conducted a campaign no less violent against Piedmont. Buol, however, was not satisfied, declaring that he might have been more impressed by Cavour's assurance of wishing to maintain friendly relations with Austria, had it been given sooner and more spontaneously.[26] As it was, he could not find in the reply the least regret for the wrongs committed nor any guarantees that Piedmont intended to put an end to the intolerable state of affairs which had produced the crisis. He had learned, moreover, that Cavour had recently welcomed a delegation from Modena with the statement that Piedmont had not forgotten the events of 1848. Was this fulfilling international obligations, considering that Piedmont had solemnly renounced all claims to Modena? And how could one expect Austria to maintain regular diplomatic relations with a state which failed in its international duties? Buol's answer was to recall the Austrian legation from Turin.[27] Cavour followed suit by recalling the Piedmontese legation from Vienna, and diplomatic relations between the two states ceased.

In the duel of words, the Piedmontese statesman was the victor, for he created the impression of being moderate and willing to conciliate his powerful neighbor, whereas Buol's note was universally condemned. Napoleon resented it on the ground that it was not justified by Piedmont's conduct, while Cowley warned Hübner that a prolongation of the crisis would not fail to awaken the ancient rivalry between Austria and France, and since England desired to retain the friendship of the latter, she could not support Austria.[28] Even Walewski, who disliked Cavour, regarded the suspension of diplomatic relations as a grave mistake, which would hardly be to Austria's advantage. "It will," he said to Hübner, "encourage Austria's enemies in Italy, provoke excitement, perpetuate the agitation. Is the excess of the press and the alleged visit of the people of Modena to Turin a good reason for breaking off diplomatic relations?"[29] Hübner asked him what Napoleon would have done had the Belgian Minister of Foreign Affairs received a delegation of Orleanists and addressed them on the revolution of 1830 and the *coup d'état* of 1851. "The French Minister at Brussels would be recalled by telegraph."[30] Walewski admitted that Austria had grievances but feared that she would take advantage of disturbances in the Peninsula in order to intervene and to increase her influence.[31]

By his astute handling of the situation, Cavour succeeded in furthering one of his aims: the creation of a hostile attitude in Europe toward Austria's Italian policy. He now decided to take advantage of the favorable atmosphere in order to realize another of his aims, namely, the armed intervention of Napoleon in Italy. Without such intervention, he knew that Piedmont would again be crushed and Hapsburg influence in Italy would be more firmly established than ever. England could not be depended upon as she had no army strong enough to cope with the Austrians and, moreover, had effected a *rapprochement* with Austria in Near Eastern affairs. Although Clarendon was critical of Buol's action in severing diplomatic relations, he was still anxious to patch up the quarrel between Austria and Piedmont.[32] He therefore proposed to Paris that France join England in sending a joint note to Turin requesting the Piedmontese Government to make a formal declaration of its intention to respect the treaties.[33] This proposal angered Cavour, who thought he had England back of him, but now saw that she treated Piedmont like Naples, and he flatly refused to make such a declaration.[34] Though France agreed to the joint note, she did so without enthusiasm and without any expectation that it would be accepted.[35]

Cavour was now more convinced than ever that only France could win freedom for Italy. At the same time, he saw that there were in France two policies: that of the Quai d'Orsay and that of the Tuileries. Since Walewski and Gramont[36] were opposed to his aims, he decided to establish contact with the Emperor. For this purpose he could employ a number of intermediaries including Villamarina, his minister at Paris, Nigra, his private secretary, Salmour, his close friend, Dr. Conneau, Napoleon's personal physician, and Prince Napoleon, the cousin of the Emperor. In July 1857, he sent Salmour to interview Napoleon at Plombières. Invited to a private luncheon, Salmour engaged the Emperor in a lengthy discussion concerning Italian affairs.[37] He said that as Cavour believed a war with Austria to be inevitable, he wanted to prepare for it and counted on the Emperor's support.[38] To this the latter replied: "In any case, if that should arrive, tell your friend Cavour to be careful about involving me; it goes against his aim, for I wish to be the sole judge of the opportuneness of my actions." At the same time, while showing himself favorable to the Italian cause, the Emperor expressed the opinion that there were no greater or more dangerous enemies to this cause than Mazzini and the revolutionaries.[39] He blamed the Anglo-Austrian *rapprochement* for the breach in diplomatic relations between Turin and Vienna and was severely critical of England's conduct toward Piedmont. In referring to the English proposal for a joint note, he said to Salmour: "From the beginning of this affair, I understood that Sardinia would never consent to what England desired that we demand of it collectively, because if one demanded of me to declare in writing that I would never attempt to acquire the Rhine frontier, although I have no thought of doing it, I certainly would not consent to it."[40] He concluded by saying: "I do not like tortuous politics; I go straight to the point."

Salmour's mission convinced Cavour that he had set the right course. In a letter congratulating his friend, he wrote: "I now hope that you share the conviction that the Emperor is our best friend, the only power in France who is favorable to the cause of Italy, the only ruler in Europe who has a real interest in the aggrandizement of Piedmont. In marching in accord with him, we can reach our aim. This ought to be the dominant principle of our policy."[41] Thus, Cavour expected much from the French Emperor. As for England, whose political institutions he so greatly admired, he knew that he could not hope for more than moral support. Russia was not likely to oppose his aims, for since the Congress of Paris, the relations between the Russian and Piedmontese diplomats had been exceptionally cordial, owing largely to their common hatred of Austria.[42] The most important task facing Cavour was to overcome Napoleon's hesitations and to persuade him to take up arms for Italian independence. In this he was aided by a fortuitous event.

On January 14, 1858, as the Emperor and Empress were about to enter the Opera in Paris, a bomb exploded, killing several bystanders. The assassin, Felice Orsini, a former member of the constituent assembly of Rome, had planned to kill Napoleon. It was but one of several attempts made on his life by Italian revolutionaries, who never forgave him for putting down the Roman Republic. By a miracle the imperial couple escaped injury. From his cell where he awaited execution, Orsini wrote the Emperor a pathetic letter, urging him to free Italy.[43] This letter, together with a complete account of the trial, was published by Napoleon's orders in the *Moniteur* and aroused widespread sympathy in France. In a second letter, Orsini declared that the Emperor's sentiments for Italy were a source of comfort to him as he prepared to mount the scaffold, and he begged the revolutionary groups to refrain from further attempts on Napoleon's life. This letter was also published in the *Moniteur*, while the Emperor sent a copy to Villamarina, requesting that it be transmitted to Cavour and indicating that it be published. It appeared in the semi-official journal of Piedmont on March 31st. In the eyes of Italian patriots, Orsini was a great hero, a martyr who had given his life for the cause of freedom.

The Orsini affair marked a turning point in Napoleon's Italian policy. His immediate reaction, however, was one of indignation, which was cleverly encouraged by Hübner and the Papal Nuncio and which Walewski was not inclined to oppose. When General Della Rocca arrived in Paris with a letter from King Victor Emmanuel congratulating the Emperor on his miraculous escape, he was not given a cordial welcome.[44] Napoleon seemed overcome with indignation against revolutionaries and against Italy, and complained bitterly about the conditions in Piedmont. He reminded Della Rocca that alliances were not eternal and that even his friendship for England could give way to enmity.[45] "I say then to Piedmont," continued the Emperor, "I like your country, I like your King, I have great sympathy for your flag, for the cause that it represents in Italy, but if one does nothing, if one does not find the means to restrict the press, to protect morals and religion, if one cannot maintain order, my friendship will grow cool and I will be forced to ally myself more closely with Austria. Then what will happen to Piedmont? Let them think seriously about it there. Be convinced that I am your ally; do not imagine that you will be aided by England! What can she give you? Money, perhaps, but not a single man. It is necessary to choose between France and England and the choice cannot be in doubt."[46] In a letter to Victor Emmanuel, the Emperor explained that in speaking to Della Rocca about Piedment, he intended no offense but merely wanted to give a warning about "our alliance."[47] "I am prepared to sustain your cause . . . but it is just because I feel how far my sympathy for your country can engage me, that I ask you not to give the appearance of treating my most furious enemies with consideration."

In Vienna it was hoped that the Orsini affair would open Napoleon's eyes to the dangers involved in his Italian policy and that henceforth he would act more energetically on the side of law and order. Franz Joseph sent one of his great nobles, Prince Franz von Liechtenstein, to convey congratulations to the Emperor. The Prince was overwhelmed with politeness at the Tuileries and for the first time in several months, Napoleon approached Hübner.[48] The ice was broken and the tension between the two powers was noticeably relaxed.[49] Indeed, so cordial was the atmosphere that one could almost speak of a *rapprochement*. A week after Orsini's attempt, Walewski went out of his way to praise the Austrian administration of Lombardy-Venetia, characterizing it as moderate, conciliatory and liberal.[50] From his side, Buol adopted a more friendly tone and the French Chargé d'Affaires reported that his attitude was "in every respect what one would expect from an ally."[51] During an audience with Franz Joseph, to whom he remitted letters from Napoleon and the Empress Eugénie, Bourqueney declared that France had always been loyal in her policy toward Austria, that if the relations between the two powers had not been of the best, this was because ever since the Congress of Paris, the Austrian Cabinet had suspected French intentions, had taken the vaguest symptoms for realities, and had even carried its suspicions to other powers.[52] Furthermore, it had avoided a discussion of the differences arising out of the war.

Austria's efforts to capitalize on the Orsini affair fell short of the mark. While the atmosphere had momentarily cleared, the differences and suspicions which separated the two powers since the Crimean War remained, rendering a close understanding virtually impossible. Vienna still persisted in the belief that Napoleon had altered his policy in effecting a *rapprochement* with Russia. Nor was it long before he recovered from his indignation against Piedmont. Hitherto he had followed a more or less passive policy in the Italian question, and though not concealing his sympathies, had been content to permit time and circumstance to bring about a settlement. He had given moral encouragement while withholding active support and had attacked Austria's influence in the Near East rather than in Italy. But Orsini's attempt on his life convinced him that something must be done for the Italian cause if he was to escape the assassin's dagger. Once convinced, his secret dealings with Cavour's agents became more frequent and more serious in scope. Cavour was quick to take advantage of this change in attitude and redoubled his efforts to get French assistance. He persuaded Victor Emmanuel to write several flattering letters to Napoleon, while he himself presented, either by direct correspondence or through his agents, the arguments in favor of the Italian cause. In addition, he set out to prove that Piedmont was worthy of assistance. He showed himself more openly hostile to Mazzini's party, reorganized the police, amended the press law without, however, violating the principles of the constitution, and exiled a number of political refugees.[53] By such actions he hoped to demonstrate that the Piedmontese Government was orderly and efficient in contrast with the reactionary and unstable conditions prevailing in other Italian states.

During the first half of 1858 when the affairs of the Principalities and Montenegro engaged the attention of the European cabinets, the Italian question was still too far in the background to require the formulation of any definite plans, and Napoleon was careful to conceal his intentions, preferring to await the outcome of events before entering upon a struggle with Austria. When the semi-official journal of Piedmont referred to him as favorable to the Italian cause, Hübner immediately objected. He was assured by Walewski, who at this time was completely in the dark concerning his master's intentions, that France was dissatisfied with Piedmont's conduct and had entered an official protest at Turin against the objectionable reference.[54] Even Hübner, who was inclined to look at the best side of things, had to admit that Napoleon's resentment against Austria was increasing, although he attributed this to the effect of Orsini's letters and the influence of the Italian National Party, and did not believe it would lead to war.[55] He was told by Cowley that the best way to bring the Emperor to his senses was to avoid showing any distrust.[56] More or less the same advice was offered by Walewski, who said that the Emperor harbored the feeling that Austria did not show him the same benevolence as did Russia, Prussia, England and Piedmont, but instead opposed him at all times and was everywhere in his way.[57] It was enough to know that France favored a certain thing to have Austria oppose it. Napoleon attached considerable importance to good form in his relations with the powers and when this was lacking, became distrustful.

It is my personal conviction (declared Walewski) that without these little difficulties which arose immediately after the Treaty of March 30th and which since then have continued unceasingly, the power with which we would be most intimate today would be Austria, because together with England, we have a paramount interest in common with her. That is to say, we have in common with her the same enemy, which is demagogy. I adhere to the Napoleonic dynasty in every way. I should therefore know its interests, its wishes, and the dangers which threaten it. Well, the powers are no longer its enemies: in this respect the situation is completely changed. Its sole enemy, within and without France, is the demagogic party. That is why it would be easy to be in intimate relations with Austria were it not for these little difficulties. There are persons who believe that the Emperor has given himself over to profound meditations on aggression, that he entertains *arrières-pensées,* a plan to realize such or such a secret aim. If the Emperor planned to break with Austria, correct forms would do no good and bad ones no harm but it is precisely because there is no reason for a break that they are of great importance. For my part, I have the conviction that the Emperor has only one desire: that of solving amicably the political difficulties which present themselves and of living at peace with all powers.[58]

There is no reason to doubt Walewski's sincerity. In the Italian question he was by no means unfavorable to Austria, although more or less ignorant of Napoleon's secret designs.[59] Besides, one should remember that there were two policies in France concerning Italy: that of the Foreign Minister and that of the Emperor and it was the latter which counted. Buol understood this and was not convinced by the arguments of Walewski. As he saw it, Napoleon's position had become more difficult and more embarrassing than at any other time in his reign.[60] It was necessary to speak bluntly, to let Napoleon know that Austria was prepared to defend by armed force the rights and territories she had acquired in Italy by the treaties.[61] Buol refused to employ flattery and intrigue and resented Walewski's insinuations that the questions which had arisen since the Paris Congress were "little things," declaring, on the contrary, that they were of vital importance and could be settled amicably only if Napoleon recognized the Austrian viewpoint. Angered by the published statements that Piedmont could count on French support, he instructed Hübner to obtain an official disavowal of these and to learn, if possible, the real intentions of the French Government.[62]

In carrying out this assignment, Hübner had an audience with the Emperor to whom he pointed out that the situation in Italy had been relatively calm until the publication of Orsini's letters and Cavour's speeches. Then a profound change took place because the Italian revolutionaries believed that they could count on French support. Would the Emperor permit such an erroneous belief to persist? But though he protested that he was not the friend of the Italian revolutionaries and had not changed his policy, he refused to issue a public statement to this effect.[63] Nor did Hübner have any better luck with Walewski, who refused to disavow the Italian insinuations on the ground that it would give them undue importance.[64]

Deception is certainly no stranger to diplomacy but in the Italian question Napoleon revealed himself a master of the art. Although Austria knew that a crisis was bound to occur sooner or later, she did not believe that the French ruler would force the issue. Nor did she know that at the very moment he was protesting his peaceful intentions, he was actually contemplating a war for Italian independence. Just when he made up his mind to fight Austria in alliance with Piedmont is difficult to determine. It has been suggested that he came to his decision in the period between the date of Orsini's attempt (January 14th) and the opening of the latter's trial (February 25th).[65] Certainly there is nothing to indicate that before Orsini's attack, the idea of an Italian war was anything more than a rather hazy dream of the Emperor. Indeed, his Italian policy from the Congress of Paris to the beginning of the year 1858 concerned itself with the introduction, by peaceful means, of certain reforms in the Peninsula and with the establishment of an Italian confederation. The arguments of Cavour, the influence of Prince Napoleon and other partisans of the Italian cause, perhaps the realization that a popular war was needed to consolidate his power and prestige in France,[66] and that such a war might lead to the destruction of the hated settlement of 1815 and strengthen the French frontiers in the southeast—all these factors played a part in forming the Emperor's decision. His resentment against Austria made it easier, for in his eyes Austria was the symbol of the system set up in 1815. Her attitude in the recognition of the Second Empire, in the Crimean War, and in the various disputes which had arisen in the Balkans and Italy, made the Emperor more receptive to the arguments of Cavour and Prince Napoleon than he might have been had he not so frequently found her in his way.

The negotiations between Napoleon and Cavour were conducted with great secrecy behind the backs of the regular diplomats, and the war of 1859 was plotted with greater deliberation than any major conflict in modern history. At the end of March 1858, Cavour was informed by one of his agents, Alessandro Bixio, that the time had come to send a negotiator to Paris.[67] Bixio pointed out that Villamarina, the Piedmontese Minister at Paris, had obtained nothing from Walewski and that it was essential to treat directly with the Emperor outside the diplomatic channels. If Cavour could arrange to visit Paris himself, Bixio was confident that matters could be arranged within a few days. This suggestion was rejected as Cavour saw that it would arouse a great deal of suspicion and might actually hinder the attainment of his aim. Instead, he informed Dr. Conneau, the Emperor's personal physician, who played a leading role in the negotiations, that he was sending his private secretary, Constantino Nigra.[68] The negotiations which Nigra began upon his arrival in Paris concerned three points: a war against Austria by France in alliance with Piedmont, compensation for Piedmont at the close of the war and its establishment as the Kingdom of Upper Italy, and the marriage of Prince Napoleon to Princess Clothilde, the fifteen year old daughter of King Victor Emmanuel. The Emperor accepted these points with the understanding that the war must be justified in the eyes of the people and that its cause should therefore be a plausible one.[69] In addition, he stressed the importance of obtaining the support of Russia and expressed himself in favor of a division of Italy into three states, namely, Upper Italy, Central Italy, and the Kingdom of Naples.[70] Having established the basis of an agreement, Napoleon sent Dr. Conneau to Turin, where the latter arrived at the end of May and paid secret visits to Cavour and the King. He informed Cavour that the Emperor would spend a month at Plombières and would be pleased to see the minister in order to discuss the situation in Italy.[71] Cavour replied that as it was his intention to go to Switzerland for a few weeks, he would be happy to visit Plombières.

On July 11th, Cavour left Turin for Switzerland, giving as the pretext for his journey the desire to breathe the pure air of the Alps. In Piedmont, only the King and General La Marmora, the Minister of War, were informed of his real aim. He wrote to General de Bléville, the Emperor's aide-de-camp, that he would like to call at Plombières in order to pay his respects. At Geneva he received a reply from General de Bléville, stating that the Emperor would be delighted to see him.[72] Travelling incognito under the name of Benso and accompanied only by a young attaché of the Foreign Office, de Veillet, Cavour reached Plombières on July 20th. At eleven o'clock on the following morning, he was received by the Emperor.[73]

Few interviews in history have produced more momentous results than the one which took place at Plombières on that summer day of 1858. It was not only Italy that was affected by the plotting of the two conspirators. Indirectly, it brought about important changes in Germany, Austria and, indeed, in all Europe. By consenting to aid Piedmont in the struggle for Italian independence, Napoleon unwittingly started that chain of events which led to the unification of Italy and Germany and which culminated in his own downfall at Sedan a dozen years later.

The Emperor informed Cavour that he had decided to support Piedmont with all his forces in a war against Austria provided the war was not undertaken for a revolutionary cause but for one which could be justified in the eyes of diplomacy and public opinion. In other words, it was necessary to find a good pretext for war and Cavour decided to tackle this problem first of all. He suggested that Austria's violation of the trade agreement with Piedmont might serve the purpose, but Napoleon objected that this was too insignificant and could not lead to a great war destined to alter the map of Europe. The Emperor also rejected the suggestion that a cause could be found in the complaints raised at the Congress of Paris, namely, Austria's illegitimate extension of power in Italy, her prolonged occupation of the Romagna and the Legations, and the new fortifications she was erecting around Piacenza. No one, remarked Napoleon, would be able to comprehend how these complaints could justify a call to arms when they had been regarded as insufficient in 1856 to bring about the intervention of England and France on the side of Piedmont. "Besides," he added, "so long as my troops are at Rome, I can scarcely demand that Austria withdraw hers from Ancona and Bologna." Having nothing further to propose, Cavour found his position somewhat embarrassing. The Emperor, however, came to his assistance and after considering all possibilities, they finally discovered that the unsatisfactory conditions in Massa and Carrara (in Modena) could furnish a pretext. The inhabitants of these districts should be prevailed upon to petition Victor Emmanuel for protection and demand annexation to Piedmont. While the King would not accept the latter demand, he would take up the cause of the oppressed peoples and send a threatening note to the Duke of Modena who, relying on Austrian aid, would reply in impertinent manner. This would enable the King to occupy Massa and thus bring on the war with Austria. Since responsibility would rest with the Duke of Modena, for whom Napoleon had less consideration than for the other Italian princes as the Duke had never recognized any of the French rulers since 1830, the war would prove popular in France and even in England and the rest of Europe, considering that the Duke was regarded as an agent of despotism. The Emperor made it clear that no action should be taken against the Pope or the King of Naples. Both must be spared: the former in order not to alienate French Catholics, the latter in order not to offend Russia, which was favorably disposed toward Ferdinand II. It was understood that France would give the signal for the war and that at its close there would be constituted a Kingdom of Upper Italy under the House of Savoy, including in addition to Piedmont, Lombardy-Venetia, the Duchies of Parma and Modena, the Romagna and the Legations. The Pope was to retain Rome and the surrounding territory, while the remainder of his states, together with Tuscany, would form the Kingdom of Central Italy. The boundaries of the Neapolitan Kingdom were to be left untouched. Finally, it was agreed that the four Italian states would form a confederation on the German model with the Pope as president to console him for the loss of most of his territory.[74] In return for Napoleon's assistance, Savoy was to be ceded to France and a plebiscite was to determine the wishes of the inhabitants of Nice, while Victor Emmanuel was to give his daughter, Princess Clothilde, in marriage to Prince Napoleon.

Cavour's visit to Plombières, which was announced in a Belgian journal, naturally aroused much speculation in diplomatic circles. From his post in Paris, Hübner wondered what had been planned but was unable to find out, for not even Walewski could tell him.[75] Indeed, the minister assured him that there had been no discussion concerning Italy though Cavour had attempted without success to get the Emperor's support for a venture against Sicily. Hence, Austria had no reason to worry particularly since the Emperor had shown his good will by renouncing his demand for a common flag in the Principalities.[76] At the same time, however, Walewski had to admit that he was not informed about the discussions. Thirty-four years later, after he had learned the truth, Hübner commented on the part played by Napoleon at Plombières. "What a strange mixture of falsehood and frankness! What a curious lack of any kind of moral sense in regard to policy! What skill in hypocrisy, what mastery in the art of conspiracy!"[77] It reminded him of the Italian princes of the Renaissance and he attributed Napoleon's action to the contradictions in his character. "One is not at the same time the Son of the Revolution and the equal and beloved brother of the legitimate monarchs, the nephew of the Conqueror Napoleon I and founder of an 'empire which is peace,' the elect of the people and the hero (indeed only passive) of a military conspiracy, one of the five guardians of the treaties which guarantee the existence of states and the Don Quixote of national principles which overthrow them. And yet Napoleon possessed something of each."[78]

While Hübner was unable to throw light on the conspiracy, Buol suspected that Cavour had succeeded in winning Napoleon's support for a war in behalf of Italian independence.[79] His suspicions were strengthened when, with a few exceptions, the French press began a violent campaign against Austrian rule in Italy. The Austrian press replied to these attacks with equal violence. The leader of the anti-Austrian movement in France was the Emperor's cousin, Prince Napoleon, whose hatred for the Hapsburgs was only equalled by his sympathy for Italy.[80] Despite their frequent quarrels, the Emperor had great affection for his cousin and their intimacy, according to one writer, "was like that which unites two brothers."[81] Until the end of the Empire, the Prince was involved in the secret diplomacy of the Tuileries.

With the journals of the two countries indulging in mutual recriminations and poisoning the atmosphere, relations between Austria and France became more and more strained.[82] The Emperor professed to regret the new turn of affairs and assured Cowley that he had no thought of stirring up trouble in Italy but instead desired the maintenance of peace.[83] If Austria would put an end to the press attacks against him, he would promise to hold the French journalists in check. While such an arrangement would undoubtedly have eased the tension, the Austrian Government maintained that it was for France to make the first move. The *Moniteur* published a statement denying that the French Government had any connection with the press campaign but as no steps were taken to end it, the situation remained unchanged.

Meanwhile, France and Piedmont made preparations for war and took steps to convert the Plombières agreement into a formal treaty of alliance. The principal difficulty arose over the pretext. Several possibilities were considered without reaching an agreement. Finally, Cavour fell back on the original pretext relating to Massa and Carrara and this was approved by Napoleon in November

1858.[84] However, a few weeks later Cavour discovered an additional pretext in a new Austrian law providing for recruiting of soldiers in Lombardy and suggested that this might be used simultaneously with the other pretext.[85]

Negotiations relative to the pretext were conducted in the greatest secrecy. Only the Emperor, Prince Napoleon, Cavour, Nigra and La Marmora were fully informed of the plans. General Niel, aide-de-camp of the Emperor, knew of everything save the motive, while the French Minister of War was kept in the dark and merely saw that preparations were made for a great struggle in Italy.[86] The Tsar and Gortchakoff were informed of the secret plans but not of the motive. It was not until the end of December when Cavour became impatient and demanded the conclusion of the treaty that Napoleon for the first time gave Walewski partial information concerning the negotiations. Such information was necessary as the counter-signature of the Foreign Minister was required in order to make the treaty of alliance valid.[87] Villamarina was also ignored until the end of December. A letter from Cavour explained that the Emperor had exacted from him a formal promise which prevented him from informing the Piedmontese Minister in Paris, but now the Emperor agreed that he should be told part of the secret, provided he said nothing to Walewski.[88] Cavour added that Russia had been informed of the territorial arrangements, that England knew nothing but had suspicions, and that Walewski has been partly informed and was hostile. Nothing was said to the French Minister at Turin, Prince de La Tour d'Auvergne, whom Cavour distrusted.

While Cavour busied himself with the pretext for war, Napoleon took steps to see that it would be fought in the most favorable conditions. In order to accomplish this, it was necessary to isolate Austria by obtaining the good will of England, Prussia and Russia. Although Napoleon's relations with England had altered somewhat since the Crimean War, he counted heavily on the sympathy of the English people for Italy. He was aware that England resented his *rapprochement* with Russia and that she was determined to defend the treaties of 1815 but he hoped to overcome these obstacles by showing Austria as the aggressor.[89] His old friend, Lord Malmesbury, who was now Foreign Secretary, was by no means unfavorable.

Indeed, Apponyi, the Austrian Ambassador at London, complained that he was too indulgent concerning the Emperor's mistakes, and would not believe that the latter was revolutionary or that he planned to provoke disorders in Italy.[90] Despite the increasing tension between Paris and Vienna, Malmesbury did not think that Napoleon intended to go to war but held that his plan was simply the introduction of reforms in some of the Italian states.[91] In his opinion, the best solution would be for Austria to reach an understanding with France regarding these reforms. He informed Cowley that in the event of war over Italy, England would remain neutral as long as possible but would not hesitate to turn against the aggressor.[92]

In the case of Prussia, the prospects appeared somewhat less favorable for Napoleon's plans. While he had sought to win her friendship and had gone out of his way to support her in the Neufchâtel affair,[93] he realized that as a member of the German Confederation, Prussia had certain obligations towards Austria.[94] Moreover, she was highly suspicious about Napoleon's ambitions in the direction of the Rhine. In October 1858, Prince William became Regent and formed a new cabinet with Prince Hohenzollern as Prime Minister and Schleinitz, who favored harmony between Berlin and Vienna, as Foreign Minister. Thereafter the Prussian Government was more favorably disposed toward Austria.[95] When Napoleon sent his friend, Pepoli, to inquire about Prussia's attitude in the event of a Franco-Austrian war, the Prince Regent stated that he would be neutral only if France were not the aggressor, for in the other case Austria could summon the German Confederation to her aid.[96]

With regard to Russia, Napoleon had every reason to believe that she would be on his side. The Franco-Russian *entente* had already demonstrated its effectiveness in Balkan affairs, while hatred for Austria, though diminishing, still lingered in St. Petersburg. Yet, Napoleon knew that in view of internal difficulties, Russia had no desire to become involved in war. He hoped, through the conclusion of a treaty, to obtain the Tsar's approval for such changes as he intended to make in Italy and the promise of benevolent neutrality in the conflict with Austria.

The negotiations with Russia proved far more difficult than Napoleon anticipated.[97] In September 1858, he summoned Prince Napoleon to Biarritz and charged him to undertake a mission to Warsaw. After informing the Prince of his desire to obtain glory for France and the destruction of the treaties of 1815, he authorized him to conclude a treaty with Russia in which the latter should promise benevolent neutrality and agree to prevent Prussia and the German states from going to the aid of Austria.[98] The Prince was cautioned to say nothing to the Empress or Walewski concerning the object of his mission.[99]

Prince Napoleon arrived in Warsaw on September 28th and was given a royal welcome. The Russians were obviously flattered, as this was the first time Napoleon had taken the initiative of such an act of courtesy toward their ruler.[100] In his conversations with the Tsar and Gortchakoff, the Prince outlined the plans regarding the approaching war with Austria. According to his own account, he took advantage of the fear and irresolution of Alexander II and the chattering and unsteadiness of Gortchakoff, who exhausted his animation by endless digressions, in order to obtain a treaty.[101] This document recalled the *entente* established at Stuttgart, and referred to the unstable conditions in Italy and the probability of war between Austria and Piedmont in which France was obliged to support the latter.[102] It declared that Napoleon would not alter the European equilibrium to his advantage or raise pretensions which might alarm Russia, England or Germany: his object was simply to gain allies which the treaties of 1815 had rendered impossible. Upon the outbreak of war, the Tsar would proclaim an attitude of benevolent neutrality toward France and concentrate on the Galician frontier an army large enough to immobilize about 150,000 Austrian troops, while a part of the Russian fleet would be stationed in the Mediterranean. Napoleon was to make England understand that any act of aggression against Russia would be regarded as an act of hostility toward France, while the Tsar was to warn Prussia and the German states not to aid Austria. The Tsar agreed that Piedmont should be enlarged by the erection of a Kingdom of Upper Italy and approved, in advance, of the annex-

ation of Nice and Savoy to France. In case Russia became involved
in war with Austria, at its conclusion France would support demands for the annexation of Galicia to Russia and for the modification of the Black Sea Clause of the Treaty of Paris. Finally, the
two rulers were not to oppose the establishment of an independent
Hungarian state.[103]

Upon his return to Paris, Prince Napoleon informed Nigra that
his mission had been completely successful.[104] According to the
account of the Prince, the Emperor was not satisfied and insisted
upon the insertion of a clause by which Russia would promise to
sever diplomatic relations with Austria soon after the outbreak of
hostilities.[105] It was necessary to send someone to St. Petersburg to
obtain approval for this change, and as the Prince could not undertake a second journey without arousing suspicion, it was decided to
entrust the mission to Captain La Roncière Le Noury. The latter
left Paris early in November bearing with him a letter from Prince
Napoleon to Gortchakoff explaining the reason for the mission and
drafts of two treaties.[106] On December 6th he was back in Paris
with a letter and a counter-project from Gortchakoff.[107]

The Russian counter-project was a great disappointment to Napoleon for it omitted the clause relative to the rupture of diplomatic
relations with Austria, made reservations concerning the aggrandizement of Piedmont, demanded French support for the revision
of the Black Sea Clause of the Treaty of Paris, and weakened the
provision concerning a warning to Prussia. It is difficult to comprehend why Napoleon wanted a treaty in the first place and, most
of all, why he persisted in his efforts to conclude one. The *entente*
established at Stuttgart and by the exchange of letters between the
two Emperors would have been a sufficient guarantee of Russia's
benevolent neutrality. But having started the negotiations, Napoleon
was reluctant to give them up and they dragged on for several
months. At the end of December 1858, the Emperor initiated
Walewski into the great secret. Upon learning for the first time of
the negotiations with Piedmont and Russia, Walewski was furious.
"He complained bitterly, he even wept, and sent in his resignation."[108] Against the advice of his cousin, the Emperor wrote to the
minister urging him to retain his post. A reconciliation was effected

but Walewski succeeded in obtaining modifications in the treaty with Russia, particularly regarding French support in revising the Treaty of Paris. The Franco-Russian treaty was not concluded until March 3, 1859.

By the terms of the treaty, Russia promised to maintain an attitude of benevolent neutrality in a Franco-Austrian conflict and not to oppose the aggrandizement of Piedmont with the understanding that the rights of those rulers not participating in the war be respected. France would seek to keep England neutral while Russia would urge neutrality upon the German states.[109] Any further revision of the existing treaties was to be reserved until after the conclusion of peace. Actually the treaty of March 3, 1859 did little more than confirm Russia's reassurances and overcome possible wavering on her part.

During the negotiations with Russia, Cavour became more and more impatient to conclude the alliance with France. Toward the end of October 1858, he wrote to Prince Napoleon stating that it was imperative for General Niel to visit Turin in order to concert with General La Marmora, since the possibility of Austrian intervention in the Balkans would provide the opportunity for France and Piedmont to intervene in Italy.[110] He was informed by the Emperor that General Niel would leave about November 25th, after the return of La Roncière Le Noury from St. Petersburg.[111] But the difficulties which arose in connection with the Russian treaty prevented the general's departure. On December 24th Cavour transmitted to Villamarina a detailed project of a treaty, and two days later Victor Emmanuel wrote to the Emperor urging him to send Prince Napoleon to Turin about the middle of January with full powers to conclude the treaty. With the assistance of Walewski, the Emperor prepared the drafts and the instructions which the Prince was to carry with him to Turin.[112] Exasperated by the slowness in concluding the affair, Cavour begged Prince Napoleon to hasten his departure as much as possible because events were pressing and the agitation in Lombardy was increasing. Finally, on January 16, 1859, the Prince accompanied by General Niel, arrived in Turin. A week later the completed treaties were sent to Paris.[113] They were signed by Napoleon on the 26th and by Victor Emmanuel on the 28th or 29th.[114] The political treaty provided that in case war broke out between Piedmont and Austria as the result of the latter's aggression, France and Piedmont would conclude an offensive-defensive alliance; that the aim of this alliance was to free Italy from Austrian occupation and to establish a Kingdom of Upper Italy comprising eleven million inhabitants. Nice and Savoy would be ceded to France, the sovereignty of the Pope would be maintained. It was further provided that the expenses of the war should be supported by the Kingdom of Upper Italy and that neither party would conclude a separate peace. In the military convention, the allies agreed to place 300,000 men in the field; 200,000 French and 100,000 Piedmontese, with the Emperor as commander-in-chief, while a French fleet would be sent to the Adriatic.[115] Aside from the provisions relating to the Kingdom of Upper Italy, the Papacy, Nice and Savoy, no mention was made about the fate of the rest of Italy.

CHAPTER EIGHT

Drifting Toward War, 1859

THE FIRST HINT of the impending conflict came during the New Year's reception to the diplomatic corps at the Tuileries. In replying to the congratulations of the Papal Nuncio, the Emperor expressed the hope that the new year "will secure more firmly our alliance for the welfare of the people and the peace of Europe." Then, turning to Hübner, he said in a friendly and good-natured tone: "I regret that our relations are not as good as I could desire but I beg you to say that my personal feelings for the Emperor are always the same."[1] The assembled diplomats, who overheard these words, interpreted them in different ways. Cowley regarded them as an outburst of ill-humor, while to Kisseleff and Hatzfeldt they were an additional proof of the Emperor's peaceful intentions already expressed in his reply to the Nuncio.[2]

Just what Napoleon had in mind in addressing his remarks to Hübner is not certain. That it was his intention to convey a warning of the approaching war seems most doubtful considering the care he had taken to guard his secret designs. It is more probable that his words were simply an expression of his irritation against Austria provoked by the Serbian question which was still unsettled.[3] Whether they were premeditated is also difficult to answer. According to La Gorce, the Emperor's tone, gesture, and attitude showed that he had no desire to provoke a rupture and that his words were not premeditated.[4] On the other hand, Baron Beyens, the Belgian Minister to Paris, who witnessed the incident, was convinced that Napoleon spoke knowingly, accustomed as he was to weighing his words carefully.[5] When informed by Walewski of the sinister interpretation given to his remarks, Napoleon appeared to be astonished and said: "I did not wish to remain silent concerning relations between Austria and France. Thus, I had to speak to Baron Hübner about them but I thought that I had done so in an agreeable manner. . . . "[6] At the Empress' reception on the following day, he went out of his way to be friendly to Hübner, and conversed with him longer than with any of the other diplomats.[7] "All eyes were upon us," wrote Hübner, "the diplomatic corps breathes more easily. One says to himself that there will be no war."[8]

Regardless of his intentions, the Emperor's remarks created the impression that war was imminent. There was a minor panic in the Paris Bourse and a drop in French and especially Austrian government bonds. As Hübner pointedly observed, these remarks were "very imprudent if the Emperor does not want war, and very well calculated if he does want it."[9] With the aim of reassuring the public, the Government on January 7th issued a statement in the *Moniteur* that "nothing in our diplomatic relations authorizes the fears to which these reports give birth."[10] At Vienna the incident caused much commotion and several army corps were sent to Italy though Buol pretended that Austria was not offended and that he regarded the Emperor's words as spoken in a friendly manner.[11] Everywhere, but above all in Italy, the belief spread that Napoleon intended to break with Austria.[12] Addressing the Parliament of Piedmont on January 10th, the King referred to the clouds which had appeared on the horizon and said:[13]

> Strengthened by the experience of the past, we go resolutely to meet the eventualities of the future. That future will be a happy one, for our policy rests on justice, on the love of liberty and the fatherland. Our country though small in size has acquired standing in the counsels of Europe because it is great by the ideas it represents and by the sympathies it inspires. This situation is not without danger, for while we respect the treaties, we are not deaf to the cries of sorrow that come to us from all parts of Italy.

Taken in conjunction with the Emperor's remarks to Hübner, the King's speech aroused tremendous excitement through the Peninsula. A few days later, Prince Napoleon arrived in Turin where he completed the military convention between France and Piedmont.

In England the new turn of events was viewed with growing anxiety. Lord Shaftesbury, an ardent supporter of the Italian cause, asked what had happened to Cavour, whom the English had re-garded "as so cautious and so wise?"[14] The Tory Ministry was much displeased with the King's speech and Malmesbury sent a dispatch to the British Minister at Turin instructing him to advise Cavour to be more prudent and more moderate.[15] The war scare shook the complacency of the English and the *London Times*, formerly favorable to Italian unity, now began to oppose it energetically,[16] while Derby, the Prime Minister, came out strongly in support of the treaties of 1815.[17] At the same time, however, Malmesbury renewed his efforts at mediation and again suggested an Austro-French *entente* for the introduction of reforms in Italy.[18] He told Apponyi that he had written to Cowley directing him to inform the French Government that "the only saviors of Italy were France and Austria united."[19] Yet, he realized that one could not be too optimistic. "Napoleon," he said to Apponyi, "will always remain a conspirator; it is in his nature. Soon he will raise one question, then another. The essential thing is always to place him in the wrong, and for that it is necessary to be supported by the treaties and not to deviate from them an iota."[20] His proposal for an Austro-French *entente* found no support in Vienna. Buol rejected it as being of no practical value and declared that if the English Cabinet really wanted to help in calming the storm, it should act more energeti-cally in Paris and Turin.[21] He instructed Apponyi to be on his guard against the English argument that Austria should be content to defend her own territory and that intervention in another state was an infraction of international law.[22]

Among the French also the idea of a new European war found little support. There was opposition among the ministers, the financiers, the Catholic party, the bourgeoisie, the peasants and even some of the elements in the army.[23] Under the circumstances, Napo-leon had to proceed with caution while endeavoring to provoke Austria into committing overt acts which would arouse public opinion to his side. This was not an easy task as one could not point to any real issue for a conflict, not even the Italian question. Although relations between Paris and Vienna had been growing more and more strained, war-like sentiments had not been openly expressed, save in the press campaign which followed the Plombières interview. The fact that Napoleon resented Austria's policy in the east and in Italy, that he was piqued because she stood in his way, was not a sufficient reason to embark upon a great war. Indeed, it seemed to be less the tension existing between the two nations which created apprehension than uncertainty as to Napoleon's intentions. Hübner's dispatches alternated between hope for peace and fear of war, and the same uncertainty was felt everywhere. If Napoleon desired peace, why did he permit his cousin to preach war? Was this because he was afraid to alienate the only member of his family who could protect the heir to the throne in case he (the Emperor) should meet with sudden death, or did he actually share the belligerent views of the Prince?[24] In the opinion of Hübner this was the key to the question, for if Napoleon did not break with his cousin, Austria must be prepared to see the policy of nationalities and revolution prevail—a policy which meant war. Although Walewski tried to reassure the public by inserting an article in the *Constitutionnel* declaring that there was no danger of war, he privately admitted to Hübner that the situation was serious and that it was necessary to avoid any incidents which might provoke a crisis.[25] To the Ambassador's suggestion that the best means of reassuring the public was not by newspaper articles but simply by warning Piedmont against encouraging revolution, the Foreign Minister promised that this warning would be given in due time. Hübner reported that there seemed to be "a complete stagnation of affairs" in Paris, that a lively struggle went on around the Emperor between the war-hawks led by Prince Napoleon and the advocates of peace led by Walewski and that it was difficult to predict the outcome.[26] The Emperor declared that he wanted peace though admitting that he might be carried along by circumstances but he refused to listen to the peace advocates and even Persigny, the faithful friend of his exile, was unable to gain his ear and had to write to him about the dangers of war.[27] What was one to conclude from such an attitude? "Is it," asked Hübner, "that the Emperor no longer wishes to hear advice which is contrary to a decision he has irrevocably taken? Or is it simply to avoid hearing from others criticism of his conduct, which is beginning to penetrate his mind?"[28] The Ambassador described the situation as similar to that of a sick man before the crisis.

There are fluctuations, slight improvements, a little recrudescence of the fever, but no symptoms sufficiently pronounced to judge the outcome. The task of the physician charged with editing the bulletin is at once ungrateful and compromising, for he does not dare say too much and one finds he never says enough. What will the Emperor do? That is the question, for it still appears that he is master of his actions. But it will be rash to predict the resolutions which, under the sway of diverse influences and incalculable incidents, a man of the turn of mind, character and antecedents of Louis Napoleon takes in the decisive moment.[29]

Hübner was sorely perplexed by his inability to fathom the Emperor's intentions. What was he to think of a ruler who at one and the same time posed as the champion of nationalities and defender of the treaties? If Napoleon did not lift the veil concealing his plans, "Europe will be anxious, peace between the powers threatened, public order compromised, industry and commerce paralyzed."[30] Nor could Hübner see any cause for war though the French press employed the term "Italian question" as if it were a cause and called for a European congress to preserve peace. "The fact is, and we cannot hide it from ourselves, Austria and France have arrived within an ace of war without any cause! The absence of a cause is embarrassing to diplomacy, an imminent danger to peace, a grave incovenience for the Emperor from the standpoint of the internal situation. An embarrassment to diplomacy because if there was a cause, its task would be to make it disappear, but lacking a cause it can do nothing. An imminent danger to peace because the crisis can be prolonged indefinitely and we are powerless and incapable of turning it to peace."[31] Since there was no cause of war, there was obviously no need for a congress. On this point he expressed himself pungently to Walewski.

I understand perfectly the painful position in which your master finds himself. I *suppose* that he has decided to resume that policy which made his fortune and grandeur. I *suppose* because I do not know positively. If this is so, everyone will help him, and we first of all, to resume

his course; but we will help him by good means if there are any and
not by bad means. But to invent an Italian question and to regulate it
in a congress will be a bad means to which Austria will never agree.
From the first, there has been no Italian question. Aside from the occupation of the Papal States by Austrian and French troops, which could
form the subject of negotiations between the Papacy, Austria and France,
there are no open questions in Italy. To submit to a congress the internal
affairs of such and such independent states will be to change, to over-
turn the European edifice, to transform Europe into a forest, to return
not to the Middle Ages but to the migration of peoples, to anarchy,
to chaos.[32]

Although both the Emperor and Empress were extremely gracious
to him when he attended a ball at the Tuileries, Hübner did not
believe that this signified a change in policy but was rather an
attempt to make amends for the New Year's incident.[33] Such information as he was able to gather regarding Napoleon's intentions
came to him indirectly. Persigny told him that the Emperor had
been deceived by the situation in Italy: at first believing that a
revolution was imminent and that something had to be done but
later, on discovering his error, seeking to find a way out of his
embarrassment and to effect a reconciliation with Austria. In order
not to give the impression of drawing back, however, Napoleon
encouraged the journals to continue their anti-Austrian campaign.[34]
The idea that the Emperor was anxious to find a way out of his
embarrassment appealed to Hübner, who reported it in several of
his dispatches. It seemed to explain the uncertainties and fluctuations
of French policy, and convinced him that a war on behalf of the
Italians would find little sympathy in France.

If it were a question of conquering Belgium or the Rhine frontier
or fighting for Poland, it would be a different thing. Then, perhaps, one
could expect to find the ancient chord of military chauvinism awakened
and surmount the interests of commerce, industry and capital, which
demand peace. But a disinterested war and one designed merely to
create an Italian nation, is decidedly repudiated by the country.[35]

Hübner, of course, was not blind to the effects of newspaper propaganda. He saw that the French press was arousing old prejudices
against Austria, accusing her of violating treaties, of subjecting the
Italian people, and of controlling Parma, Modena, Tuscany, Naples

and the Papacy. "France, it is said, is at Rome, but Austria is at the Vatican."[36] He knew that such propaganda could create a state of mind favorable to a war against Austria.

Early in February there appeared in Paris a brochure entitled "L' Empéreur Napoléon III et l' Italie," which had been authorized by Napoleon soon after the Plombières interview.[37] It made a bitter attack on most of the Italian governments and on Austrian influence in the Peninsula. The Duke of Modena was referred to as a lieutenant of Austria; the Duchess of Parma as bound to Austria by treaties; the Grand Duke of Tuscany as maintaining himself in power by means of Austrian bayonets; the King of Naples as isolated not only in Italy but in Europe as well; and the Pope as opposed to reforms. Only Piedmont escaped criticism and thus stood forth in shining colors. Austrian influence was labelled as an evil which could no longer be tolerated. The brochure advocated an Italian confederation under the presidency of the Pope, who was to reform his government in return for this honor. The Emperor's aim in launching this highly provocative document seems to have been twofold: to explain the reasons which necessitated a political change in Italy, and to present the idea of an Italian confederation.[38] But the "policy brochures" was an important feature of the Second Empire and was employed not only to ascertain internal and external reaction to a particular scheme but to indicate unofficially the course of action the Emperor intended to follow. In this instance, however, Napoleon appears to have sensed the inopportuneness of pushing matters too far, for on February 7th, three days after the publication of the brochure, he addressed the *Corps Législatif* and while describing the situation in Italy as abnormal in view of the foreign troops stationed there, declared that this was not a sufficient cause of war and that his policy was peaceful and not provocative.[39]

This speech helped somewhat to offset the tone of the brochure and to ease the tension which had existed since the New Year's incident. Walewski, Persigny, the Empress and other friends of peace gained new hope, while the Emperor, who had been very gloomy and irritable, was now so happy that he seemed to Hübner like a man relieved of a burden; whereas Prince Napoleon could not conceal his ill-humor.[40] Attending a dinner at the Tuileries,

Hübner noted the general air of optimism. The Empress was particularly cheerful and her face was wreathed in smiles as she withdrew to a window recess where she conversed with the Austrian Ambassador. "On my part," wrote Hübner, "I permitted myself to hint to the wife of the Sovereign of France that I considered myself fortunate not to be forced to draw the sword against such a charming person."[41] Such, he added, was the confidential court style at the Tuileries in the year of salvation, 1859. Toward the close of the evening the Emperor came to him and in a voice loud enough to be heard by the others, explained the New Year's incident and expressed his astonishment at the false interpretations given to it.[42] Hübner replied that he had not been surprised by these interpretations since it was known for more than a year that relations between Austria and France were not of the best. He warned the Emperor that Vienna would not welcome proposals for a revision of the boundaries of northern Italy.

While Hübner busied himself in diagnosing Napoleon's intentions, Malmesbury continued his efforts in behalf of peace and asked Russia and Prussia to join England in overtures to Austria and France.[43] Prussia was willing but Gortchakoff declined on the ground that the moment was inopportune and that the role of counsellor had never brought Russia good luck.[44] On February 4th Queen Victoria urged Napoleon to avoid a war which would cause a rift in the Anglo-French *entente*. She pointed out that he had a splendid opportunity to demonstrate his respect for the treaties, to calm apprehensions, and to reëstablish confidence.[45] Though Napoleon was disturbed by this appeal, he refused to make any promises. Instead, he replied by calling attention to the dangers of insurrection in Italy against which he had to be prepared and complained of the attitude of Germany and the suspicions of England.[46] Undismayed by this rebuff, Malmesbury still hoped to bring about an understanding between Austria and France as the best means of preserving peace. Having failed to persuade either of these powers to take the initiative, he decided to offer England's mediation. On February 13th he requested Cowley, after learning the nature of the French complaints against Austria and what concessions France expected of her, to go on an unofficial mission to Vienna.[47] Napoleon approved of the mission and set forth the following terms for Austria's acceptance: abrogation of the treaties concluded by Austria with Naples, Tuscany and the Duchies; the establishment in the Italian states of governments in which taxes would be voted by assemblies; a separate administration for the Legations headed by a Roman prince to be named by the Pope; and financial assistance to the Pope by Catholic states.[48] With the way thus cleared, Malmesbury instructed Cowley to proceed to Vienna and obtain Austria's approval of four points: the withdrawal of Austrian and French troops from the Papal States; reforms in the Papal States; a guarantee of better relations between Austria and Piedmont; and the abrogation or modification of the Austro-Italian treaties of 1847.[49]

The prospects for an Austro-French understanding were not promising. It is true that Napoleon was finding his position rather uncomfortable in view of the attitude of England and Prussia. The latter, he wrote to Victor Emmanuel, threatened to aid Austria if France intervened in Austrian affairs, while England was jealous of France and not well-disposed toward Italy.[50] Napoleon advised the King to continue to prepare slowly but seriously for war while avoiding anything that might precipitate a conflict. Yet, though Napoleon hesitated to break the peace, he was pledged to liberate Italy from Hapsburg control, and only a war could accomplish this. Nor was the situation in Austria favorable to the English plan. In view of the agitations started by Piedmontese agents in Lombardy-Venetia and Tuscany, and the heavy financial burden required to support her armaments, the desire to cut the gordian knot by means of the sword was becoming stronger each day in Austria.

Cowley arrived in Vienna on February 27th and on the following day was received by Franz Joseph and had several conversations with Buol. He informed the latter that he brought with him no definite proposals and had no power to negotiate. His purpose was simply to learn the views and intentions of the Austrian Cabinet and to see if there was not some way of bringing about an *entente* and thus preventing a disastrous war. Buol replied that he had already made known Austria's peaceful intentions and that there was nothing he could add in this respect.[51] He was willing, however, to discuss the difficulties affecting Austro-French relations. In regard to the withdrawal of troops from the Papal States, he pointed out that this question could not be considered a cause of conflict since Austria had expressed a willingness to put an end to the occupation, whereas France had discontinued the negotiations started after the Paris Congress.[52] The second and more important difficulty concerned the treaties of alliance between Austria and some of the Italian states. Not only was Buol unwilling to comply with the request that Austria abrogate these treaties but he declared that any discussion as to their validity was inadmissible.[53] He pointed out that Austria had never attempted to interfere in Parma and Modena and that the secret article in the Austro-Neapolitan treaty of 1815 which bound the King not to alter the institutions of his Kingdom without Austria's permission, was a dead letter. Indeed, he insisted that the treaties in question had been concluded solely for the protection of the Italian princes at their own request. At the same time, he was quite willing to entertain some other arrangement, providing it would protect these princes, and suggested two possible alternatives: a league of small Italian states or the neutralization of Piedmont. As to the question of introducing reforms, Buol stated that he was prepared to cooperate to the extent of advising their acceptance but not to impose them. Finally, he assured Cowley that Austria would not begin hostilities provided Piedmont refrained from any attack against her or her allies, Parma, Tuscany and Modena.

Except for the assurance that Austria would not attack Piedmont, Cowley's mission accomplished nothing in resolving the difficulties in Austro-French relations.[54] As a matter of fact, neither the English nor the French had entertained much hope of success. Apponyi reported that very few persons in England believed that the mission would result in the maintenance of peace and that almost everyone was agreed in thinking that Napoleon had irrevocably decided on war.[55] Cowley mentioned among the difficulties he encountered the fixed idea in Vienna that Napoleon was determined on war and that concessions would merely postpone the event, the resentment of Austria at being made the target of attack, her desire to profit from the growing tension in Franco-German relations, and the absence of any real issue which could be regarded as involving a *casus belli*.[56] Yet, he expressed the firm conviction that Austria was

prepared to accept any overtures for a reconciliation with France
compatible with her honor but that she would not enter any negotiations so long as Piedmont remained armed.[57] Austria insisted
upon the disarmament of Piedmont as a pledge of French sincerity.
Cowley apparently believed that his mission provided the basis of
an understanding between Austria and France.[58] The French Chargé
d'Affaires at Vienna was more pessimistic. In a dispatch to Walewski,
he wrote that the Austrian Government had become less conciliatory,
less willing to make concessions or to seek friendly relations with
France, while there was much talk about the patriotism of the
provinces and the anticipated support of the German states.[59] This
attitude, he reported, was due to the personal initiative of Franz
Joseph and the influence of the military entourage. "It seems that
he has come to consider any attempt at conciliation, any concessions,
as henceforth useless in view of the resolution taken by the Emperor
Napoleon to suppress Austrian domination in Italy. In any case,
the Emperor (Franz Joseph) is convinced that his dignity and
sovereign rights do not permit him to allow discussion of the defensive treaties concluded between Austria and the Italian states such
as Modena and Tuscany, which are governed by princes of his
family."[60] The Austrian ruler was impatient to find a prompt solution of the crisis, whose continuance increased the present uncertainties and created dangerous possibilities for the future. According
to the French Chargé d'Affaires, Buol had surrendered to the
nationalistic spirit and was no longer as confident of peace as
formerly.

Although England's attempt at mediation failed, it did make
Napoleon more hesitant to fulfill his pledge to Piedmont.[61] There
is no doubt that her diplomatic intervention together with the agitation in Germany and the provocative attitude of Piedmont, increased the Emperor's apprehensions. This was made apparent by
the publication of a note in the *Moniteur* on March 5th which stated
that the Emperor had nothing to conceal and nothing to disavow
either in his preoccupations or in his alliances.[62] He had promised
to defend Piedmont against any aggressive act by Austria, that was
all. It was time to put an end to the rumors spread by the European
press that he was planning war. Diplomacy not war would settle

the litigious questions. This note led to the resignation of Prince Napoleon as Minister of Algeria and the Colonies and produced consternation in Turin. Cavour thought of submitting his resignation while the friends of peace became more hopeful. On March 9th, however, Victor Emmanuel issued a proclamation calling out the reserves. This step, which was taken as a reply to the Austrian reinforcements, aggravated the situation, particularly when a subsequent decree established a volunteer corps composed of Lombard refugees.[63]

Napoleon had promised Cavour to open hostilities in the spring but public opinion in England and Germany was decidedly unfavorable. He was particularly bitter against the Germans who appeared to be influenced by memories of the First Empire. "But if this is so," he exclaimed to Nigra in a momentary outburst, "I will make them pay dearly someday for the bad quarter hour they have given me. They fear that after Marengo comes Jena. But if things of this sort continue, I will begin with Jena and will conduct a great war on the Rhine. In this case I could send only about 30,000 men to Italy and it would be necessary to limit oneself to a defensive war on the Po."[64] Nigra concluded that the Emperor was dominated by a "strange fatality" and would either fall or give a rude lesson to his enemies.

The "rude lesson" was not long in coming. Hardly had Cowley returned from his futile mission to Vienna, than Russia came forward (March 18th) with a proposal for a congress of the five great powers to settle the Italian question. This proposal was secretly inspired by Napoleon, who had discussed it with Kisseleff on March 15th.[65] England was not particularly pleased with the idea, suspecting that France and Russia had prepared a sort of trap. In a letter to Malmesbury, Queen Victoria wrote: "We must be careful not to be caught by the idea of a Congress getting Europe out of the present danger. A Congress has always been an alternative to war which the Emperor has put forward; but a Congress 'pour remanier les Traités de 1815.' Russia may intend to act in such a Congress the part against Austria regarding Lombardy, which Austria acted against her in the last Congress regarding Bessarabia."[66] It was clear, however, that none of the powers cared to reject the proposal altogether. Indeed, England announced her decision on the 19th: that a conference (not a congress) should meet at Aix-la-Chapelle and that its findings should be submitted to the Italian states for their consideration.[67] Malmesbury proposed that the agenda be confined to the following four items: evacuation of the Papal territories by Austrian and French troops; reforms in the Papal States and in Parma, Modena and Tuscany; the means of preserving peace between Austria and Piedmont; and the substitution of a union of the minor Italian states for the treaties of 1847 between Austria and the Duchies of Parma and Modena. This agenda received immediate approval of Gortchakoff who, however, insisted upon the term "congress" rather than "conference" in view of the gravity of the situation.[68]

The congress proposal placed Austria in a difficult position, for it appeared that she faced the alternative of a settlement imposed by the powers or isolation.[69] On March 21st Buol informed Loftus that Franz Joseph had reached a decision.[70] The Austrian ruler suggested that the first two points proposed by Malmesbury be eliminated from the agenda and that they be dealt with through negotiations carried on jointly by the great powers with the Papacy. Acceptance of the fourth point was made subject to several conditions. The first was that a substitution for the treaties of 1847 must not involve territorial changes. Secondly, Austria demanded that Piedmont disarm before the congress assemble and that she engage to respect the existing territorial treaties as well as those with her neighbors. Finally, Austria insisted upon a strict observance of the terms of the protocol annexed to the Treaty of Aix-la-Chapelle of 1818 which implied participation in the congress for the Italian states whose affairs would be discussed. If these conditions were accepted, no objections would be raised to the third point.

It seems clear that Napoleon's purpose in instigating the idea of a congress was to stall for time. By dragging out the negotiations he could prepare France morally and militarily for war while Austria's financial position became more and more desperate under the strain of maintaining her armaments. From Napoleon's standpoint it was thus a shrewd move on the European chessboard. Cavour, however was by no means pleased. Fearing that the great powers might arrange Italian affairs at Piedmont's expense, he instructed Nigra to use all his power in combatting the congress.[71] In a letter to the Emperor, he pointed out that the congress would have an unfortunate effect in Italy, particularly in the provinces subject to Austria's influence, and demanded the admission of Piedmont.[72] He rejected an English proposal of March 21st that the four great powers (excluding Austria) guarantee Piedmont against attack providing she disarm immediately. This, he declared, was tantamount to a betrayal of Piedmont.[73] If England and France insisted upon Piedmont's disarmament, it would bring about the downfall of his ministry and the abdication of the King.[74]

While Napoleon pushed his preparations for war, he found it necessary to restrain his ally. In a letter to Cavour he complained about reports which accused him of seeking in conjunction with Piedmont to find a pretext for war in order to turn Europe upside down for his own profit.[75] These reports were turning the European public against him and if he were to declare war under such circumstances, he would be compelled to fight not in Italy but on the Rhine. "My interest, my duty, thus obliges me, even in order to be useful to the cause which the King of Piedmont represents, to reassure Germany and England concerning my intentions and to prove to them, without disavowing my sympathies for Italy, that my thought is conciliatory. Russia, who . . . makes common cause with me in this circumstance, has understood the weakness, even the danger of my position. She has proposed the only means that now exists of putting me in the common right without abandoning the cause I wish to serve: it is the convocation of a congress."[76] Though Nigra demanded the immediate admission of Piedmont to the congress, with or without the other Italian states, the Emperor was not prepared to go that far. "If one desires to make an Italian congress," he wrote to Prince Napoleon, "it will be necessary to admit all the rulers of Italy. But when it is a matter of discussing a question of European interest with the great powers alone, it is impossible to make an exception."[77] In his reply Prince Napoleon accused the Emperor of acting before taking into account the reasons Piedmont had of seeking admission to a congress which would decide her fate.[78] During the Crimean War, Piedmontese soldiers were considered worthy enough to fight side by side with those of the great powers, for whom Victor Emmanuel sacrificed the blood and treasures of his people. Now, when it was a matter of deciding an Italian question, Piedmont found the doors closed while her enemy, also an Italian power, was to be admitted. He warned his cousin that England could not be counted upon, that Austria would not be satisfied, and that everyone save Russia would be discontented.

Thus, Napoleon found himself the target of suspicion from all sides. To calm public opinion while at the same time restraining Cavour from rushing headlong into war was by no means an easy thing. The heavy financial burden of maintaining an army on a war-footing was having the same effect in Piedmont as in Austria. There was the same desire to have it over with. But as the Emperor could not engage Austria in a clash of arms without a good reason, the proposed congress offered him a breathing spell.

I have no illusions concerning the difficulties which are produced from all sides. Although Piedmont and I desire the same thing, our conduct, for the moment, is diametrically opposed. In order to divide my enemies, and to conciliate the neutrality of a part of Europe, it is necessary for me to display openly my moderation and my desire for conciliation. The Piedmontese Government, on the contrary, in order to maintain its position in Italy and to preserve its influence over the minds, entertains the hope of war.[79]

The Emperor, of course, did not intend to carry his moderation to the point where it would weaken his ally. When Cowley approached him regarding the preliminary disarmament of Piedmont, he promised to join England in addressing notes to Turin but later showed extreme reluctance to keep his promise.[80] Hübner asked Walewski point-blank if the Emperor's hesitation was caused by the fact that France had concluded an alliance directed against Austria. The minister denied that such an alliance existed or that France was in any way obliged to aid Piedmont in case of Austrian aggression.[81] At the same time, however, he agreed that the preliminary disarmament of Piedmont was an indispensable condition and expressed the hope that England, Prussia and Russia would endeavor to convince the Emperor.[82]

The announcement in the *Moniteur* that Cavour was to visit Paris raised the hopes of the warmongers. Hübner immediately protested to Walewski against the visit on the ground that it would renew the alarm of those who asked nothing more than assurances concerning Napoleon's peaceful intentions.[83] There were other dangers as well to be considered. "I call your attention," he said to Walewski, "to two things your master would do well to avoid. M. de Cavour will move Heaven and earth in order to influence him; he will pose as the victim driven by despair and if he has papers with him which can be interpreted in a sense compromising for the Emperor, he will give him to understand that he will be quite capable of using them; finally, he will neglect no means of drawing some vague promise from his protector, some engagement for the future." Walewski's reply that Napoleon had invited Cavour for the purpose of persuading him that the preliminary disarmament of Piedmont was necessary, failed to reassure the Austrian Ambassador whose suspicions were by now thoroughly aroused. In a dispatch to Buol he dwelt upon the change which had taken place in the Emperor's policy since 1852.[84] At that time the chief of France was the defender of law and order; now he was simply a revolutionary conspirator. Hübner was reminded of descriptions by Tacitus and Suetonius of certain Roman Emperors who, in the early days of their reigns had been ornaments of humanity, but who suddenly became objects of alarm and disgust.

The decadence of Louis Napoleon began at the end of the Crimean War and Orsini's attempt did not check it. He is no longer the same man. To see him today, sober, anxious, taciturn, inaccessible to his friends, avoiding good advice, irritated by obstacles he himself has raised . . . trembling before the indiscretion of accomplices without finding in his own intelligence the means of imposing silence upon them nor in his heart the strength of breaking with them . . . this Prince today presents a spectacle worthy of pity. . . .

Cavour arrived in Paris on March 26th and called on Walewski. The latter informed the Piedmontese statesman that he would make every effort to dissuade the Emperor from engaging in war and would urge him to reach an agreement with Austria for the settlement of the Italian problem. Moreover, he remained firm in his belief concerning the necessity of the congress and the preliminary disarmament of Piedmont. The interview ended amicably.[85] Three days later a second interview took place which was stormy because Walewski refused to yield. Cavour also called twice on Napoleon, the first time alone and the second in the presence of the Foreign Minister. The result was not quite to his liking. It is true that he found the Emperor more determined than ever to wage war, no doubt realizing that if it were not waged he would be lost.[86] Nor did he detect any change in the Emperor's ideas regarding the future of Italy. But while he was reassured on these points, he saw that Napoleon was "in a state of perplexity and deplorable uncertainty" as to the means of putting them into practice.[87] In the opinion of Cavour, the Emperor had posed the question of an Italian war before France and Europe in a most regrettable manner. Through false prudence in trying to conceal his intentions, he had aroused the greatest apprehensions at home and the fears of other countries. French public opinion did not support him, while all Germany and a large majority in England had definitely pronounced against him. Indeed, Cavour was convinced that if war was to break out at the moment, the German states would take up arms on the side of Austria while England would also intervene, if not with her fleet, at least morally. His discussion with the Emperor dealt largely with the questions of disarmament and the admission of Piedmont to the congress. Regarding the first of these Cavour declared that only if Piedmont were admitted to the congress on a footing of equality, could she think of disarming but even then Austria would have to take the initiative.[88] In demanding the admission of Piedmont to the congress, he argued that this was necessary in order to offset the influence of Austria, who would participate in a double role, as a great power and an Italian state.[89] Napoleon replied to this demand by stating that he had requested the other powers to consent to it but that all of them, including Russia, were opposed. In desperation Cavour showed the Emperor a telegram he had just received from Victor Emmanuel. "General discontent," wrote the King, "sinister reports spread against the Emperor and myself. If war is not waged, I abdicate; tell the Emperor peace more dangerous than war at this hour."[90] Cavour hoped that this telegram would persuade

Napoleon to act but he discovered that it was impossible "to avoid the farce of the congress." In a letter to General La Mamora, he explained that the Emperor was confined to his bed and that he had not had the interview he would have regarded as decisive.[91] He summed up the situation as follows: war was inevitable; it would be delayed two or three months and would be conducted on the Rhine as well as on the Po; the greatest efforts were necessary in order to obtain a fortunate result for Piedmont and for Italy. Before leaving Paris, he wrote to the Emperor complaining about the conduct of Walewski, who was determined "to destroy us, force the King to abdicate, me to resign, and to push Piedmont toward the abyss."[92] According to his friend, Salmour, Cavour's anger was directed against the Emperor because the latter had gone back on his promises and he threatened to go to America and publish the letters he had received from Napoleon.[93] Cavour left Paris, adds Salmour, with despair in his heart, tears in his eyes, believing everything to be lost.[94]

Meanwhile, Malmesbury continued his efforts to get the congress underway. He directed Loftus to inform Buol that if Austria accepted the four points proposed for the agenda, she would find "a sincere ally" in England, whereas if she viewed them with suspicion, English public opinion would be alienated.[95] On March 31st Loftus reported that Austria accepted the four points but would not participate in the congress without the preliminary disarmament of Piedmont.[96] Loftus mentioned that little confidence existed on the part of Franz Joseph, the Government or the Austrian public in the maintenance of peace and the suspicion prevailed that the negotiations for the congress had been undertaken in order to enable the French to gain time or to isolate Austria from England and Prussia.[97] Buol looked upon the proposed congress as a Franco-Russian trick played on Austria and England which these powers should thwart if possible. In a letter to Hübner he wrote:

We understood that there was no way to refuse but I count upon the admirable efforts of Lord Cowley to prevent this double-edged weapon from being turned against us. So long as we maintain our program, the situation is not too difficult. Above all, we shall try to save the Emperor Napoleon even against his will. The congress ought to assure us of peace or furnish proof of his incorrigibility. We must insist upon the exclusion of Sardinia from the hall of deliberations and upon her preliminary disarmament. Any Austrian who consents to be seated besides a Sardinian will be disgraced.[98]

Now that Austria had accepted the English agenda, there remained the problem of obtaining the preliminary disarmament of Piedmont. Unless the congress was to be abandoned altogether, this problem had to be solved. Not only had Cavour refused to yield on this point but he insisted that Piedmont be represented in the congress on the same footing as the great powers. Malmesbury, who alone of the statesmen appeared interested in rescuing the congress from oblivion, warned d'Azeglio, the Piedmontese representative at London, that persistence in this attitude would completely alienate England.[99] But while refusing to yield to the Austrian demand for preliminary disarmament, Cavour was prepared to accept a proposal which came from Paris and was supported by England and Prussia: that the Austrian and Piedmontese armies remain a certain distance behind their respective frontiers.[100] Buol rejected it and Apponyi explained to Malmesbury that Austria would never consent to such an "undignified and humiliating proposal."[101] Despite this rebuff, Malmesbury was unwilling to give up hope of saving the peace. He had already suggested as a way out of the impasse that England would support a plan for general disarmament on condition that Austria abandon her demand for the preliminary disarmament of Piedmont and had learned that Buol was receptive.[102] On April 7th he submitted to the powers a proposal for general disarmament. This was accepted by France, who warned Austria that if she refused, the four powers might convene without her.[103] Pressure was also applied by Malmesbury, who warned Apponyi that if Austria rejected the proposal, she would lose England's moral support.[104] At the same time, he declined a request from Buol to guarantee Austria against a French attack in return for which Austria would hold up her armaments, not attack Piedmont, and not impose any conditions to the latter's admission to the congress.[105]

Upon one point Austrian statesmen were fully determined. They would make no real sacrifices merely to save the congress. They saw that a peace established by such a body would leave Austria in a

morally and materially weakened condition, especially as regarded
Italy, that her prestige would suffer, and that the discontent and
resistance in Hungary and other provinces of the Empire would
increase. On the other hand, war would serve to rally the loyalty
of the peoples of the Monarchy outside of Italy. Hence, the failure
of the congress would cause no tears to be shed in Vienna. At the
same time, however, one could not ignore the fact that rejection of
Malmesbury's proposal might lead to the loss of England's moral
support. In replying to it, Buol announced as the condition for
Austria's participation in the congress either the preliminary disarmament of Piedmont or the disarmament of all powers. This
satisfied Malmesbury, who referred to Buol's reply as "fair and
just."[106]

Having won over Austria and France to the proposal for general
disarmament, Malmesbury turned his attention to Piedmont. The
English representative at Turin was instructed to warn Cavour that
if Piedmont refused to disarm and thus prevented the meeting of
the congress, "a heavy responsibility will rest on her."[107] Cavour
was much disturbed by this warning. On April 12th he informed
Paris by telegraph that it was impossible to accept the proposal
for general disarmament without a guarantee of the right bank of
the Ticino and the principle of non-intervention.[108] The Emperor
instructed Prince Napoleon to reply that the principle of general
disarmament concerned only the five great powers invited to the
congress.[109] With this assurance, Cavour was in a position to reject
the proposal. On April 17th he issued a statement declaring that
as Piedmont had been excluded from the congress, she could not
accept the principle of general disarmament.[110]

For the moment, Buol had scored a small triumph. He had
cleverly turned the English proposal to his own advantage diplomatically and did so without dropping his demand for the preliminary disarmament of Piedmont. By indicating Austria's willingness to disarm if the other powers did likewise, he more or less
shifted responsibility to them. Yet, this merely left the situation
where it was before and did little or nothing to ease the tension.
If anything the danger of war was greater than ever. In an interview with Walewski, Hübner pleaded earnestly for peace.[111] He

even supplied the minister with arguments which should be employed to convince Napoleon. The latter's position, he pointed out, was different from that of the rulers of the older dynasties. An unfortunate war could be undertaken by a ruler of the old line but would be disastrous for the French Emperor.

The result is that the first shot of the cannon between Austria and France will be the signal for an ordinary war for my august master which, putting things at their worst, can lead for us to the loss of a province, perhaps to be retaken later; but for the Emperor Napoleon it is a war *à outrance* where the existence of his throne and dynasty is at stake. He should overcome this peril! From this viewpoint, the parties are not equal.[112]

Did Napoleon, he asked, really believe that he could defeat the strong Austrian army? And would England, Prussia and the other German states remain passive spectators if Austria suffered reverses and if France became the mistress of Italy, the Mediterranean and the Adriatic? "And Russia? Do you believe in the sincerity of all her demonstrations of tenderness? Is it natural, probable, possible that the power bled white by you, will participate in the war as your ally? That she will sacrifice the dynastic ties which unite her to Prussia and a large number of the German courts, and that she will aid you in establishing your supremacy in the center and south of Europe, and all in order to please the power which had humiliated her and had inflicted wounds upon her from which she still bleeds?" Hübner argued that while Russia spoke of vengeance against Austria, she really did not hate her.

The supposed hatred of Russia for Austria is a myth. . . . You should be prepared, if war breaks out with Austria, to see a formidable triple alliance formed against you and you must fear that sooner or later Russia will join it. In a word, if defeated the Emperor risks, I say risks, he loses his crown; if victorious he brings about a coalition and history shows that coalitions are always victorious. Thus, whatever turn affairs might take, a war with Austria is necessarily, fatally, the loss of the Napoleonic dynasty. Today, the solution of that grave and enormous problem is the disarmament of Piedmont. If Piedmont disarms and Europe, having sheathed its sword, gathers around the conference table, the consolidation of peace can result from its deliberations. If Piedmont does not disarm it means that the Emperor Napoleon has decided to wage war, and I have exposed to you what the consequences of war will be.

Hübner believed that his arguments had made a deep impression upon Walewski and that the latter might succeed in convincing Napoleon. Later in the same day, however, he learned that after a three-hour conference with the Emperor, the minister returned to his hotel "pale and defeated, completely in despair."[113]

From the very beginning of the Second Empire, Hübner had appealed to dynastic principles in his dealings with Napoleon. But while the latter was by no means impervious to such appeals, particularly since the birth of the Prince Imperial, he had based his policy upon revolutionary principles. His decision to fight Austria resulted from sympathy for the Italians as well as from certain advantages he desired for France. These advantages he set forth in a memoir to Walewski.[114] In this he pointed out that while France had succeeded in dividing her enemies, she had acquired no real allies among the great powers. A great nation, he declared, was like a star and could not live without satellites. Because of Austria's indecision and the slowness of military operations, he had failed to overthrow the treaties of 1815 during the Crimean War. "The terrain lost in the Crimea can be regained in Lombardy, if, while driving the Austrians from Italy, France protects the power of the Pope, if she opposes excesses and declares that save for Savoy and Nice she desires to make no conquests, she will have Europe for her. . . ." Napoleon was convinced that once Austria was weakened, French influence in Europe would immediately increase. But even if Europe was not satisfied, France would have nothing to fear. With Spain and Italy for allies, she would be in a stronger position than ever.

There is nothing to indicate that the French Emperor ever seriously considered the possibility of abandoning the war with Austria. On the contrary, his decision to fight appears to have been irrevocably taken. If he hesitated, it was merely that he wished to strike when the moment was most opportune and after the Austrians had taken the initiative. The Napoleonic cat and mouse game could not go on forever. Franz Joseph and his military entourage were exasperated by such tactics and by Piedmont's refusal to disarm.

Walewski, fully aware of the danger, decided to act. He

appealed to England with the suggestion that Piedmont be admitted to the congress provided she disarmed.[115] This was rejected by Malmesbury, who instead proposed the simultaneous and general disarmament of the powers before the convocation of the congress, under the supervision of a military commission, with Piedmont represented in the congress but not as a great power.[116] Cavour, however, would not agree to this scheme. On April 18th Walewski sent two telegrams to his representative at Turin, La Tour d'Auvergne. In the first he instructed the French Minister to request the immediate adherence of Cavour to the principle of general disarmament without reservations.[117] Walewski made it clear that the request came from him not as Foreign Minister but as a private individual. In the second telegram he invoked the authority of the Emperor, realizing that nothing else could persuade Cavour. "The Emperor," he wrote, "charges you to engage Piedmont to accept the principle of disarmament. . . . We will accept the congress only if Piedmont and the other Italian states are invited to take part.[118] On the following day the Emperor disavowed the steps taken by his Foreign Minister. In a letter to Prince Napoleon regarding the telegrams, he wrote: "La Tour d'Auvergne has taken for an official dispatch a personal reflection of Walewski."[119] Prince Napoleon thereupon informed Cavour, adding that the Emperor was much displeased with Walewski.[120] It has been suggested that the reason for the disavowal was that Napoleon had learned of Tuscany's decision to be neutral.[121] In any case, Cavour decided that further resistance to the principle of general disarmament was futile. On the 19th he informed Paris of Piedmont's acceptance.[122] So great was his discouragement that he informed his friends that he would resign. A note in the *Moniteur* on the 21st announced general disarmament and the approaching convocation of the congress.

Hopes for a peaceful settlement were quickly dashed, however, by Austria's precipitate action. On the very day Cavour announced acceptance of the proposal for general disarmament, a decisive meeting of the Ministerial Council took place in Vienna, presided over by the Emperor.[123] There is no doubt that Austria was finding the Italian situation unbearable. At the meeting on the 19th, Buol approved the dispatch of an ultimatum to Piedmont and declared that Napoleon, under pressure from the powers, would force Turin to yield.[124] Moreover, he asserted that if war came, Napoleon would not fight on two fronts but only in Italy. "The explanation of Count Buol," wrote Kempen, Minister of Police, who took part in the proceedings, "was clear and forcible. He urged that a demand be sent to Count Cavour to stop the Piedmontese armaments within three days, failing which the Austrian army would treat these armaments as an act of hostility. This evening this demand leaves for Milan and from there it will be sent on to Turin by a civil official. . . . Every one decided for the quickest and strongest steps and was strengthened by the belief of Buol that England and Prussia would come out more and more for Austria."[125] At a meeting on the 6th, Buol had expressed his conviction that the German states were for Austria and that England and Prussia were not opposed.[126]

The Austrian ultimatum was presented to Cavour on April 23rd and a reply was requested within three days. This was precisely the opportunity the Piedmontese statesman had been waiting for, and, assured of French support, he returned an evasive and unsatisfactory reply. This reply was discussed at a meeting of the Ministerial Council in Vienna on the 27th.[127] The prevailing opinion was that Cavour had no intention of complying with the demand for disarmament and that only one thing remained: to take military action, particularly since French troops had already entered Piedmont. Grünne, the Emperor's aide-de-camp, chided Buol for urging the dispatch of the ultimatum in the belief that France would force Piedmont to yield.[128] As it was, Austria now found herself facing a catastrophe, standing alone against France and Piedmont. What could one expect of England and Prussia, and was it true that France and Russia had concluded an alliance? Buol replied that he had no knowledge of such an alliance but if one had been concluded, he believed it would impel the German states and England to assist Austria.[129] He believed that in due course the German states, Prussia and England would declare themselves for Austria. As for Russia, she was in no condition to attack Austria for some time and in the last analysis would consider her own interests. At the conclusion of the meeting, Franz Joseph announced that he would direct a telegram to be sent to General Gyulai, Commander of the Second Army, to begin operations against Piedmont and her ally, France.[130]

Although Buol had urged the dispatch of the ultimatum, he was evidently under the impression that war would be averted. As he informed the Ministerial Council, Napoleon, who gave the impression of seeking a retreat, would force Cavour to yield. On April 22nd Buol sent a telegram to Apponyi at London instructing him to suggest confidentially to Malmesbury that the idea of a congress be abandoned in favor of an *entente* between Austria and France on the basis of the simultaneous disarmament of the two powers.[131] "But you should make him (Malmesbury) clearly understand that this is not an Austrian proposal and be quite sure that your *démarche* does not provoke an official response, in one sense or the other." A telegram of the same day, sent by Loftus to Malmesbury, stated that Buol had hinted that if Piedmont agreed to disarm, all questions could be resolved on the basis of the English agenda by direct negotiations between Austria and France under the mediation of England. [132] Malmesbury lost no time in taking up this suggestion and instructed Cowley to lay the matter before Walewski and to telegraph the answer direct to Vienna.[133] Walewski was at first receptive to the proposal but after discussing it with Napoleon, informed Cowley that in view of Austria's ultimatum, mediation should be undertaken between Austria and Piedmont.[134] At a special meeting of the Council of Ministers in Paris on the 28th, it was decided to reject the proposal because it was made contingent upon the principle of preliminary disarmament.[135]

There is no doubt that Buol had been carried away by false optimism in counting upon the support of England and Prussia. While it is true that the Derby Cabinet was not unfavorable to Austria and distrusted Cavour as the tool of the French Emperor, its weakness and the pro-Italian sympathies of the English public eliminated the possibility of aid from that quarter. The London Cabinet had refused to give Austria a formal guarantee against attack by France in exchange for which Austria promised to suspend her armaments. As a consequence, Vienna had insisted upon the reduction of the Piedmontese army as a condition for entering the congress. Of more importance to Austria, however, at least from a military standpoint, was the attitude of Prussia.[136] The clamor of the German public for aid to Austria placed the Prussian Government in a rather uncomfortable position. It neither wished to resist the popular outcry nor yield to it completely. Only if Austria was the victim of an attack, would Prussia agree to give support. This attitude did not satisfy Vienna and on April 11th the Archduke Albrecht was sent on a special mission to Berlin.[137] He was to inform the Prussian Government of Austria's intention of sending an ultimatum to Piedmont in order to compel disarmament. In case of war and in view of the certainty of French aid to Piedmont, the Archduke was instructed to propose that a German army under the joint leadership of Franz Joseph and the Prince Regent be sent to the Rhine. In his reply, the Prince Regent insisted that Austria must first make every attempt to settle her dispute with Piedmont peacefully as, for example, by means of the congress.[138] If war resulted despite such attempts and if Austria was clearly the victim of aggression, Prussian aid would be forthcoming. Thus, at the time the ultimatum was sent to Turin, Franz Joseph could not count definitely on Prussia.

Not only did Buol try to win English and Prussian support, he also made overtures to Russia. In April 1859 Count Karolyi, the new Minister to St. Petersburg, received the special mission of expressing to Alexander II the value which Austria placed on good relations with Russia.[139] He was likewise to explain Austria's attitude toward the congress and to emphasize the conservative nature of the measures Austria was taking to defend herself. All that Austria asked of the Tsar was that he would appreciate the legitimacy of her motives and would aid her morally by maintaining a viewpoint conforming to the principles "that we defend, to discourage and crush the subversive and revolutionary tendencies which could triumph in Italy." Karolyi was to appeal to the old traditions established between Austria and Russia, to explain the difficulty of Austria's position during the Crimean War, and how much she deplored the necessity of the stand she took. In return for adopting a friendly attitude, Karolyi was to offer the Tsar Austria's support in obtaining a modification of the Treaty of Paris in Russia's favor.

Rarely has a mission been undertaken with less chance of success. While it is true that there had been a softening of Russian bitterness against Austria, this had not gone far enough to produce anything like a *rapprochement*. On the contrary, Russia had definitely linked herself with Napoleon in the Italian question. On the basis of daily reports received from St. Petersburg, Franz Joseph and his Foreign Minister knew that Russia was on the side of France. In planning Karolyi's mission they probably gambled on the faint hope that the dangers of the revolutionary movement in Italy would make the Tsar think twice before giving it his support. In one of his first reports, however, Karolyi blasted this hope. He wrote that he had not expected to encounter sentiments so pronounced—sentiments which yielded to no argument.[140] This had deprived him from the beginning of any chance of success. "In sounding the terrain, I have found only obstacles, the explanations I have provoked being always varied between a frank expression of rancor and hostile dispositions, and an extreme reserve for everything which could give positive enlightenment concerning the future. In this situation, it is impossible for me to exercise here the least influence upon the course of affairs."[141] Gortchakoff told him frankly that there was no chance of reëstablishing the former intimacy between the two empires. "We are no longer disposed to act the role of the watchdog of Europe; times have changed, and these old ties have broken forever."[142] The Chancellor placed all the responsibility for the rupture of the old alliance on Austria. Karolyi concluded his report by requesting that his mission be terminated. In a private letter to Buol, he complained that he was forced to listen to sharp words from the Tsar, words which were unjust for the Austrian Cabinet and ungracious for Franz Joseph, without having the slightest influence over his mind.[143] Alexander II said bluntly that he intended to preserve freedom of action and would give no explanations concerning the future.[144] While Karolyi did not know the exact nature of the treaty between France and Russia, he was convinced that it existed and that it was hostile to Austria. "Our adversaries have all the sympathies of the Russian Cabinet, whose sentiment of rancor is more lively than ever."[145] Indeed, so hostile did he find the Russian attitude, that he decided not to bring up the proposal that

Austria would be inclined to favor a revision of the Treaty of Paris.[146] He was convinced that Austria could get Russian good will only by making concessions which would be beneath her dignity and which would deliver her hand and foot to the Tsar.[147] To seek an understanding with Russia at this time was futile.

Thus, Austria entered the war against France and Piedmont under the most unfavorable conditions. Until the dispatch of the ultimatum to Turin, her position from the legal, political and military viewpoints, appeared strong. There was every reason to expect that if France or Piedmont attacked Lombardy, the German states would have supported Austria by a war on the Rhine. A settlement of the crisis by diplomatic means would have worked to Austria's advantage as well inasmuch as Cavour would have been unable to control the revolutionary movement in Italy. Piedmont's acceptance of general disarmament seemed to portend a victory by diplomacy. The sending of the ultimatum was therefore a blunder of the first magnitude. Buol, of course, must share in the responsibility. He had suggested such a course to the Ministerial Council and had bolstered the stand of the military group by his optimism concerning England, the German states and Prussia and by his belief that Napoleon would force Cavour to yield. At the time the ultimatum was sent he did not know of Piedmont's decision to accept the proposal for general disarmament.[148] Moreover, he did not favor war and hoped that it might be averted. He explained to Count Beust, the Saxon Minister, that he did not want war but that he was unable to oppose the military men who were convinced that Austria was invincible.[149] These military men had criticized Buol's policy as being weak and indecisive and regarded all proposals to prevent war as so much wasted effort and as even dangerous for Austria's interests. The fact remains, however, that as Minister of Foreign Affairs it was Buol's task to avoid the danger of isolation. In this he failed and on May 4th he submitted his resignation and was succeeded by Count Rechberg.[150]

CHAPTER NINE

The War for Italian Independence and the Truce of Villafranca

THE WAR OF Italian independence lasted less than three months. While Austrian soldiers fought bravely, they could not overcome the incapacity of their generals. For weeks General Gyulai, who owed his appointment as Commander to Grünne, kept his armies inactive, thus enabling the Piedmontese to effect a junction with the French. Nor did the Austrians receive aid from the outside. Prince Richard Metternich, son of the former Chancellor and Hübner's successor at the Paris post, who was sent by Rechberg to observe the situation at the front, heard from all sides the same complaint. "Ah, if we had only known! We believed that England would protect our coasts, that all Germany would rise at the first shot of the cannon by France, that we would succeed in avenging ourselves on Piedmont before the entrance of the French army into the campaign, that Tuscany would hold firm, that the Pope would come to our aid with his spiritual weapons and, finally, that Napoleon would never openly dare make common cause with revolution."[1] Everything had gone wrong and only Franz Joseph refused to be discouraged. Fortifying himself in the knowledge that his cause was just, he was determined not to compromise the duty of safeguarding the treaties. "Without him," wrote Metternich, "I know positively that we would have wanted to make a thousand concessions to Prussia and even to Russia."[2] The Austrian commanders did not share their Emperor's determination and Grünne especially was deeply discouraged, complaining "of the state of our finances, the uselessness of our sacrifices, our policy in late years and even of the internal organization of the state."[3]

Worse still for the Austrian cause was the possibility of an uprising in Hungary. It was reported that Napoleon was in touch with Kossuth and other Hungarian rebels. At the moment war began, Prince Napoleon introduced to the Emperor the Hungarian General Klapka, who proposed a plan for an uprising in Hungary and who was given 50,000 francs for this purpose.[4] Klapka left for Jassy but before he could take any decisive steps, the war was over. Apponyi telegraphed to Rechberg that the English Government had been informed that Napoleon had set aside three million francs to be used in starting revolutions in Hungary, Slavonia and Transylvania. "Everything is supposed to be prepared and the word will be given after the first brilliant victories."[5] Moreover, it was rumored that Kossuth was already on his way to Hungary. Such news only added to the general discouragement. Napoleon had often threatened to invoke the aid of revolution in a war against Austria and there could be no doubt as to what this would mean. It is not likely, however, that he actually intended to produce such an uprising in Hungary since he knew that this would alarm Russia. In any case, the Hungarian project was never more than a threat because Klapka failed to win the cooperation of the civilian members of his committee.[6]

Most disappointing of all to the Austrian cause was the failure to get aid from the German allies. Despite the setback of the Archduke Albrecht's mission to Berlin, Franz Joseph confidently expected Prussian support. In the middle of May the Prince Regent sent General Willisen to Vienna as a special emissary.[7] Willisen informed Rechberg that Prussia was willing to support the Austrian position in Lombardy-Venetia providing she received command of the forces of the Confederation. To this Rechberg replied by demanding Prussian intervention not only for the maintenance of Austria's power in Lombardy-Venetia but also for the Austrian treaties with the Italian states, the defeat of Piedmont, and the overthrow of Napoleon. The Prince Regent declined to go that far. After the Austrian defeat at Montebello, Rechberg became more conciliatory and expressed himself as ready to agree to the Prussian proposal but insisted that the agreement be set forth in a written treaty. Schleinitz rejected this arrangement on June 14th, declaring that it would render it impossible for Prussia to act as mediator.[8] On the same day Prussia mobilized several army corps. On the 24th, despite the Austrian defeat at Solferino, the Prince Regent requested the support of England and Russia in an armed mediation on the basis of the territorial *status quo,* Austria's renunciation of her treaties with the Italian states, and her acceptance of reforms in north and central Italy.[9] England, however, was no longer to be counted upon. The Derby Cabinet, which had been favorably disposed toward Austria, resigned on June 10th, and the new Cabinet was headed by Palmerston with Lord John Russell as Foreign Secretary, both definitely pro-Italian. Russell rejected the Prussian request.[10] In any case, the idea of mediation did not appeal to Rechberg, who reminded Prussia of her duties.[11] The old Field Marshal, Prince Windischgrätz, was sent to Berlin with instructions to win over the Prince Regent.[12] On July 8th the Prussian Crown Council discussed the question of intervention but reached no decision.[13] Although the Prince Regent, Prince Hohenzollern, the Prime Minister, and the military men were in favor of participating in the war, other ministers as well as public opinion were opposed.[14] The mission of Prince Windischgrätz was abruptly terminated by the Truce of Villafranca.[15] Once again, as during the Crimean War, Austria failed to get the aid of her German ally.

As for England, it will be recalled that Buol had held out hopes of obtaining at least her moral support. For three years an Anglo-Austrian *entente* had functioned in the Balkans, opposing the ambitions of France and Russia but Italy was a different matter. Apponyi warned Rechberg not to count on England. "Italian sympathies and Napoleonic antipathies hold the balance in public opinion."[16] Despite this warning, Rechberg believed that it might be possible to change the attitude of England. Toward the end of May he sent Prince Paul Esterhazy on a special mission to London. While posing as a traveler visiting old friends, without an official character, Prince Paul was directed to effect such a change.[17] In order to do this he was to explain and justify Austria's actions regarding Piedmont and to point out the dangers resulting from the French policy in Italy

and the east. "What will England do in the face of French supremacy in Italy, the dissolution of the Ottoman Empire, the
weakening of Austria, and the annulment of the Treaty of 1856?
What will she do face to face with a Franco-Russian coalition in
the east?"[18] Esterhazy's visit to London extended from early June
to the middle of July. Apponyi, who was opposed to it, wrote to
Rechberg that Napoleon's military successes had made a profound
impression on the minds of the English ministers.[19] The latter
looked upon Austria as already defeated and would therefore regard
Esterhazy as coming to implore England's aid in the peace negotiations. Rechberg, however, decided to let the mission stand, believing
that through his many connections in England, Esterhazy would be
in a position to influence opinion in favor of Austria.[20] In his
reports to Rechberg, dated July 2nd,[21] Esterhazy wrote that one
could not count on any positive aid from England, that if her attitude
remained negative that was all one could expect. Only if Austria
obtained success on the field of battle was there any likelihood of
a change.

While Austria suffered defeats without the assurance of help
from her friends and allies, the victor of Magenta and Solferino
had lost his enthusiasm for the war. By instinct a humanitarian
rather than a soldier, Napoleon was disgusted by the frightful
carnage he had witnessed. Having conquered Lombardy, he knew
that the conquest of Venetia would be far more difficult and costly.
And for what was he to sacrifice the lives of more Frenchmen? It
was one thing to free Italy from Austrian domination; it was quite
another to permit the creation of a large Italian state. Napoleon
began to fear that Cavour and Victor Emmanuel were not satisfied
with a North Italian Kingdom but would seek to unite all Italy.
This would mean a strong neighbor on the southeastern frontier
and might endanger the French position in the Mediterranean.
Besides, the Emperor realized that the war had become unpopular
in France, that there was danger of losing the support of the
Catholic party in view of Piedmont's threat to the Papacy. Most important was the menacing attitude of Prussia. The latter's mobilization and the concentration of her forces near the Rhine might
mean a war on two fronts. Already the French victories had aroused

fear and distrust in England, while Russia had not proved a very satisfactory ally. Russia had not, as Napoleon expected, succeeded in holding Prussia in check. On June 23rd Gortchakoff warned France of the Prussian menace and urged peace negotiations.[22] Two days later he repeated the same thing to Montebello, the French Ambassador.[23] Russia's attitude undoubtedly influenced Napoleon in his decision to withdraw from the war.[24]

On July 4th Persigny, French Ambassador at London, was instructed by telegraph to request the British Government to propose an armistice and to approve certain proposals for peace negotiations.[25] These included the liberation of Italy from foreign control, the establishment of an Italian confederation under the presidency of the Pope, the annexation of Lombardy and the Duchies to Piedmont, the creation of Venetia as an independent state under an archduke, reforms in the Papal States, and the submission of peace terms to a European congress.[26] Though Russell and Palmerston disliked the proposals, they agreed to communicate them to Austria.[27] If the latter accepted them, a short armistice would be arranged by England alone or by England with Prussia or Russia or both.[28] Napoleon, however, decided upon direct negotiations with the enemy and, after notifying Victor Emmanuel, he dispatched General Fleury with a letter to Franz Joseph.[29] The letter stated that one of the great powers had proposed an armistice and asked what the Austrian ruler thought of it. Fleury was directed to be insistent and to say that Napoleon desired peace but that if the war continued, he would order his warships to open hostilities against Venice. Faced with the prospect of continuing a desperate struggle which might entail the loss of Austria's influence in Germany and seriously weaken her military power, Franz Joseph agreed to negotiate. On the 7th he gave Fleury a letter addressed to Napoleon which accepted an armistice and suggested a meeting of commissioners at Villafranca to fix its duration and conditions. This suggestion was accepted by Napoleon, who named Marshal Vaillant, General de Martinprey and General Della Rocca as his representatives, while General Hess and Count Mensdorff-Pouilly were chosen from the Austrian side. The armistice protocol was signed at Villafranca the afternoon of the 8th. On the same day Napoleon wrote to Franz Joseph proposing that the two rulers meet in order to discuss the basis of an arrangement. The Austrian Emperor thereupon sent Prince Alexander of Hesse to the French Headquarters at Valeggio with instructions to accept the meeting if there was an assurance of a favorable result. In giving this assurance, Napoleon stated that the moment was propitious for ending the war as neither side was decisively victorious and as a prolonged struggle might lead to the intervention of other powers.[30] It would be advantageous for the two rulers to arrange affairs directly and he promised that if Franz Joseph would agree to a settlement of the Italian question, he would gain a loyal ally in France.[31] On the 11th the two rulers conferred at Villafranca.[32] A summary of their conversation was later sent by Napoleon to Franz Joseph in care of Prince Napoleon, who was authorized to accept certain changes provided these did not distort the fundamental arrangements agreed upon. Victor Emmanuel adhered to the preliminaries of peace only in so far as they concerned him, thus keeping a free hand in other Italian affairs.

By the terms of Villafranca Austria was to cede her rights over Lombardy with the exception of the fortresses of Mantua and Peschiera to Napoleon who, in turn, would cede Lombardy to Piedmont. The other Italian states were to form a confederation under the presidency of the Pope, who would be requested to introduce reforms in his own administration. The rulers of Parma, Tuscany and Modena were to be restored without recourse to force on condition that they grant a general amnesty. A congress would be called to pronounce on the advisability of modifying the treaties of 1815 in so far as they concerned Italy. Informed by Napoleon that England, Prussia and Russia had approved these terms and that Prussia had taken the stand that if Austria refused she could no longer count on Prussian support,[33] Franz Joseph declared that he would never yield before a European areopagus and congratulated himself on having entered into direct negotiations with the French Emperor.[34]

The news of the armistice and preliminaries of Villafranca received a varied reception in the European capitals. In Russia there was undisguised joy. "The satisfaction of Prince Gortchakoff," wrote Montebello, "was complete and sincere."[35] The terms were pleasing to the Russians because they weakened Austria in favor of Piedmont and made no direct concessions to revolution. Most of all, there was a feeling of relief in St. Petersburg. There had been a real danger that Russia would have been forced to choose between France and Prussia and possibly lose the friendship of both. Villafranca removed that danger. In Berlin the sudden announcement of peace evoked a feeling of disappointment. The Prince Regent, who had expected to play a decisive role, now found his efforts at mediation cut short and his ambition for leadership in Germany thwarted. The reaction in London was even greater. "The news of the signing of the preliminaries of peace," wrote Apponyi to Rechberg, "has caused a general surprise here and a painful and humiliating impression from the viewpoint of the role or rather the absence of a role England has played in that important European transaction."[36] Prince Esterhazy referred to the astonishment, disappointment, and anger directed against Napoleon, and the blow to the Anglo-French alliance.[37] In a letter to Persigny, Palmerston declared that the plan for an Italian confederation including Venetia would prove fatal to Italy. "Once Austria is a member of an Italian confederation all Italy will be delivered hand and foot to the mercy of Austria."[38] Apponyi reported that Palmerston and Russell were displeased because they regarded the terms as too favorable to Austria and felt that they should have been concluded only after Austria had been driven from Italy.[39]

Nowhere was the deception caused by the preliminaries of Villafranca greater than in Piedmont. When Napoleon opened negotiations for an armistice, he assured Victor Emmanuel that it was simply a question of a truce and that the conditions would be so onerous it was doubtful that Austria would accept.[40] On the 8th the *Moniteur* announced that while the suspension of arms left the field free for negotiations, the end of the war was not yet in sight. Victor Emmanuel had thus been led to believe that the struggle would be continued and had repeated to his generals what the Emperor had said. Indeed, it was stated in the *Opinione* of Turin that there was little likelihood of peace and that the armistice was purely military and was concluded for the purpose of avoiding the siege of Verona during the hot weather. As soon as Cavour received the news of the armistice, he left for the front where he sought to persuade the King to continue the war even if Napoleon made peace. But neither the King nor the Emperor would listen to him. Sick at heart Cavour resigned on July 12th explaining in a letter to his friend, E. d' Azeglio, that he would not be able to deal successfully with the problems still to be settled as he had become the *bête noire* of diplomacy, detested by Walewski and Cowley, and likely to arouse nightmares among the Austrian plenipotentiaries. "In brief, I am the man least apt to obtain concessions from diplomats."[41] Cavour, however, continued to use his influence in central Italy with the result that by the end of July provisional governments were set up in Parma, Modena and Tuscany. These were directed from Turin and the inhabitants were urged to vote for annexation to Piedmont.

There is no doubt that the preliminaries worked out at Villafranca were favorable to Austria. Except for the loss of Lombardy, her position in Italy was still powerful. Hapsburg rulers were to be restored in the duchies, while Venetia would be a part of the new confederation which was to include the Papal States and Naples, both friendly to Vienna. Thus, on the morrow of Villafranca, Austrian influence in Italy appeared decidedly important. What now remained was to incorporate the terms into a final treaty of peace and to carry them into execution. This became the Austrian policy to which, for the next half year, Rechberg tried to keep Napoleon's support.

While Napoleon, however, had promised to fulfill the stipulation agreed upon at Villafranca, he no sooner returned to France than he saw that he had conceded more than could be realized. Though he regarded peace as established and had ordered the withdrawal of his fleet and most of his army, he knew that it would be virtually impossible to effect the restoration of the rulers of Modena and Tuscany.[42] He had agreed that these rulers should be restored but he felt bound to consult the wishes of the inhabitants and in no case would he permit the use of force. As a way out of the difficulty, he suggested that Franz Joseph persuade the Duke of Modena to abdicate in favor of the young Grand Duke of

Tuscany. Once this was done, the Duchess of Parma could be called to Florence and the trouble in central Italy would come to an end.[43]

Franz Joseph sent Prince Richard Metternich with a letter to Napoleon setting forth the Austrian viewpoint.[44] Recalling to Napoleon that he had engagements of honor to support the princes of his family in Italy, Franz Joseph declared that a change of dynasty in Tuscany and Modena would only complicate the situation without satisfying those who desired annexation to Piedmont. He was convinced that the great majority of the inhabitants in the duchies was attached to the former rulers but was in no position to reveal its sympathies since the provisional governments set up by Piedmont had installed their own officials. The best solution lay in a perfect understanding between Austria and France which would make the revolutionaries realize that they were lost.[45] In the instructions which Rechberg gave the Austrian plenipotentiaries to the Zürich conference, called to work out the definitive peace, he was insistent upon the restoration of the rulers of Modena and Tuscany.[46]

When Metternich arrived in Paris, he immediately discovered that the restoration of the dispossessed rulers was the most delicate and embarrassing point in the negotiations with France.[47] Walewski admitted that he could see no way by which this could be done as France would not permit the use of force. A change of dynasty might be effected in Tuscany and he thought that the best choice would be either a Piedmontese prince or Prince Napoleon. As the only means that could be employed was persuasion, two French agents, Reiset and Poniatowski, were sent on a mission to Florence, Parma and Turin in order to convince influential persons of the necessity of restoring the legitimate rulers.[48] Their efforts did not succeed.

Received in audience by the Emperor, to whom he presented his credentials as well as the letter from Franz Joseph, Metternich declared that the aim of his mission was to bring about friendly relations between the two states.[49] Both the Emperor and the Empress were charmed by the Prince and his vivacious wife, Princess Pauline Metternich. An intimacy developed which is almost without parallel in the annals of diplomacy and which proved of tremendous advantage to the youthful ambassador, enabling him to offset his deficiencies as a diplomatist. The Metternichs became frequent guests at the Tuileries, St. Cloud, Fontainebleau and Biarritz. The immediate task which faced the new envoy was to win over the Emperor to the Austrian viewpoint concerning the restoration of the rulers in central Italy and the establishment of an Italian confederation. He found the attitude of the Empress to be favorable. She asked him if the dispossessed rulers could not have done something for themselves. "I believe that if I were in the position of the young Grand Duke," she said, "I would have recalled my troops and defied Florence but in order to reach that result it is necessary to get busy. The longer they wait, the more difficult it will become."[50] She agreed that the intrigues of Cavour and his agents prevented a return to the old order of things in Italy and she spoke highly of the valor of the Austrian troops. "In summary," wrote Metternich, "I find in the conversation with the Empress the thousand contradictions which characterize the imperial policy, the mixture of good intentions and impracticable ideas, of good reasoning and utopias, the flow of wise words and empty phrases that one encounters among all the French and especially in official circles."[51]

The Emperor, with whom Metternich had a long conversation, remarked that England and Prussia already believed that something more than a simple friendship existed between Austria and France and he hoped that this would not be spoiled by questions of detail.[52] "In questions of detail rulers are somewhat the slaves of their ministers. Write to the Emperor that I seek a way out of the embarrassment and I shall prepare the means to end it. I am already unpopular in Italy. Let one give me a little more time. When I have decided on the means, everything will go all right and I shall send someone to Vienna."[53] Was Napoleon throwing out a hint of an Austro-French alliance? This was the impression of Metternich, who believed that Napoleon would try to gain prestige either by raising unforeseen questions combined with a lightning-like action or by threatening Europe with a powerful alliance.[54] Austria would be faced with the choice of allying with him or against him, for "with the Emperor of the French the *juste milieu* is impossible and always dangerous." Metternich thought that it would be a good thing to exploit Napoleon's desire for an alliance in order to derive advantage from it.[55]

The chief obstacle to a closer understanding was the Italian question and until this was settled to the satisfaction of both Austria and France any discussion of an alliance was premature. But Austria's insistence upon the execution of the terms of Villafranca rendered a solution virtually impossible. The plenipotentiaries at Zürich were at loggerheads concerning the bases to give the Italian confederation, particularly the status Venetia should occupy. Realizing that such a disagreement augured ill for Austro-French relations, Franz Joseph made a direct appeal to Napoleon. He did not wish to give Venetia a separate administration as demanded by France. Since the Austrian Empire was made up of various nationalities, a concentration of authority in the central government was deemed necessary.[56] Moreover, Austria had certain obligations as a member of the German Confederation which were diametrically opposed to those she was asked to assume in the new union. The proposal to give Venetia a separate administration and army, coupled with the grant of local autonomy, would lead the other provinces to demand the same privilege and this would mean the dismemberment of the Empire and the dissolution of the army. Franz Joseph desired therefore that the conditions under which Venetia was to be admitted to the Italian confederation should not be mentioned in the treaty.

Though the problem—the fulfillment of the terms of Villafranca—was clear enough to Austria, Napoleon was between the devil and the deep blue sea. On the one hand, he wanted to keep his word to Franz Joseph and was angered by the events in central Italy where plebiscites in Tuscany, Emilia and the Romagna (August 16-20) resulted in favor of union with Piedmont. On the other hand, he was afraid to take action lest he lose the support of the liberal groups in France. Though he still had 60,000 soldiers in Lombardy, he could not employ them to suppress manifestations of the popular will nor could he allow the Austrians to start a counter-revolution. Both Walewski and Persigny urged him to keep his word to Franz Joseph but to hide his responsibility behind a congress.[57] Anxious to escape from his embarrassment, yet unable to make up his mind, he left matters for the moment in the hands of his Foreign Minister. From the Austrian standpoint such conduct only served to increase the difficulties. "The Emperor," exclaimed Metternich to Walewski, "can no longer hesitate! It is necessary that he decide either to keep his word or declare frankly that he will assist with folded arms in the formation of the league of central Italy, the annexation to Piedmont, the dismemberment of the Papal States and, finally, a new crusade against Austria."[58] England had already condoned the events in central Italy;[59] did France intend to do likewise? Did she want to complicate affairs, asked Metternich, to the point of bringing on a new struggle? Walewski replied that reports of French agents in Italy indicated that nothing could be done to put an end to the agitation and he gave assurances that Napoleon would soon inform Austria of his policy. Metternich discovered that one reason for the Emperor's hesitation was the influence of Dr. Conneau, his personal physician and friend of his exile, who urged him to maintain friendly relations with the Italian national party.[60] On the other hand, General Fleury favored an alliance with Austria and suggested that an interview of the two rulers might settle the difficulties. Walewski promised to bring this suggestion to the attention of his master.[61]

The idea of shifting responsibility to a congress appealed to Napoleon as the best way out of his difficulties. It would relieve him of his obligations to both Austria and the Italian nationalists. But Rechberg, who perceived the Emperor's intentions, made it clear that Austria would accept a congress only if she had reached a preliminary understanding with France concerning the subjects to be regulated.[62] Without such an understanding, Austria might find herself isolated at the congress. No support could be expected from England while the attitude of Prussia and Russia was uncertain. Not only had Palmerston and Russell sympathized with Italian aspirations but they had openly applauded the events in central Italy. Rechberg warned Loftus that if England deserted Austria in Italy or openly combatted her there, Austria would cease to support England in the east.[63] This provoked a dispatch from Russell stating that England had no wish to weaken Austria or to reduce her territory in Italy but merely opposed an extension of her influence beyond her frontiers and armed intervention in other Italian states.[64] Rechberg accepted this explanation with a grain of salt and instructed Apponyi to learn the real attitude of the English Government. Above all, he wished to find out if it was Napoleon who pushed the idea of a congress in order to conceal his responsibilities or if the initiative came from England.[65] Apponyi went first to Russell, who declared that he had no objections to the restoration of the rulers of Modena and Tuscany provided this was not contrary to the wishes of their subjects and was not accomplished through the intervention of an Austrian army.[66] "What we would prefer above all," continued Russell, "is that there be no foreign influence in the Peninsula, neither Austrian nor French, and that Italy be delivered to herself." He did not seem to be in favor of a congress. Apponyi concluded that Russell was naïve and honest but not a statesman and his ideas on foreign policy were too impracticable to be feared. Palmerston, on whom Apponyi called next, combatted the establishment of an Italian confederation on the ground that the difficulties were insurmountable and that the best arrangement would be to leave the Italian states independent without armed intervention from Austria or France.[67] On the basis of his interviews, Apponyi informed Rechberg that it would be virtually impossible to win over the English ministers. "Our principles and our intentions are diametrically opposed."[68] Indeed, Palmerston seemed to favor outright annexation of the duchies to Piedmont as a counterweight to Austrian and French influence.[69] Rechberg was more convinced than ever that a direct understanding between Paris and Vienna offered the only hope of a satisfactory arrangement concerning the Italian difficulties.

At St. Saveur, Metternich had several conversations with Napoleon. He could not but admire the Emperor's charm, his genius for making bargains, and his frankness and good nature.[70] One had to be very careful, he wrote, not to be taken in by Napoleon's benevolent attitude. "He accepts everything with a marvelous humility and has a way of exonerating himself that would touch those more hardened than I." Metternich expressed himself with the utmost candor regarding the situation. He reproached the Emperor for his condescension toward the Italian delegations which had come to France to obtain approval for the annexation of the duchies to Piedmont. Napoleon promised not to receive a delegation from Modena which had requested an audience and to put an end to the criticism against Austria in the French press. When Metternich referred to the rights of reversion which Franz Joseph enjoyed in Modena and Tuscany, Napoleon appeared rather frightened and said hastily: "Believe me, do not touch this question. We did not speak of it at Villafranca and Piedmont and England would be furious. If you remain silent about this delicate question, I promise you to regard the rights of the Emperor of Austria to the succession in these duchies *as understood* between us."[71] The suggestion that he should have another interview with Franz Joseph was also embarrassing. "His Majesty has a positive fear of a new interview." The reason for this was that he did not know what compensation to offer Franz Joseph in return for the concessions he desired Austria to make in Italy. Metternich was convinced that his government must decide either to adhere rigidly to its rights in Italy or to make concessions. It was obvious that Napoleon was stalling for time and awaiting events. "If we wish to keep him in his ideas of an alliance with Austria, ideas he has once again enunciated to me and this time in view of future complications in the east or in Germany, it is necessary . . . to bind him by all possible means."[72] One could not appeal to Napoleon by setting forth logical arguments: only a "brilliant stroke" could win him over.

The concessions which Napoleon requested Austria to make comprised the formation of an Italian confederation modeled on the German Confederation, including Venetia which should have provincial assemblies and a central legislature composed of native Italians, and a native Italian army. In addition, he insisted on the creation of federal fortresses which should include the Austrian fortresses of Verona, Mantau and Peschieria; the cession of Parma and Piacenza to Piedmont; and the marriage of Princess Maria Theresa of Modena to Duke Robert of Parma, who should receive the Duchy of Modena.[73] It was understood that these concessions were to be contingent upon the restoration of the Grand Duke Ferdinand to Tuscany and the rights of Franz Joseph to send troops into Venetia in case of trouble. "Such a program," wrote Napoleon, "would solve all the existing difficulties."[74] He begged the Austrian Emperor to bear in mind that since they adhered to principles which were diametrically opposed—the principles concerning the rights of rulers and popular sovereignty—it would be necessary to compromise. Besides, would it not be worth-while to gain a faithful ally for the future?

That these concessions went far beyond any that Austria intended to make was clear even to Napoleon, who knew that they would be found too exacting. "I admit," he said to Metternich, "that I am embarrassed with all this which, in my painful position, I see myself forced to demand of the Emperor of Austria while not being able from my side to offer him just compensations."[75] Fearing the effect they would have on Franz Joseph, Metternich hesitated to send Napoleon's letter. He tried to convince the latter of the dangers of the situation and the necessity of executing the terms of Villafranca. Already the delays in concluding peace and the deplorable state of affairs in central Italy alarmed public opinion, even in France, while the attacks in the official journals of Paris against the preliminary terms, the arrival in France of various delegations representing revolutionary governments and, finally, the "exorbitant concessions" which the Emperor now demanded, were not likely to elicit friendly feelings in Vienna. Indeed, Austria was keenly disappointed by the change in Napoleon's attitude. If he persisted in the course he had followed and did not warn Piedmont against accepting the annexations, everything would be left unsettled, and in this case Austria would take steps to defend her rights.[76]

Napoleon mentioned as the principal reason why Franz Joseph should make concessions the fear which Piedmont had of Austria. Piedmont refused to be part of a confederation in which Austria would exercise control by virtue of her large army and her influence over the Pope, the King of Naples, and the archdukes. He said to Metternich that Victor Emmanuel regarded the three Austrian fortresses as volcanoes "threatening eruption at the least remark the Piedmontese representative makes which is disagreeable to the Austrian representative and, frankly, I do not believe the King is wrong."[77] Hence, if only for form, Austria should make concessions and she might find compensation in the east. *"The name 'Ost Reich' seems to indicate a predestination for the aggrandizement of Austria in the east. Would the Emperor object to an archduke at the head of the Danubian Principalities?"* Metternich was so taken aback by this suggestion that Napoleon could not help smiling. He replied, however, that before Austria could place an archduke over the Principalities, it would be necessary to possess them. At any rate, he would not dare transmit such a proposal to his government.

The idea of making concessions did not receive much favor in Vienna. Franz Joseph wrote to Napoleon announcing that counter-proposals were being sent to Metternich, while agreeing to accept a European congress after peace had been concluded at Zürich.[78] To Napoleon's assertion that the principles of the two rulers were diametrically opposed, he predicted that the Prince Imperial would one day hold the same principles as he did. "Thus it is not only for the present but, above all, for the future that I shall welcome with good will the intimate alliance of France and Austria, an alliance that I consider the best guarantee of order and progress in Europe."[79]

Napoleon now invited Metternich to continue the discussions at Biarritz. During his visit which lasted over a week, the Austrian Ambassador had a number of conversations with the Emperor, the Empress, and Walewski. The latter, who was an ardent advocate of an Austro-French alliance and who detested the intrigues of Piedmont, was charged by the Emperor to work out in collaboration with Metternich an agreement concerning the Italian question which would enable the two powers to present a united front at the congress. The result of this collaboration was a confidential memorandum which both powers accepted.[80] According to its terms, Austria, in order to facilitate the formation of an Italian confederation, agreed: (1) that Venetia, which was to be a member, should have provincial assemblies and a central legislature composed entirely of Italian residents in that province, (2) to participate in the creation of federal fortresses in case the federal assembly of the confederation should decide to create them, (3) to send only Italian regiments to the garrisons of the federal fortresses situated outside the boundaries of Austria. In addition, and with a view toward arriving at a complete understanding with France regarding the means of pacifying Italy, Austria agreed to join in persuading the Duke of Modena to recognize as his successor Duke Robert of Parma, who should marry the Princess Maria Theresa of Modena. Meanwhile, Franz Joseph reserved the rights of his House in case of the extinction of the descendants and direct issue of the projected marriage between Duke Robert and the Princess of Modena. Parma and Piacenza were to be annexed to Piedmont. These concessions, however, were made contingent upon the restoration of the Grand Duke of Tuscany. From her side, France promised to employ her influence in obtaining the concurrence of the King of Piedmont to the pacification of central Italy. The two great powers would convoke without delay a congress of the signatories of the Treaty of Vienna of 1815 in order to submit the Treaty of Zürich for its approval. In this congress Rome, Piedmont and Naples would be invited to participate for the discussion of the proper means of pacifying Italy. "The Austrian and French plenipotentiaries at the congress will act in complete accord in order to reach the aim determined by the stipulations of the Treaty of Zürich and by the *entente* consigned in the present confidential memorandum."

Metternich tried unsuccessfully to secure the insertion of a clause which would engage Napoleon "to use all his influence to put an end to the annexationist agitation, bring about the recall of the Grand Duke of Tuscany and the Duke of Modena, dissolve the league and the army of central Italy, and restore the Legations to the authority of the Pope."[81] He also attempted to persuade Napoleon to admit representatives of the Grand Duke of Tuscany and the Duke of Modena to the congress but his argument fell on deaf ears. The Emperor said that he would not object if they were summoned by the congress after it convened but he was absolutely opposed to inviting them beforehand. Metternich believed that he had obtained the maximum and was satisfied in having persuaded Napoleon to abandon the idea of inviting Piedmont alone of the Italian states to the congress. "Perhaps I deceive myself but I believe I have obtained more than the Italian tendencies of the Emperor would have warranted. In seeking to pacify Italy, I have positively succeeded in pacifying the Emperor and in accustoming him to more correct and loyal ideas."[82] The important thing was to keep Napoleon on a terrain favorable to Austria. During his sojourn at Biarritz, Metternich had to listen to all sorts of schemes proposed by the Emperor and the Empress. On one occasion the Emperor suggested that Austria adhere to a proposal from the Catholic powers according to which the Legations should be annexed to Tuscany. At another time, he proposed that the Grand Duke of Tuscany be made the governor of Venetia, while the Empress asked if Egypt might not be agreeable to Austria. Metternich was able to discount such suggestions.

The establishment of an understanding on the Italian question appeared to open the way to a new era in Austro-French relations. From his side Franz Joseph had conceded much of what Napoleon had requested. The latter was at last committed to a policy which he had resisted since Villafranca. He had leaned to the side of the Italian nationalists, had carried on an active correspondence with Victor Emmanuel behind the back of his Foreign Minister, had received Italian delegations, and had instructed his personal agents in a sense which was distinctly inimical to Austria's interests.[83] Such actions had compromised the preliminaries of peace, while the divergence between the views of the Emperor and his Foreign Minister had been so great that the latter actually threatened to resign. Nor had Napoleon hesitated to express himself in a most contradictory fashion. To the Grand Duke of Tuscany he had voiced the hope that a favorable reaction would recall him to the throne. He had urged Victor Emmanuel to take over the duchies for the maintenance of order, and Garibaldi to establish a strong army to defend central Italy against a counter-revolution. To Walewski he had said that he wanted to find a way of reconciling his sympathies for Italian unity with his engagements toward Austria, and to Metternich he had given assurances of his friendship for Franz Joseph. He had declared to Cowley that he did not favor the annexations. What was one to believe in the face of such contradictions? Was it merely indicative of the hesitations and vacillations which had plagued the Emperor since Villafranca or did it conceal a scheme of some kind? It was Metternich's opinion that Napoleon had deliberately tried to play a triple game and to keep all parties in a state of uncertainty.[84] In order to modify as much as possible the preliminaries of peace, he had urged Austria to permit Venetia to become a quasi-independent province and a part of the Italian confederation while adopting a common code of laws, a common flag and common constitutions for all the Italian states, placing the Pope at the head of the confederation, secularizing the Legations, restoring the Grand Duke of Tuscany, giving Piedmont a predominantly anti-Austrian influence and, finally, making himself the protector of the new Italy. In this way he hoped to retain the sympathies of the pro-Italian groups in France and to reconcile them with the clerical and legitimist parties. But he had found that Austria could not be won over to his views and that events had not proceeded according to his fancy. Thus, realizing that he could not push through his scheme, Napoleon had fallen back on the idea of an understanding with Austria and had permitted Walewski to draw up the confidential memorandum in collaboration with Metternich. "It took all the will-power Walewski possessed to obtain this result, which he had so long desired, of binding the Emperor, of making him enter a course which alone can bring good results, and of making him abandon that dangerous policy of expectation and hesitation."[85]

Metternich realized that the delay in concluding the negotiations at Zürich, coupled with the persistent wooing of Count Arese, the Emperor's friend, might produce an unfavorable turn for Austria, and that at best any engagement with Napoleon was likely to prove a gamble.[86] To all this Rechberg agreed, characterizing Napoleon as a veritable proteus of modern diplomacy—insatiable, incalculable, meddling, deceiving each party in turn and all together.[87] It was impossible to predict the actions of such a man. This fact was borne out by the publication in the *Constitutionnel* on November 1st of a letter Napoleon had written to Victor Emmanuel defending the Italian cause. Coming as it did at the moment when there was supposed to be the closest understanding between Austria and France, the letter produced a painful impression in Vienna and Metternich was instructed to demand explanations.[88] Napoleon admitted that he had written the letter but protested that he had done so merely to appease the Italians and that its importance was greatly exaggerated. Was he still indulging in a double or triple game? Metternich felt rather uneasy. The Emperor had just received a

telegram from Victor Emmanuel in which the latter had asked
for advice since he feared a revolution in central Italy. Metternich
warned him that if Piedmont tried to intervene in central Italy,
Austria would do likewise. "God forbid," exclaimed the Emperor,
"that will lead to war!" "Better a war for Austria," replied the
Ambassador, "than to lose all her prestige by too much weakness."
The Emperor thereupon offered to give Austria the Principalities,
the Adriatic coast and Egypt. Finally, after a heated discussion, he
promised to send a warning to Victor Emmanuel.[89]

The negotiations at Zürich were concluded on November 10th
with the signing of three treaties: between Austria and France,
France and Piedmont, and Austria and Piedmont. While these did
not expressly provide for the restoration of the rulers in central
Italy, they did reserve the rights of these princes and called for a
congress to settle the question. But a congress was something distinctly repugnant to Napoleon at this moment. Realizing the impossibility of preventing the union of central Italy and Piedmont,
he was determined to draw what profit he could by annexing Nice
and Savoy to France. He could not submit such a plan to the congress without running the risk of alienating England[90] and possibly Russia.[91] On the other hand, the pressure of his anti-Italian
ministers and of Metternich was strong enough to make him hesitate.
Metternich had a regular ordeal to bring him around to the Austrian side. "The battle of Compiègne," as the Ambassador called
it, was extremely difficult. "I owe it to my iron constitution that I
was not struck down by apoplexy. My excitement was shared by
the entire court and when I emerged with His Majesty from his
chamber, every glance was directed toward me and I heard from
right and left the words 'has he succeeded? Yes, no, et cetera,' a
real melodramatic scene."[92] According to Metternich, the members
of the court were greatly relieved to learn that he had succeeded
and he was congratulated from all sides. He had won the battle
over the intrigues of Piedmont and England, and the supporters
of the Austrian alliance breathed more easily. While the Empress
refrained from speaking to Metternich about politics, "due to orders
from higher up," she informed him through Walewski that Napoleon

would be faithful to his obligations and that she had taken as her motto "do what should be done, come what may."[93] It was evident that she had intervened in Metternich's behalf.

The Emperor was by this time, however, heartily disgusted with the whole affair. "I wish," he said, "that the Italians would wash their dirty linen among themselves."[94] He would have liked to withdraw his troops from Rome and Milan and no longer concern himself with the Italian question. Why should he support the Pope when the latter misgoverned his states? He admitted to Metternich that he himself had brought on the difficulties from which he now sought a way out. "My thought was grand and beautiful, my intentions pure and unselfish. By invading Piedmont, you gave me a good pretext to realize a desire of my life, that of giving Italy to herself. I believed that I had succeeded at Villafranca; now I see that the whole affair is more difficult than before, and I am at the end of my rope. England plays a rather singular game and my influence has completely escaped me."[95] Despite his embarrassment, he promised to be loyal to the terms of the confidential memorandum and agreed with the Austrian viewpoint that the congress should merely approve the ideas of an Italian confederation, leaving to the confederate states the task of working out the details. Nor did he see any difficulty about creating an Italian army. In the meantime, he hoped that Franz Joseph would do something about reforms in Venetia before the congress assembled. "Good politics," he said to Metternich, "consists in doing things at the right moment and the right moment is before and not after the congress."[96] If Austria would carry out reforms in Venetia, neither England nor Piedmont would have a pretext for complaining and France could then give more effective support. Metternich replied that his government would institute these reforms but it was difficult to do so before introducing reforms in the other provinces of the Empire. "I know quite well," said Napoleon, "that it is difficult in Austria to satisfy the Italians, Slavs, Hungarians, and Germans but however that may be I am sure that the Emperor will not regret the concessions he makes before the meeting of the congress. I say this because it is my sincere conviction. I do not wish to interfere in the affairs of your Emperor which do not concern me except in wishing that he promise to satisfy Venetia. The choice of the moment does not concern me."[97]

As matters stood when the Treaty of Zürich was concluded, Austria and France had formed an *entente* for concerted action at the congress. They had agreed that any departure from the confidential memorandum by either party would automatically release the other from the decisions of the congress.[98] Furthermore, if France violated the terms of the memorandum, Austria would not be obligated to fulfill her promises and would have the right to take steps to safeguard her interests. Once again Napoleon had agreed to more than he cared to execute. However, his chief concern at the moment appeared to center on the question of reforms in Venetia. The idea of proclaiming these before the meeting of the congress did not appeal to Rechberg, who felt that Napoleon had not been fully informed about the government of Venetia whose institutions, far from stifling the national spirit, really encouraged it.[99] Rechberg declared that reforms in Venetia were out of the question so long as Piedmont continued to stir up agitation.

That this attitude would not please Napoleon, who insisted upon the reforms in order to please England and Piedmont, was obvious. After all, the Italian war had not evoked much enthusiasm in France and the Emperor was denounced as a traitor by Piedmont for failing to carry out his pledge, while his conduct since Villafranca had not been such as to overcome Austria's suspicions. But though regarded by all sides with distrust, he would not abandon his *idées* and was as determined as ever to revise the treaties of 1815, particularly as they affected the security of France. "The day I have Savoy and Nice in the south and sufficient fortresses in the north," he said to Metternich, "my mission will be accomplished."[100]

The idea that Napoleon would take advantage of the congress in order to bring up the question of revising the treaties in the interest of France, aroused concern in Vienna. Rechberg did not intend to fall into this trap and asserted that the congress had only two aims: to sanction the treaties concluded at Zürich and to consider means of pacifying Italy and if any other questions were introduced, as in 1856, the Austrian delegates would leave.[101] With respect to the first aim, Rechberg would not admit that the powers could exact any revisions. As to the second, there were two points involved: to pacify Italy and to seek a durable basis for her prosperity. From the Austrian viewpoint, the pacification of Italy meant the submission of the rebellious provinces to the Pope and the return of the dispossessed rulers to their states. Rechberg realized that this could not be achieved without force, and he was prepared to recommend armed intervention by any Catholic power which offered it. The opposition of France, he thought, would vanish once the congress decreed the restoration of the rulers in central Italy.

On November 21, 1859, Walewski issued invitations for the congress. Rechberg had agreed to issue identical though not joint invitations but held back when informed that Boncompagni, a subject of Piedmont, had been named to the regency in central Italy, which he saw as the first step in the annexation of this region to Piedmont.[102] Russell accepted the French invitation, after receiving assurances from Paris that there was no question of employing force for the restoration of the dispossessed rulers.[103] Prussia and Russia also accepted but stipulated that all the great powers must be represented and that each should be free in regard to principles or measures to be adopted.[104] Rechberg, in the meantime, decided to go along and issued invitations though he refused to adopt Russell's view on non-intervention.[105] Thus the way was prepared for the convocation of the congress.

Just as public interest in the approaching congress had been aroused, there appeared in France (December 22nd) a brochure entitled "Le Pape et le Congrès." Though written by La Guérronière, who in the previous February had edited the brochure, "L'Empéreur Napoléon III et l'Italie," it was inspired by the Emperor.[105a] The arguments which it set forth were contradictory and artificial. The main theme was that the Pope should abandon the Legations as the best means of restoring order in Italy and be satisfied with the city of Rome. For the future he would be maintained by a guarantee of the great powers and by a revenue furnished by the Catholic states. Of more significance than the proposed dismemberment of the Papal States was a statement that France would not intervene in central Italy or permit Austria or Naples to do so. Thus the employment of force to restore the dispossessed princes was ruled out altogether.

The appearance of the brochure created a great stir. It naturally infuriated the Pope, Pius IX, who referred to it in his New Year's address of 1860 as "a signal monument of hypocrisy, an ignoble tissue of contradictions."[106] Indeed, it seriously threatened the relations between France and the Papacy. England was pleased, no longer fearing a war with France, and regarding the brochure as laying the basis for a closer understanding between the two powers.[107] As for Austria, she regarded it as an encouragement to the revolutionary party in Italy which not only destroyed the *entente* with France but would put an end to the congress unless the brochure were officially disavowed. Metternich hastened to point out to Walewski the serious nature of the brochure but while the minister pretended not to know the author, he promised to take up the matter with the Emperor. Moreover, he maintained that France would never abandon the principles of Catholicism and emphatically denied that there was any plan for the dismemberment of the Papal States. But Walewski had lost his influence over the Emperor and resigned on January 5, 1860. He was succeeded by Thouvenel, who was more amenable to the policy of nationalities.

The publication of the brochure gave the death-blow to the congress.[108] Rechberg was considerably upset though the French Ambassador at Vienna tried to reassure him that the brochure was after all only a brochure and had no official character and that Napoleon was sincerely desirous of a good understanding with Austria.[109] He replied that the accord between Austria and France was now destroyed since it had been based upon the maintenance of papal power. But in admitting that the congress was dead, that his efforts to keep Napoleon on a terrain favorable to Austria had ended in failure, what policy was he to follow under the circumstances? Was Austria to forsake the dispossessed rulers and permit Piedmont to annex central Italy or should she recommence the war? It was a difficult question to decide. "Either we must declare ourselves beaten," wrote Metternich, "abandon our rights and proclaim with the Emperor the principle of non-intervention, of *faits ac-*

complis, and of popular sovereignty with universal suffrage, or it is necessary to risk recommencing the struggle, to intervene on behalf of the Pope and to get back our rights or, finally, we ought . . . to protest against everything which has been done and will be done in Italy and reserve to ourselves complete freedom of action. . . . "[110] It might be possible, thought the Ambassador, to declare that Austria had ceded Lombardy on condition that the Pope be restored to his possessions although there had been no mention of this in the preliminaries of peace, the confidential memorandum, or the Treaty of Zürich. He was still confident that Napoleon did not wish to break with Austria and that new proposals concerning Italy could be expected at any moment.

While Rechberg was anxious to find a way to maintain an understanding with France and while he was willing to be conciliatory on most points, he flatly refused to countenance any scheme which deprived the Pope of his estates. What, he asked, would be the position of the Pope if he became a mere pensioner of the Catholic powers?[111] Would it not be possible for one of these powers to refuse its quota if the Pope rejected its demands? And would Prussia contribute for her eight million Catholics and England for Ireland? Was there not a danger of subjecting the Pope to the influence of these Protestant powers? To rob the Pope of his estates would be a calamity and even war would be preferable. It should not be forgotten, he declared, that Austria still had the means to fight and that a strong Austria was necessary for the maintenance of the European equilibrium.[112]

The death of the congress left unsettled the questions pertaining to central Italy. That there could be no return to the program set forth in the confidential memorandum was obvious. Napoleon had publicly announced his opposition to the restoration of the Legations to the Papacy, which amounted to a renunciation of the entire settlement since it gave the Piedmontese direct encouragement to annex not only the Legations but the duchies as well. While it is true that the territorial integrity of the Papal States had not been expressly stipulated in the agreements between Austria and France, it had been tacitly assumed.[113] In fact, when Metternich suggested the insertion of a paragraph in the memorandum concerning this,

Napoleon assured him that it was unnecessary.[114] From the Austrian viewpoint, therefore, the French Emperor had acted in bad faith. Though he expressed regret because of the agitation produced by the brochure, he refused to disavow it.

The problem which now faced Austria was to find a way out of the Italian difficulty which would keep Napoleon in check and prevent him from making further trouble or stirring up revolutions. One thing was clear: Austria did not intend to embark upon another struggle with France. Metternich believed that what was needed under the circumstances was a compromise which would give certain advantages to both parties. Accordingly, he suggested to Rechberg that a program be submitted to Napoleon representing the final concessions Austria could offer.[115] This program, as he outlined it in his dispatch, provided for the restoration of the Grand Duke of Tuscany, the marriage of Princess Maria Theresa to Duke Robert of Parma, who would succeed the Duke of Modena upon the latter's death, an arrangement whereby Venetia would have an Italian administration and enjoy the same privileges as other provinces of the Hapsburg Monarchy though it would not be defended by an Italian army, and the establishment of an Italian confederation. Austria would not oppose the annexation of Savoy to France. The approval of the Pope would be sought before submitting the program to France and Piedmont, which would be asked to accept it without reservations.

Metternich saw several advantages in his scheme. It would leave Napoleon in no doubt concerning the maximum concessions Austria could offer and would precede any proposals he might suggest. Inasmuch as the approval of the Pope was to be obtained before submitting the program to France, Austria would gain the spiritual support of the Papacy. Should Napoleon hesitate to accept, Austria could appeal to the conservative powers and win to her side Russia, Prussia, Rome, Naples, Spain and Portugal. Moreover, Austria could threaten to withhold her approval of the annexation of Savoy to France and support Spain in the latter's opposition to the annexation of Parma and Piacenza to Piedmont.

In his effort to convince Rechberg that he was in a position to gain the ear of Napoleon, Metternich pointed out that the latter literally overwhelmed him with attention, while the Empress had taken so great a fancy to his wife that almost any pretext was employed to have them both at the Tuileries. "Thus at Sylvester we were the only guests to inaugurate the new year."[116] During the evening the Emperor begged Metternich, who was an accomplished pianist, to play a waltz while he danced with the Empress. "I cannot help laughing at the situation. The Ambassador of Austria making the Emperor dance to the first moments of the new year seems quite original, to say the least. I could not resist the temptation of playing the 'Radetzky March' and our national anthem when the imperial couple had stopped dancing." This was indeed a contrast with the new year of 1859 when the atmosphere was darkened by thoughts of war. At the same time, however, the Ambassador did not permit himself to be influenced too much by this intimacy at the Tuileries. He realized that Napoleon was an incorrigible adventurer—a man with a diseased mind which could be treated but not cured.[117] This had been made sufficiently clear in the protracted negotiations since Villafranca, while further proof was furnished by the dismissal of Walewski, who had entered wholeheartedly into the difficult task of finding a solution for the problems created by the war. From the very beginning of the negotiations, it was obvious that there existed a divergence between the views of the minister and the Emperor, a divergence between conservative and revolutionary principles, but Metternich had persuaded himself that as long as Walewski remained in office, Austria had nothing to fear.[118] While Walewski's position had been rendered untenable by the publication of the brochure, Metternich concluded that his dismissal was an indication that Napoleon sought a solution of the Italian problem other than the one based upon an understanding with Austria.

Metternich's program for the solution of the Italian question was submitted to Franz Joseph who, after careful consideration, rejected it since he no longer relied on the word of Napoleon.[119] Having made important concessions in the preliminaries of Villafranca, the confidential memorandum, and the Treaty of Zürich, the Austrian ruler had no assurance that the new proposals would not meet the same fate. And how could they be carried out when

Napoleon insisted upon non-intervention? Under the circumstance, it was decided to leave the initiative to France.

As usual it was not quite clear what course Napoleon intended to follow. Baroche, who was in charge of the Quai d'Orsay pending the arrival of Thouvenel from Constantinople, declared that France still desired the congress and would convoke it as soon as Rome and Vienna showed a willingness to send delegates.[120] At the same time, there were rumors of a new Anglo-French *entente*. The pro-Italian sympathies of the English Ministry were well-known and while the Truce of Villafranca had been a great disappointment to Palmerston and Russell, Napoleon's subsequent behavior had been reassuring. In fact, the publication of the brochure and the resignation of Walewski eased the strain in Anglo-French relations for they seemed to indicate that France would follow an outright Italian policy. Finally, the Cobden Treaty (January 1860) did suggest an attempt to buy England's support in the Italian question in return for trade concessions.[121] On January 13, 1860, Palmerston's organ, *The Morning Post,* announced: "There exists—we rejoice to be able at length to proclaim the fact—a virtual alliance between the governments of France and England to recognize and protect the newly acquired independence of Northern and Central Italy."[122] Lord Cowley's abrupt departure for London and the return of Persigny to Paris early in January gave rise to reports that England and France were about to conclude a pact on the basis of non-intervention in Italy and the cession of Nice and Savoy to France. Russell denied that he had received any French proposals and explained to Apponyi that Cowley had come to London at the request of Napoleon, who wished to learn England's intentions.[123] On the other hand, Apponyi was told by Clarendon, the former Secretary of Foreign Affairs, that while no formal treaty had been signed, there nevertheless existed an Anglo-French *entente* regarding Italy based upon the principle of non-intervention.[124] There was little likelihood, however, of a complete agreement between England and France concerning Italy. Only in the aim of preventing Austria from undertaking an armed intervention was there an identity of views. Otherwise, England's policy appears to have been to widen **the breach between Austria and France, and Piedmont and the**

Papacy, in order to further her own interests and extend her influence in the Peninsula.

There is no doubt that uncertainty concerning French policy made the situation in central Italy more dangerous. Napoleon denied that he had concluded an *entente* with England or that he intended to break the engagements contracted at Villafranca and Zürich, or that he was bound to Piedmont.[125] At the same time he insisted that the Italian difficulties be settled without intervention. The question of intervention was the real crux of the entire problem as it affected relations between Austria and France. As Rechberg saw it, the dominant thought in the engagements contracted by the two states was to set up a dike against revolution by reinstating the dispossessed rulers. Both Napoleon and Franz Joseph had agreed to this and the only difference which had appeared concerned the means of execution, the question of whether or not to employ force. Both had assumed that the Legations would be restored to the Pope though this was not precisely stated in the engagements. At Zürich the French plenipotentiaries had given the most positive assurances that their government would respect the territorial integrity of the Papal States, while Walewski had been equally emphatic on this point. Consequently, before the appearance of the brochure, Austria had ample reason to assume that France intended to abide by her engagements. That document, however, had robbed the Austro-French *entente* of any meaning and mere words could not gloss over this fact. The French assurances in no way altered the situation.

In the aim of preventing the Italian problem from assuming dangerous proportions, the English Government proposed a plan to Austria and France.[126] This declared for the principle of non-intervention and suggested four points which might serve as a basis for a solution. The first called upon Austria and France to agree not to intervene by force in the internal affairs of Italy unless they received a mandate from the five great powers of Europe. The second called for an agreement between France and the Papacy for the evacuation of Rome by French troops and arrangements for the withdrawal of French forces in northern Italy. The third declared that the European powers would not interfere in any way with the internal government of Venetia. Austria was asked to assent to these three points but not to the fourth which provided that England and France would invite Piedmont not to send troops into central Italy "until its several states and provinces shall, after a new vote of their assemblies, after a new election, have solemnly declared their wishes as to their future destiny." If the elections resulted in favor of annexation to Piedmont, the latter would be free to send in troops. Austria was not asked to recognize any government in central Italy which, according to her principles, was not entitled to such recognition.

The English plan was received by Rechberg with the utmost scorn. "A power," he wrote to Metternich, "which took no part in the war, today has the pretension of regulating the results according to its fancy and its exclusive profit. To propose to us a solution which implies the most brilliant triumph of subversive principles and the most revolting contempt for our well-founded rights, and to exact by it a bargain that we engage to remain forever with arms crossed in the face of schemes so monstrous, is the height of political naïveté, if it is not the *ne plus ultra* of British egotism."[127] In other words, England had no right to interfere in the settlement of a question which belonged to Austria and France alone.

Rechberg's contemptuous attitude was not shared by Thouvenel, the new French Foreign Minister, who saw in the English plan a way out of the embarrassing problem of central Italy. In a memorandum addressed to Napoleon, he indicated the policy France should follow in this problem.[128] He regarded the Italian war of 1859 as only one incident in the long struggle between Austria and France. Since it was impossible to restore the dynasties in the duchies of central Italy or return the Legations to the Papacy, it was necessary to recognize the changes which had taken place as *faits accomplis*. The aim of French policy, therefore, should be the organization of Italy on a stable basis and the erection of a bulwark against Austrian influence. This aim could be reached, according to Thouvenel, either by creating an independent kingdom in central Italy, which would form part of the Italian confederation, or by annexation to Piedmont. While he preferred the first solution, Thouvenel recognized that there were too many difficulties in the way. As to the annexation of Central Italy to Piedmont, he thought this might be utilized by France in order to obtain Nice and Savoy. In a dispatch to de Moustier, French Ambassador at Vienna, he declared that the failure to reach a solution of the Italian problem after Villafranca was due to the neglect of the Papacy to undertake reforms, the silence of Austria concerning Venetia, and the inaction of the dispossessed rulers.[129] Now it was necessary to end the rivalry between Austria and France in Italy and this could be done if both states would voluntarily withdraw. Thouvenel concluded that the English plan offered the best means of attaining this end and he directed de Moustier to present this viewpoint to Vienna. Napoleon was also favorable to the plan though he could not agree to withdraw his troops from Rome until the safety of the Pope was assured and stated that it would be necessary for him to consult Austria, Prussia and Russia regarding the fourth point.[130].

If Thouvenel actually believed that his ideas would be favorably received in Vienna, he was soon undeceived. Not only did Rechberg flatly reject the English plan but he ridiculed the thought of establishing a durable system in Italy which violated the dynastic rights guaranteed by the treaties.[131] Instead of excluding Austria and France from Italy, as Thouvenel suggested, he declared that it would be far better to arrive at an understanding whereby they would share influence in the Peninsula. At the same time, he assured de Moustier that Austria would not employ force to realize the terms of Villafranca. Further than this, if Napoleon would be satisfied with Austria's promise not to offer opposition to the annexation of the duchies to Piedmont and of Nice and Savoy to France, an understanding might be reached.[132] But this was as far as Austria could go in order to maintain peace. She would not permit the inclusion of Venetia, the Papal States, and the Two Sicilies in a united Italy. This was indeed a rather far cry from the position Rechberg took on the morrow of Villafranca.

In the meantime, Napoleon had started secret negotiations with Piedmont for the annexation of Nice and Savoy to France. Rattazzi, who refused to cede these provinces, resigned as Prime Minister on January 20, 1860, and Cavour resumed office. Through his agents, such as Vimercati, Nigra and Arese, Cavour sought to reach a settlement regarding central Italy, Nice and Savoy.[133] In convoking the

Piedmontese Parliament, he announced that the duchies would be represented there. On February 3rd Napoleon declared that if central Italy joined Piedmont, France would reserve the right to secure a rectification of her frontiers on the side of the Alps.

Because of difficulties over Tuscany, Napoleon's negotiations with Piedmont did not progress as smoothly as he desired. He did not oppose the annexation to Piedmont of Parma, Modena and even the Legations, though he preferred that the latter province remain under the suzerainty of the Pope.[134] But the annexation of Tuscany was a more serious matter since both Prussia and Russia were opposed to it and the Emperor therefore suggested that it remain an independent state under the Duke of Genoa or Prince Eugene di Carignano.[135] Such an arrangement would give Piedmont virtual control over Tuscany, put an end to Austrian influence, and at the same time reassure those powers opposing the unification of Italy. It would, said Thouvenel, amount to a disguised annexation.[136] If Piedmont rejected this arrangement, France would not oppose the annexation of all central Italy to Piedmont but would let the Italians take the responsibility for the events that might follow. Moreover, Napoleon threatened to recall his troops from Lombardy in case Piedmont refused. On the other hand, if Cavour accepted, Napoleon promised to bring about an offensive-defensive alliance between England, France and Piedmont for the Balkans from which Piedmont would draw certain advantages, perhaps the possession of Venetia.[137]

Knowing that the Emperor was anxious to hasten a settlement of the Italian question even if such a settlement was merely a truce, Cavour rejected the French program and proceeded with plans for the annexation of all central Italy to Piedmont. He believed that Napoleon wanted to be rid of the Italian problem altogether in order to engage in Balkan affairs which might offer him the means of redrawing the map of Europe in the interests of France.[138] He considered it highly probable that Napoleon would start an uprising in Serbia where there were numerous French agents and that such an uprising would lead to a revolution in Hungary. Indeed, preparations were already under way in Paris. Kossuth and Klapka were in close touch, if not with the Emperor, at least with Prince

Napoleon. "All the ideas I have developed are in the brain of the Emperor. It now remains to be seen if Thouvenel has the necessary energy to put them into execution."[139]

It was not only Cavour's independent attitude that was disconcerting to Napoleon. The firmness displayed by Vienna was hardly less so. Apparently he had persuaded himself to believe that Austria had left him a free hand in settling the Italian question. But now Rechberg sent instructions to Metternich to inform Thouvenel that Austria still considered the rights and principles set forth in the Treaty of Zürich as valid and that while she would not have recourse to arms in order to realize them, she would refuse to adhere to any arrangement which did not take them as its point of departure.[140] Consequently, Austria would regard any state of affairs resulting from such an arrangement as existing *de facto* and not *de jure*. As to the question of Savoy, this was intimately connected with the question of central Italy and could not be separated from it. "In both cases it is the same principles which must be set aside or sanctioned. The violation of treaties, of recognized rights, is the same. It is always the same doctrines which must be applied."[141] Rechberg declared that Austria would not adhere to any scheme which threatened the territorial integrity of the Papal States or which did not take account of the rights of the dispossessed rulers expressly reserved by the Treaty of Zürich.[142]

While France could no longer entertain doubts about Austria's attitude, Vienna was not as clearly informed as to the course Napoleon intended to follow. Metternich's dispatches and letters reveal his own uncertainties. This was not surprising, for there were few, even among his most intimate advisers, who knew what went on in the Emperor's mind. There had been so many fluctuations, so many contradictions in the imperial policy, which could be explained only by the character of Napoleon and the combination of the Napoleonic cult with his personal ideas. An adventurer and a fatalist by nature, a man whose ambition and dreams of worldly power transcended all moral limits, there was no telling what he might do. "The carbonarism of Louis Bonaparte produced the Italian question; Napoleonic ambition prepared the alliance with Sardinia concerning Savoy and Nice, and decided the Emperor to provoke war. Once

that had been done, fortune favored the French army. The star of
Napoleon was made resplendent by a new state."[143] But then
Napoleon had called a halt and concluded the Truce of Villafranca.
Yet, he could not rid himself of the revolutionary forces that had
aided him. "Louis Napoleon conspired against Napoleon III, the
Carbonaro against the Emperor."[144] Metternich explained the contradictions of French imperial policy by this dualism, this struggle
between two opposing forces which became dangerous once they
found a common ground. Indeed, the Ambassador held that all
the thoughts and actions of Napoleon were contradictory. "He has
revolutionary convictions as powerful as his conservative instincts.
He can yield alternately to humanitarian thoughts *à la* Cobden and
to the immoderate ambitions of Napoleon I. He has moments of
lucidity worthy of a genius and moments of fatal blindness which
an irrefutable argument cannot overcome."[145] Metternich could find
no agreement among the Emperor's advisers concerning the course
he would follow in the Italian question. He learned from Thouvenel
that Napoleon planned to hold Piedmont in check and prevent her
from absorbing all Italy while proclaiming in principle the independence of Tuscany and the territorial integrity of the Papal States.
In case Piedmont annexed Parma and Modena, France would take
Nice and Savoy but all questions pertaining to Italy would be submitted to a congress. Others, however, believed that the Emperor
was in league with Cavour and that after having obtained his part
of the booty, would leave the Italian question open and direct his
attention to Belgium and the Rhine. Thus, carbonarism would give
way to ambition. "The Italian question," wrote Metternich, "begins
to occupy only second place in the imperial policy."[146] When he
asked Thouvenel what Napoleon would do if Tuscany and the
Romagna voted for annexation to Piedmont, the minister replied
that the elections would reveal so many irregularities that the votes
would be considered invalid; if Piedmont accepted the annexations,
the Emperor would withdraw his troops from Lombardy and let
Piedmont shift for herself.[147] Of one thing at least Metternich felt
certain. Napoleon had become indifferent to the problem of central
Italy and would accept almost any arrangement in order to be
rid of it.

Meanwhile, the inhabitants of Tuscany, Emilia and the Legations were called upon to confirm by a formal plebiscite the wishes they had already expressed. That the result of this plebiscite would be favorable to Piedmont was a foregone conclusion. Though Austria had promised not to intervene, Thouvenel was somewhat uneasy and wanted a new assurance. He therefore instructed de Moustier to inform Rechberg that having warned Piedmont as to the danger of accepting the annexations and having done everything morally to prevent them, France had decided to withdraw her troops from Lombardy and wanted an assurance that Austria would not intervene.[148] In carrying out these instructions, de Moustier expressed the hope that Austrian troops would not enter on the heels of the French and yield to the temptation of operating in the Romagna. "Certainly not," replied Rechberg very seriously. "Nothing is better than to deliver the Italians to themselves; a policy of observation is one which agrees with Austria as well as with France. I repeat, we are happy to find ourselves in agreement."[149] Franz Joseph also gave a positive assurance that Austria would not intervene.

Now that the vexatious problem of central Italy was about to be settled in one way or the other, Napoleon breathed more easily. He was extremely cordial to Metternich, who was invited to all sorts of intimate gatherings.[150] Indeed, it seemed to the Ambassador that there was a deliberate attempt to court Austria's favor. The official press ceased its anti-Austrian attacks and everyone, even Dr. Conneau, was most agreeable. It was evident that Napoleon was drawing in his claws but "in a manner to throw dust in the eyes of the most distrustful."[151] Metternich was not taken in by the air of cordiality which prevailed at the Tuileries, for he still had doubts concerning the Emperor's motives. There had been a number of hints about Venetia which indicated that Austria would again be tormented by that question.

The plebiscites in central Italy were held March 11th to the 15th and resulted in annexation to Piedmont. Victor Emmanuel accepted on the 22nd and three days later the people of Tuscany, Emilia and the Legations participated in elections for the new parliament which met on April 2nd. Piedmont had already concluded a treaty ceding Nice and Savoy to France though provision was made for plebiscites. These plebiscites were held on April 15th and 22nd and were favorable to France. Napoleon thus became an accomplice of Piedmont and could not prevent her from pursuing further aggrandizements.

While the annexation of Nice and Savoy provoked general indignation, it was not seriously opposed by any government. The English were furious though Downing Street entered no formal protest.[152] Even Palmerston, the friend and confidant of Napoleon, was unable to conceal his distrust. "One pretends," he said to Apponyi, "that the affair of Savoy was the last chapter of the Italian question. I believe, on the contrary, that it is the first chapter of a new volume with which the Emperor wishes to regale the world. It is now evident that this man who has taken for his program, 'L'Empire, c'est la Paix,' thinks only of overturning Europe, Asia and Africa. He can no longer live without war, conquests and revolutions."[153] Apponyi was astounded by the change in Palmerston's attitude and began to entertain the hope that England would now pursue a more moderate policy in Italy. His optimism, however, was not shared by Rechberg, who refused to believe that the Prime Minister had experienced a real conversion or that the English policy would be any less Italian than it had been.[154]

Piedmont's acceptance of the annexations made her responsible for future events since Napoleon had announced his intention of evacuating Lombardy. It remained to be seen what attitude the powers would take in face of the violation of the treaties. The Austrian Government realized that a mere protest of the powers would avail nothing since it would be ignored by Piedmont, while the employment of force had already been ruled out. There obviously was no way to undo the results though Rechberg was convinced that the votes had been obtained by intimidation and juggling, in short, that the plebiscites were a farce. While he still persisted in regarding the situation in central Italy as *de facto,* he saw that the annexations were accomplished facts which removed the problem from the sphere of acute diplomatic controversy where it had been since the interview at Villafranca. One phase of the Italian question had thus been settled not, it is true, in accord with the various engagements concluded by Austria and France but on the basis of the principle of nationalities which Napoleon had championed when he entered the war of Italian independence. The Italian Kingdom, stretching from the Alps to the Adriatic, which had been agreed upon at Plombières, had not been realized, for Austria still retained Venetia. Would Piedmont be content with her recent acquisitions and would Napoleon refrain from further meddling in Italy? These were the questions which interested Vienna. Thouvenel assured Metternich that Napoleon did not approve the annexations in central Italy and that he had repeatedly warned Victor Emmanuel of the responsibility Piedmont would incur.[155] So long as Piedmont confined her action to the annexed states, France would do nothing but she had warned Piedmont not to interfere with the other Italian states. Thouvenel promised to concert measures with Austria in case new complications arose.[156]

The immediate result of the plebiscites was an improvement in the relations between Paris and Vienna. Napoleon was pleased with the attitude Austria had displayed. "I am truly touched," he said to Metternich, "with the good will Austria shows us and I shall not delay in showing your Emperor my appreciation."[157] On the other hand, he was extremely irritated against England because of the outcry over the annexation of Nice and Savoy. Nigra reported that the English alliance was regarded as broken forever and that Austria was making all sorts of advances to France.[158] With the Balkans now occupying first place in the Emperor's thoughts, he wanted to be rid of the Italian problem and win the support of Austria. "It appears to me that His Imperial Majesty is now preoccupied with the east in the same manner that he was preoccupied with Italy last year."[159]

CHAPTER TEN

Rome, Naples and Venetia, 1860-1861

THE ANNEXATIONS in central Italy did not satisfy the Italian nationalists whose aim was a united nation which would include Rome, the
Two Sicilies and Venetia. It was the fulfillment of this aim that
Austria was determined to prevent, if necessary by force. Franz
Joseph would never voluntarily surrender Venetia nor abandon the
Pope to Garibaldi and his cohorts. Naples, however, presented a
different problem, for its protection might mean war with England
which Austria could not afford. Without allies, the preservation
of her remaining influence in the Peninsula would be exceedingly
difficult in view of the encouragement which England and France
might give Piedmont. The task which faced Rechberg was to keep
Napoleon within reasonable bounds, either by a direct understanding with him or by getting the support of the conservative powers,
Prussia and Russia.

In view of the danger to Venetia, Rechberg was particularly
anxious to win the support of Prussia. Negotiations were started
in January 1860 when Karolyi, the Austrian Ambassador to Berlin,
made direct overtures for a defensive alliance including a guarantee
of the territories of the two powers.[1] Karolyi warned Schleinitz
that the danger from France and revolution threatened Prussia quite
as much as Austria.[2] While the Prussian Foreign Minister agreed
that this danger existed, he pointed out that an alliance depended
upon two factors, namely, Prussian public opinion, which was not
favorable to Austria, and the attitude of Russia.[3] Karolyi reported
that the Prince Regent and Prince Hohenzollern, the Prime Minister,

were for the alliance, but that Schleinitz wished, if possible, to avoid a closer union with Austria.[4]

Making the proposed alliance dependent upon the attitude of Russia disappointed Rechberg, who regarded it as a bad omen.[5] He had learned from Thun, the Austrian Ambassador at St. Petersburg, that Gortchakoff refused to recommend to Prussia the conclusion of the alliance and had merely promised not to influence the latter against it.[6] Indeed, Gortchakoff had expressed doubt that Prussia would conclude such an alliance and had suggested that Austria attempt to reach an understanding with France.[7] Thun concluded that the Russian Chancellor was still very much under the spell of Napoleon's charm and was unwilling to do anything which might cause the least offense at Paris.[8] Support of the monarchical principle appeared to carry little weight in St. Petersburg. Having vainly sought to win Russia by holding out the bait of an agreement concerning the Black Sea and the Balkans,[9] Rechberg was now convinced that Gortchakoff would try to hinder the conclusion of an Austro-Prussian alliance. Since Russia apparently was on the side of France, it was necessary to erect a bulwark against both. How much the Russian attitude influenced Berlin is difficult to say but the alliance project seemed to be headed for oblivion. Karolyi reported that Prussia's desire for the alliance was as weak as ever, that the Cabinet did not wish to commit itself for the present, and that Schleinitz maintained that Austria no longer had to fear France and hence needed no guarantee for Venetia at this time.[10] The Prince Regent and Prince Hohenzollern were not able to overcome the opposition of the majority of the Prussian ministers. The latter were determined to advance Prussia's interests in the Confederation and demanded that the Federal Act be revised in order to give Prussia command over the confederate troops.

In Paris Metternich discussed the question of an alliance with the Prussian Minister, Count Pourtalès who, while admitting that his words might not carry much weight at Vienna in view of the fact that he had taken a stand opposed to Austria in the Italian war, was willing to work for a *rapprochement* and was prepared to go to Berlin in order to bring this about.[11] "Austria," said Count Pourtalès, "will probably need a faithful ally in order to preserve the rest of her Italian possessions and to strengthen her action internally against revolutionary tendencies fomented from the outside. Prussia, for her part, has need of increasing her influence in Germany and will gladly see Austria adopt a German policy more in line with this need." He suggested as the basis of an understanding a guarantee by Prussia of Venetia and concessions by Austria in Germany. Metternich replied that on this basis, Prussia would risk something only in case Austria were threatened in Venetia whereas Austria would be obliged to abdicate much of her influence in Germany and abandon the conservative group which relied on her for support. "The bargain does not seem very fair to me." If, however, Prussia would agree to use her influence with the aim of maintaining monarchical and conservative principles in the German Confederation, Austria no doubt would be happy to share leadership with her. As it was, Metternich believed that Prussia intended to increase her influence in the Confederation by flattering liberalism and he did not share the apprehension regarding Venetia, for he was convinced that Napoleon would never support an attack directed against that province.

Rechberg saw more in the Prussian overture than Pourtalès had revealed to Metternich. He had learned confidentially that it was Prussia's plan to offer mediation in the Italian question and that the Prince Regent intended to arrange a meeting with Napoleon and to offer himself as mediator.[12] In the event that Garibaldi attacked Venetia, Austria would have the right to attack Piedmont but must not extend her military operations beyond the duchies. A final settlement would then be concluded whereby an Italian confederation would be set up including Venetia and Nice. Prussia, of course, would expect some compensation for her efforts. Such was the plan devised at Berlin according to information which reached Vienna and Rechberg would not consent to it. He knew that a meeting of the Prince Regent and Napoleon would be interpreted in Austria and the Confederation as a Franco-Prussian *rapprochement* and as indicating a rift between Berlin and Vienna. Nor did Rechberg fancy the idea of striking a bargain with Prussia. "This is not the way the question appears to us. We see nothing to buy and nothing to sell. We see a common danger as threatening for the one as for the other, and against which we should both equally prepare, each for the care of its own preservation. If Venetia is in danger from our side, the Rhine is not less so from the side of Prussia. I do not know from which side the attack will begin; as it is, the north is as much exposed as the south to the future blows of the renascent Napoleonic system. The security of Prussia is as much in jeopardy as our own."[13] In other words, there was no need for a bargain since both powers faced a common danger. "Besides," continued Rechberg, "what are the concessions we would have to make to Prussia in Germany? Let M. Pourtalès state them and, if he dares, you will discover the secret aim toward which Prussian policy tends. You know enough of German affairs to be informed in this respect. What Prussia wants of us is not only the sacrifice of our interests but the abandonment of our confederates, that we should deliver them bound hand and foot to her ambitions. We could not do this under any circumstances and less than ever now that the German governments appear more enlightened concerning the external danger which threatens us all."

Although Rechberg rejected the idea of a bargain with Prussia, he was willing to make a personal concession to the Prince Regent. In 1859 Austria had offered him command of the federal army and had sent the Archduke Albrecht and Prince Windischgrätz on special missions to Berlin in order to secure Prussian support in the Italian war. But while the Prince Regent was flattered by this offer which appealed to his military instincts, the bait was not attractive enough to induce him to take sides in the war. Rechberg realized that the only hope of obtaining Prussia's support was in convincing her of the imminence of the danger. "When the court of Berlin becomes convinced that it has need of us to defend it from outside enemies as much as we have need of it, then there will no longer be a question of wishing to impose upon us a bargain and we could succeed in understanding each other."[14] Any attempt to win Prussian support at the moment would be interpreted as a sign that Austria was afraid that the storm was about to break and would thus increase Prussia's demands. On the other hand, by assuming an attitude of indifference, Prussia would be given time to reflect on her own dangers and would seek an *entente* with Austria without imposing conditions.

Thus Rechberg could see no immediate hope of getting Prussian or Russian support. As for England, her attitude was so unmistakably pro-Italian that even the basis for an understanding seemed to be lacking. Nevertheless, Rechberg explored the possibility of getting English support. He even tried to fan England's fear of an uprising in the Balkans by instructing Apponyi to point out to Russell how easily the principles employed in Italy could lead to the dismemberment of the Ottoman Empire.[15] But nothing would induce Russell to abandon the Italians. When asked if England would guarantee that Piedmont would not attack Austria and would promise not to intervene in case of such an attack, Russell replied that Austria could repulse the Piedmontese from her frontiers but if she crossed the Mincio and occupied Lombardy, it would mean war with England and France.[16] Rechberg regarded this reply as so manifestly hostile to Austria that he decided not to pursue the matter further.[17] In fact, he saw it as an open declaration that England would be lined up on the side of Austria's enemies.

There remained the possibility of coming to an agreement with Napoleon, whose attitude toward Austria had become decidedly more friendly since the annexations. Rechberg saw that the Roman question could be utilized for this purpose.[18] While Napoleon would not lift a finger to restore the territories lost by the Papacy, he was firmly opposed to Rome as the capital of Italy. He insisted, however, that the Pope institute reforms in his administration and desired to come to an agreement with Piedmont which would enable France to withdraw her garrison. Austria, on the other hand, upheld the Papal claims to the lost territory though she carefully refrained from active interference and raised no objections to the French occupation of Rome.

It was France, however, who took the initiative in suggesting an understanding. Persuaded that the moment had come for Austria and France to concert measures in dealing with the Roman question, Thouvenel proposed an arrangement calling for the organization of an army by the Catholic powers of secondary rank, the withdrawal of the French and Austrian garrisons, the contribution of a subsidy to the Papacy by all Catholic states, the guarantee of the remaining Papal territory, and the institution of reforms by the Pope.[19] In his reply to these proposals, Rechberg stated that while he would be glad to concert measures with France, there must be absolute silence on the question of the Romagna.[20] He agreed with the suggestion to withdraw French and Austrian troops and promised to give the proposals further consideration. Thouvenel's plan, however, was wrecked by the attitude of the Papacy. He was informed by the Papal Government that it would institute reforms when it saw fit, that it would accept no restrictions on its right to enroll soldiers anywhere, that it would accept subsidies only as compensation for annates and ancient canonical rights over vacant benefices, and that it would not accept a guarantee for the remaining territory since this would legitimize those annexed to Piedmont.[21] This obstinacy on the part of the Pope, coupled with the threatening situation in Sicily, made it impossible to proceed further, but the friendly manner in which Rechberg had received his proposals encouraged Thouvenel in the hope that an understanding with Austria on all essential questions was possible.

Meanwhile, a revolt had broken out in Sicily. The ruler of the Kingdom of the Two Sicilies, Francis II, successor to the notorious Ferdinand II, was a young man dominated by a camarilla and ill-equipped for the position. On May 5th Garibaldi and his Redshirts left Genoa and the government of Piedmont made no attempt to stop him. Indeed, Cavour gave the impression of condoning the expedition but was warned by Thouvenel of the responsibility incurred by Piedmont and asked to issue a disavowal. This Cavour did in a statement which appeared in the *Gazette Officielle* on the 18th. A few days before this he had asked England and France to mediate between the Neapolitan Government and the insurgents but Russell had demurred, maintaining that it was necessary to await developments.[22] With the arrival of Garibaldi at Palermo, the Neapolitan Government appealed to the powers to guarantee the dynasty and the integrity of the Kingdom and to send naval forces to prevent the invasion of its territory.[23] This appeal produced no results, however, and on June 1st the Neapolitan Government requested the mediation of Napoleon, who replied that before accepting it would be necessary for him to consult with England and Piedmont.[24] He suggested three bases for mediation: the separation of Sicily from Naples, under a branch of the Neapolitan dynasty, the granting of constitutions to both Naples and Sicily, and an alliance between Naples, Sicily and Piedmont.[25] Russell, who was asked by Persigny on June 5th if England was willing to collaborate, indicated his opposition by invoking the principle of non-intervention.[26] Cavour was also opposed, regarding Napoleon's bases as too favorable to Francis II.[27] Pressed by Thouvenel, however, he promised not to work against mediation at London.[28] Thouvenel warned him that Austria, Prussia and Russia would not tolerate violations of international law and that Piedmont must refrain from giving encouragement to Garibaldi.[29]

The position adopted by France in the Neapolitan affair was far from pleasing to Cavour. As conditions for an arrangement with Francis II he insisted that there should be no alliance or preliminary agreement until hostilities ceased, no intimacy with Austria, and a common attitude toward Rome[30] At the urging of Thouvenel, Neapolitan plenipotentiaries left for Turin with instructions to conclude an alliance designed to protect the independence of Italy against any foreign attack or influence.[31] Cavour now found himself facing a dilemma. "If we agree to the alliance," he wrote to Villamarina, "we are lost. If we reject it, what will Europe say? In all my life, I have never been more embarrassed."[32] Fortunately for Cavour, England's proposal for a truce tied up the alliance negotiations, while Garibaldi's progress brought on a dangerous situation. Under pressure from Russia, Napoleon asked England to join France in sending naval squadrons to the Straits of Messina in order to intercept passage but Palmerston refused to intervene.[33] Napoleon saw that there was nothing he could do without alienating England. Garibaldi completed the conquest of Sicily, crossed to the mainland and on September 7th entered Naples in triumph.

If the policy of non-intervention prevented a break with England, it also gave encouragement to revolutionaries, not only the Italians but the Hungarians and the Poles as well. Never, according to Metternich, was the agitation so great and never had he heard so much criticism of Napoleon's policy in conservative circles.[34] The announcement that Napoleon would visit the Prince Regent at Baden-Baden, coming at such a time, naturally evoked Austrian suspicions. Metternich was convinced that the Emperor would bring up the question of revising the treaties of 1815 and that while the Prince Regent was too honest to enter into such ideas, he was too weak to give explanations "concerning the duties of a prince of an old house."[35] He was instructed to learn the purpose of the interview. "There are," wrote Rechberg, "persons in the entourage of the Prince Regent who will be ready, I fear, to purchase the realization of the Prussian ideas of aggrandizement and exclusive influence in Germany at almost any price. These persons will easily make a bargain with the Emperor Napoleon, who is only too well disposed to favor anything which furnishes him the occasion of fishing in troubled waters. Whatever assurances there might be in the personal character of the Prince Regent, he will permit himself to be easily influenced. . . ."[36] Rechberg saw that Austria was practically isolated in the Italian question, powerless to act in defense of Naples, and compelled to look on helplessly while the revolution continued its onward course and threatened to strike, sooner or later, at Venetia. It was necessary, therefore, to keep Napoleon in an anti-revolutionary policy and to bring the English Cabinet to reason although Rechberg admitted that this would be virtually impossible so long as Palmerston and Russell maintained their present attitude. In the meantime, there was nothing Austria could do, at least until the Papal States or Venetia were directly attacked.

Rechberg's fears concerning the meeting at Baden-Baden were greatly exaggerated. Neither Napoleon, who had requested the interview for the purpose of removing German suspicions of his Rhine plans, nor the Prince Regent, who had no desire to be accused of entering into a private understanding with France and for this reason invited other German princes to attend, considered the moment propitious for making a bargain. The Emperor, who arrived on June 15th, assured the Prince Regent that he had no designs on German territory and that the annexation of Nice and Savoy should not be regarded as a precedent.[37]

At Fontainebleau Metternich had a long conversation with the Emperor during which he brought up nearly all important questions.

His Majesty listened in such a benevolent manner and replied to all questions with such a tone of frankness, that I employed logic, multiplied my arguments, and tried to make the chords of his true interests vibrate although long experience had proved to me that logic is powerless toward such a character, that arguments have value only when they come to the support of his desires and, finally, that his chords do not vibrate when his mind remains quiescent.[38]

Napoleon admitted that it was natural for Austria to dislike the policy he had followed in Italy but insisted that it was dictated by necessity. He repeated his favorite phrase: "I wish to get out of the scrape in Italy and leave the Italians to themselves." Metternich concluded that Napoleon's sympathies for Italy had cooled considerably. This seemed to be confirmed by Thouvenel's statement that at the Council of Ministers the Emperor had charged him to address a note to Turin that France would abandon Piedmont to her fate if she attacked Venetia.[39]

Though he was by now accustomed to the French policy of blowing alternately hot and cold, Metternich was convinced that Napoleon considered only his own interests, and that if he agreed to support Austria in Italy, the Balkans or Germany, it would be for whatever advantage he could get for himself. "I have no need to add," he wrote to Rechberg, " that it is never a question of principles, a rule of logic, European law or the treaties which motivate him. The interest of the moment, that is all!"[40] On the other hand, there was no reason to suppose that the Emperor was more hostile toward Austria than he had been previously or that he was directing his hostility toward her alone. Thus, while Russia was permitted to carry on intrigues in the east, she probably had not obtained more for her troubles than Austria. Not only that, but Napoleon was actually threatening her with the Polish question, holding it over her head like the Sword of Damocles. As for Piedmont, "I doubt that Victor Emmanuel and Cavour are anything else than puppets in his hands; and he will let them fall when it pleases him."[41] While Napoleon protected everything that was bad, everything that represented revolution outside France, he was still under the pressure of men at home and when the moment arrived, would be able to "break his chains." In presenting these views to Rechberg, the Ambassador argued for an understanding with France concerning a definite object. He pointed out that Napoleon could not understand a state like Austria which maintained a reserve on all sides. If she would only take a definite line of action in order to show that she really desired something; if she would involve the French Emperor in an affair from which he could profit, then he would understand her. "Then you will see, M. le Comte, with what zeal, what insistence and what talent for intrigue he will second us in regard to what we demand of him."[42]

This suggestion for an understanding met with a cool reception in Vienna. While Rechberg agreed that the French Emperor acted solely from motives of self-interest and was not at the moment hostile to Austria, he had no desire to repeat the experience of the previous year. The most that Austria could hope for was to maintain such relations with France as to avoid not only a rupture but a cooling off.[43]

Having turned down the suggestion for an understanding with Napoleon, Rechberg resumed his efforts to win Prussian support. He was informed by Werther, the Prussian Ambassador at Vienna, that Berlin demanded as the price of an agreement the alternation of the Presidium in the Federal Diet, the exclusive right to garrison Mainz, and Austrian support in the Holstein question.[44]

Invited by Franz Joseph to discuss the possibility of an alliance, the Prince Regent suggested a meeting at Teplitz. A memorandum intended to serve as a guide for the Austrian ruler was prepared by Baron von Biegeleben, referent for German affairs in the Foreign Office and Rechberg's chief rival.[45] On July 26, 1860 the two German rulers and their foreign ministers met at Teplitz.[46] Although the discussion covered all points at issue between the two states, the Prince Regent refused to give a written guarantee of support in the event of an attack by France. Instead, he gave Franz Joseph a verbal promise that Prussia would come to Austria's aid. The failure to reach a more conclusive agreement was due to the refusal of Franz Joseph to concede the Prussian demand for an alternation in the Presidium at Frankfurt.[47] A draft of a secret treaty was drawn up which was to be the subject of further negotiations.[48] The Teplitz meeting did little to improve Austria's position and left her no stronger than before to challenge France and the revolution.

Although the Teplitz affair followed closely on the heels of his journey to Baden-Baden, it alarmed Napoleon, who saw himself the object of distrust from all sides. Palmerston was uttering loud threats of forming an alliance against him, Franz Joseph and the Prince Regent were drawing together, and even the Tsar was beginning to entertain suspicions of France. "Everyone," he complained to Metternich, "distrusts me."[49] It was for this reason that he could not take the initiative in convoking a congress of the rulers. With a show of irritation, he declared that if instead of such a congress a coalition appeared, France would be forced to throw herself into the arms of the revolution.[50] Alarmed by Garibaldi's invasion of Sicily, the conservative powers blamed Piedmont for having tolerated it and were suspicious of Napoleon's policy. And while England favored Piedmontese success in Naples and Rome, she was opposed to an attack against Venetia.[51]

Following Garibaldi's conquest of Naples, it was feared that Rome would be his next objective. Aware that an attack against the Eternal City would lead to a clash with the French troops stationed there, Cavour took immediate steps to prevent him from carrying out his threat. He sent Farini, Minister of Interior, and General Cialdini to inform Napoleon of the urgent necessity of stopping the Red Shirt leader.[52] The Emperor agreed not to oppose a Piedmontese army sent to Naples and not to allow Austria to intervene but he advised haste. It was evident, however, that Naples could be reached quickly only by crossing the Papal States.

Rechberg, who was aroused by rumors of the Piedmontese plans, hinted at the possibility of intervention and asked France to give Austria a free hand in case of an attack against Venetia.[53] Thouvenel asked Napoleon, who was visiting southern France, for instructions. The Emperor replied by telegraph from Marseilles on September 8th. "In reply to the dispatch from Vienna, here is my idea. If Austria is unjustly attacked, I will not defend Piedmont; but if, after a victory, Austria violates the treaty of Villafranca, I will take the part of Piedmont. As to the latter, I wish to write to the King as follows: 'I am forced to acquaint you with my intentions: if, as Farini said, your troops enter the Papal States only after an insurrection, and to restore order there, I have nothing to say; but if while my soldiers are at Rome, you attack the Church's territory, I shall be compelled to withdraw my Minister from Turin and place myself in opposition.' "[54] Napoleon ordered reinforcements to Rome but these were confined to the protection of the city. Piedmontese troops under the command of General Cialdini crossed the Papal States on their way to Naples.

The Pope was convinced that Napoleon had entered into an agreement with Victor Emmanuel which tolerated the presence of Piedmontese troops in Umbria and the Marches.[55] This opinion was shared by members of the diplomatic corps in Rome, while the Piedmontese troops openly proclaimed it. General Cialdini declared to Prince de Ligne that Napoleon had given his approval of the crossing of the Church lands.[56] Though by no means unfriendly to the Italian cause, Thouvenel was a stickler for form and threatened to resign if the Emperor did not recall his representative from Turin. "He is certainly not the best of ministers for us," wrote Nigra to Cavour, "but he is a thousand times preferable to Walewski, Persigny and even Drouyn de Lhuys. We should thus avoid provoking discord between him and the Emperor. That is why I strongly insist on being recalled."[57] Realizing the need of registering an official protest against the invasion of the Papal States and of silencing rumors of his own complicity in the matter, Napoleon recalled Talleyrand from Turin, while Nigra took his departure from Paris. In October, following the annexation of Naples to Piedmont, Russia broke off diplomatic relations with Turin, while Prussia merely entered a formal protest.[58] The Tsar, who was much interested in the fate of Naples, did not regard with equanimity the indirect encouragement which Napoleon gave to the revolutionary movement. He invited the Emperor of Austria, the Prince Regent and Thouvenel to a conference at Warsaw in order to reach an understanding on the Italian problem. Thouvenel declined the invitation but agreed to have Napoleon write his views to the Tsar, who would present them to the conference.

Seeing that England's suspicions were aroused by the prospect of an Austro-Russian *rapprochement*, Rechberg gave instructions to Count Mensdorff, who was sent to felicitate Queen Victoria on her visit to Coburg. In these he directed Mensdorff to explain to Russell, who accompanied the Queen, that there was nothing in the *rapprochement* to harm England's interests.[59] "Of all the political combinations," wrote Rechberg, "the most dangerous for the peace and independence of central Europe, will be an intimate alliance between Russia and France. The price of such an alliance can only be the Rhine, on one side, and Constantinople, on the other. To prevent this combination, which would destroy the political equilibrium of Europe by increasing the two great military empires of the east and the west, appears to be an interest which is common to Austria and England. And it is precisely this interest that we pursue in seeking to ameliorate our relations with Russia." England need have no fear, continued Rechberg, that Austria would sacrifice the integrity of the Ottoman Empire in order to be on good terms with Russia. In giving these explanations Rechberg was merely abiding by an understanding which he had made with Russell in the previous year. According to this, the two powers promised to keep each other informed of any proposals which would affect the balance of power in Europe or tend to a change in boundaries.[60]

Many journals spread the report that Austria, Prussia and Russia were about to revive the Holy Alliance and that they would intervene in Italy. Cavour was greatly alarmed. "I do not think it will be impossible," he wrote to Prince Napoleon, "that Austria will obtain the consent of Russia and Prussia in order to attempt a *coup de tête* in Italy. The moment will be badly chosen for us; for a portion of our army will be found away from the theater of war."[61] Prince Napoleon urged Piedmont to take no action against Venetia and Rome but to suggest the idea that the Pope remain the spiritual leader of Rome which he would visit fifteen days in the year, and become temporal ruler over Elba or Sardinia with a guarantee and a large civil list.[62] "The Emperor is indecisive, fluctuating, well-disposed at bottom, but shaken, badly counselled. Thouvenel is not too bad, public opinion is very favorable for Piedmont."[63]

Actually there was little danger of an Austrian attack. Internal difficulties prevented Austria from engaging in a struggle with Piedmont. The unrest among her subject nationalities, particularly among the Magyars, became so menacing that Franz Joseph was compelled to make concessions. On October 20, 1860 he issued a Diploma promising a federal constitution. The Magyars, however, were not satisfied and the unrest continued. Any single-handed intervention in Italy was out of the question. If Piedmont were to be checked, it would be necessary for Austria to have the active support of Prussia and Russia. But on this point Alexander II had given assurances to Napoleon that the Warsaw meeting was not for the purpose of forming an alliance. It was known that Gortchakoff was still francophile at heart and that he hoped to find a way of bringing France in line with the conservative powers. He is reported to have said to Bismarck: "Now is a very important moment; it is necessary to make France feel that a continental coalition is on the verge of being concluded and that it merely depends on Russia to make it with or against France."[64] If Napoleon refused to break with revolution and join the conservative powers, Gortchakoff hinted that Russia might conclude a treaty with Austria and Prussia. This threat, however, had been uttered on the eve of the Piedmontese invasion of the Papal States and at a time when Russia was trying to bring pressure on Napoleon. Thun, the Austrian Ambassador at St. Petersburg, had no faith in the Russian Chancellor and feared that he might work against the Warsaw meeting in favor of a direct understanding with France. It was significant that hardly a day passed when Gortchakoff did not have a long conference with Montebello, the French Ambassador, while he maintained an air of profound mystery toward Thun.[65] What Gortchakoff really wanted was a European congress at which he would occupy the center of the stage.

The idea of playing a preponderant role in a European congress, of seeing his signature on an act destined to replace that of 1815, has always had a great attraction for his personal vanity. Besides, Prince Gortchakoff is too much imbued with liberal ideas, as he himself says, and too much a partisan of a liberal, progressive policy, to take any account of sacred principles and acquired rights. He even considered the dynastic changes in Italy as absolutely indispensable; finally, he openly hopes for good by cooperating with France and has no other desire than to isolate England. And could not a statesman of his importance, according to his own conviction, achieve this result in a congress where he would have a sufficiently vast terrain to make his indubitable superiority prevail over all other members?[66]

Thouvenel was also in favor of a European congress, it being one of the points suggested by Napoleon in his letter to Alexander II. When Austria and Spain proposed that France join in a plan to safeguard the Papal States, Thouvenel thought it would be better to await events before taking action. "What would you have us do," he asked the Spanish Ambassador, "when all Europe meets at Warsaw against us?"[67] Mülinen, the Austrian Chargé d'Affaires, got the impression that Thouvenel was afraid that France was about to be isolated.[68] In order to prevent this, the minister had said to Pourtalès that he would submit to Napoleon a plan for a direct *entente* with Austria. "We will be like witnesses to a duel, measuring the ground, challenging the arms of the adversaries, and giving Europe time to speak."[69]

No doubt Rechberg would have welcomed such an *entente* for the settlement of the Italian problem providing Napoleon was willing to follow conservative principles. But the Emperor's recent behavior had not been reassuring in this respect. Rechberg did not conceal his scorn for the feeble manner in which France had attempted to check Piedmont. He was convinced that this could have been done without the employment of force, merely by informing Victor Emmanuel that he was threatening interests which Europe could not permit.

Instead of an Austro-French *entente*, Rechberg preferred an *entente* of the four continental powers, Austria, France, Prussia and Russia. The idea of such a four-power arrangement had already been put forth by Gortchakoff, who believed it would be one way of binding Napoleon to break with revolution.[70] Rechberg saw an additional advantage, namely, that it would force England to yield in the Italian question. The French Ambassador to whom he mentioned the plan, received it with the utmost scepticism. "You desire, then, to see us break frankly and completely with England on the

Italian terrain and as compensation for the inconvenience which would result, you offer us a concert of the four great continental powers?"[71] The Ambassador wanted to know if this concert was about to take place, if Rechberg was in a position to guarantee it, and if Prussia and Russia held the same views of the Italian question as Austria. "I have always noticed much sympathy in the Prussian public for the Italian revolution and a possible intimacy between the Cabinets of Turin and Berlin. The latter has still more ties with England which you no doubt have taken into account. As to Russia, the language of the journals concerning Italian affairs is hardly in accord with your ideas and I cannot believe there is a complete community of views between you and the Cabinet of St. Petersburg."[72]

In advocating the four-power concert to deal with the Italian problem, Rechberg could hardly have expected Napoleon to join it at the price of renouncing his revolutionary principles, separating from England, and leaving Piedmont to her fate. It seems more likely that like Gortchakoff he hoped to intimidate France by hinting at the possibility of an agreement among the conservative powers. But Napoleon was no longer frightened by the nightmare of a revived Holy Alliance. He knew that there were too many obstacles in the way and, while his relations with Russia had become a little less intimate, they were still quite satisfactory. However dangerous the revolutionary movements, he could not renounce them so long as they served his purpose. To have accepted the conservative principles of law and order would have meant the *status quo* and the retention of Austrian influence in Italy.

On October 22nd the rulers of Austria, Prussia and Russia together with their foreign ministers convened at Warsaw for a four-day conference. This was the very day the plebiscite was held in Naples which favored annexation to Piedmont.[73] The situation in Italy had now reached a critical stage, for if the revolution was permitted to spread, not only would it engulf Rome and Venetia and lead to the outbreak of a European conflict, but it would threaten the monarchical principles to which the rulers gathered at Warsaw were devoted and might possibly bring about the collapse of the entire structure erected by the settlement of 1815. The conference therefore was of great importance to Austria. Should it result in an agreement of the three powers, she would then be able to face the future with greater equanimity. Rome and Venetia would be saved from the threats of Piedmont and the dangerous designs of England and France would be frustrated.

The nature of the Austrian hopes and expectations was clearly set forth in a memorandum which Rechberg prepared for Franz Joseph.[74] It began by describing the political situation in Europe as a spectacle of unspeakable confusion in principles and deplorable disorder in facts. This was attributed to "the false doctrines circulated by Bonapartism and the application which is made of them by a system of lies and hypocrisy . . . without parallel in history." Universal suffrage, upon which the Napoleonic Empire was based, was simply the right of the masses to overthrow the legitimate governments. Non-intervention was another false doctrine favoring the execution of Napoleonic projects. Was it not, asked Rechberg, the right of each independent state to call upon another for support in case of internal danger? Had France not intervened in Italian affairs by participating in the war of 1859? And did she not continue to intervene by her occupation of Rome? Moreover, Piedmont intervened with scandalous impudence in the affairs of other Italian states. Thus, the doctrine of non-intervention had come to mean that it was always permitted to intervene in favor of revolution but never in support of a legitimate power. Austria was particularly anxious to know what practical value Russia attached to the secret convention signed on October 15, 1833 at Berlin by which the three conservative powers accepted the principles of intervention. Russia's attitude toward this convention would indicate how far she would go in a joint action to check the progress of revolution and universal suffrage. Rechberg admitted that there was not much hope of success in this direction because Russia had already declared that the Holy Alliance no longer existed and that henceforth she would consult only her own interests. But was she not forgetting, he asked, that it was the permanent interest of every government to make the principles of justice and respect for treaties prevail in international relations? Did she not realize that in the absence of such principles all thrones would be endangered? And was it not evident that

Napoleon encouraged revolutions outside France under the guise of the principle of nationalities and humanitarian progress simply because he was always in need of something new in order to placate the French people and to prevent them from starting new revolutions at home by dangling before them the phantom of glory? "This fatal dilemma which faces the Emperor Napoleon makes it so that if Europe is not to resign itself to the consequences of the demagogic spirit, it will be compelled to join forces sooner or later . . . in order to offer a common resistance to the common enemy." Nor was Russia safe from this danger because the Polish question might one day arise to plague her.

Turning to the Italian question, the memorandum admitted that the agreements concluded at Villafranca and Zürich were practically dead letters. The disturbances in the Peninsula arose from the fact that while Napoleon pretended to dissuade Piedmont from violating these treaties, he actually permitted her to do so if he did not secretly encourage her. As to the congress of the powers which the French ruler suggested, what would be its task in view of recent developments in Italy? "Will it be convoked to sanction the *faits accomplis?* In this case it would irreparably compromise the dignity of the powers. . . ." On the other hand, if it were to recognize Italy on the basis of the terms agreed to at Villafranca, it would have to set forth as a condition *sine qua non* the territorial integrity of the Papal States and the restoration of the dispossessed rulers. But what chance was there of obtaining the consent of England and France to this condition? Was it not more likely that after conquering Naples, the revolution would strike at Rome and Venetia? "The issue of the struggle will then be in the hands of the gods. But if France under any pretext whatever comes a second time to the aid of the Italian revolution represented by Piedmont, it seems to me that the powers will at last be sufficiently enlightened concerning the final aim of Napoleonic policy. This will then be the decisive moment to make common cause against the common enemy. It will be of great importance to Austria to be informed of the attitude Russia expects to take in this eventuality."

Concerning Venetia, Rechberg desired to obtain Russia's adherence to the verbal agreement concluded at Teplitz between Austria and Prussia. By this the two German powers promised to make common cause in case of an attack on either one by France. In addition, Austria proposed that in the event of an attack by Piedmont against Venetia, the German Confederation should send an observation corps to the Italian frontier but on this point Prussia had reserved decision. Since the Teplitz conference the danger of a Piedmontese violation of Austrian territory had increased and, in the opinion of Rechberg, it was imperative to provide measures of defense. Russia shoud be asked to give material assistance.

Finally, the memorandum touched upon the eastern question. While both France and Russia worked to bring about the dissolution of the Ottoman Empire, the former sought to connect the Italian question with that of the east for her own profit. Napoleon realized that the program of liberating Italy from the Alps to the Adriatic would be facilitated if there was some way of offering compensation to Austria in the east. Rechberg doubted that there would be any discussion at Warsaw concerning the dismemberment of Turkey. It was more likely that Gortchakoff would bring up the question of abrogating the Black Sea Clause of the Treaty of Paris. Rechberg was quite willing to second this in return for Russia's support in Italy.

The memorandum left no doubt as to what Austria hoped to obtain from Russia. But would the latter forget Austria's "ingratitude" during the Crimean War? Was the danger of revolution likely to outweigh the particular advantages she might obtain by keeping in the good graces of Napoleon? And finally, would the conservative tendencies of Alexander II overcome his Chancellor's distrust of Austria and his attachment for France?

Much of the discussion at Warsaw centered upon four proposals submitted to the Tsar by Napoleon.[75] In the first of these the French ruler agreed to give no support to Piedmont should the latter attack Venetia provided, however, that the German states also maintained an attitude of restraint. The second proposal recognized the impossibility of reëstablishing the old order of affairs in Italy. "The guarantee against the return of that situation will be the maintenance of the bases agreed upon at Villafranca and stipulated at Zürich. Consequently, the cession of Lombardy cannot be questioned and

Italy will be constituted as a federal and national system under the protection of European law." The third proposal advocated a congress of the powers to arrange a final settlement of Italian problems; while the fourth insisted that the treaty by which Piedmont ceded Nice and Savoy to France must not be the subject of a discussion at the proposed congress even if Piedmont should lose those regions outside the provisions of the treaties of Villafranca and Zürich.

Rechberg's reaction to these proposals was not favorable inasmuch as they were based upon the assumption that an Austro-Piedmontese war was inevitable, an assumption which he refused to admit. "On the contrary," he wrote to Gortchakoff, "we think it will be worthy of the great powers to use their collective authority to prevent Piedmont from carrying out the aggressive projects upon which she meditates."[76] He added that Franz Joseph was ready to concur in any arrangements established either by negotiations or at a congress which guaranteed the execution of the terms of Villafranca and Zürich. In case of an attack by the united forces of Italy against Venetia, the German Confederation reserved the right to take such measures as provided by its constitution but a violation of the federal territory would *ipso facto* be the occasion of war.[77] Hence, the first proposal must be subject to reservations. The second was criticized because it was too one-sided. Regardless of the outcome of a war, Piedmont would be assured of Lombardy whereas Austria was asked to agree in advance not to draw any profit from victory. This would hardly be keeping the balance between the two states and would demoralize the Austrian army. As to the establishment of an Italian confederation, this would depend upon a satisfactory settlement of the boundaries. The proposal for a congress left Rechberg cold. He had never shown much enthusiasm for such gatherings and now he could see no sense in calling one if there was disagreement regarding the aims and the means of execution. The question to be decided was whether the powers upheld the treaties or recognized the accomplished facts. No objections were raised to the fourth proposal as Austria did not contest the acquisition of Nice and Savoy by France.

So far as the Italian problem was concerned, the Warsaw conference accomplished little or nothing toward its solution. Although Rechberg was far from satisfied with the French proposals, he did not reject them.[78] He agreed that they should serve as the basis for further negotiations whose aims were to be the prevention of war and the execution of the terms of Villafranca and Zürich. Realizing, however, that such negotiations were not likely to result in Austria's favor, he did nothing to promote them.

Most disappointing from the Austrian viewpoint was the failure at Warsaw to obtain from Russia and Prussia an acceptance of the principle of intervention. Whatever hope Rechberg had of reviving the Holy Alliance as a means of safeguarding the monarchical principle from the threat of revolution or of concluding a treaty of mutual assistance in order to prevent aggression by France and Piedmont was quickly dissipated upon his arrival at Warsaw. The Tsar was determined to maintain a strict neutrality so long as his own interests were not endangered, while the Prince Regent would act only in case of an Italian invasion of German territory. Prince Gortchakoff, who kept France informed of the proceedings, related to the Duke of Montebello that he had detected considerable distrust of Napoleon not only on the part of Austria but on the part of Prussia as well.[79] He attributed Prussia's distrust to the fear of French designs on the Rhine territory, a distrust which Russell had done his best to fan. "As to Austria, she arrived at Warsaw with unlimited hopes and the persevering intention of binding us by engagements which were inoffensive in appearance. She touched successively on the question of Venetia, that of Hungary, even that of the Rhine; but she obtained nothing. To everything we replied: it is a coalition that you propose to us and we do not want it, even under the eventual form in which you present it. Besides, a coalition will run counter to your aims: it will throw the Emperor of the French into the arms of revolution. Europe is sick, we regard it as you do but we believe that your remedy will hasten the crisis that you fear; we have a profound conviction that the Emperor Napoleon is the only individual with whom one can hope to escape from the chaos into which it threatens to fall."[80] Gortchakoff informed Rechberg that it was necessary to work with Napoleon and not against him if war was to be prevented. "We have removed from Austria all hope of material support from our part, and the

Emperor has declared that he will never lend his arms except for the interests of his Empire of which he desires to remain the judge. In a word, we have convinced Austria that she has no chance of drawing Russia into a coalition and that is the great result of the Warsaw conference."[81]

The failure of the Warsaw conference to sanction the principle of intervention was naturally pleasing to England, France and Piedmont. Cavour was much relieved, believing that Austria had been decisively outmaneuvered and attributing this to the firm attitude displayed by Napoleon.[82] The latter, however, did not seem much disposed to permit Piedmont to profit from the situation. When Hübner visited Paris in the latter part of October, he was received with much cordiality by the Emperor, who expressed a strong desire to maintain friendly relations with Austria.[83] Toward Piedmont, Napoleon was extremely bitter and even violent in his criticism of Cavour's conduct, which he characterized as folly, weakness and stupidity.

Metternich also, upon his return to Paris from his annual vacation, thought he detected a more cordial attitude toward Austria. Indeed, the Emperor almost immediately proposed an *entente* concerning the Italian question which he professed was necessary for the preservation of peace and the erection of a dike against the spread of revolution.[84] As the basis for this *entente,* which should be kept secret, he suggested the following points: (1) the two powers would announce their desire to avoid anything which would lead to a conflict between them, (2) non-recognition of what had taken place in Italy since the Zürich Treaty, (3) an understanding regarding effective means to prevent an attack on Venetia, (4) in case of an attack on Austria, the question of Lombardy would be left open and settled by a separate agreement with France, (5) Austria was to obtain the adherence of other powers to these bases, (6) the two governments would exchange declarations concerning the press and internal questions. Fearing that an incident might occur in Italy necessitating European intervention, Napoleon proposed a congress which should adopt as the basis for discussion the terms of the Treaty of Zürich. He insisted on the retention of Nice and Savoy but promised that he would seek no other acquisitions in Italy. Finally, he announced his willingness to support material action in Italy, providing this did not result in a break with England. He made it clear that he would not sacrifice the English alliance which he considered of vital importance.

In proposing the *entente*, Napoleon went out of his way to emphasize his good will for Austria. He was aware, he said to Metternich, that he was accused of systematic enmity toward her, that some people insinuated that he was trying to stir up revolutions in Hungary and Transylvania. "I need not say to you that these are lies invented by malevolent individuals who pursue me."[85] The Ambassador replied that the Austrian Government did not think of accusing him of such things but it wished to be enlightened about matters of greater importance.

Your Majesty knows that if we are attacked in Venetia, it will be impossible for us to take any engagements whatever either in regard to Lombardy or the conditions we would demand when the moment comes to make peace. We can admit only one thing, namely, that the balance between the two parties should be equal. The Emperor of Austria could not surrender in advance the liberty of action which international law accords to every belligerent power.

Napoleon agreed to this and stated that the question of Lombardy could only be settled by an understanding between Austria and France. Moreover, he acknowledged that Austria would refuse to recognize the changes brought about in Italy outside the treaties.

Satisfied that Napoleon really desired peace and was seeking means of preventing the outbreak of war between Austria and Piedmont, Metternich urged Rechberg to wire immediately whether or not to proceed with the negotiations as the situation could change almost any day. An understanding with France was worth the effort. "Today we know what we can expect from England, Prussia and Russia. If, by the means suggested, we could acquire some certainty regarding the intentions of Napoleon, it will, in my opinion, be a real advantage."[86] It was true, added Metternich, that one could not always take Napoleon at his word and that his indignation against Piedmont or his praise for the King of Naples must be taken with a grain of salt. And perhaps he had spoken so openly of European intervention simply because he knew that

England would oppose it. "But if he declares that he does not desire war with us, he knows quite well that public opinion in France will accept this declaration with enthusiasm and he has a great interest in spreading confidence if only to catch his breath. In any case, we risk nothing in having him promise us while our finances cannot become worse if we make the public believe that we are not about to have France on our backs."[87] As another inducement, the Ambassador mentioned that the attitude of Russia was rather disquieting. Concerning the Warsaw conference, Gortchakoff was reported to have said: "I was always opposed to the conference. I said that it was a mistake; they persisted and it took place but events have justified me. The conference resulted in drawing Russia and France a little closer. The recall of the Russian Legation from Turin signifies nothing—we are a thousand miles from wishing to prevent Italian unity." It was also rumored that Gortchakoff was conspiring with Napoleon in order to reconstruct Poland by depriving Austria and Prussia of their Polish territories and placing a grand duke over the new state. All the more reason, then, why the *entente* with Napoleon should not be delayed. The moment was opportune. Thouvenel's attitude was favorable though he did not believe that a congress could be summoned until the situation in Italy had become sufficiently anarchic to justify European intervention.[88]

Just what lay back of Napoleon's offer of an *entente* is hard to say. No doubt the difficulties in Italy, particularly the threat to Rome, was embarrassing in view of the attitude of the Catholic party in France. From the standpoint of European power politics, however, they were not unfavorable to the French Emperor. Every change in Italy represented a blow to the Vienna settlement of 1815. Austria, now the chief defender of that settlement, was forced to devote more and more attention to the Italian problem. Moreover, unlike the eastern question, Italy did not divide England and France. Russia could still be counted on to offer no real opposition, while Prussia would take no action so long as German territory was not threatened. The international situation could hardly be considered unfavorable from the vantage point of Paris. It is difficult to escape the conclusion that the Emperor's real purpose in proposing the *entente* was to involve Austria in further fruitless negotiations in order to play for time. This is evident also from the bases he suggested for the *entente*. While offhand they seem most generous, a closer examination reveals the very real difficulties they would have encountered at this stage of the game.

Metternich's eagerness for the *entente* was not shared by Rechberg, whose confidence in Napoleon was shattered by the experience of the previous year. What assurance was there that the result would be any different now? In 1859 Napoleon had backed out of his promises because of the material difficulties involved in executing the treaties. Was there any certainty, asked Rechberg, that he would now fulfill his promises when the difficulties to be overcome were even greater than before? The mere fact that he refused to break with England paralyzed in advance any engagements he might make with Austria.[89]

> To count on the assistance of France in order to reëstablish today a state of affairs in Italy based upon former treaties and upon the principles which we profess, will be to surrender ourselves to a dangerous illusion. In seeking this method it would not be long before we would be engaged in a course of transactions difficult to reject and impossible to accept. We would inevitably find ourselves facing the same danger if today we were to try to effect with the aid of a congress of the great powers that which we do not believe ourselves able to realize with the aid of France alone. We do not then desire the meeting of a congress; in general, we believe it our duty to remove from our present thoughts the idea of putting an end to the disorders already accomplished in Italy. We think it necessary to await a more opportune moment in order to act and any attempts of this kind will now be useless and will merely compromise the future.[90]

While Rechberg did not reject the proposal for an *entente,* he insisted that Napoleon must take the preliminary step of warning Piedmont of the consequences of an attack against Venetia and declare clearly and unmistakably if he was still in favor of realizing the Villafranca program or if he identified himself with the movement of Italian unification. "The traditions of French policy and the dynastic interests of the Emperor Napoleon operate in favor of the first alternative. His revolutionary instincts and passions recommend the other."[91] Hence, the question of forming an *entente* depended upon the policy Napoleon intended to follow. At the same time Rechberg saw that the two states did have certain common interests in the Italian problem. On military and religious grounds France could hardly favor Italian unification any more than Austria. For strategic reasons she desired to retain Nice and Savoy just as Austria intended to keep Venetia. Both obviously had an interest in maintaining the Papacy. "The attitude Napoleon finally adopts toward Rome will be the touchstone of our future relations with France and will determine if an *entente* between us is possible or not."[92]

Thus, Rechberg left the matter squarely up to Napoleon. The question now was whether the latter would warn Piedmont and declare his support of the Villafranca program. Although Metternich's relations with the Emperor were such that he could broach even the most delicate subjects without giving offense, he knew that it would be no easy task to obtain a categorical declaration.[93] He believed that it would be a step forward if he could persuade Napoleon to issue a written statement indicating that France had not guaranteed Lombardy to Piedmont and that this was a matter which concerned Austria and France alone. Thouvenel had already assured him that no such guarantee existed. "The word 'guarantee,' " he said, "has never been pronounced or written."[94]

Invited by Napoleon to a hunt at Rambouillet, Metternich had the opportunity of chatting with him during the two hour journey from Paris. He discovered that the Emperor had not changed either for good or evil.

He is embarrassed by the Italian question and as always, he arranges to leave all doors open. He said about himself, and I found this admission curious: 'I am reproached for having two policies; it is true. I am obliged to have two since I cannot be reactionary in view of my origin, and I cannot be revolutionary because of the danger it has for me. I cannot fight Piedmont for the cause of the Pope or Austria, and I cannot direct my arms against Rome and no longer wish to direct them against you.'[95]

Metternich did not believe that the Emperor was really hostile toward Austria. Indeed, if she succeeded in recovering her strength, he might actually begin to court her in his own interest. On the other hand, it could not be said that he cared for Austria, for he did not care for anyone, not even for Piedmont.

He wishes to reign, to live and continue to live, and he employs the means he judges proper in order to maintain himself in power. If he is mistaken, he will employ others . . . He does not admit principles, he does not admit rights; he admits success. There is no doubt about it, and if we do not implore his support before victory, he will propose it to us afterwards. Let us first triumph at home, then in Italy, without disturbing him too much, but let us be clever and prudent when we chant victory.

Metternich concluded from his conversation that while Napoleon did not know what he really wanted in Italy, he no longer smiled on unification and would hardly wage another war in its behalf. As for the *entente* with Austria, there was no hope of getting the Emperor to take the initiative and still less chance of persuading him to issue a written declaration regarding Lombardy.[96]

Once again the prospect of bringing Austria and France together on the Italian problem failed to materialize. Rechberg was by no means disappointed, for he had placed little stock in Napoleon's protestations of good will. Nor did the latter's admission that he pursued a double policy tend to increase the minister's confidence. How could one think of establishing an *entente* with a man who was unable to make up his own mind? This deplorable dualism, complained Rechberg, characterized all of Napoleon's actions but sooner or later he would have to choose between the two policies. For the moment the fear of avenging daggers outweighed the appreciation of dynastic interests.[97]

Meanwhile, events in Italy were taking their course. The soldiers of Victor Emmanuel joined the Redshirts of Garibaldi in Naples and Francis II with the remnant of his army fled to Gaeta where he was besieged. Napoleon decided that the time had come to act. The successes of Victor Emmanuel aroused considerable dissatisfaction in France, particularly in clerical circles. Bixio, the Piedmontese Chargé d'Affaires at Paris, reported to Cavour that the Empress spent her days "in tears, complaints and recriminations."[98] To quiet resentment at home, as well as to please the Tsar, who considered

Francis II his protegé, Napoleon sent a naval squadron to Gaeta and thus prolonged the siege.[99] This action, however, produced strong protests from England, which insisted upon non-intervention. Napoleon thereupon warned Francis II that he could do nothing more for him except to offer diplomatic support. An armistice was arranged but when this expired on January 9, 1861, Napoleon recalled his squadron and a few weeks later Francis II surrendered. The conquest of Naples was completed and Italian unification moved a step nearer to realization.

Rome and Venetia now remained as symbols of the hateful settlement of 1815. The former offered little chance of conquest so long as French troops were in occupation. Whatever his personal feelings toward the Papal States, Napoleon was too shrewd a stateman to alienate the Catholic world by permitting them to be devoured by the Italian nationalist movement. For the moment, at least, the Eternal City was safe. Venetia, on the other hand, seemed to offer more hope either of actual conquest or of voluntary relinquishment by Austria. At various times Napoleon had tried to induce Austria to consider an exchange of Venetia for compensation in the east but to all such efforts the Vienna Cabinet had turned a cold shoulder.

The possibility that Venetia would be the next goal of the Italian nationalists and thereby precipitate the outbreak of war increased the pressure on Austria. Early in November Cavour was informed by his representative at Paris that the Emperor had dined at the home of Princess Mathilde with Metternich, Kisseleff and Cobden and that the question of an arrangement relative to Venetia had been discussed.[100] Napoleon had not actually pronounced the words "cession" or "purchase" but had expressed the hope that a way would be found of reconciling Austria and Piedmont and that the great powers would prevent further bloodshed for a "lost cause." It was said that Metternich had been partly won over to the idea and that Cobden left for England in order to propose to the London Cabinet a plan for the cession of Venetia. Moreover, the Russian Ambassador had the air of believing that Austria would agree.

In St. Petersburg Gortchakoff broached the subject to Thun, the Austrian Ambassador.

I have reasons to believe that the greatest efforts will be made from all sides to engage you to cede Venetia in exchange for a large sum of money. This plan seems to be concerted between France and England and I am convinced that it is the principal reason for the nomination of an English Ambassador to Vienna. Lord Bloomfield will be instructed to spare no efforts to bring about this result during the winter and before war breaks out in Italy. This has been mentioned to me indirectly but you can be quite certain that you will never hear a word on this subject from us. I said to Count Rechberg at Warsaw that in my opinion if Austria did not exist, it would have to be invented for the tranquillity and equilibrium of Europe. I am equally convinced that Venetia is a necessity for Austria and for Germany in order that their southern frontiers will not be completely exposed. Thus, you have nothing to fear from our part on this subject.[101]

While Russia kept hands off, France and England endeavored to persuade Vienna to part with Venetia. A brochure appeared in France entitled: "L'Empéreur François-Joseph I et l'Europe," which proposed that Austria sell Venetia to Piedmont and at the same time purchase Bosnia and Herzegovina from Turkey.[102] This proposal was favored by Palmerston and Russell but vigorously opposed by Queen Victoria on the ground that it would encourage Piedmont to take aggressive measures.[103] Napoleon also considered it a good idea but refused to press it on Austria.[104] In any event, the Vienna Cabinet would not think of ceding Venetia and Rechberg cynically remarked that the proposal "offers us spoiled fish sweetened with honey."[105]

Although Austria's opposition was a foregone conclusion, Palmerston and Russell were reluctant to give up the idea of working out some sort of an arrangement concerning Venetia. Palmerston was particularly outspoken and in a letter to Apponyi declared that Austria hoped by means of Venetia to restore the situation in Italy as it was in 1858.[106] "Be convinced," he wrote, "that this idea is only a dangerous illusion which can never be realized. The division of Italy is a thing relegated to times past and can never be re-established. Italy will never permit it, France will not permit it, and I am convinced that England will not permit it." Apponyi replied that any discussion concerning Venetia was futile as Austria would not give it up voluntarily. "You regard Italian unity as an irrevocable fact. I would not allow myself to contradict a man of a political experience as accomplished as yours. I can only ask you to note that hardly eighteen months operate in favor of your thesis, while fifteen centuries contradict it."[107]

Russell tried to break down Austria's resistance and urged Clarendon to undertake a mission to Vienna with the object of proposing the sale of Venetia to Piedmont.[108] Upon hearing of this, Apponyi addressed a letter to Clarendon pointing out that it would be a mistake for him to go to Vienna as it would lead to a misunderstanding.[109] Clarendon replied that he had never thought and could not think of being charged with such a mission.[110] He admitted, however, that the subject had been raised. Later, in a conversation with Apponyi, he explained the matter more fully.[111] He had received a letter from Russell informing him of disturbing reports concerning Austria's declared intention of holding Piedmont responsible for any attack of volunteers coming from Italy and directed to any point whatever of her territory. Russell considered the Austrian declaration as dangerous and insisted that something would have to be done to deter the Vienna Cabinet from it. He therefore proposed that Clarendon accept an official mission to Berlin whose aim would be to compliment the King of Prussia on his accession to the throne and to return by way of Vienna where he could see Franz Joseph and confer with Rechberg. While in Vienna he would seek to dissuade Austria from her avowed intention of holding Piedmont responsible for the attack of volunteers, press for reforms, and treat confidentially on the question of ceding Venetia. Clarendon admitted that he was tempted by the proposal but after giving it some thought, decided to decline.

Looking back, one feels that it would have been wiser for Austria to have accepted an arrangement concerning Venetia. Financially, the addition of twenty or thirty million pounds sterling, the figures Russell had in mind,[112] would have been a boon to the Austrian treasury. An exchange of Venetia for Bosnia and Herzegovina, providing Turkey was agreeable, would have avoided considerable difficulty in later years. It is easy to speculate on such possibilities.

In the 1860's, however, before the disaster at Sadowa, Austria still regarded herself as an Italian as well as a German power. Franz Joseph would never have thought of giving up Venetia, the brilliant jewel of his heritage. His honor, the honor of a Hapsburg, simply would not permit it. From his viewpoint, this was a purely internal question, not to be discussed by others.

CHAPTER ELEVEN

Recognition of the Kingdom of Italy, 1862

THE HIGH HOPES which Prince Metternich entertained when he began his mission in August 1859, of establishing a close understanding with France, were still far from being realized. For a fleeting moment success seemed to be within his grasp only to be dashed to the ground by the famous brochure the Emperor so unexpectedly launched upon a troubled Europe. Walewski, who had cooperated so faithfully and with such evident sincerity in promoting the understanding, had been summarily dismissed from his post as Foreign Minister. This was a severe blow to the Austrian cause which was not compensated for by Walewski's reentry into the Government in 1861 as Minister of State. Since Thouvenel's appointment to the Foreign Office, Metternich had met with little success. To be sure, the obstacles to be overcome were sufficient to dampen the hopes of the most optimistic champion of an Austro-French understanding. At the moment the two powers were separated in all the important questions of the day: Italy, Rome, Venetia, Germany and the Balkans. But it was not simply the number of divergencies which constituted a barrier to warmer relations. In the twentieth century England and France patched up their differences which were far more numerous. What kept Austria and France apart, aside from certain conflicts of interest, was the fundamental difference in principles: principles which were, indeed, diametrically opposed. When Metternich entered upon his duties in 1859, there seemed to be every reason to suppose that Napoleon had turned his back on revolution. The historic meeting at Villafranca was thought to be the turning point which would bring the erstwhile Carbonaro into the respectable circle of his fellow monarchs. Events had demonstrated the futility of such hopes.

Metternich was not one to be held back by difficulties. Despite his youth and lack of experience, he had a kind of dogged tenacity and a buoyant optimism which helped to offset his deficiencies as a diplomatist. Moreover, his intimacy with the imperial couple provided him with the necessary *entrée*. As it was, his desire to reach an understanding with France was as keen in 1862 as it had been in 1859. It now occurred to him that he might accomplish his purpose by making direct overtures to Napoleon and thus offset the opposition of Thouvenel. With this in mind, he drafted a confidential letter to Rechberg which he showed to the Emperor before transmitting it to Vienna. In this letter he set forth the desirability of an understanding and the obstacles confronting it. There was no question, he wrote, of a treaty between the two parties.[1] It would be enough if Austria and France would agree to certain general principles. The moment was opportune as there was a lull in foreign affairs. Austria was preoccupied with internal problems, while France awaited events. Would such an understanding be difficult to establish? "I do not think so," declared the Ambassador, "always admitting that we would meet here the same desire, the same good will, and the same frankness." Without an understanding circumstances could lead to new complications and again place the two powers in opposite camps. Hence, to be sure of the future, it was necessary to face the facts frankly, to attack the difficulties and, if possible, to foresee the events. The first step in this direction would be to set forth the principles which would guide the two governments in the face of future events. In the Italian question Metternich held that Napoleon would intervene only when it appeared absolutely necessary and would adopt a decisive attitude only if the interests of France peremptorily required it. It was far from the Emperor's thought to adopt a personal policy hostile to Austria. In eastern affairs the interests of Austria seemed to be in fairly close accord with those of France, while in Germany the situation made an understanding desirable. However, as these problems had not yet reached the stage where they could be settled, Napoleon did not find it necessary to take the initiative toward an understanding. "As for us," continued Metternich, "our policy is so simple and so natural that we lose nothing in issuing our profession of faith." Austria wanted the establishment of a durable state of affairs in Italy and a guarantee of peace which would enable her to complete the work of internal reconstruction. An understanding with France based upon a broad interpretation of the Treaty of Zürich would safeguard the dignity of both powers and would remove dangers and misunderstandings in case the Italian nationalists should have the folly to attack Austria. The situation was no less serious in the Balkans where revolutions in Serbia, Montenegro and Herzegovina would constitute a grave threat to Austria's security. What better guarantee of peace was there, asked Metternich, than a friendly understanding with France whereby the two governments would take it upon themselves to warn those who fomented disturbances and keep them within prudent limits? "Why should we not submit to the Emperor our desires and our way of thinking? His Majesty will accept our overtures or will advance arguments upon which they could be discussed confidentially. His Majesty has shown me too much personal confidence that I fear to be refused an attempt of this kind and I know enough of your good intentions to hope that you will give an indulgent reception to my sincere efforts at conciliation."

Such were the ideas set forth by Metternich. In submitting the draft of a confidential letter to Napoleon, he made it clear that the views were his own and that they might not be completely shared by his government. Hence, his overture was strictly unofficial. "The pleasure," he wrote to Rechberg, "that he (the Emperor) revealed in making small kitchen politics in secret, the complacence that he shows whenever it is a question of speaking behind closed doors, proved to me once more that this is the way it is necessary to act with him and I permit myself to call this fact to your attention. It is possible that it will profit us someday."[2] After reading the draft letter, Napoleon praised its amicable tone and said that he also desired a general understanding but saw difficulties in questions of detail. He then referred to the subject of alliances based on mutual interests and recalled that in 1854 he had taken the initiative of proposing one to Franz Joseph who, like himself, had mounted the throne on December 2nd after breaking the back of revolution. This analogy impressed the Emperor as significant. But his attempt to conclude a durable alliance with Austria had been frustrated. Again in 1859 he had proposed an alliance to Russia only to see it checked. Since then he had made numerous advances to England with no better results. Nothing remained then but to carry on alone. However, it was not because of these failures that he had not concluded an *entente* with Austria. Rather it was that the situation favored a policy of gaining time and awaiting future events. This was the policy each power had adopted for the moment. He had no desire to recommence 1859. At present it was necessary to maintain the *status quo* in Italy and to see what would happen there. He assured Metternich that he had abandoned his idea of a bargain concerning Venetia, for he realized that this would be out of the question for the time being. But he still felt that Austria would gain much by giving up Venetia in return for an alliance with France concerning the Balkans and an arrangement enabling her to intervene in Italy in order to restore the Papal States and the King of Naples. As for the idea of establishing in advance the bases for action to be taken in case of a revolutionary attack, this would be extremely difficult. Napoleon professed a desire to concert measures with Austria in the Balkans and hoped that she would try to reach an understanding with Serbia, Montenegro and Rumania. The discussion was confined to generalities as Metternich intended it to be. There were no specific proposals, no promises, and the confidences exchanged were entirely unofficial. But Metternich hoped that this overture would pave the way for an understanding which would guarantee peace between the two states.

Rechberg did not respond with much enthusiasm to these hopes. He dispatched two letters to Metternich: one apparently destined to be shown to Napoleon which expressed in generalities the desire for an understanding, and the other intended for the Ambassador himself.[3] In the latter, Rechberg approved the idea of dealing secretly with the Emperor in order to offset the unfavorable attitude of Thouvenel but he had no illusions concerning the practical value of this exchange of intimate communications.

I do not believe that this can bring a positive result other than that of flattering the inclination of the Emperor to make a personal policy behind the back of his minister. Besides, I do not know if we should desire that it be otherwise. We place much value in preserving the best possible relations with the Sovereign of France, but rather to prevent him from hurting us than in the hope of being actively aided by him. It seems improbable to me that France can free herself entirely from ties with the revolutionary party whether in the east or in Italy, in order to be able to reach an accord with us toward a definitive solution of the questions submitted to our examination. All that we can reasonably hope for at the moment is that the Emperor Napoleon does not encourage the secret intrigues of our mortal enemies and that he does not precipitate events in a sense opposed to our wishes. In directing his attention toward the possibility of a future *entente* with us, we offer sustenance to his covetous mind for schemes and we remove perhaps, for sometime at least, more dangerous ideas. In any case, I believe that we should maintain ourselves as long as possible on the basis of generalities and refrain from entering further into the examination of special questions.

Rechberg admitted that something might occur to facilitate an *entente* with France but until the moment was more opportune, Austria should avoid tying her hands. She was not now in a position to treat advantageously the questions which concerned her future and it was better therefore not to make engagements which might prove onerous when she recovered her strength and was able to exert a greater influence. There was still another consideration.

It is the absolute impossibility for us to associate ourselves in a policy which rests on the principle of nationalities. We can always show ourselves accommodating when it is a question of forming combinations on purely political calculations. We can rigorously support the momentary ascendancy of such and such a power and accept the territorial alterations which will be the consequence of it. But we can never consent to such alterations made in the name of the principle of nationalities for we would thus sign our own death warrant. This should be well understood whenever it is a matter of envisaging the different eventualities which a near future can bring forth.

Rechberg's skeptical attitude did not leave Metternich much upon which to proceed in his efforts to achieve an understanding with

France. Apparently all that he could do was to dangle the idea before Napoleon in order to keep him within bounds.

For the moment, the Italian problem continued to be the most disturbing factor in the relations between Austria and France. It was Rome rather than Venetia which occupied the attention of the statesmen during 1861. In a memoir which he addressed to Thouvenel in December 1860, Napoleon pointed out that Rome was the great obstacle to Italian independence and urged a reconciliation between Piedmont and the Papacy.[4] Although Thouvenel attempted to effect such a reconciliation in 1861, he failed because of the uncompromising attitude of the Papacy. In April of that year the Austrian and Spanish ambassadors at Paris submitted notes to the French Government proposing an understanding of the Catholic powers to protect the Papacy against any threat from Piedmont.[5] This proposal was rejected by Thouvenel, who declared that the Papacy had nothing to fear since the French garrison in Rome had been increased and would remain.[6] Despite the pleas of Prince Napoleon and the insistence of Piedmont, the French Emperor saw that there was no alternative for the maintenance of the *status quo.* His obvious reluctance to be drawn again into an adventurous policy aroused great dissatisfaction among the Italian sympathizers. Austria, on the other hand, was relieved by Napoleon's determination to keep the French garrison in Rome. From her viewpoint, Rome and Venetia constituted parts of one problem inasmuch as an attack against one would almost immediately endanger the other. For the defense of Venetia it was necessary to support the Papacy. No one believed that the Italian nationalists would remain content without Rome and Venetia and the opinion prevailed in some quarters that war was almost inevitable. At the end of December 1861, Cowley received from Russell a letter written by Palmerston in which the Prime Minister expressed the belief that Napoleon intended to go to war in the spring.[7] Palmerston predicted that France and Piedmont would attack Austria in Venetia, Dalmatia and Hungary. This would be followed by a French attack against Prussia on the Rhine and the outbreak of an insurrection in Poland. "The only thing we can do to avert these impending evils would seem to be to urge Austria and Prussia to acknowledge the King of Italy and to press Austria to cede Venetia for an adequate sum of money." Cowley was requested by Russell to give his opinion concerning Palmerston's letter, which he did in a memorandum of January 10, 1862. He declared that neither Napoleon nor his ministers were contemplating war, that a war undertaken for Venetia would be very unpopular in France, and in any case the money was not available.[8] Palmerston's letter reveals his distrust of Napoleon which was brought on, at least in part, by the events in Italy. Rechberg had been kept informed of Palmerston's views by reports he received from a secret agent, Mr. George Klindworth. The latter was a sinister figure in European diplomatic circles for nearly a half century.[9] The son of a mechanic, he studied at the University of Göttingen and later went to Berlin where he became the private secretary of the Portuguese Minister and through the latter made the acquaintance of a number of diplomats.[10] Later he was employed on secret missions by Count Apponyi, then Austrian Minister at Paris, Guizot, Prince Clemens Metternich, Manteuffel of Prussia, Gortchakoff and the King of Würtemberg. He was well known to Bismarck and King Leopold of Belgium and acted as a sort of middleman between Palmerston and Rechberg.[11] An extremely strange person, small in stature, ugly and neglected in appearance, dressed like an English dissenting minister, with a penetrating glance like a hypnotist— such is the description given of this secret agent of European statesmen.[12] Though aware that Klindworth was not wholly trustworthy and that he was capable of serving as a spy for anyone who paid him the price, Rechberg found it worth-while to employ him on a number of occasions.[13]

Early in January 1862, the French Government sought to reach an agreement with the Papacy concerning Rome. M. de Lavelette, the French Ambassador, was instructed to request the Papal Government to formulate its ideas of a future arrangement and he was to declare that Napoleon was not bound in any manner to Turin and was prepared to impose upon Italy any condition which appeared acceptable.[14] The Papal Government replied firmly but courteously that it would enter into no negotiations which had for their basis the cession of even a single village from the Roman territory.[15] This was equivalent to saying that the Pope would agree to negotiate only if his territories were restored.

The peremptory refusal of the Papacy to enter into discussions which would imply a recognition of the lost territories, produced a sensation in France. The clerical party took the position that after this refusal there was nothing for the French Government to do but to give back to the Pope all his possessions.[16] The pro-Italian party, on the other hand, argued that since the French overture had failed, it was absolutely necessary to put an end once and for all to the pretensions of the Papacy and to recall the troops from Rome. Under the circumstances the French Government decided to await a change in the Papal attitude before making further overtures. Thouvenel considered the Papal pretensions of regaining the lost territories as inadmissible as the pretensions of Italy to have Rome for the capital, both of which he consigned to the realm of impossibilities. The best scheme, he thought, would be an Italian confederation with a hereditary secular vicar to govern the Roman states for the Papacy.[17] Rome should become a free city like Frankfurt, garrisoned by Catholic troops. The Pope should retain his private possessions in Italy and elsewhere which would give sufficient revenue for his position. This plan, moreover, would offer the non-Italian cardinals a better chance of being elevated to the Holy See.

Thouvenel's manner of envisaging the Roman question found no favor in Vienna. The problem, according to Rechberg, was not a mere matter of a political combination or of momentary convenience.[18] It was far more important than that. Indeed, it was a matter of deciding if the temporal power of the Papacy was incompatible with the exercise of spiritual power, or if, as Austria firmly believed, it was indispensable for the independent exercise of the vast authority vested in the Pope as head of the Catholic Church. "In asking the Pope to recognize the *faits accomplis,* one asks him much more than a sacrifice of territory, for in yielding he will abandon the principle upon which the edifice of the Papacy has rested for centuries. We cannot believe that the French Government has any illusions concerning the real value of the theories emitted by M. de Cavour and his successors regarding a free church in a free state. No moral guarantee, no promise on paper could replace for the Papacy the independence which the possession of the temporal sovereignty assures it and a sovereignty not reduced to derisory proportions."[19] Rechberg instructed Metternich to make it clear to the French Government that Austria insisted upon the maintenance of the principle of the temporal sovereignty of the Papacy in all its extent and that she would reject any plan which did not have the spontaneous assent of the Holy See.[20]

This decisive attitude did not mean that Austria deluded herself with extravagant hopes of undoing what had been done in Italy or of regaining her former influence there.[21] The problem was how to prevent any further aggressions by Piedmont. Rechberg assured Gramont in the most positive manner that Austria had no belligerent intentions. "If Austria," he said "had had the thought of intervening in the affairs of Italy, she would have done so at the time of the invasion of the Roman provinces and the Kingdom of Naples; then the occasion was favorable; since she had not done so at that moment, it would be insane to wish to compromise her position today by an aggression which no new circumstance can justify."[22] But it was nonetheless true that the large army Austria was compelled to maintain by fear of an attack against Venetia, did make it appear that she contemplated aggression. Austria needed peace, however, perhaps more than any other power in Europe at the moment. The enormous task of reconstruction, the ever-present problem of finances as well as the threats from Italy, Germany and the Balkans, made peace an imperative necessity. Important in the eyes of the Austrian statesmen was the attitude which France would adopt toward the great problems of the day. Would Napoleon abandon his role of *l'enfant terrible?* That was the question. Austria needed time to put her house in order by conciliating the restive Magyars, by restoring her depleted finances, by reorganizing her armed forces. But would Napoleon give her the time necessary to accomplish all this or would he take advantage of her difficulties in order to launch another of his pet schemes? It was impossible to say. Metternich, whose intimacy with the Emperor afforded him an opportunity to discover the way the wind was blowing, admitted that for the moment the Napoleonic thought was unfathomable.[23]

One could not tell from the various declarations whether or not the French Government expected to evacuate Rome or desired the completion of Italian unification. Yet, the Ambassador was convinced of one thing: the internal consolidation of Austria, which would naturally increase her influence in international affairs, had made a profound impression in France and tended to improve relations with that state. Once the crown of Hungary had been placed on the head of Franz Joseph, Austria would be in a position to make her own terms with Napoleon. And the more Austria's prestige increased, the more that of Piedmont would decrease. "If the Emperor," wrote Metternich, "leaves us tranquil today this is certainly not out of sympathy for us. He knows too well that we form and will form still more his most formidable adversary, his political antipode."[24] It was Napoleon's habit to compromise with the opposition which was most dangerous for him. There was hope, then, that he would feel less inclined to take issue with a regenerated Austria. But Austria's enemies were not pleased to see her growing influence. In a speech before the French Senate on February 23rd, Prince Napoleon made a bitter attack against the Hapsburg Monarchy. Metternich handed Thouvenel a formal protest against the speech.[25] Napoleon expressed his regrets. "My cousin," he said to Metternich, "permits himself to be drawn along by his words to please a party with which I have nothing in common and whose gratitude and devotion are more than doubtful."[26] He then praised Austria's work of reconstruction and referring to the Italian question said: "I wish that the King of Naples were a man of action and would begin to head the militant reaction. I am pleased that Garibaldi has the cholera. I wish to know how to leave my embarrassment with Rome."[27] From these statements Metternich concluded that the Emperor had no interest in seeing the achievement of Italian unification, that he regarded the Garibaldi party as his most dangerous enemy, and that he did not know how to terminate the Roman question.

In several of his conversations with Metternich, the Emperor had expressed a desire for an understanding with Austria. The Ambassador had replied that such an understanding would depend on its aim. If it were a question of Germany, Poland or Venetia it would be difficult to achieve, but if Napoleon merely wished to declare himself in a conservative, anti-revolutionary sense toward Austria, there was no doubt that an understanding could be established. "The Emperor did not explain his real thought. He only said that the complications arising on all sides render an understanding necessary."[28] Another suggestion which Napoleon advanced was of a congress of the European rulers to reach a settlement of the difficulties. The idea was deeply rooted in his mind and he had mentioned it on numerous occasions in the past. It found no favor at Vienna where it was regarded as impracticable. As Rechberg pointed out, there was a profound difference between the situation in 1862 and that in 1815.[29] At the time of the Congress of Vienna all the governments were in agreement concerning the principles which would serve as the basis for the negotiations. Before the Congress met the statesmen knew the aim that would be followed and the directions the negotiations would take and it was only necessary to agree on the means of execution. Hence, it had been comparatively easy to reach an understanding. But such was not the case at the moment.

Today the most opposite principles and interests are found in conflict. The points of departure are so different that it will be scarcely possible to find a compromise satisfactory for all. The collision of opinions so contrary will soon lead to a rupture, at least since from one part or the other one cannot resign oneself to sacrifices too painful to be accepted without *arrière-pensées.* In one way or the other one will thus arrive at compromising much more than consolidating the peaceful relations of the governments and the tranquillity of Europe.

The uncertainty concerning French policy, as well as the lack of confidence in Napoleon and the dangerous potentialities in the European situation in 1862, kept the powers in a state of suspense. Especially in Austria was there an unwillingness to take positive action in the important problems of the day. Paris and Vienna were suspicious of each other's intentions. Rechberg had not forgotten the experiences of the past and was not disposed to go out of his way in order to assist Napoleon in finding a means of leaving his embarrassment. "Confronted by the heated complications that his policy has made or let grow," he wrote to Metternich, "exposed to the most contradictory demands invoked by the most opposite parties, attracted and repulsed in turn by the most diverse elements, the Emperor Napoleon seeks an issue or rather awaits that chance offers him one from which he can profit, in order that he can open a way across the difficulties which encompass him."[30] Not knowing where Napoleon would find this issue, Rechberg followed each of his moves with "scrupulous attention." He discounted reports from Metternich that the French ruler was on the verge of adopting a conservative policy.

We are too habituated, in fact, to sudden changes of Napoleonic policy not to require the most convincing proofs before believing in a complete conversion, I do not say to our ideas, but to ideas acceptable to us. The half-confidences which are made to us, the vague assurances that he desires an *entente* . . . finally, the official remonstrances he addressed without much effect to the court of Turin and to the Prince of Montenegro, all this does not suffice to inspire in us a positive confidence and to engage us to leave a prudent reserve. So long as French policy remains placed on a basis so shifting, we should guard ourselves from being drawn into its path in order to venture into the unknown by abandoning the principles which serve as our fulcrum and under the shelter of which we can, without too much inconvenience, watch the events come.[31]

Indeed, Rechberg declared that if Napoleon really desired an understanding with Austria he would have to make the first move and break definitely with the revolutionary party. The condition for an understanding concerning Italy was nothing less than a mortal blow directed against the idea of unity which constituted a permanent menace to Austria. Let Napoleon openly proclaim himself as opposed to Italian unification and he would find Vienna ready to join him. Or better still, let him come to the defense of the temporal power of the Papacy and Austria would be convinced of his good intentions. Rechberg was aware that in thus entrenching himself behind immovable principles, he was exposing himself to the charge of not profiting from the momentary good will shown by Napoleon in order to win him to the side of Austria at the price of some concessions, and that he might actually drive him into the enemy camp. However, he was convinced that this danger was less to be feared than that of delivering Austria into the hands of her enemies.

While Rechberg persisted in his distrust of Napoleon, there was some doubt in France concerning Austria's good intentions, particularly toward Italy. Had Austria really abandoned the idea of regaining her former influence in the Peninsula or did she cloak sinister designs behind her reassuring statements? Gramont, the French Ambassador at Vienna, tried to find the answer to this question. He saw that there were two different interpretations, each of which had its *raison d'être*.[32] According to the one, Franz Joseph had by no means renounced the thought of revenge. His present inactivity was simply the policy of watchful-waiting, traditional with the Hapsburgs, and was imposed upon him by the requirements of the internal situation. There was a large and influential group who made constant efforts to influence the Emperor along the ideas of reaction. According to the other interpretation, which Gramont himself believed to be the true one, Austria had definitely renounced the hope of regaining her influence in Italy and thus had broken with her traditional policy. Austria's attitude concerning Italy would be passive unless an attempt was made against Venetia. Gramont seemed to be absolutely convinced of this and expressed the belief that if Austria were compelled by the aggressive tactics of Piedmont to take action, she would first inform France of her intentions. But while the French Ambassador refused to accept the view that Austria entertained sinister designs on Italy, he was doubtful about her benevolence toward France. He learned that Klindworth was at the moment in the pay of Palmerston and was attempting to bring about an Anglo-Austrian *entente* regarding Italy and the Balkans directed against France.[33] Gramont related that Klindworth's negotiations were carried on behind the back of the English Ambassador to Vienna.[34] Klindworth was said to have declared to Rechberg that England's principal interest in Italy was to check the influence of France. Rechberg apparently made no attempt to reject Klindworth's overtures. According to Gramont, the latter had a number of interviews with Rechberg and Count Moritz Esterhazy, Minister without Portfolio, and had even been received by Franz Joseph.[35] Right in the midst of these secret doings, Palmerston made a speech in Parliament against the temporal power of the Papacy. This was hardly the right method to use if he was sincere in trying to reach an understanding with Austria. But like all other statesmen, Palmerston was no doubt sparring for time. Convinced that things would happen soon each power was busily maneuvering for a position which would give it the advantage.

At Paris the idea of an Austro-French *entente* on Italy found an ardent advocate in the Empress. She was impatient with the Austrian delay in reconciling Hungary—a problem in which she took a keen interest.[36] The sooner the Hungarians were pacified, she maintained, the sooner Austria would be in a position to cope with the difficulties in Italy and the east and to come to an understanding with France. Her dislike for Piedmont was revealed in a conversation she had with Nigra, the Piedmontese Minister, whom Metternich referred to as "this unfortunate representative of the pseudo-Italian Kingdom."[37] The Empress was not very cordial to Nigra. "Your Majesty," said Nigra, "is really too unjust and in order to defend myself I would ask if the King of Italy has not today done at Naples what the Emperor had previously done in France." These words made the Empress furious and she replied: "Oh, do not say that, do not compare the Emperor to your highwayman; the Emperor has robbed no one, he found France abandoned, the throne vacant, and he saved France by driving out men of your kind." Thereupon Nigra took his hat and dashed out of the room. Metternich standing nearby, overheard the conversation.

Hübner, the former Ambassador, who visited Paris in May 1862 had a number of conversations with leading figures and at the suggestion of Metternich sent his impressions to Rechberg.[38] He was told by Drouyn de Lhuys, who was soon to take up again the post of Foreign Minister, that Napoleon was "tormented" by his embarrassment in the Italian question.[39] Drouyn de Lhuys was very critical of the Emperor's Roman policy which he declared was dictated by fear of alienating the Catholic party on the one hand, and fear of vengeance from the revolutionary party on the other. But the Emperor had really lost all interest in Italy, which had become only a source of difficulty. Once Nice and Savoy had been acquired, Italian affairs filled him with disgust and he now had no other desire than to let the Italians "stew in their own juice." But in view of his great embarrassment, the Emperor required a success elsewhere and Drouyn de Lhuys believed that he would seek this in Germany or in the east. Prince Napoleon had recently tried to persuade his cousin to adopt a policy whereby France would withdraw her troops from Rome and thus enable Piedmont to squeeze out the Pope by degrees until nothing remained to him but "a palace and a garden with the right of extraterritoriality." Thiers, who was interviewed by Hübner, accused the Emperor of neglecting the interests of France.[40] Napoleon worked for the creation of a united Italy which could only become a natural enemy of France; he championed a united Germany under Prussian leadership which would constitute a perpetual menace to France; and in the east he weakened the Ottoman Empire which merely served the greed of Russia. In all three regions, according to Thiers, the interests of France were the same as those of Austria. Hübner summarized his impressions as follows.[41]

The Emperor is still much stronger in the country than the leaders of the old parties seem to think, except that his power is neither extended nor consolidated since the war.

But the real danger is not the weakness of his position in France; it is the loss of his credit in Europe and the consciousness of his isolation, of the gap he has created around him despite all the brilliance of his reign. For not being held back by any scruple he can, in order to leave his embarrassment, undertake anything, attempt anything and dare anything; there is only one thing he cannot do: he cannot give back to Europe the confidence lost in his loyalty; but without confidence no serious arrangement is possible. He is thus in the unfortunate position of men who are capable of anything but who are also capable of nothing.

Hübner's analysis of Napoleon's position did not differ in essentials from that contained in the reports of Metternich. That the Emperor was in a dilemma concerning the Italian question, he himself had admitted on a number of occasions. Pressed from both the conservative and revolutionary sides, it was difficult to take a decisive stand one way or the other. If he supported the conservative-Catholic group, he would alienate the liberal and revolutionary elements and vice versa. Better then to mark time and await circumstances which might extricate him from his embarrassment. While it was regrettable to see with what ease concessions could be obtained from the Emperor, to see the growth of the influence of Prince Napoleon, "it is very evident on the other hand, that neither the influence of Prince Napoleon nor the recent concessions of the Emperor have as yet won over the latter to make him leave this enigmatic calm and this indecision which forms the object of general distrust but which always permits us to hope that the definitive triumph of the revolution is not as near as the abettors and their dupes predict."[42] Two days after he had penned these words, Metternich learned from the Empress that Napoleon had written a letter to Victor Emmanuel in which he said: "Have no illusions, I will never abandon the Pope to his enemies."[43] Garibaldi had been laying plans for an invasion of Rome but was held back by this clear warning.

Though circumstances prevented the Emperor and his Foreign Minister from taking a decisive stand in the Roman question there was no doubt that their sympathies were on the side of Piedmont. Thouvenel was certainly pro-Italian and expressed himself strongly against the Papacy. He believed that a compromise was possible whereby Italy would guarantee Rome against invasion, while the Pope recognized the seizure of his estates.[44] Such a compromise, admitted Thouvenel, might be temporary but it would be a way out of the difficulties for the moment. Later, an arrangement could be concluded whereby Piedmont would undertake to guarantee Venetia to Austria. The idea of a compromise on the Roman question made a powerful appeal to Napoleon. Was it not, after all, only common sense that two parties so diametrically opposed in their views, so absolute in their hatreds, and so deaf to all appeals to the common welfare, must make concessions in order to reach a settlement? Napoleon declared that it had been his constant aim in the Italian question to support the national aspirations and to persuade the Pope to support them rather than hold out against them—"in a word, to consecrate the alliance of religion and liberty."[45] But his efforts had failed; each party substituted its own exclusive sentiments for the true principles of equity and justice. Thus, one of them forgetting the recognized rights of a power which had endured ten centuries, proclaimed without regard for a consecration so ancient, the dethronement of the Pope; the other, careless of the legitimate claim of popular rights, condemned without scruple a part of Italy to an immobility and an eternal oppression. It was the duty of statesmen to study the means of reconciling the two causes and even if reconciliation proved impossible of achievement, the attempt would be worth-while. At least there would be the advantage of proclaiming the aim toward which it was necessary to work. And what was this aim? It was to persuade the Pope to adopt modern ideas such as the right of national self-determination, and to persuade the Italian people to recognize as salutary the temporal power of the Papacy whose influence extended over the entire globe. To be sure, it seemed hopeless to obtain such mutual concessions considering the prejudices and the bitterness involved, but might not circumstances, might not self-interest oblige the two groups to effect a reconciliation? It was the first interest of Italy to remove the dangers which threatened her, the enmity which she had aroused, in fact, everything which opposed her legitimate ambitions to reconstruct herself. Italy was a new state and thus had against her all those who clung to the institutions of the past. Having called revolution to her aid she naturally inspired distrust among all men of order. Moreover, she had at her very gates a redoubtable enemy whose strong army would constitute an imminent danger for a long time. And to cap it all, she had earned the enmity of the Catholic Church and hence of Catholics all over Europe. Certainly it was to Italy's interest to pacify the Church. But it was no less the interest of the Church to be reconciled with the Italian people. Did the Church not have against it all the liberals of Europe? Was it not regarded as the representative of the old regime, the most devoted partisan of reaction? Many sincere Catholics who had accepted modern ideas, declared Napoleon, were alienated by the attitude of the Papacy. "The interests of the Holy See, that of religion, thus require that the Pope be reconciled with Italy; for this will mean to be reconciled with modern ideas, to retain in the bosom of the Church two hundred million Catholics and to give a new lustre to religion by showing faith supporting the progress of humanity!" Napoleon's plan of reconciliation was simple: the

Pope should accept everything which would attach him to the rest
of Italy, while the latter should adopt guarantees necessary for the
independence of the Papacy and its free exercise of power. But in
order that the Pope be master in his own states, his independence
should be assured and his power accepted freely by his subjects.
In other words, Napoleon demanded that the Pope carry out certain
reforms in government. Proposals were drawn up and sent to Rome
and Turin. These called upon the Papacy to renounce any rights to
the lost provinces while demanding that Italy abandon her pretensions to Rome and promise to respect its territorial integrity under
the Papacy. The major part of the public debt of the Papal Government was to be borne by the Kingdom of Italy. France agreed to
take the initiative in securing from the signatory powers of the
Treaty of Vienna a guarantee of the territory which remained under
the control of the Papacy. She also agreed to propose to the Catholic
powers a civil list for the Pope toward which she would contribute
three million francs annually. The question of reforms was not to
be insisted upon since the Pope was the only judge of their opportuneness. In replying to these proposals, Cardinal Antonelli, the
Papal Secretary of State, declared that the Pope would never renounce the territories taken by force and would refuse a civil list.[46]

The attitude of the Papacy was but one more indication of the
futility of trying to settle the Roman question by means of an
understanding between Rome and Turin. Meanwhile, with the departure of Prince Napoleon for Italy, the influence of the Empress
over Italian policy increased and she was able to obtain from
Napoleon a promise not to abandon the Pope, to guarantee the latter
his present possessions, and to engage the great powers to join
France in this guarantee.[47] To the Papal Nuncio the Emperor said
that he would try to preserve the *status quo,* that he would evacuate
Rome but not without the certainty that the Pope would be protected.[48] "I regard as a real triumph of the Empress," wrote Metternich, "having led the Emperor to renounce entirely the demand for
utopian concessions on the part of the Holy Father."[49] Metternich
had a lively discussion with the Empress regarding the proposal
for a European guarantee of Rome, which he characterized as being
as utopian as all other French proposals.[50] He declared that the

fate of Rome did not depend on France alone and if Napoleon would openly break with the Italian revolution, the Roman question could be quickly settled. In the course of the discussion he gathered the impression that the French Government no longer insisted upon the collective guarantee but desired that the Pope should demonstrate his sympathy for the Emperor and use his influence to effect a reconciliation between the latter and the French clergy. "The Pope," said the Empress, "ought to do something for us, if only to encourage the Emperor in his good intentions by showing him a little more gratitude. If the Emperor and I should be assassinated, which can happen any day, Prince Napoleon will be the regent and perhaps then the Holy Father will miss us." Only a few days before the Emperor had made the same melancholy declaration. Metternich found this state of mind rather curious and saw in it an indication that the edifice of glory which Napoleon had so daringly erected could not endure the least reverse without being shaken. Never had the Ambassador seen the Emperor so dull, so apathetic, as he was at this time. The Italian question was apparently insoluble, while circumstances rendered the difficulties more aggravating.

Napoleon's problem, as Metternich saw it, was to reconcile the conservative, religious and dynastic interests with the ever-increasing demands of the revolution.[51] "From the insolubility of this problem results the grievances, the bitterness of the Emperor against the resistance of the principle represented at Rome and his fear of threats coming from Turin. From it the unavailing, fumbling efforts today, abandoned tomorrow, from it a universal discontent, an anxiety, an insurmountable uneasiness and finally, an apathetic expectation."[52] But Metternich was of the opinion that Napoleon had not the least desire to attack Catholicism or to deprive the Pope of his power though he had done nothing to discourage the spoliators. If only Turin would be satisfied with the *status quo* or if only the Pope would agree to share Rome with Victor Emmanuel! Napoleon knew that neither of these possibilities held any hope.

While the Emperor had run into a snag in his Roman policy, he was more fortunate in the question of according recognition to the Kingdom of Italy. England and France had already recognized the new kingdom but the conservative powers held back. Austria had taken the stand that to recognize Victor Emmanuel as "King of Italy" was to sanction the usurpations in Italy. Yet, there was no intention of actively combatting recognition and Rechberg merely entered a formal protest and let it go at that. Prussia and Russia, on the other hand, were somewhat more amenable. Indeed, they saw an opportunity of deriving some profit by adopting a more benevolent attitude toward Turin. There was a chance that Napoleon might recognize Prussian aspirations in Germany and Russian aspirations in the Balkans. The possibility of a triple alliance of France, Prussia and Russia could not be overlooked. "Between France and Prussia," wrote Metternich, "there is neither an Italian nor an eastern question—there is only the Rhine, and if the spirit of M. de Cavour descends upon the House of Hohenzollern, the second part of the Italian political comedy will not be delayed."[53] Bismarck's nomination to the Paris post in May was hardly reassuring to Austria. "We see in it," wrote Rechberg, "an alarming symptom that the second great German power has decided to pursue the policy of encroachment. . . . "[54] Rechberg had learned that Bismarck accepted the Paris post only on condition that he should direct Prussian policy toward an understanding with France and Russia. But he underestimated the skill of the new Prussian Minister to Paris. He said to Gramont: "If M. de Bismarck had had a complete diplomatic education, he would be one of the first, if not the first, statesmen of Germany. . . . "[55] But he went on to say that Bismarck was incapable of sacrificing a preconceived idea, was too much of a party man, and besides was hostile to Austria. "Napoleon III," he predicted, "will find in M. de Bismarck a docile instrument who, if he cannot reach his ends at the price of slight sacrifices merely by abandoning the territories taken from France and joined to Prussia by the Second Treaty of Paris, will not hesitate to draw anew on Germany the misfortunes of a period mournfully celebrated."[56] Metternich was instructed to counteract as much as possible the maneuvers of Bismarck and to prevent the conclusion of an alliance directed against Austria.[57]

The fact that Baron Budberg, the Russian envoy, was visiting Paris at this time lent some support to the rumor of a triple alliance.

No doubt Bismarck would find a zealous collaborator in Budberg. "I need hardly tell you," wrote Rechberg to Metternich, "that we cannot permit the realization of such an alliance even if its frustration must be purchased with sacrifices."[58] Metternich tried to discover if there was a connection between the mission of Budberg and "the precipitous arrival of the envoy of Prussia" but concluded that both had personal aims.[59] He believed that Budberg was seeking to replace Kisseleff, while Bismarck desired to reach an understanding with Napoleon in order to act more freely when he entered the Prussian Cabinet.[60] "I do not doubt," added Metternich, "that M. de Budberg has a secret mission either officially to replace M. de Kisseleff in the questions of the east and the recognition of Italy, or concerning the affair of Poland and the recent measures which have been taken there, or finally, in a special aim that I have not been able to divine. As to M. de Bismarck, his nomination appears to have been solicited secretly by M. Thouvenel. I have never doubted the desire the latter has of seeing arrive here a Prussian diplomat of the temper of M. de Bismarck. . . . "[61] Nor did Metternich believe that there was any connection between the appointment of Bismarck and Napoleon's desire to redraw the map of Europe but attributed it solely to the Italian policy of Thouvenel.[62] "M. Thouvenel, it is clear, works with all his might for the recognition and desired to be able to act on Prussia in conjunction with an active man like M. de Bismarck."[63] He concluded that Austria had nothing to fear from the arrival of the two diplomats. In fact, Napoleon had already adopted a sphinx-like attitude toward Bismarck, which dispelled any adventurous attempts, while Budberg was not especially pleased by the Emperor's policy in the Polish problem.

There was no doubt that recognition of the Kingdom of Italy by Prussia and Russia would leave Austria isolated in the Italian question. This danger was pointed out to Rechberg by Lord Bloomfield, the British Ambassador to Vienna, who urged Austria to recognize the *faits accomplis* in the Peninsula.[64] Rechberg replied that Austria's interests and dignity as well as the rights set forth in the treaties prevented her from according recognition. Informed that Russia had extended recognition, Rechberg declared that it merely offered one more proof of the duplicity of Gortchakoff's policy.[65] He suspected that Russia had a hidden motive in thus abandoning conservative principles and predicted that instead of deriving any profit from it, the act of recognition would precipitate an internal crisis which would shake the Russian Empire to its foundations. Although Russia's action had been expected,[66] it nevertheless produced a painful impression at Vienna and Rechberg studiously avoided any reference to it in his conversations with members of the diplomatic corps.[67] Metternich learned that Alexander II had written a flattering letter to Napoleon stating that Russia had recognized the new kingdom because France desired it.[68] The Tsar probably hoped that he could win over Napoleon on the Polish question.

The recognition of the new kingdom by Prussia[69] and Russia was a severe blow to the conservative principles to which Austria still adhered. The flimsy excuse that Gortchakoff advanced, namely, that the Cabinet of Turin had given satisfactory assurances of order,[70] did not deceive Rechberg, who felt that such assurances must be taken with a grain of salt. Moreover, he was inclined to give Napoleon rather than Thouvenel credit for the actions taken by Prussia and Russia.

> The recent success won by the revolution is incontestably a result of the policy of fumbling followed by the Emperor Napoleon. Called upon by M. Rattazzi to make a concession to the Italian cause in order to strengthen the position of the Piedmontese Government, undermined by Garibaldi, the Emperor of the French, who desires to quit Rome, who fears to see the Venetian question arise, believed he could leave his embarrassment by offering as compensation for the *status quo* the recognition of Italy by the Cabinets of St. Petersburg and Berlin.[71]

Of greater danger to Austria than this attack on conservative principles was the possibility of an understanding or an alliance of France, Prussia and Russia. At first Metternich had been skeptical of this possibility but recent developments had persuaded him of the danger. The pretext for the *rapprochement* of the three powers was the recognition of Italy. Metternich did not believe that they had common interests of sufficient importance to form the basis for an alliance.[72] However, it was possible that they might reach an understanding which would be detrimental to Austria's interests in Germany, Italy and the Balkans. Already it appeared that Russia had obtained certain promises from Napoleon regarding Poland and the east, while Prussia, having recently concluded a commercial treaty with France, hoped to win the Emperor's sympathies and thus remove the danger that he might pursue a policy of annexation in Germany, "The French Government, on the other hand, is not displeased with being able to boast of its good offices to the Cabinet of Turin on the subject of the recognition; it flatters itself in weighing on England in the question of the east and of arriving at a more effective protection of the Slav and Rumanian populations whose emancipation offers it no danger and whose gratitude can furnish it in good time a moral and material force which it is pleased to be able to assure itself in advance."[73] Furthermore, Thouvenel was only too satisfied in having united Prussia and Russia to France in the question of recognition not to seek to maintain the *rapprochement,* while Bismarck and Budberg were sufficiently ambitious to employ all their efforts in the same direction. There was reason, therefore, to believe that Austria would meet with further opposition, if not with open hostility, from France in the affairs of Germany, Italy and the Balkans. England would probably support Austria to a certain extent but the past had revealed that English statesmen could not be relied upon. "The isolation which the approaching autumn could lead us to does not frighten me for I have the conviction that there are always means of coming to an arrangement with the Emperor Napoleon. . . ."[74] What these means were Metternich did not indicate but that they would involve concessions on Austria's part was obvious. Much would depend upon the nature of these concessions. Rechberg had already opposed any further sacrifices and he now rejected in advance the idea of a European congress if Napoleon should think of proposing one on the Roman question.[75] "It will be superfluous to develop for you here the motives which render a meeting of a congress undesirable for us at this time. If you see the Emperor Napoleon, he no doubt will speak to you of the difficulties which the present situation in Italy has created for him. Make every effort, if the word 'congress' is pronounced, to dissuade your interlocutor from such an idea. . . ."

In the face of the isolation with which she was threatened, Austria adopted a more conciliatory attitude toward France. Gramont detected unmistakable, if rather vague symptoms, of a desire to effect a *rapprochement* in the Italian question.[76] Rechberg said to him: "I do not say that we will never recognize Italy; I do not have this thought; quite the contrary; but at this time we cannot think of it. It is necessary that Italy ceases to be hostile to us and one cannot ask us to recognize the right of taking from us Venice, which forms a part of the rights Italy proclaims." He admitted that the Italian Government represented in the Peninsula, at least in a relative sense, the principles of monarchy and order as opposed to revolution and anarchy.[77] No doubt Victor Emmanuel would remain master in the north but Garibaldi would succeed in revolutionizing the south, which would raise the question of European intervention. Austria would defend herself but would not intervene in Italy except in concert with France "and after having regulated with her all the clauses of a common action."[78]

Metternich had several conversations with the Emperor and Empress at St. Cloud in regard to Italian affairs. The Emperor assured him that he would not evacuate Rome until he could leave honorably.[79] Encouraged by this assurance, the Ambassador approached the problem of a settlement of the Italian question. The Emperor, however, did not reply to this but after a moment's hesitation changed the subject. This incident struck Metternich as rather curious and it was only later that he learned the reason. In speaking to Metternich about the Italian question, the Empress suddenly asked if Napoleon had mentioned his idea of three kingdoms. When the Ambassador answered in the negative, she continued: "I know quite well that he did not speak to you of it; it is because he is bound by a promise he made to you." "You wish to speak again of Venetia," replied Metternich, unable to hide his disappointment. "Do not be angry," exclaimed the Empress smiling. "I will not speak of it since it displeases you and since you resume your character of an Ambassador. Here is the point: the Emperor promised you not to speak any more about Venetia and not to permit the question to be raised. Has he kept his promise?" Metternich had to admit that Napoleon had shown the most perfect loyalty in this respect. "Oh well," added the Empress, "I can assure you that the day Austria takes the initiative either of placing an archduke in Venice in order to make it an Italian province or abandons it, which I believe will be wiser, the Emperor will yield to all conditions, even the hardest, that you would make whether in regard to the Pope and Naples or to obtain concessions in Germany, the east or where you wish. If you were to ask me what I would do in your place, I would reply that one does not bargain away a province, that the great power which calls itself 'Austria' cannot make policy à la Cavour—I would do as you—I would probably refuse and would get myself much just pride and dynastic grandeur but perhaps I would admit to myself that I am not very clever." Metternich asked the Empress if she really believed that it was in the interest of France to have Austria abandon Venetia and if a Franco-Austrian understanding could restore to Italy the prosperity which Austria's domination had given her. The Empress replied: "The Emperor is pledged by the blood which has flowed in Italy—as long as he lives. He could not come to an understanding with you if you desire to maintain your influence there. Italian unity is certainly not what he desires, and I hope that this utopia will never be realized for it will be a misfortune for France. Rightly or wrongly the Emperor entered Italy in order to make you leave. He could not permit you to reënter and I, who detest the Italians and who am known in the Peninsula to be pro-Austrian and am honored thereby, I understand and I am obliged to share the views of the Emperor. After our death, the deluge, but before that we will be against you if you wish to annul the effects of the unfortunate war which cost me so many tears. We will be your faithful allies if you would leave Venice or make it a place as independent as possible. You have handled Prussia well enough; resume then your 'Roman' position in Germany and get your hands across Bavaria and Würtemberg. If you do not wish Italian unity, German unity with Prussia repels you even more."

No doubt the Italian question could have been settled had Austria been willing to pay the price. And, after all, would it not have been wiser to have done so? In looking back it is easy to see that the Hapsburg policy of holding on to both Germany and Italy was doomed to failure. If she had abandoned Venetia, as the Empress suggested, and in doing so paved the way for an alliance with France, Austria might have kept her influence in Germany or strengthened her position in the Balkans. But she preferred to hang on to the bitter end and thus lost out in both Italy and Germany. In the fall of 1862 one could not have foreseen the epoch-making changes which were to occur within the next decade. Outwardly, Austria's position was no worse than it had been for some time, if indeed it was not actually stronger as a result of internal reconstruction. Moreover, her hopes were raised by the ministerial change which took place in France. On September 10, 1862, General Durando, who was Foreign Minister in the Rattazzi Cabinet, issued a circular demanding Rome as the capital for the Italian Kingdom.[80] This increased Napoleon's embarrassment. The pro-Italian group led by Prince Napoleon urged him to accede to the Italian demand, but the conservatives with the Empress and Walewski combatted it vigorously. In view of the approaching elections for the *Corps Législatif* and his realization that the majority was likely to oppose the evacuation of Rome, Napoleon yielded to the conservatives. Thouvenel, whose "passion for Italian unity had increased in proportion to the mortifications he had endured and the hesitations he could not conquer,"[81] was relieved of his post and was succeeded by Drouyn de Lhuys. This was a welcome change to Austria and to Metternich in particular. Thouvenel had done everything possible in order not to be agreeable to the Austrian Ambassador. "His mild manners, his amicable protestations toward us, did not prevent him at the same time from working with the Cabinets of Berlin and St. Petersburg directly counter to our policy; finally, he was able to flatter the known instincts of the Emperor in order to counteract our most conciliatory *démarches* regarding the east and to encourage the movement patronized by the revolutionary party and by Prince Gortchakoff." Thouvenel had a way of escaping any serious discussion, which made it difficult to transact affairs with him. Metternich was not the only one to complain of this attitude: Lord Cowley and the Papal Nuncio were apparently no better pleased.[82] The new Foreign Minister, on the other hand, was regarded as friendly to Austria, and Rechberg held out high hopes of establishing more cordial relations with France.[83] When Metternich returned to Paris after a vacation spent in Bohemia, he found the situation considerably improved and believed that a real *rapprochement* was now possible.[84] Drouyn de Lhuys expressed himself in the most "cordial fashion" on all questions. "Questions of the east, of Greece, of Germany and Italy—everything which interests our policy were treated by the minister in the sense which can be agreeable to us. I believed that I was dreaming in finding myself back in the same place where I had heard the utopias inspired by the Palais Royal and Turin—I believed that I was dreaming, I say, in hearing come from the mouth of the minister words so correct, so sensible. Time and things have indeed changed since my departure from here and were this not an anomaly in seeing seated at the same green table Drouyn de Lhuys and Walewski, Fould and Persigny, one would believe himself on the eve of an era of peace and prosperity. Let us await results."[85]

Drouyn de Lhuys assured Metternich that France would maintain the *status quo* in Italy and follow a policy sympathetic toward the Pope but "positively hostile toward Turin." [86] This was sweet music to Metternich but it was tempered by the realization that the minister was after all a good Frenchman and a Bonapartist and therefore influenced by the *Idées Napoléonienne*. It would be his duty to work for the glory of France and the achievement of her natural frontiers. Since the arrival of Bismarck the subject of natural frontiers had been receiving greater attention. "What do you think," Walewski asked Metternich, "of the propositions that M. de Bismarck could make? You know that Drouyn de Lhuys agrees with me that the alliance with Austria will be the means for us to save all." [87] When he heard the word "alliance" Metternich's first thought was about the price France would demand. "Do you not believe," continued Walewski, "that the affairs in Germany will become complicated to the point of making necessary to you our neutrality if not our moral support? And if that is so, be assured that in what con-

cerns the Rhine, the Emperor will like nothing better than to
arrange with you rather than once more with revolution." Metternich took advantage of an interview with Drouyn de Lhuys to
inquire what Bismarck had offered Napoleon for the support of
France against the small German states and perhaps against Austria.
He was assured that Bismarck had not even tried to hint at an
arrangement of this kind. Speaking confidentially as an old friend
rather than as Foreign Minister, Drouyn de Lhuys declared that
had he remained in office since the Crimean War the "revolutionary
and Italian intermezzo" would not have taken place.[88] He preferred, he said, a Franco-Austrian alliance to any other. When
Metternich inquired what could be done to prevent the Emperor
from again allying himself with revolution, Drouyn de Lhuys mentioned the powerful influence which the idea of a rectification of
frontiers had on the mind of Napoleon. Perhaps Austria might see
her way to offer France something along this line. The Ambassador
replied that this suggestion could lead to no results at the moment
but when the time came he would recall it to the minister. Metternich concluded that Drouyn de Lhuys preferred arrangements with
Austria to the advances of Prussia and would give a complete explanation of his theories of natural frontiers when the right moment
appeared.

The Italian question, which for more than three years had held
the center of the stage in European diplomacy, was being unceremo-
niously pushed into the background. In France it was already considered of secondary importance and the Emperor seldom referred
to it in his conversations with Metternich. While the questions of
Rome and Venetia still remained and were far from settled, other
problems were forging their way to the front line. "The year
1862," wrote Metternich, "ends in the midst of growing complications, insurmountable difficulties, and a situation always indecisive
—a sad heritage of their predecessors."[89] As far as relations between Austria and France were concerned, the one bright point
in the year was the appointment of Drouyn de Lhuys.

The new minister proceeds with prudence and with a timidity that
I find quite natural but at the same time with a great logic in the way
which permits us not only to lessen the distrust only too justified that

the Napoleonic policy inspires in us but of foreseeing in some manner the moment when it will be possible for us to draw near a power whose good offices are not to be disdained. If I believe M. Drouyn de Lhuys literally, his personal aim will be to lead the Emperor to inaugurate an era of confidence and peace which will exclude neither the necessity of maintaining French power at the height of its aspirations, nor the opportunities to profit from the future in order to increase still more its range. Instead of running the risk of weakening . . . discipline and internal peace by seeking allies among the supporters of revolution, the new minister only tends to raise up as much as possible the principle of authority by sustaining it wherever it is attacked. He has repeated to me quite frequently that the real interests of our two countries call for an intimate and cordial *entente* bearing inscribed on its flag the monarchical principle, mutual frankness and loyalty. He thinks that as much as it is possible England ought to be admitted as a third party.

Metternich did not place too much credence in the assertions of the new Foreign Minister, for he was by now accustomed to consider only the results which depended upon what course was followed in the future. As it was, the appointment of Drouyn de Lhuys had already led to an important change in the Italian policy of France. "We see the Italian alliance fall today to a very moderate temperature."[90] Relations between Paris and Rome had improved, the attitude of the press was more reasonable, and positive steps had been taken to check the influence of the pro-Italian group in France.

CHAPTER TWELVE

The Question of an *Entente* on Eastern Affairs, 1859-1863

ALTHOUGH ITALIAN affairs occupied the center of the European stage during the three years following Villafranca, there was considerable interest in the Near East. Indeed, as far as Austria and France were concerned, this interest was closely tied up with the problem of Italy. After the war of 1859 and the subsequent events in the Peninsula, Austria sought to emerge from her isolation and to extend her influence in the east. At the same time, Napoleon hoped that he could induce Austria to find compensation in the Balkans or in Egypt for the loss of her influence in Italy.

The Austrian Government no longer displayed that self-righteous indignation toward the question of dismembering the Ottoman Empire that had characterized its attitude before the Italian war. Rechberg was more receptive than his predecessor to Napoleon's insinuations though no less determined to maintain Austria's rights. He was aware that the Anglo-Austrian *entente* on eastern affairs, which had functioned rather well during the period following the Crimean War, was no longer in good working order. England's encouragement of the Italian nationalists and of the liberal and revolutionary movements in the Balkans made it difficult for Austria to count any longer on her support. Rechberg therefore decided upon another course and soon after Villafranca set about to establish an *entente* with France and Russia concerning the share each power should receive in the event that the Ottoman Empire crumbled. In September 1859 Prince Alexander of Hesse was sent on a mission to St. Petersburg. As brother-in-law of the Tsar, it was thought that he might succeed in bringing about a warmer atmosphere between the two courts. Rechberg, of course, had no illusions concerning the difficulties. He knew that the Russians had not forgotten Austria's conduct during the Crimean War and her subsequent defense of the Porte in Balkan affairs. On the other hand, he believed that the progress of the revolutionary movement in Italy was certain to antagonize the Tsar, while self-interest could make Russia look with favor upon an agreement with Austria. The principal stumbling block would be the attitude of Gortchakoff, who continued to exercise a great influence over the mind of the Tsar.[1] But even Gortchakoff appeared somewhat less bitter in his hatred for Austria and less ardent in his affections for France. In any case, Prince Alexander's report was so encouraging that Rechberg decided to go ahead with the efforts to conclude an agreement with Russia in eastern affairs.[2] In October the Archduke Albrecht and Baron Werner, Under Secretary of State in the Foreign Office, visited the Tsar at Warsaw. The ostensible object of this visit was to compliment the Tsar on his sojourn near the Austrian frontier.[3] Its real aim, however, was to sound out the attitude concerning an *entente* and to secure Russian cooperation at the proposed congress on Italy. In his instructions to Werner, Rechberg indicated that Austria was prepared to support a proposal to revise the Black Sea Clause of the Treaty of Paris. He directed Werner to remind Gortchakoff of the Münchengrätz Treaty of 1833 which Austria regarded as embodying the only rational means of dealing with Turkey. It was Rechberg's belief that Gortchakoff desired the reëstablishment of the alliance of the conservative powers.

The Albrecht-Werner mission failed to obtain the desired agreement. The price offered by Austria was not high enough from the Russian standpoint. Gortchakoff wanted more than a mere passive support of the revision of the Black Sea Clause; he wanted Austria to take the initiative.[4] Furthermore, Russia insisted upon the restitution of Bessarabia. In return, Gortchakoff promised that Russia would not vote for the principle of popular sovereignty at the proposed congress.[5]

In Paris Metternich was instructed to inform Walewski concerning the visit of the Archduke and Baron Werner and to broach the subject of a triple *entente*.[6] Both Napoleon and his Foreign Minister appeared sympathetic.[7] Walewski admitted that France and Russia had already discussed the possibility of the dismemberment of Turkey and had agreed to do nothing to precipitate it.[8] "The Emperor," continued Walewski, "will welcome, if not with complete disinterestedness, at least with the greatest desire any proposal coming from the Emperor of Austria which has for its aim an understanding concerning this eventuality [Turkey's dismemberment]. If Austria, Russia and France come to an agreement, this question, so delicate, long foreseen but justly feared, will be solved the day it presents itself and no one, not even England, will be able to resist the immense force of our action." Metternich tried to get further details from the Foreign Minister regarding Napoleon's attitude but did not succeed. He believed that the Emperor had not expressed himself completely to the Minister and awaited definite proposals from Austria. In any case, Napoleon did not wish to include England in the *entente*.[9] Metternich's opinion was that the time had not yet arrived when an agreement of the three powers could be achieved. He argued that it could be established only on a dynastic-conservative basis which would mean that Austria and Russia must take the restless ruler of France in tow and tear him away from his democratic and nationalistic utopias.[10] Had it not been seen how easy this man of Strasbourg and Boulogne escaped from the well-meaning hands that had been extended to him? "Indeed, like any other necessary evil, the Emperor Napoleon must be watched and even nursed."[11] Left to himself, he would continue his hobby of sowing discord, whereas a firm alliance of Austria and Russia could be used to guide him when he was peaceful and oppose him whenever he transgressed.

As the price for her participation in the proposed *entente,* Russia demanded the revision of those clauses of the Treaty of Paris which were humiliating and onerous for her. These included not only the Black Sea Clause but the restitution of Bessarabia. Rechberg was not disposed to quibble too much about the price. "To refuse categorically," he wrote to Metternich, "or not to take account of his (Gortchakoff's) demands, will be to create, at the very moment he seems desirous of drawing near to us, an irreconcilable enemy in Gortchakoff, whose friendship can be very useful to us in the present condition of Europe."[12] Moreover, the revision of the Treaty of Paris would set a precedent which Austria might utilize in regard to the Treaty of Zürich. "The analogy is evident and our interests indubitable."[13] This was indeed a far cry from the sanctity of treaties which Vienna had so arduously defended. Nor could Rechberg see any reason for maintaining the Black Sea Clause since its stipulations could be easily evaded by Russia. It was otherwise with the question of modifying the frontiers of Bessarabia, particularly if this should bring Russia to the left bank of the Danube.[14] Austria could not permit the Russians to dominate the Danube but as she could count upon England's cooperation in resisting such a change, it was not deemed necessary to raise the question at the moment. Instead, Rechberg believed that by displaying a willingness to satisfy her demands, he would gain Russia's support at the congress on Italy. Moreover, if she did not fall in line on eastern affairs, what would be easier than to let her know that Austria would not back up the revision of the Treaty of Paris?

In view of these considerations (wrote Rechberg to Metternich) I have decided to charge you, ostensibly on behalf of the Russian Government, with secret negotiations with the Cabinet of the Tuileries. . . . The hints which have recently been given you concerning the establishment of an *entente* for the affairs of the east, will provide the occasion to broach this subject. You will state, as coming from yourself, that in order to bring about a perfect accord among the three imperial courts, it seems to you urgent to modify a treaty directed against Russia, which evidently humiliates that power so much that one can hardly expect her to enter into our views frankly and without *arrière-pensées*. You know that St. Petersburg desires only the abolition of two clauses of this treaty. That regarding the neutralization of the Black Sea contains illusory provisions; the pronounced prohibition against Russian war vessels being so easily evaded by merchant vessels which could be armed with engines of destruction, without counting that it is quite difficult to exercise a sufficient surveillance over the dockyards. Referring to the territorial cession in Bessarabia, you will appear less indulgent because of the rights acquired by the Porte and by Moldavia. In treating this latter point you would do well to support yourself principally on the difficulties of execution.[15]

Rechberg was anxious to learn the reaction of France to this proposal before continuing the negotiations with Russia. He thought it advisable to reach an understanding concerning the distribution of the spoils while Turkey was still in existence instead of leaving this to chance after she had disintegrated. In case the subject was mentioned, Metternich was instructed to say that Austria was opposed to the establishment of small independent states in the Balkans, which sooner or later would become the prey of the northern colossus.[16]

It is principally for this reason that it seems urgent to us to agree in advance on a just method of partition. What are the provinces coveted by France? Try to discover this before you express yourself concerning our intentions which are not yet sufficiently matured in order that I can give you precise instructions in this respect. The idea of making Constantinople a free city appears good to us; it is the only possible expedient so as not to give one or the other of the great powers too marked a preponderance. But in order that Constantinople be a free city, we cannot permit the Russians to establish themselves along the coasts of the Black Sea as far as the walls of the present capital of the Ottoman Empire. Does Paris desire an aggrandizement of the Kingdom of Greece? For us it seems important that we immediately gain Scutari and Salonika in order to establish important maritime outlets and, on the other hand, the possession of the Danubian Principalities would offer us a guarantee against the encroachments of Russia. But, I repeat, these are merely my personal ideas and I have not had time to deliberate upon them with justice.[17]

Acting upon his instructions, Metternich obtained an interview with Walewski. From him he learned that while France wanted a peaceful revision of the treaties of 1815 in so far as they were directed against her and the Napoleonic dynasty, she would not bring up for the moment the question of her natural frontiers.[18] "Your Excellency," he wrote to Rechberg, "sees that the question of the east could well play a great role in the west and that accommodations, if not completely disinterested, have become a bargain."[19] It seemed rather significant to Metternich that both France and Russia demanded revision of the treaties. Might this not prove providential for Austria in the future? In any event, Rechberg could now come to the congress prepared to deal directly with Gortchakoff and Walewski. Indeed, the latter assured Metternich that Napoleon would be very moderate, even modest, in his demands and once he had obtained them France would be as conservative as any other power.[20] On one point, however, Metternich ran into difficulty. Count Kisseleff, the Russian Ambassador, had informed Walewski that Austria had been asked by Gortchakoff to take the initiative in proposing a revision of the Treaty of Paris.[21] As a matter of fact, Kisseleff actually informed Walewski of the discussions between Gortchakoff and Werner at Warsaw. Rechberg was indignant when he learned of this breach of faith and declared that he had no illusions regarding Russia.[22] Walewski gained the impression that Austria and Russia had already reached a preliminary agreement. He was quite peeved and when Metternich attempted to enter upon a discussion of the question of revising the Treaty of Paris, he showed no enthusiasm and held that the moment was inopportune.[23]

This seeming indifference of the French Minister to his overtures, did not please Rechberg. He complained that Walewski had been altogether too vague in indicating the compensations France desired in return for a territorial increase for Austria in the Balkans.[24] While Austria, he pointed out, did not wish to hasten the dissolution of the Ottoman Empire nor deviate from the principles to which she had adhered so scrupulously, she could not shut her eyes to reality. "However profound our respect might be for an order of things to which we have contributed so much to maintain, whatever danger we might see in the complications which can result from redrawing the map of the east, we cannot deny that the structure of the Ottoman Empire, undermined by so many different causes, threatens to fall. . . . It is our duty to consider in advance anything which can render this catastrophe less perilous for the peace of Europe."[25] The greatest danger for Austria would be the division of the Ottoman Empire into small independent states and it was to forestall this that Rechberg considered it urgent to reach an understanding with France and Russia. Such states, he reasoned, would inevitably be plunged into civil war which would lead to the intervention of their more powerful neighbors and sooner or later be absorbed by them. It would be far better to arrange affairs in advance in order to prevent a period of painful uncertainty. Rechberg was particularly desirous of obtaining an arrangement which would favor Austrian commerce and shipping. But it was necessary to make one thing clear to France, namely, that Austria's desire for aggrandizement in the Balkans was not so strong as to lead her to make concessions in Italy.[26] "The regulation of the affairs of the Peninsula [Italy] is today our first and foremost interest and it is not some vague hope that can make us sacrifice it."[27] So long as France continued to speak in generalities, Austria must do likewise. Rechberg did not feel that it was for him to suggest what compensations France should obtain. Napoleon had already hinted that Austria might take Egypt. While Rechberg admitted that this would be a valuable acquisition, particularly for commerce, he knew that the Austrian navy was too weak to defend it against a great maritime power. He was prepared to accept it only if England and France would guarantee its peaceful possession to Austria. "However, we have interests nearer home of which we should take account. The banks of the Danube, the coast of the Ionian Sea, will procure advantages for us less brilliant but more certain."[28] In any case, Rechberg regarded an *entente* with France as the first essential. Once the two powers had reached an agreement, he felt confident that Russia's adhesion would be forthcoming. Indeed, Walewski suggested that the entire affair might be concluded if Rechberg would visit Paris a few days before the opening of the congress and treat directly with Napoleon and Gortchakoff.[29] Before Rechberg could act upon this suggestion, the publication of the brochure, "Le Pape et le Congrès," put a damper on further negotiations. In January 1860 he took up the subject of revising the Treaty of Paris with Prussia and agreed to make another overture to France as soon as the situation permitted.[30] Nothing more could be done for the moment.

Following the settlement of affairs in central Italy, Rechberg again took up the threads of the negotiations. He found a pretext in a letter written by Mocquard, Napoleon's secretary and an intimate confidant of his thoughts, to a French journalist. In this,

Mocquard predicted that the eastern question would soon reappear.[31] Rechberg felt that there must be something to this prediction since Mocquard was so well informed about Napoleon's policies. Reports he received from Austrian agents in various provinces of the Ottoman Empire revealed that the French were carrying on subterranean intrigues. "Everything indicates," he wrote to Metternich, "that Napoleon's attention is directed toward the east and that he is preparing an explosion there with the object of getting new territorial aggrandizements for France." According to Rechberg's viewpoint, it was impossible to ignore the question. Both ethnographic and geographic considerations involved Austria in any crisis which might occur in the Balkans. The important thing was to see that it did not operate to her detriment.

Convinced that Napoleon would not attempt to act alone, Rechberg's greatest fear was the prospect of an *entente* between England and France. "Encouraged by English liberal ideas, the democratic instincts of the Emperor Napoleon will prevail, the revolutionary spirit will receive a new impulse from it, and the territorial changes which follow, effected under this influence, will be conceived in a sense hostile to the principles upon which the very existence of the Austrian Empire rests. Our cooperation in such a solution will be suicidal, and if we wished to oppose it by force, it would result in a formidable struggle in which we would run the risk of succumbing."[32] A Franco-Russian *entente* would be less dangerous as this would tend to separate Napoleon from democratic and revolutionary ideas and restrict him to a purely political alteration in the east. But in order to counterbalance the influence of Russia and prevent her from extending westward, Rechberg was anxious to have Austria participate in the *entente*. He instructed Metternich to redouble his vigilance, to do everything possible to prevent an *entente* between England and France, and at every occasion which presented itself to mention to Napoleon that a tripartite agreement of Austria, France and Russia was less dangerous.[33] "Do not lose sight of the fact that this is for us a vital question which can be fatal or damage us far more than the losses we have sustained."[34]

Metternich lost no time in acting upon these instructions. Thouvenel, with whom he discussed the situation, assured him that since the Italian war, Napoleon had made up his mind not to weaken Austria further but, if possible, to compensate her for the loss of influence in Italy.[35] Moreover, Thouvenel declared in the most categorical manner that France would not attempt to work out a settlement of the eastern question with England alone as this would lead to opposition by both Austria and Russia. Nor would she establish a direct *entente* with Russia for this would result in an Anglo-Austrian alliance and consequently in war. What Napoleon desired most of all, according to Thouvenel, was a sincere understanding with Austria. Not only was he prepared to reach such an understanding but he would oppose any attempt by Russia to expand westward. As Metternich feared, however, Thouvenel did not confine himself to a discussion of the eastern question but insisted on taking up the subject of compensation for Austria's losses in Italy. He informed the Ambassador that Napoleon was most anxious to do something for Austria relative to Lombardy and even Venetia. In fact, it was Venetia which troubled him most. This effort to make Italy the bargaining point for an understanding on the eastern problem did not please Metternich, who warned Thouvenel that Franz Joseph would never consider an arrangement for exchanging Venetia.[36]

Metternich also discussed the question of an *entente* with Baron Budberg, who was soon to succeed Kisseleff as the Russian Ambassador to Paris. Budberg expressed a profound admiration for Napoleon but referred to the danger of permitting him to act as dictator of Europe.[37] In order to prevent the formation of an Anglo-French alliance it was necessary, according to Budberg, to bring Napoleon into an *entente* with Austria, Prussia and Russia. One of the objects of this *entente* would be a revision of the treaties of 1815 in the interest of France. When Metternich informed Thouvenel of his conversation with Budberg, the Minister declared that an *entente* could not be established on the basis of what the interested powers wanted but rather on what they did not want.[38] France, for example, knew that Austria did not want the formation of small independent states in European Turkey under Russian tutelage. What struck Metternich as curious in his conversations with Budberg and Thouvenel was the fact that neither mentioned the questions in which their governments were directly interested. Budberg had said nothing about the Russian aims in the Balkans but had referred to the necessity of revising the treaties of 1815 in the interests of France. Were the objectives which the two powers desired to achieve so opposed to Austrian interests that it was better not to mention them for the moment?

On the whole, Rechberg appears to have been reasonably satisfied with the attitude of France. He believed it would be easier to reach an understanding with that power, whose interests in the east did not differ too sharply from those of Austria, than with Russia. The latter favored the establishment of small Balkan states under her influence. England, who desired to keep Russia out of the Middle East, was also in favor of such Balkan states. Hence, the aims of England and Russia differed from those of Austria and France, who preferred that Russia expand eastward rather than westward. Mindful of the fact that Austria was being pressed from the north by Prussia and from the south by Piedmont, Rechberg wanted to avoid such pressure from the east. Since Austria and France apparently had similar interests in the Balkans, he still clung to the hope of establishing an *entente.*

So far as Russia was concerned, Rechberg was less optimistic. Prince Gortchakoff was still the most formidable obstacle to the establishment of an Austro-Russian *entente.* The influence which the Chancellor exercised over the Tsar, his anti-Austrian bias, his conviction that the only alliance worth seeking was one with France, made it exceedingly difficult for the Austrian representatives to make much headway. When Thun, the newly appointed Ambassador to St. Petersburg, discussed with Gortchakoff the possibility of concluding an eastern *entente,* the latter made it appear that it was Austria's duty to take the initiative in revising the Treaty of Paris and by so doing she would not be rendering a great service to Russia but would merely perform an act of contrition for past wrongs.[39] Indeed, only after Austria had employed her good offices to obtain this result, would Russia decide on her attitude. Thun saw that the eastern question was the most delicate that could be treated with Russia, the one issue that would present the greatest difficulty in reaching an understanding, and the one upon which

Austria could take no steps without being certain that she was completely within her rights.[40] In summing up his opinions concerning Gortchakoff, he wrote: "I would find nothing more dangerous than if my reports created the illusion at Vienna that our position is essentially ameliorated and that Prince Gortchakoff has changed his views toward us. This is not the case and never will be so long as Prince Gortchakoff remains at the head of the Russian Cabinet. All his efforts tend to lead to an intimate *entente* with France. He is completely under the charm of the Emperor Napoleon and the experiences of the last year and especially the last months, have changed nothing. He remains just as bitter an enemy of Austria and he will remain so during his life. It seems to me important that Your Excellency should be convinced that I have my eyes open from this side and that the cajoleries of Prince Gortchakoff have not had the least influence upon me. If I am wrong in my judgment [of him], this will be an error without serious consequence."[41]

In May 1860, Revertera, the Austrian Chargé d'Affaires at St. Petersburg, sent a lengthy dispatch to Rechberg dealing with Gortchakoff's policy.[42] He referred to Gortchakoff's indifference toward the overthrow of legitimate governments, his renunciation of conservative principles, his ambition, and his cult of material interests. The chief aim of the Chancellor was to establish an alliance with France whereby Russia would give Napoleon a free hand in the west in return for a free hand for Russia in the east. "One can say without the risk of deceiving oneself that if the Emperor Napoleon agrees to give it a *carte blanche* in the east, he can count on the connivance of the Russian Government not to concern itself with such changes as he considers it useful to bring about in other parts of Europe. At this price, he will be assured of the complete abstention of Russia regarding the affairs of Italy and Germany (the latter being transformed into the 'German question') and perhaps even of her active support if it is a matter of conquering the Rhine in Turkey."[43] Revertera then mentioned Gortchakoff's suggestion to call a conference to settle the eastern question. The reasons were threefold. First, it would give him the opportunity of showing his preference for France by addressing the first overtures to her while merely sending simple notifications to the other powers. Secondly, he would be able to assume a disinterested attitude before Europe. Finally, it would give him the chance of presiding over a conference and hence satisfy his vanity. In a second dispatch, Revertera declared that it was an illusion to think of Russia as a conservative power.[44] "Russia is not European, she is not civilized. Russia is schismatic in religion, with the immoral despotism of Asia in her internal policy, and Slav in her external action. These three principles have founded the Russian Empire and it is their development which preserves it, makes it live and grow." France alone could reach an understanding with such a state—a commentary on how low France had fallen in Revertera's eyes.

Only gradually did Rechberg abandon the idea of a tripartite *entente* with France and Russia. In view of the actual state of affairs in Europe at the time, it is somewhat surprising that Vienna should have entertained hopes in this direction. The interests of Austria and Russia were by no means the same in the eastern question. Just how far Rechberg would have gone in meeting Russia's demands, is uncertain because the negotiations did not get that far. From the various Austrian documents bearing on the subject, including those on the Warsaw conference in 1860, it is difficult to escape the impression that Vienna placed altogether too much reliance on Russian conservatism. Actually, Russia was revolutionary rather than conservative in eastern affairs. Because Alexander II was known to be more attached to conservative principles than Gortchakoff, Rechberg apparently clung to the forlorn hope that the Tsar could be won over the head of the Chancellor. Moreover, there still existed an *entente* between France and Russia. Though badly shaken by the events in Italy, it continued to be one of the cardinal principles of Gortchakoff's policy up to the Polish uprising of 1863. While the Franco-Russian *entente* by no means precluded a tripartite *entente* dealing with eastern affairs, it nevertheless made it difficult so far as Austria was concerned. Napoleon was far more interested in Italy than in the Balkans. It was easier for him to bargain with Russia than with Austria because of the latter's unwillingness to make the necessary concessions in Italy. In June 1860 Metternich informed Rechberg that Napoleon was preparing to make concessions to Russia in the Balkans in return for her promise not to meddle in Italian affairs.[45] This was substantially what Revertera had reported from St. Petersburg.[46]

Napoleon's attitude at this time was by no means reassuring to the Vienna Cabinet. Though Metternich had several lengthy discussions with him on the subject of an *entente,* they were barren of any concrete results. In one of these discussions, Napoleon compared the diplomacy of Austria and Russia since the Crimean War.[47] He pointed out that once the Treaty of Paris was signed, Russia showed remarkable cleverness in her foreign policy. "In fact, Russia saw Germany hesitant and divided, Austria hostile and imposing the most onerous conditions upon her, England dissatisfied with the peace and eternally jealous of her power; consequently, she sought the friendship of France by all possible means with extraordinary suppleness and an admirable *savoir faire.*" Austria, on the other hand, had struck blows right and left and balked France on every occasion and ended by forcing her into the arms of Piedmont which led to the war in Italy. After making this comparison, the Emperor offered his friendly advice concerning the best means for Austria to expand either in the direction of Germany or the Balkans. In Germany, she ought to range herself on the side of Prussia, while in the Balkans it would be necessary to make concessions to Russia. He promised not to oppose her in either direction.

After reading Metternich's report, Rechberg was convinced that Napoleon intended to draw still farther away from Austria.[48] He saw in the comparison between Austrian and Russian diplomacy an attempt to make Vienna feel how strong were the ties uniting France to Piedmont and Russia. "This resembles an indirect manner of warning us that we are far from having such rights and that we should not expect a friendship so useful and so proven to be given to us who have done nothing to merit this favor." Nor was Rechberg particularly impressed with the so-called friendly advice offered by Napoleon. It appeared to him rather singular that Austria should be told to place herself on a footing of equality toward Prussia in Germany and inferiority toward Russia in the Balkans. Rechberg concluded from Metternich's report that Napoleon intended to throw his support to Piedmont in Italy and to Russia in the eastern question.[49]

In another discussion of eastern affairs with Metternich, the Emperor pointed out that Russia was revolutionary in the east, Prussia in Germany, England in Italy, while Austria alone did not deviate from her conservative principles.[50] He again brought up his favorite idea of giving Egypt to Austria. Metternich realized, however, that such an offer would have significance only if it were part of a bargain. But although Napoleon was very fond of striking bargains, he had not proposed one to Austria.

On the basis of reports from Paris and St. Petersburg, Rechberg was finally convinced that there was little chance of realizing his plan for a tripartite *entente*. He believed that Napoleon was determined to prevent a *rapprochement* between Austria and Russia.[51] Yet, despite Gortchakoff's attitude, Rechberg did not completely abandon hope that Russia would one day join Austria in a common front against Napoleonic ambitions and revolution. Alexander II had lost much of his bitterness against Austria and had less confidence than formerly in the French ruler. The events in Italy and particularly in Naples, as well as the rumblings in Poland, aroused the Tsar's fear of revolution.[52] As the Polish question became more critical, this fear increased and along with it a distrust against the champion of nationalities. While Gortchakoff, whose policy was anti-Austrian and pro-French, still retained his influence over Alexander II, it was not unlikely that circumstances would compel him to turn tables in order to continue in office. At any rate, Rechberg was far more optimistic than the Austrian representative at St. Petersburg, Count Thun. The latter became so discouraged with the apparent hopelessness of seeking to establish an *entente* with Russia, that he suggested to Rechberg that it might be advisable to be replaced by a man of high military reputation.[53] Nothing could be achieved so long as Gortchakoff remained in power. "This Minister—if I am not mistaken—is a man of such personal vanity, of such confidence in his superiority, and in his infallibility, that any discussion with him becomes perfectly impossible or at least completely useless and even dangerous."[54] Rechberg, however, believed that Russia would have to abandon the policy she had pursued and rally to the defense of the monarchical principle, and he urged Thun to persevere in his efforts.[55]

Meanwhile, the attention of the powers was directed to certain problems connected with the Balkans, Syria and Poland. In the Principalities, Serbia and Montenegro there was considerable unrest, much of it the result of outside propaganda. A revolt in Syria had led to military intervention by France, while in Poland the nationalists, encouraged by the success of the revolution in Italy, had begun an agitation against Russia.

The attitude of the Vienna Cabinet toward these problems varied according to their proximity. So far as Syria was concerned, the French intervention was regarded as a distinct advantage to Austria since a French corps engaged in a distant region meant fewer soldiers for Europe and since it threatened to disturb relations between England and France.[56] England was opposed to the French action in Syria. According to Rechberg's viewpoint, whatever loosened the ties between the two maritime powers was worth-while as it made their cooperation in favor of revolution less likely. Austria's benevolent attitude in the Syrian question was naturally appreciated at Paris where a conference had been convoked to consider a solution. Thouvenel suggested that the two powers act together in opposing England and in making it clear that only French or Austrian troops should be permitted in Syria.[57]

Of more immediate interest to the Austrian Government were the disturbances in the Balkans and the nationalistic fervor in Poland. Whereas Russia would be directly threatened only by a revolution in Poland, Austria was vulnerable to disturbances in both Poland and the Balkans. As for France, she had nothing to fear unless the revolutionary movements produced a European conflagration. Indeed, Napoleon could possibly derive some profit from fishing in troubled waters. His sympathy for the Poles and the Balkan Slavs would not permit him to remain indifferent. He said to Metternich that of late the Tsar had become very suspicious concerning French connivance with the revolutionary agitators and had tried to get him to enter into a loyal alliance.[58] As the proposed alliance would merely further Russian interests in the Balkans, Napoleon rejected it. However, the mere mention of an alliance encouraged Metternich to suggest one between Austria and France as the best safeguard for European peace. There were a thousand considerations of common interests, said Metternich to Napoleon, which would draw the two powers together while such divergences as existed, would disappear in time. But the Ambassador was quite aware of the fact that an alliance based upon an abstract devotion to peace would have no appeal for the Emperor. "It is," he wrote, "as if some person showed his friend a beautiful fruit hanging very high on a tree in his garden, representing to him all the succulence and exquisite goodness but making him understand this: 'You would like to taste this fruit but it is necessary that you promise me before I give it to you to do something which I can tell you only when the moment arrives.' "[59]

Napoleon knew, of course, that he held trump cards against both Russia and Austria. He could threaten the former with the Polish question, the latter with difficulties in the Balkans, Hungary and Italy, and even drive a hard bargain over Venetia. The dangers facing Austria were thus very great indeed. "The terrain on which I find myself," wrote Metternich to Rechberg, "is the most difficult, the most dangerous, and the most thankless."[60] Convinced that Napoleon intended to reopen the eastern question and, by employing revolutionary methods, obtain an aggrandizement for France in the west, Metternich maintained that in order to safeguard her interests, Austria must either join Napoleon or try to form an *entente* with England, Prussia and Russia to oppose him. There were indications that France desired either Austria's support or at least her friendship in the eastern question. Thouvenel informed Metternich that Napoleon would offer no objection to an Austrian intervention in Herzegovina: in fact, he would strongly approve it.[61] Moreover, in referring to the possibility of Turkey's dismemberment, the Minister declared that Austria stood to gain more than any other power and that she need have no fear of finding France in her way.

Having by this time become distrustful of the French, Rechberg instructed Metternich to adopt a prudent and passive attitude and not to engage his government in any way.[62] Austria, he added, would base her policy on the treaties, however weak they might be, and only when they no longer were recognized, would she consult her own interests exclusively. For the time being, she preferred to have the downfall of the Ottoman Empire delayed as long as possible.

Though at the moment not in favor of Austrian intervention in Herzegovina, Rechberg refused to rule out the possibility for the future. He believed that Thouvenel was deliberately trying to direct attention to Herzegovina as a compensation for the exchange of Venetia. Furthermore, he suspected that the French were planning to set up a Hungarian-Rumanian state. Information reached him that the French Government had advanced two million francs to Louis Kossuth to enable him to settle his debts.[63]

To follow the trends of French policy under Napoleon III and to predict what action the latter intended in any given situation was by no means a simple task. That the Austrian statesmen did not always succeed and that they were deceived by straws in the wind, is not surprising. Thus, the belief that Napoleon intended to re-open the eastern question was not borne out by events. It is true that there were fluctuations and contradictions in the French policy concerning the east just as there were about Italy but Metternich thought he detected a difference. "I do not believe myself mistaken," he wrote to Rechberg, "in affirming that if in the great complications in Italy the Emperor Napoleon carried on behind the back of his minister a policy hostile to Austria, today in eastern affairs it is Monsieur Thouvenel who makes the revolutionary and anti-Austrian policy behind the back of his master."[64] He had learned that Thouvenel instructed French agents in Montenegro and Serbia to support the national aspirations of the Christians against the Sultan.[65] This was in direct contradiction to assurances which Napoleon had given Metternich. Yet, considering how tightly the Emperor held on to the reins of foreign policy, the Ambassador's assertion that Thouvenel actually conducted affairs behind the back of his master is rather difficult to believe.

It was no easy task for Rechberg to map out a satisfactory policy for eastern affairs. He knew that England and France preferred Austrian to Russian influence in the Balkans. But he wondered how he could make Austria's influence predominate when, on the one hand, he desired to maintain the integrity of the Ottoman Empire and, on the other, to protect the Balkan Christians.[66] So long as there was no satisfactory substitute for Turkish rule, Austria was forced to defend it. Moreover, while she could not renounce the conservative principles which formed the basis of her policy, she had to treat England with respect for some day she might have need of an English alliance. Finally, she could not afford to alienate the Balkan Christians whom she might in the future desire to bring under her control. "Placed between interests so contradictory," wrote Rechberg, "it is difficult for us to avoid offending equally the one and the other. We are thus led to follow a double policy hardly favorable to our influence."[67]

At the beginning of 1863 Balkan affairs appeared to be nearing a crisis. Difficulties in Greece, the Danubian Principalities, Montenegro and Serbia threatened to bring on a renewal of the eastern question and to endanger the security of both Austria and Turkey. In the circumstances, it was natural that Austria should support the Turk in the face of disturbances whose origin she attributed to revolutionary agitation, aided and encouraged by Russia, and to some extent by England and France. As the principal threat now appeared to come from Russia, Rechberg was anxious to bring about an understanding with the western powers in order to maintain peace and the *status quo*. The replacement of Thouvenel, who had leaned to the side of revolution, particularly in the Balkans, by Drouyn de Lhuys whose principles were conservative and whose sympathies pro-Austrian, encouraged Vienna in the hope of reaching such an understanding with France. Despite Napoleon's well-known dislike of the Turks and his warm sympathy for the Balkan Christians, Rechberg was given to understand that France intended to abide by the treaties.[68] This, of course, was not the same thing as saying that France would cooperate with Austria in maintaining the *status quo*. While Drouyn de Lhuys shared Austria's view that no encouragement should be given to revolutionary elements in the Balkans, he admitted to Metternich that he had many difficulties to overcome "here and elsewhere."[69] It had been necessary occasionally to put a little water in the Emperor's wine in order to counteract the influence of Budberg, the Russian Ambassador to Paris.

Napoleon declared to Metternich that the only influence in the Balkans that appeared legitimate to him and that did not in any way interfere with the interests of France, was Austrian influence and he regretted that Austria had not succeeded in taking root among the inhabitants.[70] He pretended to be greatly alarmed by the dangers of revolution, which was the cause of his own embarrassment and which disgusted him with Italy and Poland. Drouyn de Lhuys was also most conciliatory and assured Metternich that any proposal which would put an end to the differences and rivalries of the powers in the east would be welcomed by France.[71] He declared that the Emperor was free from engagements of any sort and believed that he could be persuaded to contribute to the maintenance of Turkey as long as possible.

There is no doubt that Drouyn de Lhuys was sincerely desirous of coming to an agreement with Austria on all important questions. Rechberg, however, was not convinced that Napoleon could be persuaded to cooperate toward the maintenance of the *status quo* in the Ottoman Empire.[72] As had already happened in Italy, the uncertainty concerning French policy gave encouragement to the subversive elements in the Balkans and hindered a peaceful solution, while it explained to some extent the oscillations of England's attitude. Rechberg believed that if France would openly declare herself against the intrigues which boasted of the secret and powerful protection of the Emperor, the difficulties would vanish and it would then be comparatively easy for the three powers to establish an accord. He instructed Metternich to call the attention of the French Government to the critical position of Cuza, ruler of the Principalities, and the need for an understanding concerning his successor.[73] There were rumors that Napoleon was planning to nominate his cousin as ruler of Rumania.

Another supporter of a close understanding with Austria was Gramont, French Ambassador at Vienna. To him such an understanding was more attractive than ever in view of the internal reforms in the Hapsburg Monarchy. "Austria," he wrote to Drouyn de Lhuys, "has advanced along the path of liberal ideas as quickly as it has been possible to do without a revolution. Without renouncing her past which had its *raison d'être,* the Austrian Government does not for a single moment think of returning to it. Today, it could not do so without struggles and dangers from which it will abstain, for henceforth this past is radically incompatible with its new institutions and the spirit which inspires them. . . . Hence, the enemies of yesterday no longer exist. It is a new Austria for whom the French alliance is the most desirable of alliances and whose government does not hesitate to declare it. . . . France and Austria, united by ties of mutual and enlightened confidence, cannot fail to exercise a powerful influence over the British Government and to temper the spirit of enterprise with which it appears to be animated in regard to the east; before such an *entente* Russia itself will even renounce the exaggeration of her desires and no doubt will cease to pursue by indirect means an aim which can be reached only with the general consent of the powers."[74] Franz Joseph expressed the same idea to Gramont. "I am really happy," he said, "with the thought that our two governments tend to draw closer each day. My greatest desire is that the Emperor Napoleon III and I be more and more united. I fear that he does not prepare himself for the serious embarrassment in the Principalities, but if we are together, everything will be arranged, and for my part, I will do everything that depends on me in order that our union be intimate and lasting."[75]

While Austria was endeavoring to reach an agreement with France concerning the east, at the same time she was being courted by Russia. Thun, who was on the point of leaving his post in St. Petersburg, was the recipient of unusual attentions by Gortchakoff. So extraordinary was the attitude of the Chancellor, whose lack of veracity was proverbial and whose character had filled Thun with disgust, that it was difficult to tell what lay behind it. Gortchakoff depicted himself as a statesman of the most correct principles from which he could deviate only with the greatest repugnance when forced by absolute necessity.[76] In the questions relating to Greece, Italy and Montenegro, he had upheld the principle of legitimacy and it was the mistakes committed by other powers which had checked his policy. He was convinced, he said to Thun, that Austria and Russia by virtue of their geographic positions, interests and principles, were the two empires destined to unite intimately and to erect a barrier to the revolutionary tendencies of the age. It was particularly in the Balkans that they would make their principles prevail. Gortchakoff pretended that such had always been the main lines of his policy but, unfortunately, he had been misunderstood in Vienna. For example, Austria still believed that Russia wanted the downfall of the Ottoman Empire, and that she employed all sorts of intrigues in order to bring this about; even the protection of the Christians was considered a means toward this end. On the other hand, it was generally believed in Russia that at all times Austria pursued her traditional policy in the east, that she upheld the Turks in all questions and to the very limit, not in order to maintain their rights but simply to wipe out the Christians she regarded as supporters of Russia. Gortchakoff was now ready to admit that both sides were mistaken. He contended that the aim the two powers had in mind was the same; there were merely differences of opinion as to the means to be employed.

The common aim is to preserve and sustain the Ottoman Empire as long as possible because its downfall will be equally embarrassing for both neighboring states and will present grave dangers for the peace of Europe. There is one difference on this subject: Russia wishes to preserve the Porte, to uphold it in its European political position and in its acquired rights on the sole condition that it respects the rights of the Christian subjects and that it gives them an assured means of existence, physical as well as moral and religious. Thus, Russia subordinates her interests for Turkey to her solicitude for the Christians of this vast empire. This is a cardinal point from which no government in Russia could deviate even if it wished. Austria, on the contrary, appears to have for a supreme principle always to uphold Turkey on every occasion even when she is wrong and even if it is to the detriment of her Christian subjects.[77]

Gortchakoff admitted that he personally did not believe that such was Austria's intention but the Russian public held to this view. Much of the misunderstanding between the two powers, he said, arose from the inflammatory articles in the press and he was prepared to do his part to eradicate this evil. As for alliances, he professed that he preferred Austria to France, whose political attitude disgusted him not a little.

Thun was not deceived by these fine phrases nor did he believe that Gortchakoff was so naïve as to think that he had really made an impression. What puzzled him was Gortchakoff's motive. He found part of the answer in the character of the Russian statesman. "Prince Gortchakoff has a truly fabulous vanity and an insolent arrogance with respect to the judgment of persons with whom he discusses affairs. He has so high an opinion of his mind, of the wisdom of his expedients, and at the same time such a contempt for the judgment of others, that he does not even admit the possibility that one can resist the charm of his words and that one does not accept, without reflecting, everything that is incoherent, even contradictory in his proposal."[78] More important was the fact that Gortchakoff's personal position was much weakened because of the diplomatic setbacks he had experienced in recent months. In order to retain favor with the Tsar, he threw blame for his mistakes on Budberg, Russian Ambassador at Paris, whose influence at the Russian court caused him much concern. Thun had heard rumors that Gortchakoff's downfall was imminent. "In any case," he wrote to Rechberg, "I believe that the outburst of heart with which Prince Gortchakoff favored me has a certain interest for us. If I am not mistaken, it apprises us of a certain change which is in the air."[79] Thun was apparently convinced that a change in the Russian Foreign Office was very likely. The question was who would be Gortchakoff's successor? The logical choice was Budberg, who in many respects was more capable, less vain, and also less tractable than Gortchakoff though he was just as ambitious and intriguing. As far as Austria was concerned, the appointment of Budberg would be no cause for rejoicing, for he was no more friendly to her than Gortchakoff. Indeed, the latter was more preferable since, finding his position in danger, he would do the only thing possible to save himself and that was to ally Russia with Austria.

Rechberg took Gortchakoff's overture with a grain of salt. He did not deny the possibility of a future understanding but he believed that nothing could be done in that direction for the time being as Austria favored the maintenance of the *status quo* in the Balkans.[80] While the outbreak of the Polish revolt and the conclusion of the Alvensleben Convention tended to draw Austria closer to England and France, her efforts to conclude with them an *entente o*n the eastern question had made no appreciable headway. Metternich could report only negative results. Though he found Drouyn de Lhuys, who favored such an *entente,* rather easy to deal with, the Ambassador had more difficulty with the Emperor.[81] The latter could be won over only by striking a bargain with him involving the acquisition of territory or a deal on Venetia. Metternich was of the opinion that Austria could aid Drouyn de Lhuys to overcome the hesitations of Napoleon if she would come out more openly in support of the Balkan Christians. In the event of another Russo-Turkish war it was most unlikely that France would participate, while England alone would not undertake another Crimean campaign. Thus, Austria might find herself compelled to draw the sword against Russia under conditions far less favorable than in 1854. Metternich declared that she could save herself from this eventuality by imposing her influence in all possible ways on the peoples of the Balkans.

Not until the Polish question had actually assumed dangerous proportions, did Napoleon abandon his attitude of indifference regarding an understanding with Austria. Then he was anxious to effect a *rapprochement* and made an offer of an alliance. Metternich was astonished by the utter frankness employed by the Emperor in discussing the prospects of such an alliance. "His language recalls the great epochs of his reign, epochs which preceded the wars of the east and Italy. His words breathed political passion and made a much greater effect since they were in sharp contrast with his habitual attitude. In these moments, one perceives the unbounded ambition and the indomitable energy of this extraordinary man."[82] The Emperor declared his adherence to dynastic and anti-revolutionary principles but admitted that he had not always inspired confidence at Vienna and for this reason he wished to bring England into the alliance. "The marriage of reason which bound the two western powers in all the great questions which presented themselves did not prevent, in his opinion, a narrow and devoted union between the two greatest states of the continent."[83] Napoleon asserted that with the conclusion of an Austro-French alliance all the important problems would be settled amicably and that for such sacrifices as Austria made, she would be amply compensated in the Balkans and in Germany. Metternich reminded the Emperor that what seemed to him a beautiful horizon in the distance would appear to Austria as a mirage of the desert if she would be the only one to submit to a surgical operation. Why, he asked, was it always necessary whenever it was a question of an alliance to precipitate events and foresee the need of amputations? "Let us understand one another tranquilly, I beg of you, Sire, without doing something tragic when we do not know if the curtain will not be lowered before the second act."[84] The Emperor admitted that France would gain more than Austria from an alliance.

With the powers devoting more and more attention to the Polish question, Balkan affairs were pushed to the background. Rechberg's efforts to conclude an *entente* with France and Russia and later with France and England were not realized. Nor did Napoleon succeed in obtaining an alliance with Austria or in inducing her to sacrifice her Polish territory or Venetia in return for compensations in the Balkans or Germany. Vienna was never certain that Russia might not make concessions in Poland in order to win over the Emperor and perhaps strike a bargain concerning the Balkans. Finally, the dismemberment of Turkey, which provided the principal motive for Rechberg's overtures, was still in the distance. As Russia's influence in the Balkans increased, Austria insisted upon the maintenance of the *status quo* and support of the Dying Turk.

CHAPTER THIRTEEN

The Polish Question, 1863

THE POLISH REVOLT of 1863 was the culmination of a long struggle against Russian domination. In the eighteenth century Poland as an independent state disappeared from the map of Europe following its partition by Austria, Prussia and Russia. The Kingdom of Poland, which had been set up by Tsar Alexander I of Russia after the Congress of Vienna and to which he gave liberal concessions, was destroyed by his successor, Nicholas I, following an insurrection in 1830. Thereafter Poland formed a mere province of the Russian Empire and was ruled with the greatest severity.

With the accession of Alexander II to the Russian throne there seemed to be a promise of better things to come for the Poles. The emancipation of the serfs and the influence of the idea of nationalities, which had made rapid headway among oppressed peoples everywhere, gave new hope to the Polish leaders. Indeed, there were rumors that the new Tsar planned to revive the Polish Kingdom of 1815.[1] Unfortunately, the Tsar's policy of alternating liberalism with oppression served to agitate and arouse the Poles and led to an insurrection in the spring of 1861 which was quickly suppressed. Aware that the Polish cause evoked widespread sympathy in France,[1a] Alexander II hastened to grant some concessions to the Poles. But these concessions merely whetted the appetites of the Polish leaders, who were determined to make Poland an independent nation. A decree of October 6, 1862, which provided that Polish revolutionaries be conscripted into the Russian army and the occupation of Warsaw by Russian troops infuriated the Polish nationalists. The Polish revolt broke out on January 22, 1863 and soon became a major problem of European diplomacy.

On February 8th Prussia concluded with Russia the Alvensleben Convention.[2] By this Prussia promised military assistance in order to suppress the insurrection. News of the Convention aroused Napoleon from his attitude of seeming indifference. Hitherto he had hesitated to declare himself in favor of the Poles and, indeed, had refrained from giving any official encouragement to their cause. But Prussia's intervention changed the character of the crisis, transforming it from a domestic to a European question. Still anxious to avoid a rupture with the Tsar, Napoleon decided upon a diplomatic campaign against Prussia rather than Russia.[3] On February 21st Drouyn de Lhuys proposed to London and Vienna the dispatch of identic notes to Berlin protesting against the Alvensleben Convention.[4]

This attempt to make Prussia rather than Russia the target of a diplomatic campaign did not meet with favor in London and Vienna. While the Polish cause elicited widespread sympathy in England, the Cabinet had no desire to become too deeply involved in the affair and both Palmerston and Russell had already made it known that no material assistance would be given to the Poles.[5] The English were not especially anxious to see Poland reconstituted as an independent state, for they suspected that such a state would be allied to France. Moreover, they saw that the Polish question was likely to bring about a rupture between Paris and St. Petersburg— a prospect by no means displeasing to Downing Street. On the other hand, England had no quarrel with Prussia and no desire to provoke that power. Although a note was sent to Berlin, March 2nd, this was merely to please the French.[6]

Austria's interest in the Polish question was far more important than that of England.[7] Along with Prussia and Russia she had shared in the partitions of the old Poland during the eighteenth century. The Austrian province of Galicia, inhabited by both Poles and Ruthenians, had not given much trouble for a number of years and the outbreak of the Polish insurrection caused no immediate alarm in Vienna. On the contrary, the Austrian statesmen were rather pleased to see Russia experiencing the dangers of nationalism. They had not forgotten that the Tsar declined the suggestion of Franz Joseph at the Warsaw conference in 1860 for an understanding concerning Poland. During the first period of the insurrection, Austria adopted a rather indulgent attitude toward the insurgents.[8] But in view of the general principles of her policy and her special interests in the Polish question, she refused to participate in the action suggested by France.[9] As far as these special interests were concerned, Austria could not ignore the fact that the insurrection was the work of revolutionaries, who only awaited a favorable moment to stir up the Galician Poles. In declining the French proposal, Rechberg made it clearly understood that Austria's sympathies were with the western powers.[10] As it was, the importance of the Alvensleben Convention was greatly exaggerated and its duration was very brief.[11]

The failure of the French move left the situation unchanged. Napoleon was still reluctant to bring about a rift with Russia and hoped to reach an understanding with the Tsar which would settle the Polish question. However, as Russia appeared determined not to reconstitute the Polish Kingdom, Napoleon decided to turn his attention to Austria. His aim was to utilize the Polish question in order to conclude an alliance with Austria through which he hoped to persuade the latter to give up both Galicia and Venetia and thus solve the Italian and Polish problems at one stroke. The general idea was set forth in a memorandum which was submitted to him by Prince Napoleon.[12] After reminding the Emperor of the enthusiasm evoked by the Polish insurrection among all classes of French society, the memorandum went on to suggest a wholesale revision of the European map including the reëstablishment of the old Polish kingdom, the cession of Venetia to Italy, a Balkan confederation, the erection of Constantinople as a free city, compensation for Austria in Germany for the loss of Galicia and Venetia, cession of the left bank of the Rhine to France, and the return of Finland to Sweden. Austria was the pivot of this grandiose scheme and the Prince urged the Emperor to dispatch a personal agent to Vienna.

No doubt Austria's attitude in the Polish question stimulated the French desire for an alliance. Metternich reported that the moment had never been more favorable to conclude an *entente* with France on all questions.[13] Public opinion, Catholic and revolutionary journals, conservative statesmen and even radicals like Prince Napoleon leaned to the side of an alliance, while Walewski, who could now give free rein to his Polish sympathies, was so enthusiastic that Metternich had to beg him to set limits to his dreams.[14] Though Drouyn de Lhuys favored the idea, he preferred to have England included, believing that only such a triple alliance could destroy the old pact between Napoleon and the revolutionary movement.[15]

On February 21, 1863, Metternich had a three-hour conversation with the Empress Eugénie on the subject of Poland.[16] She began by saying that the Emperor was greatly preoccupied with the question of an *entente* of Austria, England and France, an *entente* which would lead to the solution of all problems, the consolidation of his dynasty, and the happiness of the world. Meantime, she desired to throw caution to the winds and to say what she thought even if the Ambassador regarded her as a fool. "In order to make you understand what I desire," she said, "the ideals of my policy, it is necessary that we take the map." Metternich's curiosity was aroused in the highest degree at the thought of journeying with the Empress "across a map so frequently travelled over by the imperial couple." The Empress took a large map and for more than an hour explained her curious plan. "I could not follow in all its details the peregrination . . . of the Empress and I finally arrived at this which appeared to me the positive aim, the decisive arrangement. . . ."

Here Metternich set forth the territorial alterations suggested by the Empress. Russia should be driven out of the Balkans and remunerated for the loss of Poland by compensations in Asiatic Turkey. Poland should be reconstituted with a Hapsburg Archduke as king, if Austria desired, but preferably with the King of Saxony resuming his dynastic rights for the cession of his kingdom to Prussia which, in turn, would cede Pomerania to Poland, Silesia to Austria, and the left bank of the Rhine to France but would obtain in addition to Saxony, Hanover and the duchies north of the Main. Austria would cede Venetia to Piedmont and a part of Galicia (Cracow and Lemberg) to Poland, but would take a line of frontiers across Serbia along the Adriatic, Silesia and all that she wanted in Germany south of the Main. France would cede nothing but would get the left bank of the Rhine, while respecting the independence of Belgium because of England. Italy was to have Lombardy, Venetia, Tuscany, Parma, Piacenza, Bologna and Ferrara but was to restore the Two Sicilies to the King of Naples, who would enlarge the Papal States. Turkey would be suppressed in the interest of public utility and Christian morality and allow herself to be partitioned by yielding her Asiatic possessions to Russia, the coastline of the Adriatic to Austria, Thessaly, Albania and Constantinople to Greece, and the Principalities as an independent enclave to a native prince. The dispossessed princes and kings would go to civilize and monarchize the American republics which would follow the example arranged for Mexico. "There is the plan of the Empress and I beg you, Monsieur le Comte, not to consider it a joke; I believe the Empress and even the Emperor are convinced of the possibility and the necessity of realizing it some day." Putting aside "these Napoleonic phantasmagoria," Metternich firmly believed that Austria could reach an understanding with France but thought it quite important to include England in order to moderate French influence.[17]

The idea of an alliance with France found favor in Vienna. In writing to Metternich, however, Rechberg stated in the official dispatches, which were to be shown to Drouyn de Lhuys, that it should put off until later, while in a private letter he directed the Ambassador not to let the moment go by.[18] Metternich was to use his discretion as to whether it was advisable to adopt an active or passive attitude in the matter. Rechberg pointed out that in return for support in the Polish question, Austria expected concessions in the Balkans and in Italy.

Drouyn de Lhuys, to whom Metternich submitted the official dispatches, appeared somewhat vexed, but the Emperor who received the Ambassador's "small mysteries" set to work immediately.[19] "I spent three days running from the Tuileries to the ministry and from the ministry to the Tuileries in order to reëstablish the equilibrium." Metternich could not tell what would result from his efforts but he was convinced that only the two rulers could place the alliance on a solid and durable basis and that the difficulties

confronting it would be solved by events. Since Napoleon demanded
a definite pledge of support from Austria before deciding on compensations, it was necessary to devise a formula. He promised that
if Austria would abandon Galicia and Venetia, he would support
her in finding compensations in the east and in Germany. Metternich
did not care for this approach and replied that Austria had no
particular desire to reconstitute Italy and Poland. "Why," he asked
Napoleon, "do you wish to force us to engage ourselves in advance
when we are not certain that the sacrifices . . . will be necessary?
Why not go back to what will be the more simple question and
and engage yourself to aid us in getting compensations if the
necessity arises?" The Emperor argued that events could compel
Austria to give up either Galicia or Venetia before she had time
to save them or to prepare an understanding with France. However,
he agreed not to couple the question of Austria's support with that
of compensations and not to accept any proposition without first
notifying Vienna. Finally, he assured the Ambassador that if Austria
would state her wishes more clearly, he would take them under
consideration and reply to them frankly and honestly.

While the Emperor's tone remained calm throughout the discussion, the Empress, with whom Metternich also conversed, was
all "fire and flame."[20] She could not comprehend why Austria would
not make every sacrifice in order to bring about the alliance.
Believing that she had not succeeded in making clear her viewpoints orally, she wrote Metternich a letter.[21] In this she conceded
that the Ambassador probably found the *furia francese* rather
strange, that it may have frightened him, and that he may have
preferred abstention to a rapid decision. But the more she thought
about it, the more she asked herself what means would be found
to conclude an alliance if this opportunity were lost. Should the
insurrection in Poland be suppressed and order reëstablished, would
it be possible again to bring up the question of an alliance? Would
not France reply that she had no further need of an ally? And
where would one find the point of contact to cement the alliance
if the two powers abstained from any common action? If France
demanded sacrifices of Austria, were these not accompanied by
compensations?

The marriage of inclination is with you; we do not make a marriage of reason. But if you were to tell me to be specific, I could not say much; what I fear to lose is the opportunity. You are nearer the events and can even judge the development they take. But, above all, let us specify, that is more practical. I have reread my letter thoroughly and I do not know if it has a *raison d'être*. I believe it is by habit that I again speak of the affair, but, above all, keep it to yourself. I decidedly do not wish to have it made part of a fairy story or of the *Thousand and One Nights.*

From all this it was clear to Metternich that if she so desired, Austria could conclude an alliance with France. The eagerness displayed by the imperial couple left no doubt on that score. That the Empress did not intervene in the affair without the knowledge and approval of the Emperor is unquestionably true. She was the medium frequently employed by Napoleon in dealings with the Austrian Ambassador. This is understandable considering the intimate friendship existing between the Empress and the Metternichs. In connection with the alliance project, Napoleon also employed the services of Bourqueney, who was well-liked in the Austrian capital, having acted there as French Ambassador for a number of years. Bourqueney was requested to give Metternich a detailed exposition of the imperial viewpoint.[22] The Emperor also asked Bourqueney to undertake a special mission to Vienna in order to exert an influence favorable to the alliance project but the former ambassador declined.[23] Metternich himself was an ardent advocate of a *rapprochement* with France but now when suddenly confronted by the offer of an alliance, found it difficult to make up his mind in view of the sacrifices Austria was asked to make. As it was, he decided to recommend the alliance to his government. "I maintain," he wrote to Rechberg, "that the occasion is propitious for us to draw enormous advantages from the French alliance as the terrain has never been and, perhaps, will never be better prepared."[24]

Metternich was summoned to Vienna in order to give an oral account of his impressions. He was instructed to announce his departure in such a manner as to give it the least possible importance and thus avoid the danger that the Tuileries would attach hopes to it which Austria might not be in a position to fulfill.[25] Upon learning of the summons, the Empress hastened to send Metternich a draft of a secret treaty.[26] The Emperor approved the draft, which was couched in general terms and made no mention of pledges or concessions, and it was understood that Metternich was free to submit it to his government or not, as he saw fit. However, he sent a copy to Rechberg and on March 12th left for Vienna. He took with him a letter from Napoleon addressed to Franz Joseph[27] and a very brief draft of a treaty which he himself had prepared and which the French ruler accepted in principle.

Metternich's mission to Vienna did not escape the attention of the European cabinets. Occurring at such a time, there was considerable interest and not a little suspicion aroused by it. Though Cowley had kept Russell well informed about the affair, the latter was nevertheless apprehensive lest Austria conclude an alliance which might serve the ambitious designs of Napoleon in redrawing the map of Europe.[28] Prussia was also alarmed and Bismarck instructed Werther, Prussian Ambassador at Vienna, to ask Rechberg if it were true that France had made proposals concerning an alliance.[29] Rechberg did not deny that negotiations had taken place between the two governments " by the ordinary diplomatic way" about events in Poland but he did not believe that he had the right to communicate the substance of these to a third power.[30] The Austrian Ambassador in Berlin was instructed to decline any request Bismarck might make regarding the subject. There was such a sharp contrast between Rechberg's tone of defiance toward Prussia and his friendly attitude toward France, that Gramont was encouraged to enter upon a frank discussion of the alliance project. By allying with France, he said to Rechberg, Austria would divorce her past and embrace a new future. But she would have to take France as she was, bearing in mind the origins, principles and interests of the Emperor Napoleon. Gramont tried his best to reassure Rechberg concerning the latter's policies. He argued that France was progressive but not revolutionary and that her policy was not dominated by a spirit of adventure. Rechberg's reply was encouraging. He offered not the slightest objection to the views set forth by the French Ambassador. On the contrary, he expressed himself as being perfectly reassured regarding French policy and professed to see in an Austro-French alliance the best guarantee for the present and, above all, for the

future. But it was necessary to call a spade a spade and before
Austria could join France in a common action, she must have
guarantees concerning compensations. "I do not think," replied
Gramont, "that my government has ever understood otherwise."[31]

Metternich's sojourn in Vienna in March 1863 was an important
event in the annals of European diplomacy. Unfortunately, the
documents do not give a full account of what transpired there. The
official Austrian reaction to the alliance proposal is fairly well
presented in a number of papers.[32] One of these is a memorandum
drawn up by Rechberg, an extract of which was presented to
Napoleon. After expressing appreciation for the frankness with
which the French Government had made known it views to Metternich, the memorandum set forth the reasons why Austria could
not accept the offer of an alliance. It pointed out that such an
alliance would compel her to follow an active policy which was
not in accord with her interests. It would involve her in long and
costly wars which would more than offset any contemplated advantages. At the moment, Austria was engaged in a laborious task of
internal reconstruction absorbing all her cares and thus had need
of peace. In declining the offer of an alliance, Rechberg wanted
Napoleon to understand that Austria was not contemplating any
other combination.

In a personal letter to Drouyn de Lhuys, Rechberg endeavored
to soften the effects of Austria's refusal.[33] He praised the efforts of
the French Minister in establishing closer relations between the
two governments and expressed the hope that he would continue
to give his support to Metternich. However, Austria could not
renounce her traditions and principles without sacrificing her moral
strength. The difficulties inherent in her geographic position, the
presence of her numerous nationalities, and the work of internal
reconstruction—all these factors forced Austria to maintain an
attitude of reserve which the interests of France did not require
in the same degree.

Besides Rechberg's letter, Franz Joseph wrote one to Napoleon
in which he expressed the hope that the French ruler would
appreciate Austria's difficulties and continue to show the same
confidence that inspired his offer of an alliance.[34] In his reply,

Napoleon declared that since his accession to the throne, he had always sought to establish a durable alliance with one of the great powers but had been checked by some incident or other.[35] When there appeared the possibility of resurrecting Poland, he saw an opportunity of concluding a real understanding with Austria which would put an end to all uncertainties of the present and all dangers of the future.

We find the real motives for Austria's rejection of the alliance in the secret instructions which Rechberg prepared for Metternich.[36] Once it had been accepted in principle, said these instructions, that Austria had need of peace, that she could not engage in an active policy, and that circumstances alone could compel a change in her attitude, it was clear that these circumstances must be present before determining the kind and degree of influence they would exert on her policy. Furthermore, while it was recognized that events could bring about an agreement between Austria and France, yet, the nature of such events, the regions where they occurred, and the manner in which they engaged the interests of Austria, should be taken into consideration before indicating what compensations could offset the burdens of the proposed alliance. Any attempt to stipulate the concessions beforehand would be purely conjectural. The instructions discussed some of the eventualities upon which an alliance with France depended. The first of these concerned the cession of Venetia. Considering that Austria had spent hugh sums of money and sacrificed thousands of lives for the defense and prosperity of this province, that its geographic position assured her free access to the only sea open to her and served as the principal outlet for the trade of southern Germany, the possibility of its cession could never be presented as advantageous or admissible to the Austrian people. Not until the European equilibrium had been completely changed and Austria had acquired new possessions and real advantages in the Balkans and in Germany, would she agree to abandon Venetia. No doubt there would be advantages in obtaining compensations in Germany but there would also be grave responsibilities. And if France should direct her gaze toward the Rhine and annex the German provinces, would this not be giving the lie to the principle of nationalities? Would it not be a denial of the pretext that Austria should exercise exclusive influence in Germany? As for the reconstruction of Poland, sooner or later this would mean the loss of Galicia. But how could one expect Austria to support a plan which would inevitably engage her in a war against Russia alone or against Russia and Prussia—a plan which would involve the loss of one of her finest provinces? Galicia had certain advantages for Austria which could not easily be replaced.[37] Not only was it an essential line of communication between Vienna and Transylvania but it was of the highest strategic importance. It provided the Emperor with 100,000 troops and a substantial revenue and at the same time required little expense for administration. Besides, France did not control provinces in either Germany or the Balkans which could be regarded as acceptable for the loss of Galicia. In regard to compensations in the east, Austria did not favor the aspirations manifested by countries subject to Turkish sovereignty for complete independence. And in return for compensations, she would be expected to embark upon an adventurous policy, involve her finances, run the risk of fighting for the principle of nationalities abroad while arousing nationalistic tendencies at home.

While Paris and Vienna were engaged in the alliance negotiations, the Polish question was given a new turn by an English proposal that the signatory powers of the Treaty of 1815 make representations at St. Petersburg calling on Russia to restore the constitution granted by Alexander I. Rechberg did not favor this proposal, it being his opinion that it would not pacify the Poles since they would not be content with the constitution of 1815 but actually desired the establishment of an independent state comprising all districts once part of the old Poland.[38] Furthermore, such a step by the powers was likely to bring on war and entail the loss of Galicia, while there was also the danger that Russia would throw herself into the arms of France and promise the latter compensations in the east.

Checked in his attempt to embroil Austria in his plans for solving the Polish question, Napoleon now faced the alternative of remaining silent or of accepting the English proposal. Silence, however, was impossible in view of the pressure of French public opinion. Yet, while anxious to do something for Poland, the Emperor was not yet ready to break with Russia. The hints thrown out regarding the possibility of an understanding with Russia appeared to have some foundation. The Emperor read to Metternich a long letter from Montebello, French Ambassador at St. Petersburg, relating conversations with Gortchakoff. The latter had declared that if Napoleon was thinking of direct advantages for France in the Polish question, he should state them and then he would see that his real friends were in St. Petersburg.[39]

The proposal for a collective *démarche* at St. Petersburg was accepted by France and an effort was made by Drouyn de Lhuys to obtain's Austria's support. The latter found the situation especially trying. Just as she had hesitated during the Crimean War, she now endeavored to avoid a decision that would force her into an active policy. Rechberg refused to depart from the attitude of reserve he had adopted at the beginning of the crisis. However, Drouyn de Lhuys was anxious to have Austria demonstrate her solidarity with the western powers and he urged Rechberg to address a circular dispatch to all powers declaring that the autonomy granted to Galicia in February 1863 had secured the tranquillity of that province and suggesting that Prussia and Russia make similar provisions for their Polish subjects.[40] It was understood that England and France would support Austria in this move and there would thus be established the semblance of an *entente* of the three powers. Rechberg rejected this suggestion, viewing it as a veiled attempt to shift responsibility for taking the initiative.[41] He also turned down the proposal for a collective note to St. Petersburg on the plea that this would be interfering in Russian internal affairs.[42] Instead, he offered to direct the Austrian Chargé d'Affaires at St. Petersburg to submit a note to the Russian Government protesting against the insurrection and urging a restoration of order and an improvement in the condition of the Poles.[43] The proposal for a collective note was finally dropped though a common action was established when Austria agreed to submit her note at the same time as the western powers. England was particularly anxious to have Austrian support in order to prevent Napoleon from going too far in behalf of the Poles.[44] With the presentation of the notes early in April the *entente* of the three powers was finally established.

The Polish question awakened the distrust of all the powers. Rechberg learned that at the very moment Napoleon was making advances to Austria, he was trying to drive a bargain with Russia whereby the Duke of Leuchtenberg would become ruler of an independent Poland, excluding Galicia and Posen.[45] According to information he received from Berlin, Prussia hesitated to express herself too openly to Russia, believing that Gortchakoff would return to his old French sympathies as soon as the Polish question had been half-way arranged. At Paris, von der Goltz, the Prussian Minister, was endeavoring to cast doubts about the sincerity of Austria's policy by emphasizing her supposed *rapprochement* with Prussia and Russia.[46] Napoleon began to fear that the Holy Alliance was about to be revived. He told Metternich that von der Goltz "praised enormously Austria's benevolent attitude toward Prussia."[47] The Emperor also learned that Rechberg had asked the Russian Ambassador, de Balabine, *à propos* the French offer of an alliance, "how can you expect to come to an understanding with a power which desires to take two provinces from us?"[48] At St. Petersburg, Alexander II spoke very favorably of Austria's policy and expressed the hope of establishing an *entente* with her.[49] Actually, Franz Joseph and his minister were not thinking of reviving the Holy Alliance. In view of Russia's internal weakness and her Balkan aspirations, they saw little advantage in joining Russia, while their suspicions of Prussia did not encourage much hope in that direction.

Just what action would be taken in the event that Russia returned unsatisfactory replies to the notes, was uncertain. Apparently France considered the possibility of intervention and it was noticeable that Napoleon spoke in a more belligerent tone about Russia.[50] He asked Cowley if England would join France in a naval expedition to the Baltic in case war broke out and even went so far as to say that it would be a good plan to occupy one of the Russian islands as a pledge of obtaining results in Poland.[51] However, Metternich advised Rechberg to reject equally those reports which pretended that Napoleon was on the point of embarking upon war or those which pretended a false optimism to the contrary.[52] The truth of the matter was that the Emperor saw that the Polish crisis might last and that he could derive certain advantages from it. But Rechberg did not discount the possibility of a Franco-Russian war over Poland nor did he believe that such a war could be localized or that Austria could remain neutral. It was practically certain that Prussia would join Russia in the event of a French expedition to the Baltic. Rechberg's chief preoccupation at the moment was to prevent France from dragging Austria into a course which would threaten peace and he hoped that England would regulate her conduct in such a way that Napoleon would hesitate to draw the sword.[53]

In his reply (April 26th) to the notes of the three powers, Gortchakoff showed a disposition to negotiate and invited them to make known their ideas. On the surface it appeared that the Polish question was about to be settled by diplomacy. Actually, however, the Russians were playing for time, realizing that with the Baltic open to a naval expedition, they were vulnerable to attack. But Drouyn de Lhuys preferred to look upon Gortchakoff's willingness to exchange views as a diplomatic victory and declared that not even Louis Philippe had been able to obtain such a concession.[54] As the best means of getting something "serious" for the Poles, he suggested the convocation of a European congress—a favorite idea of Napoleon's. He hoped that England would accept such a congress, while there were rumors that Gortchakoff would welcome it in order to introduce questions which would divert attention from the Polish problem. "The idea of a congress," wrote Metternich, "has again inflamed the minds at the Tuileries and they almost seem to count upon it."[55] Indeed, the Emperor felt quite sure that even Austria would accept it with certain reservations concerning the agenda. The liberal and seemingly sympathetic attitude Austria displayed toward the Poles at the beginning of the crisis and the language of her press, led Napoleon to believe that she intended to take decisive action and this encouraged him to propose an alliance though it is true that these illusions had evaporated since Metternich's return from Vienna. In any case, Rechberg turned down the idea of a congress, preferring ordinary diplomatic negotiations, and insisted that he could not ask Russia to do more for her Polish subjects than Austria had done for hers in Galicia.[56]

No doubt Austria's position in the Polish question was somewhat anomalous. By participating in the *démarche* at St. Petersburg and by implication thus upholding the principle of nationalities, she appeared to be contradicting her traditional policy. Actually there was no intention of compromising with a principle which would lead to the disintegration of her empire. In May 1863 Rechberg explained to the Austrian Council of Ministers that in view of internal conditions, the maintenance of peace was absolutely necessary and that Austria could not make demands on Russia which that power would reject and thus provide France with the occasion for war.[57] It is not surprising that the Russians had their doubts about Austria's sincerity in supporting the Poles or the solidarity of the triple *entente.* They knew that if Austria could be won over to their side, the western powers would not be likely to carry matters too far. It was with this in mind that on June 1st Alexander II wrote to his uncle, William I of Prussia, begging him to use his influence at Vienna in order to detach Austria from the *entente* and join Prussia and Russia in a conservative alliance.[58] Though the Prussian King made the overture in Vienna, the attempt to destroy the *entente* did not succeed because Austria was firmly resolved not to separate herself from England and France.

As the Polish affair dragged on during the spring and summer of 1863 the triple *entente* of Austria, England and France became more and more feeble. In May the English Government submitted to Paris and Vienna a four-point program which called for a one-year armistice, turning over the civil and political administration to Poles enjoying the confidence of the Polish people, retention of the fortresses by Russia, and a guarantee that no Pole be arrested or indicted before tribunals for acts committed during the insurrection.[59] Though accepted by France, Rechberg did not approve this program. He maintained that acceptance of the first point by Russia would be an acknowledgment of an independent Poland, while the second would consecrate its existence.[60] Moreover, to demand an armistice was to establish a parity between the Russians and the Poles, which the former could not accept without giving the appearance of recognizing the insurrection as a legally constituted force.[61] Convinced that Russia would not accept this program and that its presentation would merely aggravate the situation, Rechberg submitted a substitute program to London and Paris which he regarded as the maximum that could be attained.[62] The Austrian program provided for a complete and general amnesty, national representation, the admission of Poles to administrative functions in the interior of Poland, complete freedom of conscience and the suppression of all legal restrictions which existed in this respect and to which the Catholic religion and clergy were principally subjected, the recognition of the Polish language as the official language of Poland and to be employed as such in the administration, justice and instruction, and the establishment of a regular and legal system of recruiting. Rechberg declared that this program constituted the *ne plus ultra* of what Russia could grant to friendly demands made in a pacific spirit. Any attempt to exceed them would sooner or later provoke an open rupture and possibly war and in view of her geographic position and special interests in the Polish question, Austria could not run the risk of a conflict in favor of Poland without obtaining positive guarantees. These guarantees, which was the price England and France must pay for Austrian cooperation were as follows: (1) England and France must consider as a *casus belli* for themselves any act of hostility directed against Austria by any power whatever which was provoked by Austria's attitude in the Polish question, (2) in case of war they should participate in the same measure as Austria by placing in line equal forces or by giving subsidies to make up for the inequality of their contingents, (3) to guarantee the entire solution of the Polish question and in the arrangements terminating it to respect the territorial integrity of Austria or to procure for her territorial compensations fully equivalent to the regions she might be induced to cede to Poland should the course of events favor the reconstruction of a Polish kingdom and (4) in the definitive settlement of the Polish question to permit such an extension as the signatory powers of the Treaty of Vienna would accept.[63]

Neither England nor France was disposed to accept the Austrian program.[64] Indeed, Drouyn de Lhuys ridiculed the fear of war and asked what this program contained which the Russians had not already offered the Poles.[65] Though Metternich made valiant efforts to defend the program and to combat the idea of an armistice, he made no headway. In fact, he found the situation in Paris so complicated and so difficult that it was virtually impossible for him to exercise any influence.[66]

In a series of dispatches to Metternich, Rechberg took great pains to explain the policy he had followed in the Polish question from its beginning. Austria's moderation, he said, did not result from any excessive desire to spare the feelings of the Tsar but from the fact that she could not demand more of Russia than she herself was willing to give.[67] France had raised the question of a congress which Vienna could not accept since it would establish an unfortunate precedent. If disturbances occurred in Hungary or Venetia, might these not be regarded as European in character and a congress summoned to interfere in Austria's internal affairs? In reply to the insinuations made by France that Austria had altered her policy, Rechberg emphasized that it had been Austria's constant preoccupation to prevent the outbreak of war and all her actions had been consistent with this aim.[68] Turning to the question of an independent Poland for which the western powers apparently were working, he saw that Austria might not be able to evade the issue but would have to oppose it if it were a disadvantage to her.[69] Meanwhile, Galicia was an excellent bargaining point which should not be ceded without an equivalent compensation. In any case, Rechberg was convinced that Austria could not remain passive while England and France effected a reconstruction of Poland. Such a course would be just as dangerous as an attempt on her part to offer opposition. France would certainly fight Austria and summon the revolution to her side; Italy would attack from the south, while the Slavs of the Hapsburg Monarchy would revolt. Nor would Austria gain anything by joining Prussia and Russia. The latter was too weak, the former too untrustworthy. Therefore, if it came to a showdown on the Polish question, Austria could not refuse to support England and France but this decision should be delayed as long as possible.

Realizing that Austria could not be persuaded to accept the English program, the western powers displayed a more conciliatory attitude. In order to preserve the appearance of an *entente,* these powers accepted the Austrian proposals as the basis for notes to be presented to Russia but in addition insisted upon an armistice and a conference of the signatory powers of the Treaty of Vienna.[70] Rechberg realized that Austria could not afford to separate herself from the western powers, that if she did, she would lose the moderating influence she had exercised over them and probably find a war at her very doorstep.[71] Therefore, the *entente* must be maintained and the Polish question kept on the terrain of diplomacy as long as possible. He was willing to accept a conference provided its deliberations were restricted to the Polish problem but an armistice was quite another matter and he flatly rejected it on the ground that it implied equality between the two contestants.[72] Indeed, Franz Joseph considered this demand incompatible with the rights and the dignity of a sovereign power.[73]

The three powers presented their notes to St. Petersburg in the middle of June.[74] In the meantime, the obvious weakness of the *entente* had caused the Russians to stiffen and even before the presentation of the notes Gortchakoff let it be known that he would not consider a conference on the Polish question alone as this would bring Russia before a European tribunal.[75] This was contrary to what he had given the three powers to understand in the notes he had addressed to them in April and it increased the possibility that Russia would refuse the demands of the *entente* altogether. Convinced that Russia would yield only if the *entente* were maintained and strengthened, Drouyn de Lhuys proposed that the three powers bind themselves by means of a convention or a protocol.[76] This was rejected by Austria and England, the latter because she feared Russia might decide to fight rather than yield to the demands of the three powers. Drouyn de Lhuys was frankly disappointed with this lukewarm attitude and especially peeved with England which he described to Metternich as "an old woman who no longer has any humor, who sulks at every moment, and who when she tries to carry on an antiquated flirtation must disgust us as quickly as possible by her impotence."[77]

On July 13th Gortchakoff replied to the notes of the three powers. While accepting in principle the six points of the Austrian program, he rejected an armistice and a conference of the signatory powers of the Treaty of Vienna, and placed responsibility for the continuance of the insurrection on the moral and material assistance it received from without.[78] Finally, he argued that the part of the old Poland acquired by Russia in the partitions was in the same class as those parts belonging to Austria and Prussia and suggested an *entente* with these powers to regulate the affairs of their respective Polish subjects. Rechberg hastened to repulse this obvious attempt to separate Austria from the western powers. He denied that there existed any similarity between Russian Poland and Galicia. "Galicia," he declared, "belongs to Austria without conditions while the Kingdom of Poland belongs to Russia under conditions stipulated and guaranteed by a treaty of which the contracting powers have the right to demand execution."[79] He was indignant because Gortchakoff professed to see in the wording of the Austrian note a tacit recognition that a conference was undesirable. Yet, despite the unsatisfactory tone of Gortchakoff's reply, Rechberg thought it might be used as the basis for further discussions.[80] However, England and France were no longer in the mood to reopen negotiations. Instead, Drouyn de Lhuys proposed that the three powers send short identic notes to St. Petersburg for the purpose of closing the discussion.[81] The refusal of Austria and England to accept this proposal gave the death-blow to the triple *entente* and early in August the three powers sent separate notes to St. Petersburg. On September 7th Gortchakoff replied in a manner which discouraged further negotiations. There was a note of finality in his statement that the Tsar knew what to do with Poland.

While for all practical purposes the *entente* had been shattered, none of the three powers had modified its attitude in any degree toward the Polish question. The divergence among them was largely over the means to be employed toward Russia. From the beginning of the crisis, France had been the most active champion of the Poles and it was her activity that aroused suspicion in London and Vienna. The fear that Napoleon was pushing his two partners into a war against Russia explains their hesitation to follow him in a forward policy. England had no desire to pull the chestnuts out of the fire for France, while Austria was held back by her own peculiar interests in the Polish question. The failure to present a common front at St. Petersburg demonstrated only too eloquently the weakness of the *entente* and gave Gortchakoff the opportunity to reply in his highhanded manner. Even then a semblance of unity might have been maintained had London and Vienna agreed to the proposal for identic notes. But the realization that nothing short of war would induce Russia to grant concessions as well as the weariness engendered by months of tortuous and futile diplomacy made Austria and England only too glad to let the matter drop.

So far as Austria is concerned, one cannot escape the conclusion that she accepted simply as a theory the principle of humanity and justice which the French Government raised on behalf of the Poles, while in practice she worked for the maintenance of the *status quo*. Hence, she participated in the diplomatic maneuvers at St. Petersburg in favor of the Poles, but only in order to restore the administrative and legal conditions of the past. In this way she probably hoped to raise herself morally in the eyes of European liberal opinion while escaping the inconveniences and complications of a conduct conforming to the principles she enunciated. This policy had not been without its difficulties, however, for the Poles of Galicia were naturally sympathetic to their fellow kinsmen under Russian rule and quite as naturally desired that Austria combine theory with practice. In other words, the Poles of Galicia wanted nothing less than that the Austrian Government give aid to the insurrection. Confronted by such an attitude on the part of her own subjects, Austria took steps to repress their enthusiasm and regarded as criminal any attempt to show open sympathy for the Russian Poles. The presence of revolutionary agitators in Galicia made it all the more necessary to adopt stern measures. The greater the sympathy revealed for the Polish cause, the greater the repression and consequently the more reluctant Austria became to follow the lead of France.

At a Ministerial Council in Vienna on November 1st presided over by the Emperor and attended by Prince Metternich, a discussion took place concerning the policy Austria should adopt in the Polish question. The following decisions were arrived at: (1) the retention of Galicia and opposition to any plan which had for its object the reëstablishment of the Polish Kingdom even within the limits of the Treaty of 1815, (2) cooperation with England in order to maintain peace, (3) in case war became inevitable, Austria would join the side of the western powers.[82] The various aspects of the Polish question were reviewed in a memorandum prepared by Rechberg.[83] In this he declared that the Russian replies could be considered as closing the period of diplomatic intervention of the three powers and removing any hope of settlement by means of negotiations. He expressed the belief that France had no intention of dropping the Polish question but on the contrary would do everything to bring about a settlement which would permit the realization of at least a part of the plans she pursued, and that while England did not want war, she would probably be dragged into it. In this case, Austria sooner or later would be compelled to take part in the struggle. While the memorandum did not indicate which side Austria would take, it implied that an alliance with the western powers was less dangerous for her position than any other combination.

Meanwhile, all Europe waited for Napoleon to speak. His silence raised all sorts of conjectures. What schemes had he concocted during his sojourn in Biarritz? Was he planning war or peace? Nobody knew but everyone felt that he would have something important to say to the *Corps Législatif*. In the Polish question his hands were more or less tied, for he could not abandon it without danger to himself. The French press was critical of the failure sustained by the government in this question and there were some which did not hesitate to place the blame on the Emperor.[84] Thus, it was reasonable to expect that he would do something to retrieve this failure. "The reserve," wrote the Austrian Chargé d'Affaires, "followed by his government in the later phases of the [Polish] question ought to prepare us for some sort of a *coup de théatre*."[85]

The *coup de théatre* came on November 5, 1863, in an address delivered by the Emperor at the opening session of the *Corps Législatif*. Referring to the Polish question, he recalled the friendly relations existing between France and Russia since the Crimean War and his hesitation to compromise these relations by taking a decisive stand in favor of the Poles but the question touched too many interests to be treated by France alone.[86] As the efforts of Austria, England and France to obtain concessions for the Poles had ended in failure, what were these powers to do under the circumstances? Was there nothing left for them but the alternative of war or silence?

Without having recourse to arms while without remaining silent, one means remains to us; it is to submit the Polish cause to a European tribunal. Russia has already declared that conferences where all other questions which concern Europe will be debated, will in no way offend her dignity.

Let us take note of this declaration. Let it serve us to extinguish once and for all the fermentations of discord ready to break out on all sides and let it, from the very uneasiness of Europe wrought by so many elements of dissolution, create a new era of order and peace.

Has not the moment come to reconstruct on new bases the edifice undermined by time and destroyed piece by piece by revolutions?

Is it not urgent to recognize by new conventions that which is irrevocably accomplished, and of accomplishing in common accord that which the peace of the world demands?

The Treaties of 1815 have ceased to exist. The force of things has overthrown them or tends to overthrow them almost everyhwere. They have been broken in Greece, Belgium, France, Italy as well as on the Danube. Germany is agitating to change them; England has generously modified them by the cession of the Ionian Islands, and Russia crushes them under foot at Warsaw.

In the midst of this successive tearing of the fundamental pact, ardent and overwrought passions, and in the south as in the north powerful interests, demand a solution.

What is then more legitimate and more sensible than to convene the powers of Europe in a congress where prestige and resistance would disappear before a supreme arbitration?

Such was the substance of the speech which Napoleon launched like a bombshell on a startled Europe. The Vienna Settlement was dead, a new one must be created by a congress of the powers. Here, indeed, were the *Idées Napoléonienne* challenging the old order. And here was a way out of his difficulties. Finding the Polish question in an impasse and having suffered diplomatic setbacks which threatened to undermine his popularity in France, while faced with the alternative of taking isolated action and the possibility of raising a coalition against him, or of maintaining silence which might lead to internal complications, the Emperor cleverly discovered a middle-way by proposing a congress. That this was simply a maneuver to gain time in the Polish question was the opinion expressed in diplomatic circles in Paris.[87] Should the *entente* with Austria and England be reëstablished and strengthened and should it succeed in extracting concessions from Russia, the Emperor would endeavor to have them submitted to the congress for approval. On the other hand, if the *entente* failed to revive, he would be in a position to prove to France that he had done everything possible to maintain peace. So skillfully had he concealed his real thought, that his speech was applauded by both militarists and pacifists. Yet, the speech could be interpreted as a warning to Austria and England that if they refused to cooperate in the Polish question, he would mix up the cards and complicate affairs.

Nowhere, perhaps, was the reaction to Napoleon's speech so great as in Vienna. Writing three days after the event, Gramont found that the public and the government had not yet recovered from the shock.[88] Rechberg was in a dilemma. Faced by a possibility which he had always feared and yet unwilling to compromise relations with France by refusing to accept the congress, he had to map his course with great care. He explained to Gramont that in principle Austria was not opposed to a congress and did not refuse to be represented but he wanted to know what questions would be treated there.[89] Before the congress met he desired that Austria and France should reach an understanding to the end that they would maintain the same language or at least support the same proposals. He insisted that such an understanding was an indispensable preliminary for any deliberation of a general character. In addition, he wanted the French Government to explain its intentions more specifically. How, for example, did it interpret the Emperor's declaration relative to the treaties of 1815? Was this to be taken in its literal sense? If France would indicate those parts of the treaties she considered defective or incomplete, and the changes she desired to make, Austria would welcome such overtures with the aim of expediting the *entente.*

The idea of a European congress was one which Napoleon had entertained for years. Whenever a crisis arose which threatened to disturb the harmony of the powers, he almost invariably suggested a congress as a way out. From the first Austria repulsed the idea as an ineffective means of solving existing difficulties and as likely to threaten her special interests. This attitude remained unaltered though now she hesitated to reject Napoleon's invitation. "Such a rejection," wrote Rechberg to Metternich, "without doubt would have offended him [Napoleon] grievously and would thus have provoked complications still more disastrous. We have been confirmed in this view by the British Government which, little inclined from its side to favor the meeting of the congress, however, like us has considered it necessary to give a dilatory reply."[90]

On the day following Napoleon's speech, Rechberg telegraphed Wimpffen, the Austrian Chargé d'Affaires at London, instructing him to see Russell immediately and to insist upon the establishment of an agreement.[91] Wimpffen replied on the 8th that Russell desired to establish a close *entente* with Austria concerning the proposed congress.[92] The result was that London and Vienna cooperated in opposing any attempt to overthrow the Settlement of 1815 and each promised to keep the other informed of its actions. At Rechberg's suggestion, Russell gave Cowley instructions similar to those which Metternich received.[93]

While Austria and England took the same position concerning the wisdom of convoking a European congress, they were not in agreement as to the questions which might be discussed at such a gathering. Russell suggested, for example, that the question of Venetia might be considered for the agenda. Before his departure from Vienna for London Count Apponyi received oral instructions from Rechberg to prevent the congress, if possible, by inducing England to take the initiative of a refusal.[94] If the congress became inevitable, he was directed to concert with the English Cabinet in order to neutralize the dangers which could result from it. At the same time, he was to leave the English Government in no doubt concerning Austria's firm intention not to make territorial sacrifices and to decline any discussion of this nature at the congress. Upon his arrival at London, Apponyi acted upon these instructions and vigorously combatted Russell's suggestions about bringing up questions relative to an independent Poland and Venetia.[95]

The more Rechberg studied the question of a congress, the more convinced he became that it would threaten Austria's interests. If the congress were to constitute itself a supreme tribunal assuming the right to announce and to impose its decrees, adopted by a majority vote, Austria might find herself deprived of Galicia and Venetia. He was determined not to accept, under any circumstances, a discussion of territorial modifications.

The French Government, on the other hand, did everything in its power to prevent the failure of the congress. All the arguments it could think of were set forth in order to convince the hesitant powers that they had nothing to fear. Drouyn de Lhuys informed Cowley that what France proposed was a new edition of the Treaties of Vienna to date from 1864 instead of 1815, a date odious to all Frenchmen, and the congress should proceed by examining in turn each article of the treaties, confirming some, modifying others, and abrogating those which had ceased to have any value.[96] In a dispatch to Gramont, the minister asserted that the congress was intended to settle peacefully questions of a threatening nature.[97] "It is because of his solicitude for the peace and prosperity of Europe and not because of any personal view, that the Emperor addresses this generous call to the powers."[98] From his side, Napoleon tried to sound a reassuring note by expressing his willingness to have questions of a delicate nature relegated to the background and declared that he would pronounce in favor of the *status quo* after the congress.[99] In other words, as soon as another settlement replaced that of 1815, France would become a conservative power.

Disillusionment appeared in Paris sooner than such observers as Metternich expected. England definitely declined to accept the congress, while both Prussia and Russia accepted with reservations.[100] England's rejection was a severe blow to the Emperor who until now had hoped that all the great powers would at least accept the principle of a congress even though they made certain reservations. Nor did the Austrian reply help matters. In a dispatch which Metternich was instructed to show to Drouyn de Lhuys, Rechberg set forth the ostensible reasons for declining the invitation to the congress.[101] He declared that he did not doubt the sincere desire of the French Government to consolidate European peace but he was not convinced that a congress was the only sufficient and effective means of reaching this aim. France had left to the powers the task of determining the scope of the congress. However, Austria had made it clear that a preliminary *entente* with France was an indispensable condition of her acceptance. It was not so much the type of questions that mattered as the manner in which they would be discussed and on this point France had given no assurance. He concluded his dispatch by declaring that Austria was always ready to discuss with France in a spirit of equity and conciliation the various questions which disturbed European peace and to form a close *entente* with her.

The real reason for rejecting the congress, which Rechberg apparently considered too delicate to set forth in an official dispatch, was communicated to Metternich in a private letter.[102] In this he pointed out that the two principal subjects which would be introduced in the congress concerned Poland and Italy. If they were brought up, Austria could hardly avoid proposals relative to Venetia and Galicia. Even if these questions were definitely excluded from the agenda, what guarantee was there that the experience of the Paris Congress of 1856 would not be repeated? Hence, it was the determination to avoid any discussion regarding Venetia and Galicia which formed the most important reason for Austria's refusal to accept the congress. Aware that in his present state of mind Napoleon might vent his spleen on Austria, Rechberg took great pains in wording his official dispatch in order to soften its effects as much as possible. He used the most courteous and conciliatory forms, assumed an air of complete frankness and sincerity, and did not intrench himself behind England's refusal. Metternich was directed to employ all his influence at the Tuileries in order to soothe the Emperor's feelings.[103] At the same time, Rechberg tried to convince Gramont that there had been no connivance with England.[104]

Napoleon was deeply disappointed when he learned of Austria's refusal. While Drouyn de Lhuys held out the hope of maintaining the slender wire between Paris and Vienna, the Emperor considered it broken.[105] "I have never seen the Emperor so discouraged," wrote

Metternich, "and giving himself so little trouble not to show it. Everyone at Compiègne is struck by it. Our friends as well as our enemies find him impenetrable."[106] Metternich himself was pessimistic and considered it highly probable that Napoleon would create more difficulties for Austria in Italy. In fact, the dangers seemed to be accumulating on all sides. The agitation in Germany and the bad humor of Napoleon did not augur well for the future. "The atmosphere seems to me strongly impregnated with revolutionary and belligerent storms."[107]

The year 1863 ended with a double defeat for Napoleon. Despite the popularity of the Polish cause among the French and his own resolve to obtain concessions from Russia, he was compelled to abandon the Poles to their fate. To sacrifice this *Idée Napoléonienne* was a bitter pill for the champion of oppressed nationalities to swallow. No less bitter was the rejection of his proposal for a congress to revise the treaties of 1815, another *Idée*. On top of it all was the realization that he had lost his *entente* with Russia without having obtained a substitute for it. Austria had declined his offer of an alliance, while England's attitude in regard to Poland and the congress had proved painfully disappointing and disillusioning. Diplomatically, it was the lowest point in Napoleonic policy in nearly a decade. The only bright spot in the picture was the success of French arms in Mexico.

Austria's position was little better. Though she still clung to Galicia and Venetia, her hold was rather precarious. The future seemed doubtful, for with the exception of England, her relations with the great powers left much to be desired. Her attitude in the Polish question created suspicions everywhere. The fact that she had sided with the western powers was not appreciated at St. Petersburg nor at Paris either. Napoleon placed much of the blame for his defeats on Austria and regarded her more or less with the same distrust as in 1856. Austria in his eyes represented the system of 1815—a constant reminder of humiliation for France and the Bonapartes. Since his accession to power, it was the same issue, modified by circumstances, of *status quo* versus the *Idées Napoléonienne,* of conservative and dynastic interests versus revolution. Franz Joseph could never become a frank believer in the principle of nationalities nor could Napoleon accept the Settlement of 1815. Only if one or the other changed his viewpoint or abandoned his principles, would it have been possible to establish an intimate alliance between them. The more Napoleon urged Austria to make territorial sacrifices in order to attain this or that objective, the more stubbornly she clung to her possessions. Just as the French Emperor would not or could not completely abandon his *Idées.* so Franz Joseph could not surrender the conservative and dynastic principles which, from the beginning of his reign, had formed the basis of his foreign policy.

CHAPTER FOURTEEN

Conclusions

IN LOOKING back over the period from the *coup d'état* of December 1851 to the proposed congress of November 1863, one sees that the relations between Austria and France were beset with many difficulties. These are traceable in part to the events of 1815—the defeat of the first Napoleon, the exclusion of the Bonaparte family from the throne of France, the assignment of Lombardy and Venetia to Austria, and the establishment of a loose confederation in Germany—and in part to the ideas and principles of Louis Napoleon and Franz Joseph. Of the five great powers of the period, Austria and France stood forth most prominently as champions of different systems.

Austria defended the arrangements of 1815 upon which rested her position in both Germany and Italy. As a *status quo* power she opposed attempts to alter these arrangements. Until the Crimean War, she was supported by her allies Prussia and Russia. Not only did these three powers defend the *status quo* but they upheld dynastic interests against revolution, monarchical sovereignty against popular sovereignty, and intervention against non-intervention. The Crimean War was an event of major importance for it ended not only the alliance of the northern powers but the isolation of France and paved the way for the Italian upheaval. More than that, it elevated France to a position of leadership such as she had not enjoyed since the days of the first Napoleon. Having restored his dynasty, destroyed the Holy Alliance, and acquired friends, Louis Napoleon was in a position to challenge the system of 1815.

Among the various factors which influenced Austro-French relations in the dozen years from the *coup d'état* of 1851 to the close of the Polish question in 1863, five were of particular importance. These were the treaties of 1815, the *Idées Napoléonienne*, the character of Louis Napoleon, the northern alliance, and the principle of nationalities. The first remained a continuously operating factor throughout the period. Its major influence appears in the establishment of the Second Empire, the problem of Italy and the question of Poland. The determination of Louis Napoleon to alter the system set up in 1815 was a challenge to all the great powers but Austria emerged as its principal defender. It was a role which she found increasingly difficult after the Crimean War. The revision of the treaties of 1815 was a cardinal point in Napoleonic policy and one which made a powerful appeal to French sentiment. The destruction of the conservative alliance of Austria, Prussia and Russia was a necessary step to the achievement of this aim. In the principle of nationalities, Louis Napoleon found a weapon of vast possibilities. Of all the great powers, Austria was most vulnerable to this weapon in view of her ethnic composition, her influence in the Balkans, and her position in Germany and Italy. Moreover, England supported the principle of nationalities in Italy, Prussia in Germany, and Russia in the Balkans. Whether Louis Napoleon espoused the cause of oppressed nationalities out of real sympathy for them or merely to advance the interests of France, made little difference to the position of Austria. It threatened her existence as a great power and the continuance of the system of 1815.

In the last analysis, however, it was the character of Louis Napoleon which exerted the greatest influence on Austro-French relations. It was always a question of how far he would go in a given situation, particularly in the problems of Italy and Poland. Moreover, the uncertainties regarding his actions, despite his well-known adherence to the *Idées,* increased the difficulties of dealing with him. The many references in the dispatches and letters of Buol, Hübner, Rechberg and Metternich to Napoleon's character, indicate the importance which Austria attached to this point. Indeed, the main problem in her relations with France throughout the period was the problem of how to deal with Louis Napoleon. Since the latter, in view of the principles he represented, was her greatest threat, every effort was made to keep him in a "safe" course. Convinced of the correctness of their own principles, the Austrian statesmen sought to persuade him to adopt them. Had he been willing to abandon the demand for treaty revision and the cause of nationalities and revolution and to accept a conservative, dynastic policy, the history of the period would have been very different. The war in Italy, the disturbances in the Balkans, and the uprising in Poland might have been avoided altogether. Austria's difficulties in the Crimean War would have been lessened and her position in Germany strengthened. The very fact that one could not predict how far Louis Napoleon would go in a given situation made him the enigma of European diplomacy.

Both Franz Joseph and Napoleon III were the chief instruments in determining the foreign policies of their respective countries. After the death of Schwarzenberg, the Austrian ruler assumed control, guided by his own conscience and by the influence of his ministers and such intimates as his mother, Cardinal Rauscher, Count Grünne and the elder Metternich. It was unfortunate that Franz Joseph was dependent upon ministers who lacked the skill and the firmness of Metternich and Schwarzenberg. Neither Buol nor Rechberg were first-rate men. While both had a fairly good understanding of Louis Napoleon, they were not sufficiently clever in exploiting his weakness or in capitalizing on situations. Buol, in particular, was somewhat too inflexible in his approach to the French ruler. The latter, in turn, was not a master of the art of diplomacy nor were his foreign ministers men of great distinction. It was perhaps less a matter of superiority in the conduct of foreign policy which led to French success and to Austrian failure than it was the manner in which events unfolded. In the recognition of the Second Empire, Louis Napoleon was aided by England's position and by the unwillingness of the northern powers to push matters too far. The Crimean War was ideally suited to his purpose of smashing the conservative alliance, while the Italian question effectively isolated Austria. The very nature of the problems which arose were favorable to the position of France as they were unfavorable to that of Austria. The two rulers followed principles which responded more or less to the public sentiment of their states—Franz Joseph in defending his possessions, his influence in Germany and Italy and his opposition to revolutionary agitation, and Napoleon in seeking to liberate France from the restraints of the Settlement of 1815 and in seeking a position of leadership on the continent. There was, it is true, unrest among the Magyars of Hungary and division in Austria regarding the Crimean War and in France regarding Italy. Though neither ruler was blind to public opinion, Napoleon was more sensitive to its influence.[1]

When one considers all factors—the position of the Hapsburg Monarchy, the principles of its foreign policy, the character of Franz Joseph and his advisers, and the principles and character of Louis Napoleon, it is clear that difficulties in the relations between Austria and France were unavoidable. The question is whether Austria could have prevented the misfortunes which befell her during the period. Were these misfortunes due to errors of policy or were they due to circumstances beyond her control? The Crimean War was the first of them since it ended the alliance of the conservative powers, increased Austria's internal difficulties, brought on the Franco-Russian *rapprochement,* and made France the leading continental power. In this case the choice which faced Austria was an exceedingly difficult one. Her slowness in concluding the treaty with the western powers and her dependence upon Prussia no doubt made matters worse in the long run. Buol, as we know, was prepared to align with England and France without Prussian support but was held back by the Emperor. Yet, could Austria have escaped unscathed whatever course she had followed? In one way or another, this war which she did not want, would have affected her adversely. As a neutral position was ruled out because of her interests in Italy and the Balkans, Austria could not have avoided alienating Russia by siding with England and France, or of alienating the western powers by siding with Russia. While active participation against Russia might have hastened the latter's defeat and placed Austria in a stronger bargaining position vis-à-vis France, it would not necessarily have altered Napoleon's determination to revise the treaties or caused him to abandon interest in Italy or Poland. Nor would it have strengthened Austria's position in Germany. At best, it might have prevented the Franco-Russian *rapprochement* and postponed the events in Italy and the Balkans. The Crimean War illustrates the basic reasons for Austria's difficulties: her internal weakness and her determination to hold on to her influence in Germany and Italy.

The rising tide of nationalism was also a force beyond Austria's control. Again she could not remain neutral in view of her vital interests. In this instance only one course seemed open to her: to oppose it. The presence of various national groups within her empire, the maintenance of her influence in the Balkans, Germany and Italy, left her no other choice. It is true that by abandoning her position in Italy, she might have strengthened it in Germany or vice versa. But here again much depended on Napoleon's intentions. Indeed, there appeared to be no escape from the dilemma in which she was placed because of internal conditions and her policy concerning Germany and Italy. An alliance or an arrangement with Napoleon would have entailed sacrifices on her part. This was so because the French ruler would not or could not adopt a conservative policy and because Austria could follow no other. Besides, Napoleon knew that Austria was more or less isolated in the problem of nationalities in view of the attitude of England regarding Italy, Prussia in Germany and Russia in the Balkans. Only in the Polish question was Napoleon left virtually unsupported.

In the Italian problem Austria upheld the treaties by upholding her own interests. From the diplomatic veiwpoint, the sending of the ultimatum to Piedmont in April 1859 was a blunder since it left her isolated and since it enabled France to enter what appeared to be a defensive war. One may assume that if the ultimatum had not been sent and if Austria had assured herself of the military support of Prussia and the German states and the moral backing of England, the war would not have come. But this does not take into account other factors: the strain on Austria's finances due to military preparations, the probable sacrifice of her influence in Germany in return for Prussian support, and the diplomatic defeat which would have fallen to Napoleon in yielding in the Italian question. It would not have ended the revolutionary agitation in Italy nor Napoleon's insistence on revising the treaties of 1815 or his encouragement of nationalities. Moreover, it is not unlikely that a diplomatic defeat in the Italian question would have spurred on the French ruler to discover the means of weakening his enemy. The fact that of all the great powers in Europe, Austria was the one most vulnerable to the rising tide of nationalism, placed her on the defensive. Only by means of a strong alliance could she have checked the threat of France. But where and how could she have found allies after the Crimean War without sacrifices on her part?

Following the military disaster of 1859 Austria stood alone in the Italian problem, unable to prevent infractions of the Truce of Villafranca or the Treaty of Zürich. No support could be obtained from England in view of the pro-Italian policy of Palmerston and Russell, nor from Prussia without the sacrifice of leadership in Germany, while Russian bitterness was still too deep to admit of hope from that quarter. France alone seemed to offer the best, if not the only means, of safeguarding Venetia and the integrity of Rome. The attempts to conclude an *entente* with France proved futile. Neither side was prepared to go far enough. Napoleon still preferred his ties with England and Russia and was reluctant to abandon the Italians, while Austria refused to pull out of Italy altogether by sacrificing Venetia. Thus, the combination of circumstances forced Austria into a defensive position.

The Balkan problem was closely linked with that of Italy in view of Napoleon's penchant for territorial bargains. On a number of occasions he sought to persuade Austria that it would be to her advantage to exchange Italian for Balkan possessions. Though she did not rule out the possibility of acquiring Balkan lands, Austria would not sacrifice her Italian holdings. Two courses were open to her: to maintain the Ottoman Empire or to arrange with powers for its dismemberment. Both were logical in view of her geographic position and the Russian threat. The first prevailed until the close of the Italian war when Rechberg, in the aim of strengthening Austria's position in Italy and preventing the spread of revolutionary agitation, opened negotiations with France and Russia pointing toward the dismemberment of Turkey. The Anglo-Austrian *entente,* which had operated successfully in Near Eastern affairs, had not functioned in Italy. French policy was more fluid for although

Napoleon appeared to uphold the integrity of the Ottoman Empire during the Crimean War, he entertained ideas of ceding the Principalities to Austria. Following the war, he joined Russia in encouraging the establishment of independent Balkan states. It was his insistence upon linking Italy and the Balkans which precluded an Austro-French agreement.

The Polish question had important consequences. It undermined the Franco-Russian *entente* and in the end saw Napoleon virtually isolated in Europe. His offer of an alliance to Austria was rejected since it involved a revision of the map and the possible sacrifice of Galicia and Venetia. Common interests drew together Austria and England and Russia and Prussia. Checked in his aim of aiding the Polish nationalists, Napoleon fell back on the idea of a congress to revise the settlement of 1815. The failure to win approval of the powers was a serious blow to his pride and to the ideas he had pursued since his accession to the throne. For Austria, on the other hand, the discomfiture of Napoleon and the decline of his prestige and influence together with the appointment of Drouyn de Lhuys as Foreign Minister produced a sense of relief.

Thus, the twelve years from the establishment of the Second Empire to the close of the Polish affair brought significant developments in European diplomacy and in the relations between Austria and France. Within this brief period occurred two major wars, the rise and decline in the power and prestige of Napoleon III, the beginning of the dismemberment of the Austrian Empire, the appearance of a new Italian Kingdom, revolts in the Balkans and Poland, and the intensification of Austro-Prussian rivalry for leadership in Germany. Although Napoleon had a hand in all these developments, he was assisted by other factors—the policy of Tsar Nicholas in the conflict with Turkey, the procrastination of Austria in connection with the Crimean War, the astute diplomacy of Cavour, the pro-Italian attitude of England, the rivalry of Austria and Prussia in Germany, the policy of Prince Gortchakoff, the rising tide of nationalism, and the popular opposition in France to the Settlement of 1815. Inspired by the *Idées Napoléonienne* as well as by his ambition, the French ruler exploited these other factors in order to advance the interests of France and the Bonaparte dynasty. That his policy coincided for the most part with the desires of the French people made its execution so much the easier. One cannot escape the conclusion that Napoleon was Austria's misfortune to a greater degree than her policy, her ruler or her ministers. Considering the principles which guided Louis Napoleon, his reluctance to abandon them, and the steps he took to advance them, it is doubtful if Austria could have maintained the high position she enjoyed in the days of Prince Clemens Metternich or Prince Schwarzenberg. While one cannot predict what would have happened had France not been governed by Louis Napoleon, there is little doubt that his influence was of major importance in the developments which affected Austro-French relations.

Notes

Chapter One: THE END OF THE METTERNICH SYSTEM AND THE EMERGENCE OF NEW LEADERS

1 At a congress held at Aix-la-Chapelle. France had by this time paid up the indemnity and was freed from military occupation.

2 The protocol was not signed by England and France. For the Troppau Congress and Protocol as well as the reasons for England's refusal to sign, see Gooch, G. P. and Ward, A. W. (eds.): *Cambridge History of British Foreign Policy, 1783-1919,* 3 vols., London, 1922-23, II, 36-38.

3 By a treaty concluded at Münchengrätz, September 18, 1833. See Martens, F.: *Recueil des traités et conventions conclus par la Russie avec les puissances étrangères,* 15 vols., St. Petersburg, 1874-1909, IV, 444. For a brief account of the Münchengrätz conference, see *Cambridge History of British Foreign Policy,* II, 167.

4 Born in Bohemia in 1800 of a distinguished noble family, Prince Schwarzenberg entered the Austrian diplomatic service and held posts in the legations at St. Petersburg, London, Paris, Berlin, Turin, Parma and Naples. In 1842 he became a Major-General in the Austrian army and served with distinction at Custozza. For his statesmanship, see especially Oberst Dr. Edward Heller: *Mitteleuropa Vorkämpfer, Fürst Felix zu Schwarzenberg,* Vienna, 1933, and the more recent study by Adolf Schwarzenberg: *Prince Felix zu Schwarzenberg. Prime Minister of Austria, 1848-1852,* New York, 1946.

5 Joseph Redlich: *Emperor Francis Joseph of Austria,* New York, 1929, 47.

6 Only a third of the Austrian territories had been admitted to the Confederation established by the Federal Act of 1815. Schwarzenberg's plan provided for the inclusion of Lombardy-Venetia.

7 Haus-, Hof-, und Staatsarchiv, Vienna (hereafter cited as HHSA), no. 29 B, secret, Paris, February 23, 1851, Hübner to Schwarzenberg.

8 HHSA res., Vienna, February 14, 1851, Schwarzenberg to Hübner.

9 HHSA nos. 1 and 2 secret, Dresden, January 12, 1851, Schwarzenberg to Hübner.

10 HHSA no. 2 secret, Vienna, March 7, 1851. Hübner was not in favor of Schwarzenberg's plan. "It is the first time," he wrote, "that I find myself in opposition to Prince Felix on a question of foreign policy." Hübner, J. A. Graf von: *Neuf ans de souvenirs d'un ambassadeur*

d'Autriche à Paris sous le second empire, 1851-1859. Publiés par son fils Le comte Alexander de Hübner, 2 vols. Paris, 1904, I, 14, March 31, 1851.

11   HHSA Vienna, April 17, 1851, Schwarzenberg to Hübner.

12   It should be noted, however, that Louis Philippe started France on her North African Empire.

13   Upon the death of the Duke of Reichstadt, son of Napoleon I. For a good account of Louis Napoleon see: Robert Sencourt: *Napoleon III, The Modern Emperor.* London, 1934.

14   Napoleon denied that he had ever been a Carbonaro. He related to Mme. Carette that this legend arose from his brother's connection with the Italian revolutionists, and that he was often confused with the latter. This brother, Prince Napoleon, died in April 1831 in Italy. (Mme. Carette: *Souvenirs intimes de la cour des Tuileries,* III, Paris, 1891, 131.)

15   P. La Gorce: *Histoire du Second Empire,* 4th ed., 7 vols., Paris, 1899-1905, I, iv.

16   F. A. Simpson: *Louis Napoleon and the Recovery of France, 1848-1856,* New York, 1923, x.

17   HHSA no. 38 G, Paris, February 28, 1852, Hübner to Schwarzenberg.

18   HHSA no. 137 B secret, Paris, October 25, 1852, Hübner to Buol.

19   For the ideas and principles which governed the foreign policy of Louis Napoleon see the excellent article by A. Pingaud, "La Politique Extérieure du Second Empire," in *Revue Historique,* vol. 156, 1927, 41-68.

20   He was also mindful of the importance of strengthening the frontiers of France.

21   Pingaud, *loc. cit.,* 47.

22   *Ibid.*

23   Pingaud, *loc. cit.,* 42-43. On one occasion Napoleon said to von der Goltz, the Prussian Minister: "A declaration from one of my ministers would have no importance. I alone know what the foreign policy of France will be." (Émile Ollivier: *L'Empire Libérale. Études. Récits. Souvenirs,* 17 vols., Paris, 1895-1915, III, 135.)

24   Vitzthum von Eckstädt, K. F. Graf: *London, Gastein und Sadowa, 1864-1866,* Stuttgart, 1889, 202.

25   *Ibid.,* 203-204. For a sketch of the career of Drouyn de Lhuys see: Paul Louis Pradier-Fodère: *M. Drouyn de Lhuys,* Laval, 1871.

26   Heinrich Ritter von Srbik: "Franz Joseph I. Charakter und Regierungsgrundsätze" in *Historische Zeitschrift,* vol. 144, 1931, 513.

27   A brief summary of the character of Franz Joseph is given in J. Redlich: *Francis Joseph of Austria,* 251.

28   Chester W. Clark: *Franz Joseph and Bismarck,* Cambridge, Harvard Univ. Press, 1934, 514. The same author gives an excellent description of Austrian diplomatic technique, 489ff.

29   "If we are to seek for the individual who had the most lasting effect on his (Franz Joseph's) personal character we must study Charles Grünne." (Redlich, *op. cit.,* 43.)

30 Until his death in 1859, Prince Clemens Metternich frequently advised Franz Joseph and Buol on foreign policy. Buol was in the Foreign Office from 1852-1859, Rechberg from 1859-1864.

Chapter Two: THE ESTABLISHMENT OF THE SECOND EMPIRE AND ITS RECOGNITION

1 Nesselrode to Meyendorff, PL, St. Petersburg, December 23, 1851, cited in E. Bapst: *Les Origines de la guerre de Crimée. La France et la Russie de 1848 à 1854,* Paris, 1912, 203.

2 *Ibid.,* 218, Castelbajac to Turgot, St. Petersburg, January 29, 1852. For an account of the recognition question based on Russian documents see the article by Richard Salomon, "Die Anerkennung Napoleons III" in *Zeitschrift für Osteuropäische Geschichte,* II, 1912, 312-366.

3 HHSA no. 1, Vienna.

4 HHSA no. 1, Vienna, December 18, 1851, Schwarzenberg to Hübner.

5 HHSA.

6 Heller, *op. cit.,* 157.

7 HHSA no. 12 G, Paris.

8 *Ibid.*

9 In Berlin it was asserted that Schwarzenberg failed to take into account either the imprescriptible law of legitimacy or the solemn obligations of the treaties and the Tsar agreed with this view. (H. Friedjung: *Historische Aufsätze,* 2 vols., Stuttgart, 1919, II, 146.) On the other hand, Friedjung exaggerates in stating that the memorandum produced great opposition in Berlin and St. Petersburg. On this point see Heller, *op. cit.,* footnote, 235.

10 HHSA no. 22 B, St. Petersburg, March 12/February 29, 1852, Lebzeltern to Schwarzenberg.

11 King Leopold declared that if the powers did not stand together against Napoleon it would be the ruin of Europe. (Ernest II: *Memoirs of Ernest II, Duke of Saxe-Coburg-Gotha.* Trans. by P. Andreae, 4 vols., London, 1888-90, III, 16, Leopold to Prince Clemens Metternich, November 17, 1852.)

12 Malmesbury had no intention of entering any alliance and did not believe a French invasion of Belgium likely. (Earl of Malmesbury: *Memoirs of an Ex-Minister,* 2 vols., London, 1884, I, 52, Malmesbury to Lord Bloomfield.)

13 The difference between the Austrian and Russian viewpoints was clearly explained in the instructions given to Count Mensdorff at the time of his departure for St. Petersburg to take the post of Austrian Ambassador. Dated April 19, 1852, two weeks after the death of Schwarzenberg, these instructions follow closely the latter's principles. They pointed out in regard to France, that whereas Austria considered the parliamentary system as the most dangerous factor, Russia's apprehensions arose over the known friendliness of the Bonapartes for the Polish cause. (HHSA Varia, 1852, Instructions pour M. le Général

Comte de Mensdorff, Vienna, April 19, 1852.) Austria, of course, was no less concerned over the safety of her Italian possessions.

14   HHSA enclosure: copy of dispatch of Nesselrode to Meyendorff, St. Petersburg, January 9, 1852.

15   F. Schnürer: *Briefe Kaiser Franz Josephs I an seine Mutter, 1838-1872,* Munich, 1930, 143, date of letter, April 6, 1852.

16   Friedjung: *Historische Aufsätze,* II, 147, exaggerates in stating that during Schwarzenberg's administration "the best relations" existed between Paris and Vienna. Actually there were rather sharp differences over the questions of admitting all the Austrian provinces to the German Confederation and over the questions of Italy and Switzerland. (*Cf.* Heller, *op. cit.,* footnote, 236.)

17   H. von Srbik: *Metternich der Staatsmann und der Mensch,* 2 vols., Vienna, 1925, II, 465.

18   From Vienna Nicholas went to Berlin where he persuaded Frederick William IV to agree to the protocol.

19   HHSA enclosure in no. 2 res., Vienna, November 8, 1852, Buol to Hübner. The assertion of Friedjung, *Historische Aufsätze,* II, 146, that Schwarzenberg would never have signed the protocol because of the demand for guarantees regarding Napoleon's policy and the territorial boundaries established by the treaties, is difficult to comprehend. In his memorandum, Schwarzenberg made recognition of the empire conditional upon guarantees regarding the treaties. Moreover, it is clear from the instructions given to Count Mensdorff, April 19, 1852, the main lines of which were traced by Schwarzenberg before his death, that the three powers were in substantial agreement as to these guarantees. The attempt of some writers to show that there was a radical change in Austrian policy after the death of Schwarzenberg is a distortion of the facts. At no time did Schwarzenberg actually encourage Louis Napoleon to take the imperial crown. Indeed, he instructed Hübner not to take sides and to follow the same course as Kisseleff, the Russian envoy. So far as the reëstablishment of the empire is concerned, Buol's attitude was more or less passive. He did not send Hübner instructions to combat the empire as such but only the title "Napoleon III." In his journal, Hübner deliberately exaggerated the differences between Schwarzenberg and Buol because of his dislike of the latter. Friedjung's discussion of Buol's attitude is found on pp. 212-16 of his *Historische Aufsätze,* II. For the correct viewpoint, see Heller, *op. cit.,* footnote 38, 235-236.

20   HHSA no. 1, Vienna, May 29, 1852, Buol to Hübner.

21   HHSA Russie Expéditions. Copy of a dispatch of Nesselrode to Kisseleff, Potsdam, May 1852, enclosed in a dispatch of Buol to Mensdorff, Vienna, May 29, 1852.

22   In connection with the recognition of Louis Philippe in 1830, Prince Clemens Metternich had tried to get the quadruple alliance to present a united front and to extract pledges from the new French ruler concerning the treaties of 1815. He had abandoned this plan when England and Prussia insisted upon immediate recognition.

23 HHSA no. 34 B, St. Petersburg, 18/6 April 1852, Lebzeltern to Schwarzenberg and no. 2 B, St. Petersburg, 3 May/21 April 1852, Mensdorff to Buol.

24 HHSA no. 1, res., Vienna, May 26, 1852, Buol to Mensdorff.

25 HHSA no. 5 A, London, June 16, 1852, Colloredo to Buol.

26 HHSA no. 7, res., Vienna, June 11, 1852, Buol to Colloredo. The French representative at London, Count Walewski, was confident that England would not join the continental powers in a war against France. "I have every reason to believe," he wrote to Drouyn de Lhuys, "that the English Ministry will miss no opportunity to make clear to all the Cabinets that the policy of England today has no analogy to the policy followed by this power at the beginning of the century and it is convinced that a war against France will be the greatest calamity." (Vicomte E. de Guichen: *Les Grandes Questions Européenes et la Diplomatie des Puissances sous la Seconde République Française*, 2 vols. Paris, 1929, II, 429.)

27 HHSA no. 7 res., Vienna July 11, 1852, Buol to Colloredo.

28 Nicholas was deeply offended by parts of the Bordeaux speech. See F. A. Simpson, *op. cit.*, 194.

29 He succeeded the Marquis Turgot at the end of July 1852.

30 France. Archives des Affaires Étrangères (hereafter cited as Fr. Doc.) vol. 448, PL, Fontainebleau, Nov. 15, 1852, Drouyn de Lhuys to Lacour.

31 *Ibid.*

32 HHSA no. 2, Vienna, November 26, 1852, Buol to Hübner.

33 Hübner complained that the instructions he received from Buol were "distinguished by a despairing lack of clarity" but were mild in comparison with the orders from the Berlin Cabinet which were "confused, contradictory, breathing anger mitigated by fear. . . ." (Hübner: *Neuf Ans,* I, 82.)

34 *Ibid.,* p. 90. *Cf.* Sir Ernest Satow: *An Austrian Diplomatist in the Fifties,* Cambridge, 1908, which gives a good summary of Hübner's position based on the latter's journal.

35 HHSA PL, Vienna, September 1, 1852, Buol to Hübner.

36 Hübner: *Neuf Ans,* I, 90.

37 *Ibid.*

38 *Ibid.*

39 HHSA no. 1, Vienna, November 18, 1852, Buol to Colloredo, enclosure.

40 HHSA no. 2, Vienna, November 27, 1852, Buol to Colloredo. *Cf.* Guichen, *op. cit.,* II, 444.

41 "As to calling him Napoleon III, when we had never recognized Napoleon II, it seemed absurd, inasmuch as we accepted Charles X and Louis Philippe during the life of the Duke of Reichstadt." (Malmesbury, *op. cit.,* I, 361, October 31, 1852.) Queen Victoria did not wish to oppose either the title or the empire. (Benson, A. and Esher, Viscount: *The Letters of Queen Victoria. A Selection of Her Majesty's Correspondence between the years 1837 and 1861,* 3 vols., New York, 1907, II,

482, Queen Victoria to the Earl of Malmesbury, Windsor Castle, November 8, 1852.)

42 Malmesbury, *op. cit.*, I, 361. Lord Derby, the Prime Minister, wanted to refuse recognition of the title "Napoleon III" (*ibid.*, 363). For the diplomatic correspondence between England and Russia regarding the question of the empire, see Martens, *op. cit.*, XII, 287-92.

43 Malmesbury, *op. cit.*, I, 367.

44 *Ibid.*, 372, Malmesbury to Queen Victoria, F. O., December 3, 1852.

45 Wellesley, Hon. F. A. (editor): *The Paris Embassy during the Second Empire: Selections from the Papers of the first Earl Cowley*, London, 1928, 11-12. *Cf.* F. C. Palm: *England and Napoleon III. A Study of a Utopian Dictator*, Duke Univ. Press, 1944.

46 A copy of this memorandum was enclosed in a dispatch, no. 46, from Mensdorff to Buol, dated St. Petersburg, 29 October/10 November, 1852, HHSA.

47 HHSA no. 1, Vienna.

48 Heller, *op. cit.*, 174, who adds that Buol in his dispatch suggested the title "Mon bon ami" which is incorrect.

49 Such is the viewpoint held by Heller, *op. cit.*, 175.

50 HHSA enclosure in no. 57 A-B, St. Petersburg 13/1 December 1852, Mensdorff to Buol. The Russian Chancellor would have preferred the salutation "Mon Frère," fearing serious complications if it were refused. (Peter von Meyendorff: *Ein russischer Diplomat an den Höfen von Berlin und Wien. Politischen und privater Briefwechsel 1826-1863*. Hersg. und eingeleitet von O. Hoetzsch, 3 vols., Berlin, 1923, III, no. 422, pp. 3-5.

51 That is "Sire et bon ami."

52 HHSA no. 2 A-D, secret, St. Petersburg, 7 January/26 December 1852, Mensdorff to Buol. *Cf.* Vitzthum von Eckstädt, K. F: *St. Petersburg and London in the Years 1852-1864*, London, 1887, 13.

53 Hübner: *Neuf Ans*, I, 93-94. Russia had refused the customary salutation to Louis Philippe.

54 HHSA no. 164, Paris, December 13, 1852, Hübner to Buol.

55 HHSA no. 167 A-D, Paris, December 17, 1852, Hübner to Buol.

56 Hübner: *Neuf Ans*, I, 95. It should be remembered that the Russian instructions differed from those of her allies.

57 Drouyn de Lhuys to Castelbajac, Paris, January 12, 1853, cited in Bapst, *op. cit.*, 300.

58 Bapst, *op. cit.*, 303. *Cf.* Hübner: *Neuf Ans*, I, 98.

59 HHSA no. 4 A-B, Paris, January 5, 1853, Hübner to Buol.

60 This announcement caused Drouyn de Lhuys to submit his resignation which, however, was not accepted. (Hübner: *Neuf Ans*, I, 98.)

61 In accordance with procedure outlined by Morny.

62 Until January 11, 1853.

Chapter Three: BEGINNINGS OF THE CRIMEAN WAR

1 HHSA no. 41 A-E res., Paris, March 16, 1853, Hübner to Buol.

2 HHSA no. 29 E res., Paris, February 23, 1853, Hübner to Buol.

3 V. J. Puryear: *England, Russia and the Straits Question, 1844-1856,* Univ. of California Press, 1931, 244-248.

4 HHSA no. 76 B, Paris, June 2, 1853, Hübner to Buol.

5 For the correspondence between the two Emperors carried on during this period, see Dr. Hanns Schlitter: *Aus der Regierungszeit Franz Joseph I,* Vienna, 1919, especially 92-102.

6 Great Britain. *Accounts and Papers. Blue Books* (hereafter referred to as BB), LXXI, pt. 1, no. 277, Vienna, June 17, 1853, Westmorland to Clarendon.

7 *Ibid.,* pt. II, no. 156, Vienna, October 15, 1853, Westmorland to Clarendon.

8 *Ibid.,* no. 204, Paris, November 5, 1853, Cowley to Clarendon.

9 At Clarendon's suggestion, the note was prepared in London and then submitted to the conference for signature. (*Ibid.,* no. 282, FO, November 29, 1853, Clarendon to Westmorland.)

10 *Ibid.,* no. 315, Vienna, December 6, 1853, Westmorland to Clarendon, enclosure.

11 *Ibid.,* no. 396, Constantinople, December 31, 1853, Stratford de Redcliffe to Clarendon, enclosure.

12 *Ibid.,* no. 403, Vienna, January 13, 1854, Westmorland to Clarendon, enclosure.

13 Austria was asked to promise neutrality not only for the duration of the Russo-Turkish War but for the duration of the impending struggle between Russia and the western powers as well. Orloff was in Vienna from January 29 to February 8, 1854.

14 F. Eckhart: *Die deutsche Frage und der Krimkrieg,* Berlin, 1931, 32.

15 The draft treaty which Orloff brought with him envisaged only the third course. It provided that in case England and France entered the war against Russia, Austria and Prussia would observe strict neutrality and, if necessary, defend this neutrality by force of arms. In case of an attack against the territories of Austria or Prussia or any of the German states, the three powers (including Russia) would take steps to repulse it. Russia promised that she would conclude peace only in agreement with Austria and Prussia. (HHSA enclosure: copy of drafts sent by Nesselrode to Meyendorff at Vienna and Budberg at Berlin, dated St. Petersburg 8/20 January 1854.)

16 HHSA no. 2, Vienna, February 7, 1854, Buol to Hübner.

17 Eckhart, *op. cit.,* 32, letter dated St. Petersburg, 4/16 January 1854. This was a reply to a letter of Franz Joseph sent January 7, 1854.

18 Franz Joseph demanded the maintenance of the *status quo* in the Balkans in return for benevolent neutrality. (Orloff to Nesselrode, January 22/February 3, 1854, no. II, A. N. Zaïonchkovskii: *Vostochnaya Voina, 1853-1856* (1903-1913), Documentary Appendix II, 268, cited

in G. Henderson: "The Diplomatic Revolution of 1854" in *American Historical Review,* vol. XLIII, no. 1, October 1937, 23. Orloff replied to Franz Joseph that this demand was impossible as it would paralyze Russia's military operations. (*Ibid.,* no. 1.)

19 Orloff warned Franz Joseph that rejection of the Russian proposal would mean the end of the alliance. (HHSA no. 3, Vienna, February 5, 1854, Buol to V. Esterhazy at St. Petersburg.)

20 On January 31st the Austrian Council of Ministers rejected the proposal. (HHSA Protokoll der Ministerkonferenz, January 31, 1854, Vorträge 1854.)

21 H. R. von Poschinger (ed.): *Preussens auswärtige Politik, 1850 bis 1858,* 3 vols., Berlin, 1902, II, 290-93.

22 The Vienna Conference rejected the conditions which Russia had made known to Berlin and Vienna through Budberg and Orloff. These provided for direct negotiations between Russia and Turkey, confirmation of all former conventions between the two states, a declaration by the Sultan to maintain the privileges of Greek Christians, and evacuation of the Principalities by Russia.

23 HHSA PL, Vienna, June 21, 1853, Buol to Hübner.

24 HHSA no. 87 B secret, Paris, June 22, 1853, Hübner to Buol.

25 HHSA no. 153 A-B res., Paris, October 10, 1853, Hübner to Buol.

26 HHSA no. 159 A-C res., Paris, October 22, 1853, Hübner to Buol.

27 HHSA no. 151 A-N, Paris, October 3, 1853, Hübner to Buol.

28 HHSA no. 174 B secret, Paris, November 20, 1853, Hübner to Buol.

29 HHSA PL, Vienna, November 29, 1853, Buol to Hübner.

30 HHSA, Vienna, November 29, 1853, Buol to Hübner.

31 HHSA PL, Vienna, November 29, 1853, Buol to Hübner.

32 Fr. Doc., vol. 453, Vienna, January 14, 1854, Bourqueney to Drouyn de Lhuys.

33 *Ibid.,* no. 11, Vienna, January 21, 1854, Bourqueney to Drouyn de Lhuys.

34 *Ibid.*

35 F. Engel-Jánosi: *Der Freiherr von Hübner,* Innsbruck, 1934, 111-115, throws new light on Hübner's attitude in 1853 toward the eastern crisis. This is based upon a memorandum of October 8, 1853, which Hübner sent to Count Rechberg and which is found in the Rechberg archives. In this Hübner criticized the course followed by Buol in 1853 and favored the maintenance of the alliance with Russia provided the latter would give a binding promise not to seek aggrandizement from the war. He believed that such a promise would have calmed English public opinion and brought peace in the winter of 1853. There is no mention in the memorandum about joining the western powers. Engel-Jánosi states that Hübner continued to believe in the maintenance of the alliance with Russia and in the possibility of peace among the great powers throughout the year 1853. Hübner urged Rechberg to get

the memorandum before Franz Joseph. No mention is made in Hübner's journal of this memorandum. Indeed, Engel-Jánosi asserts that Hübner was far less anti-Russian in 1853 than the journal indicates, particularly the *résumé* for that year. He states that Debrautz, the Director of the Austrian Consulate-General in Paris, had secret information that at this time Hübner was anti-French. But Debrautz, who was in the pay of Drouyn de Lhuys and who submitted reports to Kübeck, the Austrian Minister of Commerce, is hardly a reliable source. His reports were submitted by Kübeck to Franz Joseph behind the back of Buol and had no influence on the determination of Austrian policy. (*Cf.,* Heller, *op. cit.,* footnote 34, 235, concerning the reports of Debrautz.) By January 1854, according to Engel-Jánosi, Hübner had changed his attitude and openly favored an alliance with the western powers. The reason for this change, states Engel-Jánosi, was the fear that the western powers would stir up revolutions against Austria. But just as it is probable that Friedjung, Stern and others have given too much emphasis to Hübner's anti-Russian attitude and to his advocacy of an alliance with France in 1853, it is no less probable than Engel-Jánosi gives too much weight to the memorandum to the exclusion of other evidence, such as Hübner's official reports and private letters.

36 Buol had proposed such an orientation on January 16, 1854 (HHSA Buols Vortrag of January 16th and Protokoll der Ministerkonferenz, January 23, 1854) but Engel-Jánosi, *op. cit.,* 115-116, points out that it was retarded by the influence of the Prussian Government. Hübner, however, had not been informed of this proposal or of the meeting of the Council of Ministers of January 23rd.

37 HHSA no. 15 G secret, Paris.

38 HHSA no. 23 C secret, Paris, February 14, 1854.

39 *Ibid.*

40 *Ibid.*

41 *Ibid.*

42 HHSA no. 4 A-B, Paris, January 7 and no. 9 B res., Paris, January 17, 1854, Hübner to Buol.

43 "What is clear to me," wrote Hübner in his journal on January 7, 1854, "is that Drouyn de Lhuys seeks in the Austrian alliance a remedy against the revolutionary tendencies of his master and at the same time a counterweight to the English influence which weighs upon him." (Hübner: *Neuf Ans,* I, 198.)

44 HHSA no. 15 B, Paris, January 30, 1854, Hübner to Buol.

45 HHSA enclosure: Projet de Convention, in no. 1, Vienna, February 25, 1854, Buol to Hübner and Colloredo. (*Cf.* Henderson, *loc. cit.,* 24 and F. H. Geffcken: *Zur Geschichte des orientalischen Krieges, 1853-1856,* Berlin, 1881, 75-76.)

46 Both Austria and Prussia supported the ultimatums at St. Petersburg. (*Cf.* K. Borries: *Preussen im Krimkrieg,* Stuttgart, 1930, 101 and Geffcken, 73.)

47 Borries, 96-99, Geffcken, 76, A. Stern: *Geschichte Europas seit den Verträgen 1815 bis zum Frankfurter Frieden von 1871,* 10 vols.,

Stuttgart, 1894-1924, VIII, 63-68, and *Memoirs of Ernest II, Duke of Saxe-Coburg-Gotha,* III, 63.

48 HHSA no. 1, Vienna, March 11, 1854, Buol to Hübner.

49 B. Schmitt: "The Diplomatic Preliminaries of the Crimean War" in *Am. Hist. Rev.,* XXV, 1919, 60.

50 HHSA no. 35 D, Paris, March 5, 1854, Hübner to Buol.

51 HHSA no. 35 G secret, Paris, March 5, 1854, Hübner to Buol.

52 *Ibid.*

53 HHSA no. 1, Vienna, February 25, 1854, Buol to Hübner and Colloredo.

54 Fr. Doc., vol. 453, no. 45, Vienna, March 14, 1854, Bourqueney to Drouyn de Lhuys. According to Hübner, Bourqueney reported to his government that at a ball on February 20th, Franz Joseph said to him: "Austria will sign the Quadruple Treaty. A time-limit will be set for the evacuation of the Principalities; if Russia refuses he (Franz Joseph) will soon open hostilities. In return, he demands guarantees relative to Italy." (Hübner: *Neuf Ans,* I, 214, February 21, 1954.) Hübner himself, as is clear from his journal, regarded Bourqueney as inclined to be somewhat too optimistic in his reports. That the Emperor intended to go as far as Bourqueney indicated is not substantiated by the Austrian documents.

55 HHSA PL, Vienna, March 7, 1854, Buol to Hübner.

56 *Ibid.* (*Cf.* Engel-Jánosi, *op. cit.,* 117.)

57 Buol drew up a draft convention relating to Italy which he sent to Hübner. (HHSA res., Vienna, February 25, 1854.)

58 HHSA no. 4, Vienna, March 11, 1854, Buol to Hübner.

59 Hübner reported that Napoleon, while wishing to keep the convention a secret, had said to the Duke of Saxe-Coburg: "Austria and France will march together in the east but in return I will aid in suppressing disturbances which break out in Italy." (HHSA no. 35 D, Paris, March 5, 1854, Hübner to Buol.) The Duke visited Napoleon in March 1854. (*Cf. The Memoirs of Ernest II,* III, 62-69.)

60 HHSA enclosure in no. 35 C, Paris, March 5, 1854, Hübner to Buol.

61 HHSA no. 47 C, Paris, March 21, 1854, Hübner to Buol.

62 Eckhart, *op. cit.,* 25.

63 H. von Sybel: *The Founding of the German Empire by William I,* 7 vols., New York, 1890-98, II, 216-217. (*Cf.* C. Friese: *Russland und Preussen von Krimkrieg bis zum polnischen Aufstand,* Berlin, 1931, 56-64.)

64 Borries, *op. cit.,* 155; Geffcken, *op. cit.,* 79-80.

65 Poschinger, *op. cit.,* II, 359, letter dated March 11, 1854. (*Cf.* Borries, 161 and Geffcken, 94.)

66 HHSA Protokoll des Minist. Rates, March 22, 1854, Pol. Arch. Vorträge. An excellent account of the meetings of the Crown Council is given in Eckhart, 49-54. *Cf.* Engel-Jánosi, *op. cit.,* 119.

67 Kriegsarchiv, Vienna, Feldakten 1854. Memorandum of General Hess, March 22, 1854. (*Cf.* Eckhart, 53.)

68   HHSA Protokoll des Minist. Rates, March 25, 1854. (*Cf.* Eckhart, 54.)

69   *Ibid.*

70   H. Friedjung: *Der Krimkrieg und die österreichische Politik,* 2nd ed., Stuttgart and Berlin, 1911, 21. The most rabid of the Russophiles was Baron Kempen, Minister of Police. (*Cf.* Joseph Karl Mayr: *Das Tagebuch des Polizeiministers Kempen von 1848 bis 1859,* Vienna, 1931.)

71   V. Bibl: *Der Zerfall Österreich. Von Revolution zu Revolution,* 2 vols., Vienna, 1921, II, 244. In March 1855 Bruck became Minister of Finance.

72   Friedjung, *op. cit.,* 28-29. Metternich still exercised some influence at the Ballplatz and sought to guide Buol in the conduct of foreign affairs. (*Cf.* Carl J. Burchhardt: *Briefe des Staatskanzler Fürsten Metternich-Winneburg an den österreichischen Minister des allerhöchsten Hauses und des Äussern, Grafen Buol-Schauenstein, aus den Jahren 1852-1859,* Munich and Berlin, 1934.)

73   Friedjung, *op. cit.,* 30.

74   See especially Borries, 14-55 and Stern, VIII, 63-66.

75   Borries, 36-43 on Manteuffel.

76   For the Prussian side of the negotiations see Borries, especially 167-181. Frederick William appointed Prime Minister Manteuffel and Adjutant Generals Groeben and Gerlach to negotiate with Hess. Manteuffel handled the political details, Groeben and Gerlach the military. The King's instructions to his negotiators are given by Borries, 167-168 and Poschinger, II, 391-393.

77   BB, LXXI, pt. VIII, protocol signed at Vienna, April 9, 1854. On May 23rd the Conference concluded a protocol declaring that the aim of the four powers was the integrity of the Ottoman Empire and the evacuation of its territory by Russian troops. After that date Prussia was no longer represented.

78   HHSA enclosure in no. 2, Vienna, May 10, 1854, Buol to Hübner.

79   BB, LXXXI (1854), pt. X, text of additional article. It was further agreed that Austria would station 100,000 men on the Galician frontier and that Prussia would station an equal number on her Polish frontier, if Vienna requested it.

80   Eckhart, 52.

81   Poschinger, II, 415-417, April 29, 1854.

82   Friese, *op. cit.,* 65, letter of Tsar dated April 27/May 9, 1854.

83   Poschinger, II, 422-426.

84   The King declared that he would not be able to place simultaneously 250,000 men in the east and 100,000 in the west.

85   Friese, 86. *Cf.* Borries, ch. 6 for the attitude of the German states.

86   Borries, 217-220, Geffcken, 97 and Stern, VIII, 77.

87   Borries, 191. Prussia was also informed by General Mayerhofer, who was sent to Berlin to request military support. (Geffcken, 108-109).

88 Borries, 194; Poschinger, II, 448-450; letter of Frederick William to Tsar, June 15, 1854.

89 Poschinger, II, 440ff., Sans Souci, June 6, 1854.

90 Friedjung, *op. cit.*, 64, asserts that Nicholas seriously thought of going to war with Austria. (*Cf.* Henderson, *loc. cit.*, 26.)

91 Terms in BB, LXXI, pt. VII.

92 HHSA no. 60 A-F, St. Petersburg, 6 July/24 June, 1854, Esterhazy to Buol.

93 Eckhart, 81.

94 This called for guarantees to regulate political relations with Turkey in order to safeguard the European equilibrium. Although it was the most important demand in the protocol, the Tsar simply ignored it.

95 Eckhart, 81-82.

96 Poschinger, II, 457ff., Sans Souci, July 6, 1854.

97 *Ibid.*

98 Eckhart, 82.

99 *Ibid.*

100 *Ibid.* Bismarck, the Prussian delegate to the German Diet, was not in agreement with the King's policy, holding that it gave Austria the idea that she could count on Prussia and the Confederation in all circumstances. He believed that it was necessary to put an end to this "irresponsible and unwarranted hope," that Prussia's aim should be to win over the German states to her viewpoint and not to aid Austria in drawing advantages from Russia's difficulties. In his opinion, Austria would never have taken a strong stand against Russia if she had not felt certain of Prussian support (*ibid.*, 91).

101 See chapter 4, pp. 76-83, for a discussion of these negotiations.

102 The Duke of Saxe-Coburg referred to the four points as "a sort of diplomatic magic wand by means of which the friends and the enemies of Russia might be united in happy concord." (*Memoirs of Ernest II*, III, 122.)

103 HHSA no. 1, Vienna, August 10, 1854.

104 HHSA PL, Vienna, August 10, 1854, Buol to Esterhazy.

105 HHSA no. 3, Vienna, August 10, 1854, Buol to Esterhazy.

106 Prussia, however, did not officially adhere to the four points. (*Cf.* Guichen, *op. cit.*, 180.) Bismarck found the King's action incompatible with the honor "which His Majesty used to call the honor of an officer." (Eckhart, 98.)

107 Eckhart, 99.

108 Austria's position in the Diet had been rendered exceedingly difficult by the rivalry which existed between Bismarck and Prokesch-Osten. The latter was not in agreement with Buol's policy and in January 1855 was transferred to Constantinople, being replaced as Austrian delegate at Frankfurt by Count Rechberg. Bismarck distrusted Prokesch-Osten and showed a decided preference for Rechberg. In his journal for June 28, 1855, Kempen relates that Prokesch-Osten complained bitterly of the "miserable viewpoint" which Austria had adopted toward the great powers and declared that Buol was hostile to any decision and was

unable to get along with the military men. (Mayr: *Das Tagebuch des Polizeiministers Kempen von 1848 bis 1859,* 368.)

109   Eckhart, 106.

Chapter Four: THE ALLIANCE OF DECEMBER 2, 1854

1   HHSA no. 54 E, Paris, March 30, 1854, Hübner to Buol.

2   HHSA no. 59 D, Paris, April 9, 1854, Hübner to Buol.

3   HHSA no. 78 E, Paris, May 21, 1854, Hübner to Buol.

4   Austria had no desire to see the reëstablishment of an independent Poland and Buol directed Hübner to warn the French Government against encouraging the hopes of the Poles as this would cast doubt upon the principle of maintaining the territorial boundaries. (HHSA no. 8, Vienna, June 8, 1854.)

5   HHSA no. 83 A-D, Paris, May 31, 1854, Hübner to Buol.

6   Hübner: *Neuf Ans,* I, 237, May 14, 1854. This was a rather frequent complaint and is not entirely convincing. While Buol's dispatches and private letters were not masterpieces of composition, they were by no means incoherent or contradictory. It is difficult to escape the conclusion that at least in part Hübner's criticisms of Buol were due to jealousy.

7   *Ibid.,* 229. This statement was made to Franz Joseph during an audience on April 27, 1854. Hübner was in Vienna attending the wedding of the Emperor and the Princess Elizabeth.

8   HHSA no. 87 E secret, Paris, June 14, 1854, Hübner to Buol.

9   Hübner rejected the idea of dismembering Russia.

10   *Ibid.*

11   HHSA no. 1 res., Vienna.

12   HHSA no. 3, Vienna, Buol to Hübner. (*Cf.* Henderson, *loc. cit.,* p. 26, who mentions secret conversations which took place at the beginning of July in Paris between Drouyn de Lhuys, Thouvenel, the Political Director of the French Foreign Office, and Hübner, which resulted in an elementary form of the four points. He does not cite any documents for these conversations. Buol's dispatch, in which he refers to the bases of peace as suggested by Drouyn de Lhuys, was dated July 2nd.)

13   HHSA PL, Paris, July 9, 1854, Hübner to Buol. Henderson, *loc. cit.,* 28 mentions Cowley as stating that Buol was "pressed through Hübner by Drouyn de Lhuys to sign a treaty." (Cowley to Clarendon, July 27, 1854, no. 937, FO 27/1019.)

14   HHSA no. 104 B secret, Paris.

15   HHSA PL, Paris, July 22 and 27, 1854. Hübner to Buol. In his letter of the 27th, Hübner urged Buol to recommend to Franz Joseph that a decision be taken promptly regarding the treaty of alliance, "for if one delays, France and England will escape us. I am at the end of expedients."

16   HHSA res., Vienna, July 21, 1854. Hübner received this on the 24th. He had been instructed to enter into discussions for the treaty in

Buol's own name, a point which is repeated in his private letter of July 27th. (*Cf.* Henderson, *loc. cit.,* 28.)

17 Henderson, *loc. cit.,* 29, who points out that England was not a party to the negotiations but that Clarendon learned of them through a French source. According to Hübner, Clarendon approved. (*Neuf Ans,* I, 257.)

18 *Ibid.,* p. 30. Henderson concludes that the draft treaty was proof at this time that Austria was prepared to fight Russia to secure the evacuation of the Principalities.

19 HHSA no. 55 A-C, June 21 and no. 60 B, July 6, 1854, St. Petersburg, V. Esterhazy to Buol, reporting that the Russians were likely to retreat from the Principalities. (*Cf.* Henderson, *loc. cit.,* p. 31.) On August 8th Buol was informed by Gortchakoff, the Russian Minister at Vienna, that Nicholas had ordered the complete evacuation of the Principalities. Hübner attributed the failure of Franz Joseph to sign the tripartite alliance to the bad impression produced by the reports of Colloredo. Dispatches from the Austrian Embassy in London were first sent to Paris where they were read by Hübner before being forwarded to Vienna. According to Hübner, Colloredo took fright at the thought of breaking with Russia and in his private letters to Buol pointed out dangers of war with that power. (Hübner: *Neuf Ans,* I, 261, August 5, 1854.)

20 See chapter 3, pp. 69-70.

21 According to a dispatch of Werther, the Prussian envoy at St. Petersburg, to Frederick William IV, dated August 26th, Russia's chief objection to the four points was in the fact that they were presented at the very moment she was evacuating the Principalities. (Preussisches Geheimes Staatsarchiv, Auswärtige Amt, Politischer Bericht, no. 13, 1ABq, Turkei 44, vol. 19, cited by Henderson, *loc. cit.,* 36.) Nicholas toyed with the idea of declaring war upon Austria but was dissuaded by Nesselrode, who submitted a memorandum stating that this would involve Russia in a struggle against all Europe. (Nesselrode, Comte A: *Lettres et Papiers du Chancellor Comte Charles de Nesselrode,* 11 vols., Paris, n. d., XI, 74-77, memoir, September 7, 1854.)

22 Nor of Hübner. (*Neuf Ans,* I, 266.) In a letter to General Hess, Buol stated that if Russia rejected the four points, it would be necessary for Austria to conclude an alliance with the western powers. (HHSA Nachlass Buols, Vienna, August 12, 1854.)

23 Fr. Doc., vol. 456, no. 151, Vienna, September 4, 1854, Bourqueney to Drouyn de Lhuys.

24 HHSA no. 1, Vienna, September 14, 1854.

25 Henderson, *loc. cit.,* more or less ignores the influence which Prussia exerted on Austrian policy.

26 HHSA Nachlass Buols, Vienna, September 16, 1854.

27 Fr. Doc., vol. 456, no. 91, Paris, September 13, 1854, Drouyn de Lhuys to Bourqueney and HHSA no. 122 B res., Paris, September 12, 1854, Hübner to Buol. Clarendon was highly indignant and wrote to

Aberdeen that the Austrians "intended to throw us over in the most complete and impudent manner." (September 10, 1854, quoted in Henderson, *loc. cit.*, 37.)

28 *Ibid.*, HHSA. In a subsequent conversation with Hübner, Drouyn de Lhuys acknowledged that by means of her armaments and her strategic operations, Austria had compelled Russia to withdraw from the Principalities. He also agreed that no act of diplomacy of which she was a signatory obligated Austria to go to war because of the rejection of the four points. On the other hand, he insisted that Austria was under a moral obligation to join those powers whose cause she shared. He regretted that she had not seized the occasion to assert her leadership in Germany instead of drawing back before the hesitations of Prussia. Indeed, he exhausted his vocabulary in showing his disdain for the Prussian Government. (HHSA no. 128 B, Paris, October 1, 1854, Hübner to Buol.)

29 *Ibid.*, no. 122 B res.

30 *Ibid.*

31 HHSA no. 1, Vienna, September 23, 1854, Buol to Hübner.

32 HHSA Vorträge, Buol to Franz Joseph.

33 Eckhart, 109.

34 Concerning this influence and the relations of the Archduchess with the Empress Elizabeth, see: Corti, Count Caesar E: *Elizabeth of Austria*, London, 1936, chs. 3 and 4. Corti (p. 59) shows that the Archduchess was the Emperor's adviser, even in matters of high politics.

35 No doubt Franz Joseph became more favorably disposed to the alliance by the events taking place in the Crimea. On September 20th the battle of Alma was fought and a false report was circulated concerning the fall of Sebastopol. (*Cf.* Henderson, *loc. cit.*, 38.)

36 HHSA Vienna, October 3, 1854. Colloredo received similar instructions.

37 "Though drawn up by the allied ambassadors, it was fundamentally an Austrian scheme, and was regularly referred to as such." (Henderson, *loc. cit.*, 39, who adds that Buol wished to conceal his initiative in the affair and have the proposal come from the western powers. In his instructions to Hübner, Buol did not refer to this draft treaty.)

38 HHSA no. 131 A-B, Paris, October 8, 1854, Hübner to Buol. Hübner referred to the attitude of Drouyn de Lhuys as "pure comedy." (*Neuf Ans,* I, 268.)

39 The draft treaty drawn up by Bourqueney and Westmorland did not bind Austria to take an active part in the war. While Franz Joseph had agreed to the conclusion of the alliance, he was not yet prepared to indicate the time when Austria would become an active belligerent. This explains the attitude of Drouyn de Lhuys. England was even more skeptical of Buol's proposal and Clarendon showed such hostility to Austria that Aberdeen was disturbed. Drouyn de Lhuys told Cowley that both he and the Emperor "thought the propositions de-

testable and that they could not be seriously entertained." (*Cf.* Henderson, *loc. cit.*, 39-40.)

40 *Ibid.*, 41.

41 HHSA no. 133 F secret, Paris, October 11, 1854, Hübner to Buol.

42 *Ibid.* Here again Hübner minimized the difficulties.

43 HHSA no. 133 B, Paris, October 11, 1854, Hübner to Buol. Napoleon told Cowley that he thought it would be a good idea to have Poland as a buffer state but would not actually go so far as to make it a matter of war. (Wellesley, Sir Victor and Sencourt, R. (eds.): *Conversations with Napoleon III*, London, 1934, 64, October 6, 1854, Cowley to Clarendon.) The Emperor had also discussed the Polish question with Prince Albert at Boulogne in September, 1854. (T. Martin: *The Life of His Royal Highness: The Prince Consort,* 5 vols., New York, 1875-1881, III, 119.)

44 HHSA no. 137 C, Paris, October 22, 1854, Hübner to Buol.

45 HHSA PL, Paris, October 22, 1854, Hübner to Buol.

46 HHSA no. 140 B secret, Paris, November 3, 1854, Hübner to Buol.

47 *Ibid.*

48 HHSA PL, Paris, November 21, 1854, Hübner to Buol. In a telegram of November 13th, Hübner mentioned as another argument for hastening the alliance the fact that the prevailing opinion in France was that it was Austria's attitude regarding the Principalities which had permitted Russia to send reinforcements to the Crimea. Drouyn de Lhuys was accused of having been duped by Austria.

49 HHSA telegram, St. Petersburg, November 17, 1854, Esterhazy to Buol.

50 The new engagement was actually an extension of the Additional Clause of April, 1854.

51 Henderson, *loc. cit.*, 45, who adds that Buol drew up a new draft which became the basis of the treaty.

52 The text is given in HHSA no. 2, Vienna, December 3, 1854, Buol to Hübner and Colloredo.

53 This was signed at Vienna. (HHSA enclosure in no. 2, Vienna, December 23, 1854, Buol to Hübner.) In the British House of Commons on February 10, 1857, Disraeli referred to the convention of December 22nd. Palmerston at first denied that it had been formally concluded or signed. A day or so later, however, he admitted that it had been signed but declared that as it was made contingent upon Austria's participation in the war against Russia, the convention became a dead letter. (HHSA nos. 9 and 10, London, February 11 and 13, 1857, Karolyi to Buol.)

54 Henderson, *loc. cit.*, 46-47.

55 Eckhart, 132-137.

56 *Ibid.* Von Arnim's story was taken over by Helmut von Lucius: *Le rôle politique de la Prusse pendant la guerre de Crimée,* Paris, 1903,

61, while Friedjung: *Der Krimkrieg,* 122, followed the account of Lucius. According to Eckhart, 134, Friedjung's entire account of what happened at Vienna during the last days of November and the first days of December is incorrect since it is based to a large extent on the journal of Hübner, who knew little of what went on in Vienna at this time. On the other hand, Hübner mentions (*Neuf Ans,* I, 282-283) that he was informed by Drouyn de Lhuys on November 29th that Bourqueney considered the treaty as good as signed and this was confirmed by a dispatch from Buol on the 30th. There seems to be no reason, therefore, for an Anglo-French ultimatum. But Friedjung evidently tried to reconcile the account given by Lucius with that of Hübner. "Following the ultimatum of the western powers," he states, page 123, "days of dire distress arose for the Vienna Cabinet. Count Buol was enmeshed in his own pledges and if the Emperor did not sign the treaty, he saw only one escape: his resignation. He could have rendered the best service to his ruler if he had not placed him before the alternative but instead had asked for his dismissal immediately and without any subterfuges." Friedjung maintains, page 124, that Buol should have realized that the Emperor had no intention of taking up arms against Russia and hence should have made way for someone willing to compromise with the Tsar. Among those who accepted Friedjung's version are: Stern, *op. cit.,* VIII, 95, T. Schiemann: *Geschichte Russlands unter Kaiser Nikolaus I,* 4 vols., Berlin, 1904-1919, IV, 327, A. O. Meyer: *Bismarck's Kampf mit Osterreich am Bundestag zu Frankfurt,* Berlin, 1927, 232, and Redlich, *op. cit.,* 152. In Poschinger, II, 579, an account is given of an interview on December 1st between Count Georg Esterhazy, the Austrian Ambassador at Berlin, and Manteuffel. The Ambassador showed Manteuffel a dispatch from Buol, dated November 28th, stating that the western powers had desired to make stronger demands than those included in the four points, that Austria had disapproved of this but was convinced that her disapproval would be effective only if she entered into closer relations with the western powers. In his dispatch Buol made it clear that while the treaty had not yet been signed, complete agreement had been reached concerning its terms. He made no mention of the treaty to Gortchakoff when the latter, on November 28th, presented the note accepting the four points because, he said, the secret was not his alone. (HHSA no. 1, Vienna, December 8, 1854, Buol to V. Esterhazy.)

57   HHSA Vienna, December 14, 1854, Buol to Georg Esterhazy.

58   Von Arnim's deafness was a great handicap in his work as a diplomatist. It is said that at the time of his transfer from Paris to Vienna in 1851, he received a written assurance from the King that he could remain at his new post until he himself requested a recall. (Eckhart, 135. *Cf.* Borries, 44, who says that von Arnim had requested that he be recalled but that the King and Manteuffel preferred to have him remain.)

59   Meyendorff, *op. cit.,* III, no. 490, 144, Vienna, March 30/April 11, 1854, Meyendorff to Nesselrode.

60   Eckhart, 135.

61   Kempen relates that in order to prevent his aide-de-camp, Count Grünne, from opposing the treaty, Franz Joseph ordered him to go hunting. (Mayr, *op. cit.*, 346, entry of December 3, 1854.) Kempen mourned over the "humiliating" alliance and the loss of Austria's "greatness." There are other references in Kempen to Buol's ascendency over the Austrian generals, for example, that the journal "Lloyd" was suppressed because of its pro-Russian sympathies. (*Ibid.*, 349, entry for December 21, 1854.)

62   Eckhart, 136.

63   Quoted in Redlich, *op. cit.*, 155. (*Cf.* Friedjung, *op. cit.*, 110.)

64   HHSA PL, Paris, December 3, 1854, Hübner to Buol.

65   HHSA no. 154, Paris, December 13, 1854, Hübner to Buol.

66   Hübner: *Neuf Ans,* I, 284.

67   HHSA PL, Paris, December 6, 1854, Hübner to Buol.

68   HHSA no. 150 B, Paris, December 6, 1854, Hübner to Buol.

69   HHSA no. 156 B, Paris, December 17, 1854, Hübner to Buol. Palmerston told Hübner that the treaty of alliance would be "a stillborn child," adding: "By alliance, I understand your participation in the war. Oh well, you will never fight Russia, and the only result of this treaty will be a tension in the relations between you and the western powers." (*Neuf Ans,* I, 282, November 27, 1854.)

70   On Prussia's reaction see Borries, 250-253.

71   In a dispatch to Hatzfeldt, dated December 20, 1854, Manteuffel stated that it was best to remain cool-headed and not to set too small a value to Prussia's aid. This value would increase within a few weeks, particularly if Prussia succeeded in placing herself in a stronger military position. (Poschinger, III, 5.)

Chapter Five: THE CLOSE OF THE WAR AND THE CONGRESS OF PARIS

1   Text is given in BB, LV, pt. xiii.

2   Puryear, *op. cit.*, 363.

3   "My name," said Franz Joseph on January 2, 1855, "will never be affixed to a condition which would wound the honor and dignity of Tsar Nicholas." (S. Goriainov: *Le Bosphore et les Dardanelles,* Paris, 1910, 99, Gortchakoff to Nesselrode, Vienna, January 3, 1855. *Cf.* Puryear, 367, who points out that this promise enabled Gortchakoff to maintain a firm stand in the negotiations.)

4   A. J. Whyte: *The Political Life and Letters of Cavour, 1848-1861,* London, 1930, 130. For an account of Piedmont's actions see: F. Valsecchi: *L'Alleanza di Crimea. Il Risorgimento E L'Europa,* Arnolda Mondadori, 1948, pp. 377-406 and 415-463, and the article by Paul Matter, "Cavour et la guerre de Crimée," *Revue Historique,* vol. 145 (1924), 161-202.

5   The treaty was accepted by Piedmont on January 9th and ratified on the 26th.

6 HHSA no. 6, Vienna, January 4, 1855, Buol to Hübner and Colloredo. Hübner saw no danger in the Piedmontese alliance, believing that it would place Piedmont under Austro-French influence. (HHSA no. 51, Paris, January 16, 1855, Hübner to Buol.)

7 Sybel, II, 256-257, Borries, 329 and Geffcken, 159.

8 Borries, 285-90 for details.

9 Eckhart, 154.

10 This resolution prevented Napoleon from carrying out a plan to send French troops across Germany to attack Russia and thus make Austria and the Principalities theaters of war.

11 Fr. Doc., vol. 458, no. 6, Paris, January 10, 1855, Drouyn de Lhuys to Bourqueney.

12 HHSA no. 5 B, Paris, January 16, 1855, Hübner to Buol. Drouyn de Lhuys believed that Russia had accepted the four points merely to prevent Austria from entering the war. (*Ibid.*, no. 5 A-N.)

13 Fr. Doc., vol. 458, confid., Paris, January 24, 1855, Drouyn de Lhuys to Bourqueney.

14 HHSA autograph letter, dated Tuileries, January 26, 1855.

15 HHSA autograph letter, Vienna, February 4, 1855. Puryear, 353, points out that Austria signed the treaty of December 2nd without knowing the British interpretation of the third point. "The British interpretation of the most important point in the negotiations for peace had not yet been formulated for communication to Austria. Yet Francis Joseph signed an alliance which provided for war against Russia if England failed to get satisfaction on that point." (*Ibid.*)

16 HHSA no. 18 A-J, Paris, February 10, 1855, Hübner to Buol.

17 *Ibid.*, no. 18 C secret.

18 Napoleon announced his intention in a letter of February 26th to Palmerston, declaring that it was "the only way to bring to a rapid conclusion an expedition which otherwise must result in disaster to England as well as France." (Martin: *Life of the Prince Consort*, III, 228.)

19 They declared that they were not answerable for internal peace and that the finances were in a most dangerous state. (Wellesley and Sencourt, *op. cit.*, 80, citing Cowley to Clarendon, April 23, 1855.)

20 HHSA no. 24 A-D res., Paris, February 27, 1855, Hübner to Buol.

21 *Ibid.*

22 HHSA autograph letter.

23 Martin, *op. cit.*, III, 241.

24 In March 1855 Clarendon visited Boulogne where he tried to dissuade the Emperor. (*Ibid.*, 231-34, memorandum prepared by Prince Albert, March 6, 1855, based on Clarendon's report.) By the end of April the plan had been abandoned. Various reasons are given for this. La Gorce, I, 367, believes that the attempt made on Napoleon's life in the Bois de Boulogne on April 28th caused him to abandon the plan. Hübner, *Neuf Ans*, I, 323, April 16, 1855, states that Napoleon gave up the plan because it was impossible to form a regency strong enough to paralyze the influence of Prince Jerome Napoleon and his son. On April

26th Cowley wrote to Clarendon that the plan was abandoned. "The real reason I take to be that the Emperor has been alarmed at the state of France and what might happen in his absence." (Wellesley and Sencourt, 81.) In any case, the matter ended with the appointment of Marshal Pelissier to succeed Canrobert as Commander-in-Chief of the forces in the Crimea.

25　Eckhart, 167.

26　*Ibid.,* 169. (*Cf.* HHSA telegram, Paris, January 8, 1855, Hübner to Buol.)

27　*Ibid.,* 170, citing report of G. Esterhazy to Buol, March 28, 1855.

28　HHSA no. 39 D, London, March 28, 1855, Colloredo to Buol and no. 34 D, Paris, March 30, 1855, Hübner to Buol.

29　Stern, VIII, 95, asserts that Buol had lost the confidence of Franz Joseph after the conclusion of the treaty of December 2nd, and that the Emperor took personal charge of foreign policy without consulting his minister. In this connection, however, see Eckhart, 170.

30　Because Prussia had not adhered to the treaty of December 2nd, England and France insisted upon her exclusion from the Conference.

31　Fr. Doc., vol. 459, no. 45, Vienna, March 14, 1855.

32　Schlitter, *op. cit.,* 102, autograph letter, Vienna, February 24, 1855.

33　*Ibid.,* 103, letter dated St. Petersburg 5/17 March 1855.

34　*Ibid.*

35　It was a five-power conference with delegates from Austria, England, France, Russia and Turkey. Prussia was not represented though Buol had favored her participation. (HHSA Vienna, March 14, 1855, Buol to G. Esterhazy.)

36　Details of the Conference together with the protocols are given in BB LV, pt. xiii. *Cf.* Puryear, *op. cit.,* especially 342, 370-402. The fourth point by which Russia was to renounce any claims to a protectorate over Turkish subjects was not of sufficient importance to cause difficulty.

37　Puryear, 371.

38　It was said that Palmerston found Russell an "inconvenient colleague" and was glad to get rid of him for a while. (Vitzthum von Eckstädt, *op. cit.,* 150.) The other delegates at the Conference were Buol and Prokesch-Osten for Austria, Gortchakoff and Titov for Russia, Ali Pasha and Fuad Effendi for Turkey, Bourqueney and later Drouyn de Lhuys for France. Westmorland was the other British delegate. In a letter to Russell, March 15, 1855, Palmerston gave his opinion of the Austrian delegates. "Buol I believe to be as honest as an Austrian Minister can be, but Prokesch is on the whole the most roguish diplomatist I ever had to do with. He is a consummate hypocrite, an accomplished actor, destitute of all principle, and utterly regardless of truth." (G. P. Gooch (ed.): *The Later Correspondence of Lord John Russell,* 2 vols., London, 1925, II, 198.) On the other hand, Friedjung, *Der Krimkrieg,* 151-52, states that Franz Joseph did not wholly trust Buol and secretly gave his confidence to Prokesch-Osten.

39 BB LV, pt. xvi, Clarendon to Russell, FO, February 22, 1855. *Cf*. Puryear, footnote 373-74 for a detailed account of these instructions.

40 *Ibid.*, pt. xv, no. 1, Clarendon to Russell, FO April 3, 1855. Buol suggested that the counterpoise plan might be applied either by means of a Russo-Turkish agreement not to maintain more than an equal number of warships in the Black Sea, or by giving Turkey the right to call into the Black Sea as many warships as she required from her allies in time of danger without alluding to the relative strength of the Russian and Turkish forces. *Cf*. Puryear, 379.

41 *Ibid.*, telegram, FO, March 24, 1855, Clarendon to Russell.

42 From Paris Cowley wrote to Russell that the Emperor was disappointed with the results of the Conference and not satisfied with the conduct of Bourqueney, who had not shown enough firmness toward Russian pretensions. It was therefore decided that Drouyn de Lhuys should go to Vienna. "He (Drouyn de Lhuys) hopes to shame the Austrian Government into active cooperation with the Allies. I believe myself that the only chance of obtaining it is by plain language. From the beginning of the Eastern Question I have myself never had the slightest hope of Austria. . . . " (Gooch: *The Later Correspondence of Lord John Russell,* II, 202.)

43 La Gorce, I, 374.

44 BB LV, pt. xv, no. 2, Clarendon to Russell, FO, April 3, 1855.

45 *Ibid.*

46 Harcourt, Comte Bernard d': *Diplomatie et Diplomates, Les Quatre Ministères de M. Drouyn de Lhuys,* Paris, 1882, 113-120, letter of Drouyn de Lhuys to Napoleon, April 1, 1855.

47 *Ibid.*, 125.

48 BB LV, pt. xv, no. 3, Russell to Clarendon, Vienna, April 10, 1855.

49 *Ibid.*, no. 4, Russell to Clarendon, Vienna, April 12, 1855.

50 Russell warned Buol that Austria's attempt to escape from her engagements of December 2nd would endanger her relations with England. (*Ibid.*)

51 D'Harcourt, 130-33, report of Drouyn de Lhuys to Napoleon. *Cf*. La Gorce, I, 359 and Sybel, II, 266.

52 Russell and Clarendon were of the opinion that Buol, in refusing to yield, was attempting to force the abandonment of the neutralization plan. (BB LV, pt. xv, no. 3, Russell to Clarendon, Vienna, April 10 and no. 5, Clarendon to Russell, FO, April 16, 1855.)

53 *Ibid.*, no. 8, Russell to Clarendon, Vienna, April 16, 1855.

54 *Ibid.*, no. 9, Russell to Clarendon, Vienna, April 18, 1855. When asked by Russell if Austria would enter the war in case Russia rejected all limitation plans, Buol refused to answer. (*Ibid.*)

55 *Ibid.*, no. 11, Clarendon to Westmorland, FO, April 21, 1855.

56 *Ibid.*, no. 10, Russell to Clarendon, Vienna, April 18, 1855. *Cf*. Puryear, 401.

57 *Ibid.*, no. 13, Clarendon to Westmorland, FO, April 24, 1855.

58　Drouyn de Lhuys was informed of the Emperor's decision on April 23rd. (D'Harcourt, 143.)

59　HHSA no. 45 B res., Paris, May 9, 1855, Hübner to Buol. Lord Cowley had warned Napoleon that an unsatisfactory peace would destroy the Anglo-French alliance. (Wellesley and Sencourt, 78, Cowley to Clarendon, March 25, 1855.) In a letter to Stratford de Redcliffe, May 5, 1855, Cowley wrote: "Drouyn de Lhuys has been playing old gooseberry at Vienna and agrees with Buol to support terms it would be disgraceful for us to accept and I have taken the liberty of exposing him to his Imperial Master to his great discomfiture." (*Ibid.,* 82.) Hübner attributed the defeat of the plan to the direct influence of Cowley, "who during the absence of Drouyn de Lhuys became, so to say, the Minister of Foreign Affairs of the Emperor Napoleon," and who went beyond his instructions in working against the Austrian alliance. (*Neuf Ans,* I, 327, May 5, 1855.)

60　HHSA rapport très secret de M. de Lightenveld, Ministre des Pays Bas à M. Van Hall, Ministre des Affaires Étrangères, Paris, June 4, 1855, enclosed in a private letter from Prince Richard Metternich to Rechberg dated Paris, February 23, 1863.

61　In a letter addressed to Napoleon, which Drouyn de Lhuys carried with him to Paris, Franz Joseph explained his refusal to fight Russia by stating that he had been compelled to direct his attention to the German problem and this had made it impossible for him to engage in a war over the limitation of Russian warships in the Black Sea. (Eckhart, 175.) On April 27th Drouyn de Lhuys sent Napoleon a report of a conversation with the Austrian ruler. "I sincerely regret," said Franz Joseph, "that it is impossible for me to go beyond the plan that you have sent to Paris. But when the Emperor knows what has been decided in the last instance, I hope that he will agree with me that a permanent alliance between us to defend the Ottoman Empire against Russia by land and sea, is better than a figure." (d'Harcourt, 144.)

62　HHSA no. 43 A-D, Paris, April 30, 1855, Hübner to Buol.

63　HHSA no. 43 B secret, Paris, April 30, 1855, Hübner to Buol.

64　HHSA telegram chiffre, Vienna, May 8, 1855, Buol to Hübner. (*Cf.* Fr. Doc. vol. 459, Vienna, May 14, 1855, Bourqueney to Drouyn de Lhuys.)

65　HHSA no. 1, Vienna, May 20, 1855, Buol to Hübner.

66　*Ibid.,* no. 4, Vienna, May 20, 1855, Buol to Hübner.

67　After the departure of Drouyn de Lhuys and Russell from Vienna, Buol made several other proposals which Clarendon rejected.

68　E. Ashley: *Life of Henry John Temple, Viscount Palmerston, 1846-1865,* 2nd ed., 2 vols., London, 1876, II, 94, date of letter May 28, 1855.

69　HHSA no. 50 D res., Paris, May 28, 1855, Hübner to Buol.

70　HHSA PL Paris, May 28, 1855, Hübner to Buol. Napoleon asked the Duke of Saxe-Coburg, who visited Paris in May 1855, if he was still of the opinion that Austria was prompted by sincere and honest intentions. The Duke replied in the affirmative, giving various reasons as to why Austria could not take offensive measures. The Emperor admitted every point but added: "Enfin un manque de courage." By contrast, he spoke favorably of Prussia. The Duke concluded that Napoleon in his heart had already "completely broken with the Austrian alliance." (*Memoirs of Ernest II,* III, 176-177.) Napoleon admitted to Cowley that his faith in Austria "was nearly gone." (Wellesley and Sencourt, 78, March 25, 1855.)

71 HHSA no. 54 B, Paris, June 15, 1855, Hübner to Buol.

72 Walewski assured Hübner that the four points would be maintained in the peace treaty. "They will be part of it. That goes without saying. It is even impossible that it should not be so." (HHSA no. 68 F, Paris, July 13, 1855, Hübner to Buol.)

73 HHSA no. 57 A-B, Paris, June 22, 1855, Hübner to Buol.

74 F. Charles-Roux: *Alexandre II, Gortchakoff et Napoléon III,* Paris, 1913, 30.

75 Friedjung, *op. cit.,* 109, Bibl., II, 244.

76 Bourqueney reported that Franz Joseph was deeply offended by the rejection of the Austrian proposals not so much because it diminished the prospects for peace but because the allies did not seem to appreciate the value of his sword. (Fr. Doc. vol. 460, no. 88, Vienna, June 3, 1855, Bourqueney to Walewski.)

77 HHSA PL, Vienna, June 6, 1855.

78 HHSA PL, Vienna, July 3, 1855, Buol to Hübner.

79 Charles-Roux, *op. cit.,* 27.

80 HHSA no. 74 B secret, Paris, August 3, 1855, Hübner to Buol.

81 HHSA no. 89 A-H secret, Paris, September 21, 1855, Hübner to Buol.

82 *Ibid.*

83 HHSA no. 1, Vienna, August 13, 1855, Buol to Hübner.

84 Napoleon discussed peace with the Duke of Saxe-Coburg in September 1855, and said that those problems such as Poland and Italy which had either been badly settled at the Congress of Vienna or which had arisen since then, should be brought up. "The Emperor thinks of a Congress, at which all the great and small sovereigns would have to appear in person." (*Memoirs of Ernest II,* III, 194-195.) Napoleon repeated the same idea to Cowley. "Among the dreams, was the possibility of saying to Europe that events had clearly proved that the balance of power in Europe was neither established nor could it be maintained under the Treaties of 1815, and that it was necessary to call a congress in order to resettle the map." (Wellesley and Sencourt, 95, Cowley to Clarendon, October 25, 1855.) The questions of Poland and Italy were among those he mentioned to Cowley.

85 Through the intermediary of Seebach, Nesselrode began direct negotiations with Paris on the basis of the four points. Moreover, Napoleon permitted the Duc de Morny to carry on a strictly secret and private correspondence with Gortchakoff regarding point three, which Russia had rejected. On the Franco-Russian *rapprochement* during the

Crimean War see Charles-Roux, *op. cit.*, 48-54, 62 and Morny: *Extrait des Mémoirs. Une Ambassade en Russie en 1856*, Paris, 1892, 19-23, 43.

86 Buol was vacationing in the Alps and only learned of the allied victory from Baron Beust, the Saxon Minister of Foreign Affairs. This was one reason for the delay though Buol offered the excuse that it was necessary to await news concerning the extent of the victory—an excuse which Napoleon regarded as worse than the omission itself. (*Memoirs of Ernest II,* III, 195.) Napoleon told the Duke of Saxe-Coburg that he definitely preferred Prussia to Austria. "It is quite clear," he said, "that it is better to attach oneself to a woman who hates us, than to one who has cheated us once before and that is the case with Austria." (*Ibid.,* 196, September 1855.)

87 Hübner: *Neuf Ans,* I, 351. *Cf.* Friedjung, *op. cit.,* 172.

88 Beust, Friedrich Ferdinand Graf von: *Aus drei Vierteljahrhunderten,* 2 vols., Stuttgart, 1887, I, 159. *Cf. La* Gorce, I, 457 and Friedjung, *op. cit.,* 43.

89 Hübner's position at Paris had become so bad that he requested the Duke of Saxe-Coburg to intervene in Vienna in order to induce the Austrian Government to act. The Duke agreed and on October 5, 1855, wrote to Buol that the relations between Austria and France were cooling and that if Franz Joseph still regarded himself as an ally of the western powers, "it would be very desirable to give the Emperor of the French some outward sign of the fact." (*Memoirs of Ernest II,* III, 197.)

90 As Friedjung suggests, it is likely that Buol had got wind of the secret Franco-Russian negotiations and this spurred him to act. (*Der Krimkrieg,* 173-174.)

91 Fr. Doc. vol. 461, no. 142, Vienna, October 7, 1855 and no. 146, Vienna, October 14, 1855, de Serre to Walewski.

92 *Ibid.,* no. 146.

93 *Ibid.,* no. 149, Vienna, October 22, 1855. Buol appeared willing to concede that England and France were entitled to a reward for their sacrifices providing this did not jeopardize European interests.

94 Goriainov, 127-129, Puryear, 410-411.

95 Fr. Doc. vol. 461, no. 160 confid., Vienna, November 14, 1855, Bourqueney to Walewski and HHSA no. 1 secret, Vienna, November 17, 1855, Buol to Hübner and Colloredo.

96 HHSA Vienna, November 17, 1855.

97 HHSA no. 108 A-G secret, Paris, November 26, 1855, Hübner to Buol. It has been pointed out that Napoleon was really playing a double game. "While seducing Russia by the possibility of a direct *entente* with France, he negotiated behind the back of the Russian Government with Austria. . . ." In this way, he hoped to place himself in a better position to overcome Palmerston's opposition to peace. (V. Boutenko, "Un projet d'alliance franco-russe en 1856 d'après des documents inédits des archives russes," *Revue Historique,* vol. 155 (1927), 283.) Napoleon told Cowley that "a rupture of diplomatic relations between Austria and Russia was at this moment more valuable than a declaration of war by Austria, for in the latter case he must

prepare to go to her assistance, and this he was hardly prepared to do." (Wellesley and Sencourt, 98, Cowley to Clarendon, November 18, 1855.)

98 England was irritated because Napoleon had negotiated with Vienna without her participation. (Martin, III, 524-526.) On November 24, 1855, Clarendon wrote: "Cowley's letter was again most unsatisfactory today. Those French are mad with fear and roguery, and I am afraid that the Emperor is almost as much demoralized as his government. I am sure that if we rejected the terms, the French would make peace on their own hook, and our position would then be a miserable one. The French have been screaming so loudly for peace that I expect Austria will be frightened by the hard conditions she has offered to impose on Russia and may want to back out of them." (H. Maxwell: *The Life and Letters of George William Frederick, Fourth Earl of Clarendon,* 2 vols., London, 1913, II, 104.)

99 Sweden joined the Anglo-French Alliance on November 21, 1855, and it was agreed that fighting be resumed in the spring.

100 Walewski appeared to attach much significance to the acceptance of the proposals by England. "We enter a new era," he said to Hübner. "Whether peace follows immediately or is obtained only after a long struggle, the relations between Austria and France are henceforth truly intimate. It is a different world." (HHSA no. 113 A-E, Paris, December 17, 1855, Hübner to Buol.) On the other hand, Palmerston was particularly loath to yield. On December 13th Clarendon wrote: "Palmerston is very rabid, and his feelings about Austria are so savage that he almost compels me to take her part." (Maxwell, II, 107.)

101 HHSA no. 6 E, Paris, January 17, 1855, Hübner to Buol.

102 Fr. Doc. vol. 463, telegram, Vienna, January 12, 1856, Bourqueney to Walewski.

103 HHSA St. Petersburg, January 17, 1856, V. Esterhazy to Buol.

104 Napoleon prevailed upon Palmerston to soften the special conditions that England proposed to present to Russia. See Boutenko, *loc. cit.,* 283 and A. Jomini: *Étude diplomatique sur la guerre de Crimée,* 2 vols., St. Petersburg, 1878, II, 380-383.

105 A. Debidour, *Histoire diplomatique de la Europe, 1814-1878,* 2 vols., Paris, 1891, II, 147, states that while Austria protested her good dispositions in favor of Prussia, she secretly intrigued to exclude her from the peace congress. It is probably true that Friedjung, *Der Krimkrieg,* 178, exaggerates the willingness of Austria to aid Prussia in this matter. Borries, 328-329, admits that Buol did intervene in Prussia's behalf with Napoleon but maintains that he did so in a dilatory fashion as if to punish her for the attacks Austria encountered in the German Diet.

106 A full account is given in BB, LVI: Protocols of Conferences held at Paris relative to the General Treaty of Peace. (*Cf.* H. T. Hagg: *The Congress of Paris of 1856,* typed thesis, University of Iowa, 1936, and E. Gourdon: *Histoire du Congrès de Paris,* Paris, 1857.)

107 Cavour wrote that the Russian delegates said horrible things about the Austrians. This was particularly true of Orloff, "whose eye is

ferocious when he speaks of these gentlemen." (V. E. d'Azeglio: *Cavour E L'Inghilterra. Carteggio con V. E. d'Azeglio,* 2 vols., Bologna, 1933, I, #275, p. 216, Paris, February 26, 1856.)

108　HHSA, Congress of Paris, report of Buol to Franz Joseph, Paris, February 24, 1856.

109　*Il Carteggio Cavour-Nigra, Dal 1859 al 1861,* 4 vols., Bologna, 1926, I, first series, no. 3, 40.

110　BB, LXI, protocol #22, Hagg, *op. cit.,* 143-146. A revolt had broken out in Greece during the war. The question of Poland was omitted because of Russia's opposition. (Boutenko, *loc. cit.,* 291.) France, of course, had grievances against the Belgian press.

111　BB, LXI, protocol #22. As Whyte, *op. cit.,* 218, points out, Clarendon expressed only his personal views. (*Cf.* Hagg, 144.)

112　HHSA no. 21, Paris, April 9, 1856, Buol and Hübner to Franz Joseph.

113　*Il Carteggio Cavour-Nigra,* I, no. 4, 41, Paris, April 12, 1856.

Chapter Six: NEAR EASTERN AFFAIRS, 1856-1859

1　HHSA no. 88 A res., Compiègne, October 22, 1856, Hübner to Buol.

2　Pingaud, *loc. cit.,* 59.

3　In this connection see F. Charles-Roux, *op. cit.,* 179-180.

4　Nesselrode, *op. cit.,* XI, 112-116, memoir dated February 11, 1856. *Cf.* Meyendorff, *op. cit.,* III, 217ff. and Ernst Schule: *Russland und Frankreich vom Ausgang des Krimkrieges bis zum italienschen Krieg, 1856-1859,* Berlin, 1935, 126. It should be remembered that Nesselrode had been the first Russian statesman to work for a *rapprochement* with France.

5　Friese, *op. cit.,* 17.

6　For a detailed account of Morny's mission consult F. Charles-Roux, *op. cit.,* especially book II, chapters 1 and 2, which is based not only on Morny's *Une Ambassade en Russie* but also on unpublished documents. *Cf.* the article by F. Charles-Roux, "La Russie et l'Alliance Anglo-Française après la guerre de Crimée" in *Revue Historique,* vol. 101, 1909, 272-315.

7　Charles-Roux, *loc. cit.,* 279.

8　Boutenko, *loc. cit.,* 290.

9　Charles-Roux, *op. cit.,* 162.

10　*Ibid.,* 164-165. Not all of Napoleon's advisers were in favor of the *rapprochement* with Russia. Thouvenel, the Ambassador at Constantinople, opposed it because he distrusted the Russians and saw that underneath their politeness they concealed ambitious schemes. (L. Thouvenel: *Trois Années de la Question d'Orient,* Paris, 1897, 45). He agreed with Persigny, the Ambassador at London, that the Anglo-French alliance should be kept intact. Walewski, on the other hand, was a warm advocate of a Franco-Russian *entente.* According to Hübner, Napoleon had no idea that Walewski intended to substitute a Russian alliance for the alliance concluded on April 15, 1856 by Austria, England and France. The Emperor was visiting Plombières and Biarritz and left foreign policy to his minister. When he returned to Paris, he was astonished and indignant to learn that Walewski had abused his confidence. (*Neuf Ans,* I, 452.) Hübner, however, was too optimistic about Napoleon's attachment to the alliance of April 15th. It was not this but his ties with England which concerned the Emperor. He would have preferred a tripartite alliance of England, France and Russia.

11 Boutenko, *loc. cit.,* 294. *Cf. Memoirs of Ernest II,* III, 230.

12 BB, LXI, pt. xviii, for text of treaty. *Cf.* H. Temperley, "The Treaty of Paris and Its Execution," *Journal of Modern History,* vol. 4, 1932, 527 and W. E. Mosse, "The Triple Treaty of 15 April 1856," *English Historical Review,* April, 1952, 203-229.

13 In view of the Franco-Russian *rapprochement,* the new treaty did not conform to the realities of the situation. Though it was supposed to be secret, Napoleon revealed its existence to the Russian delegates at the Congress. (Charles-Roux, *op. cit.,* 106.) Count Valentin Esterhazy reported from St. Petersburg that the Russian Cabinet was greatly disappointed upon learning of the treaty and that it had a disillusioning effect upon advocates of a *rapprochement* with France. (HHSA no. 34 A-C, St. Petersburg, 24/12 May 1856, to Buol.) It should be said that Napoleon was obligated to conclude the treaty by the terms of a protocol signed at Vienna on November 14, 1855. This called for a new treaty of alliance in order to safeguard the peace from infractions by the Russians.

14 HHSA Congress of Paris, no. 24 A-B, Paris, April 16, 1856. There is no doubt that Franz Joseph sincerely desired the friendship of Napoleon providing the latter would respect Austria's interests. In reply to a remark of de Serre, French Chargé d'Affaires at Vienna, that the Crimean War should not be regretted since it served to establish an alliance between Austria and France, Franz Joseph exclaimed: "You are right; that alliance will be eternal. It is based upon the mutual interests of the two empires, upon the confidence and friendship of the two sovereigns!" (Fr. Doc. vol. 463, no. 32, Vienna, March 26, 1856, de Serre to Walewski.)

15 In this connection see Charles-Roux, *op. cit.,* 131-132, 160-161, and the excellent article by Temperley, *loc. cit.,* 387-415. The aim of article 20 was to exclude Russia from the Danube.

16 Serpent's Island was of no value in itself but in the possession of Russia, it would have violated the express purpose of the Paris Congress. (*Cf.* T. W. Riker: *The Making of Roumania,* London, 1931, 63.)

17 Austria saw in the difficulties over Bolgrad and Serpent's Island a pretext for prolonging her occupation of the Principalities and held that the withdrawal of her troops was contingent upon a settlement of all the clauses of the Treaty of Paris. By Article 31 of the Treaty, Austria was to withdraw her troops from the Principalities as soon as possible after the exchange of ratifications. This she was most reluctant to do particularly as she was planning a system of railways in the Prin-

cipalities and wanted to interest European capitalists. Her withdrawal would have weakened her influence and hence her ability to get foreign capital. (*Cf.* Riker, 47.)

18   Charles-Roux, *op. cit.*, 169. The settlement was worked out in a conference which met at Paris on December 30, 1856, which Napoleon had persuaded Austria and England to accept. In addition to the questions of Bolgrad and Serpent's Island, those relating to the evacuation of the Black Sea by England and the Principalities by Austria were settled.

19   HHSA No. 95 A-L secret, Paris, November 7, 1856, Hübner to Buol.

20   HHSA PL, Vienna, November 26, 1856, Buol to Hübner.

21   HHSA no. 101 A-G res., Paris, December 5, 1856, Hübner to Buol. In a letter to Buol, Franz Joseph revealed his concern over the new situation. "The reports from Paris," he wrote, "are interesting but sad. The eyes of Hübner are opened and he no longer writes in rosy colors. . . . The procedure of Walewski is an open deception and the Emperor is also not far from it. How this man has changed since the conclusion of peace! The best thing is to wait and stand with England." (HHSA Nachlass Buols, Venice, December 15, 1856.)

22   For a detailed discussion of this question consult Riker, *op. cit.*, and W. G. East: *Union of Moldavia and Wallachia,* New York, 1929.

23   *Cavour E. L'Inghilterra, Cavour con V. E. d'Azeglio*, I, no. 251, 194, Cavour to Victor Emmanuel, Paris, February 22, 1856.

24   This scheme had been suggested to Napoleon by Cavour some months previously. (*Cf.* Riker, 40.)

25   *Cavour E. L'Inghilterra,* I, no. 275, 216, Cavour to E. d'Azeglio, Paris, February 26, 1856.

26   Articles 22-25 of the Treaty provided that the Principalities were to retain their existing autonomy, subject to the suzerainty of Turkey, that an international commission should inquire into the conditions and sentiments of the people and report to the powers, who would determine the final organization of the Principalities. On March 14, 1856, the Congress accepted a protocol which provided for a plebiscite.

27   Not all of the French diplomats were in favor of the union. Bourqueney, Persigny and Thouvenel were opposed to it although the last-named became more favorable when he saw that France might be forced to accept a Russian alliance. (L. Thouvenel: *Trois Années de la Question d'Orient, 1856-1859,* Paris, 1897, 31.) To Persigny the union was far less important than the maintenance of good relations with England, and he believed that Napoleon should remain aloof from the struggles of the powers and assume the role of arbiter. (Ollivier, *op. cit.,* III, 411.) It was incomprehensible to him that the Emperor should become involved in questions in which he had no direct interest.

28   On Gortchakoff's attitude see Charles-Roux, *op. cit.,* 182-184, who points out that Russia hoped to see the union checked through the opposition of Austria and England. (*Cf.* Riker, 40-41.)

29   At the Paris Congress, Clarendon at first seemed opposed to the union and then later accepted it. (Riker, 42, who does not offer any

satisfactory reason for this change.) Buol, however, believed that Clarendon wanted to please France. (HHSA, Vienna, June 28, 1856, Buol to Prokesch.) After the Congress, Clarendon again changed his attitude. On August 22, 1856, he wrote to Cowley opposing the union. (Riker, 61, who gives a detailed discussion of Clarendon's attitude, especially footnote 3, p. 42.) Clarendon might have been influenced by Palmerston's opposition. England's earlier support of the union disgusted Franz Joseph. He wrote to Buol that Austria should not lose time in trying to bolster up England or in awaiting concessions from France but should show Turkey that "she still has one friend." (HHSA Nachlass Buols, Pressburg, Augus 25, 1856.)

30 Riker, 27.

31 *Ibid.* (*Cf.* Friedjung: Der Krimkrieg, 184-185.)

32 Fr. Doc., vol. 464, no. 69, Vienna, June 22, 1856, Bourqueney to Walewski.

33 Riker, 86.

34 Fr. Doc., vol. 464, Vienna, July 1, 1856, Heeckeren to Walewski.

35 *Ibid.*

36 *Ibid.*

37 HHSA no. 42 A-N, Paris, May 13, 1857, Hübner to Buol and Fr. Doc., vol. 467, no. 59, Paris, May 27, 1857, Walewski to Bourqueney.

38 Riker, 125, calls the plebiscite "a farce."

39 HHSA PL, Vienna, May 27, 1857, Buol to Hübner.

40 See Riker, especially 125-131 and his article, "The Concert of Europe and Moldavia in 1857" in *Eng. Hist. Rev.,* XLII, 1927, 227-244.

41 On the Osborne memorandum of August 9, 1857, see W. G. East, "The Osborne Conference and Memorandum of August 1857" in *Eng. Hist. Rev.,* XLIII, 1928, 409-412, T. W. Riker, "The Pact of Osborne" in *Am. Hist. Rev.,* XXXIV, 237ff., and H. Temperley, "More Light on the Pact of Osborne, 9 August 1857" in *Cambridge Hist. Journal* V, 1937, 315-323. The mutiny in India overshadowed the question of the Principalities in England at this time. "It was under cover of this distraction that Palmerston and Clarendon could plan the nature of their retreat." (Riker, *op. cit.,* 131.) No document was signed at Osborne although the British understanding of the agreement was set forth in a memorandum which was presented to Walewski, who assented to its accuracy. (*Ibid.,* 133.)

42 HHSA no. 62, Paris, August 13, 1857, Hübner to Buol.

43 HHSA PL, London, August 12, 1857, Apponyi to Buol.

44 HHSA no. 55 B secret, London, August 12, 1857, Apponyi to Buol.

45 *Ibid.*

46 *Ibid.* When Napoleon complained to Cowley about the intimacy of Anglo-Austrian relations, the latter reminded the Emperor of the intimacy between France and Russia. "England and Austria agreed together on most questions arising out of the Treaty of Paris. France differed from them and shared the opinions of Russia. Hence, we were naturally

obliged to hold the same language as Austria; but whose fault was that?" (Wellesley and Sencourt, 124, Cowley to Clarendon, June 19, 1857.)

47 HHSA PL, Paris, October 28, 1857, Hübner to Buol.

48 *Ibid.*

49 On the Stuttgart meeting see the article by G. Rothan, "Souvenirs Diplomatique. L'Entrévue de Stuttgart," in *Revue des Deux Mondes,* vol. 90, Nov.-Dec. 1888, 555-586. *Cf.* S. Goriainov, "Les Étapes de l'Alliance franco-russe" in *Revue de Paris,* January 1, 1912 and Charles-Roux, *op. cit.,* 211-213, 219-223. The King was a persistent advocate of a Franco-Russian *rapprochement.*

50 Rothan, *loc. cit.,* 584, is incorrect in stating that an accord was signed. The agreement is recorded in minutes found in the Russian archives. See Charles-Roux, 219-220 and Goriainov's article. In a conversation with Hübner in May 1858, Napoleon declared that at Stuttgart the Tsar had proposed the conclusion of an alliance which the French ruler declined. (HHSA no. 54 A-K, Paris, May 23, 1858, Hübner to Buol.)

51 Charles-Roux, *op. cit.,* 223, who corrects the account by Rothan.

52 *Ibid.,* 221.

53 Buol pretended not to be alarmed by the Stuttgart meeting. He said to Bourqueney, before it took place, that it would not disturb the European equilibrium because, while Napoleon wanted peace but could make war, the Tsar wanted peace and could not make war in view of the conditions of Russian finances and the development of reforms. (Fr. Doc., vol. 469, no. 160, Vienna, September 14, 1857, Bourqueney to Walewski.)

54 Russia had put out feelers regarding a meeting at Warsaw. Franz Joseph believed that Gortchakoff was behind this idea and that he had an ulterior motive in view. "My dignity," he wrote to Buol, "will not permit me to go to Warsaw and I will not accept an invitation to Weimar." (HHSA Nachlass Buols, Laxemberg, September 13, 1857.) Buol managed to overcome the Emperor's objections to a meeting at Weimar. Charles-Roux, *op. cit.,* 213; states that Franz Joseph solicited an interview with the Tsar "in a pressing manner" and that the latter hesitated but yielded to Gortchakoff who represented the *démarche* as an "honorable amend." This seems to be contradicted by Buol's Nachlass.

55 HHSA no. 6 A-B, Moscow, 21/9 September 1856, Prince Esterhazy to Buol.

56 HHSA PL, Vienna, October 20, 1856, Prince Esterhazy to Buol.

57 It is interesting to note that the Austrian Ambassador suggested that a decoration be conferred on Gortchakoff in order to modify the latter's attitude. Gortchakoff did receive an order from Franz Joseph at Weimar. (HHSA no. 2 res., St. Petersburg, 3 January 1857/22 December 1856, Count V. Esterhazy to Buol.)

58 *Ibid.* According to Baron Budberg, Russian Ambassador at Vienna, the reëstablishment of friendly relations between Austria and Russia could take place only with the resignation of Buol. (Fr. Doc., vol. 469, no. 181, Vienna, October 31, 1857, Bainville to Walewski.)

Bourqueney reported that there was some talk in Vienna that Buol would resign because of his unpopularity in Paris and St. Petersburg. It was even said that Franz Joseph was displeased with the conduct of his minister, who had severed the old ties without having obtained effective substitutes. (*Ibid.,* confid., Vienna, September 29, 1857, Bourqueney to Walewski.)

59   It should be noted that Austria's relations with Prussia were none too good at this time, while England had been diverted from European affairs by her difficulties in India.

60   HHSA PL, Vienna, April 26, 1857, Buol to Hübner.

61   *Ibid.*

62   HHSA PL, Paris, May 13, 1857, Hübner to Buol.

63   Born during the Congress of Paris, March 16, 1856.

64   HHSA PL, Vienna, May 27, 1857, Buol to Hübner.

65   HHSA. While the memorandum is not signed, there is no doubt as to its authorship. A copy was sent to Hübner and also to Apponyi at London, who wrote concerning it: "The portrait you have made of the secret tendencies of Louis Napoleon is traced with the hand of a master and, moreover, it seems to me a striking resemblance." (HHSA PL, London, December 16, 1857.) The memorandum is mentioned by Engel-Jánosi, *op. cit.,* 139, and reproduced by C. W. Hallberg in *Revue d'Histoire Diplomatique,* Oct.-Dec., 1939, 353-360.

66   Hübner, who visited Vienna in September 1857, found Buol in poor health, very irritable and greatly excited against Napoleon and the French Government. Buol asserted that Napoleon was an inveterate enemy of Austria, and wanted to degrade her and rob her of Lombardy-Venetia. Indeed, the minister asserted that should the interests of Austria demand it, he would not hesitate to recommend an alliance with Russia. Hübner attempted to "correct" these ideas but without success. "I shall try to lead him back to a saner judgment of the situation, for as long as he is minister, I owe him the aid of my position and shall offer him this as much as possible. But he precipitates matters head over heels into a fatal course." (*Neuf Ans,* II, 49-50, September 22, 1857.) There were rumors that Buol would resign. In a lengthy conversation with Franz Joseph, Hübner tried to prove that Napoleon was not an inveterate enemy of Austria and that he had no fixed plans to deprive her of Italy. The French ruler employed foreign affairs simply as an instrument in order to secure dominance in France and to strengthen his throne. It would be as dangerous a mistake to consider him a pronounced, embittered enemy of Austria as to think of him as a sincere and reliable ally. Hübner urged that there be more indulgence toward Napoleon and greater respect for his egotism. In any case, Austria should not accustom him through systematic opposition to regard her as an enemy. (*Ibid.,* 50-52, September 23, 1857.) It should be mentioned that Buol's position was extremely difficult in view of the continual attacks on his policy by the military clique at the court, which advocated an alliance with Russia and war against France. His bitterness against the French can also be explained by the fact that he felt himself to have been unjustly treated

by them. Having worked for an alliance with France, he discovered at the Paris Congress that this was not appreciated by Napoleon. On the other hand, considering what is known about the latter's intrigues with Cavour, Buol had sufficient reason to suspect Napoleon. Keen observer that he was, Hübner was slow in recognizing the danger.

67   HHSA no. 1, Vienna, March 9, 1858.

68   Charles-Roux, *op cit.*, 188-189.

69   T. von Sosnowsky: *Die Balkanpolitik Österreich-Ungarns seit 1866*, 3 vols., Vienna, 1913-14, I, 61. *Cf.* R. Charmatz: *Geschichte der auswärtigen Politik Österreichs in 19 Jahrhundert*, Leipzig, 1914, 37.

70   Charles-Roux, *op. cit.*, 189. While the question of Montenegro was not discussed at the Paris Congress, the Turkish delegate, Ali Pasha, found the opportunity to explain that the Sultan, without altering the *status quo*, intended to make Montenegro an integral part of the Turkish Empire. On May 31, 1856, Prince Danilo protested to the great powers and demanded not only the independence of Montenegro but the rectification of the frontier toward Albania and Herzegovina and the port of Antivari. (*Cf.* Stern, VIII, 211.)

71   Prince Danilo rejected the arrangement and instead suggested the delimitation of frontiers to which France agreed. The French and Russian ambassadors were thereupon instructed to concert measures for this delimitation. (*Cf.* Charles-Roux, *op. cit.*, 192.)

72   Charles-Roux, *loc. cit.*, vol. 101, 277.

73   *Ibid.*, 278. Russia at this time was not reconciled to Prince Danilo.

74   Fr. Doc., vol. 470, no. 33, Vienna, March 16, 1858.

75   Charles-Roux, *op. cit.*, 232.

76   *Ibid.*, 233.

77   HHSA no. 1, Vienna, April 19, 1858, Buol to Hübner. According to Hübner, Walewski showed ill-humor and defiance toward Austria, and it was probable that the same attitude existed at the Tuileries, since the minister was a faithful interpreter of Napoleon's impressions. There were two reasons for this attitude: first, the firm and independent policy which Austria followed in eastern affairs, and the influence she exercised at the Porte, aroused jealousy at Paris which Russia capitalized upon by insinuating that Vienna contemplated isolated intervention in the Balkans; second, the fact that Napoleon's desire to do something for the Italians was thwarted by the realization that he was not prepared to fight Austria. In addition, Cowley told Hübner that the Emperor was peeved because he had promised Prince Danilo protection and was unable to keep his word. (HHSA PL, no. 1, Paris, April 9, 1858, Hübner to Buol.)

78   HHSA no. 11 res., Vienna, April 19, 1858, Buol to Hübner.

79   Russia refused to recognize Turkish sovereignty over Montenegro. Gortchakoff said to Count Valentin Esterhazy that Russia "will not associate herself in any act which will place a Christian population . . . under Moslem domination." (HHSA no. 20 A-F, St. Petersburg, 3 April/22 March 1858, V. Esterhazy to Buol.)

80   HHSA no. 1, Vienna, May 17, 1858, Buol to Hübner.

81   This gave Grahavo to Montenegro. At the same time, France made preparations to send two cruisers to the Adriatic as a demonstration in favor of the Montenegrins. (*Cf.* Charles-Roux, *op. cit.,* 233.)

82   HHSA no. 54 A-K, Paris, May 23, 1858, Hübner to Buol. Hübner's position was far from comfortable. He was not invited to the hunts at Compiègne in October 1857 and certain journals predicted his recall. He placed some of the blame for Napoleon's resentment on Buol's policy and was severely critical of the latter's handling of the question of the Principalities. Once he described Buol's dispatches bearing on this question as written with spleen instead of ink and became so angry because of them that he had an attack of dyspepsia. (*Neuf Ans,* II, 12, February 19, 1857.) There are other examples of Hübner's critical attitude given in his journal. On December 23, 1857, he wrote: "Preoccupied with the conduct of Buol, who will finish by embroiling us with all Europe." (*Ibid.,* 75.) In his *résumé* for 1857, he again complained of the bad temper of Buol, "who loses no occasion in order to be disagreeable." (*Ibid.,* 79.) Hübner's relations with his chief became rather delicate. "He considers me too prudent, not energetic enough, too much the man 'des bonnes rélations.' From my side, I find him tiresome and arrogant." (*Ibid.,* 82.)

83   HHSA no. 2, Vienna, June 1, 1858.

84   *Ibid.*

85   The sessions of the conference lasted from May 22 to August 19, 1858. For a detailed account see Riker, *op. cit.,* 158-180. The question of the navigation of the Danube was also discussed. In regard to this, Hübner wrote: "What a sad task to pass in review all the faults one has committed in Vienna in this question and it is I who must wash the dirty linen, not *en famille,* but before Europe." (*Neuf Ans,* II, 205-206, August 11, 1858.) The fact that Austria stood alone in this question at the conference was most annoying to Hübner.

86   HHSA no. 69 E, Paris, June 29, 1858, Hübner to Buol. The white flag referred to was the symbol of the Bourbons.

87   To Baron Heeckeren, who came to Vienna in order to discuss Austro-French relations, Buol declared that in upholding the cause of the oppressed Balkan nationalities, Napoleon was playing Russia's game. For years it had been Russia's aim to bring about the dismemberment of the Ottoman Empire by the formation of independent Christian states. "Austria is inflexibly opposed to a common flag for Rumania. If Rumania is united as Napoleon desires, it will be the prelude to the dismemberment of the Ottoman Empire and he will demand compensation by redrawing the map of Europe." (HHSA no. 7, Vienna, July 9, 1858, Buol to Hübner.) Buol wrote to Hübner that if Napoleon dropped the demand for a common flag, Franz Joseph would regard this as a sign of friendship. (HHSA no. 6, Vienna, July 9, 1858.) Riker, *op. cit.,* 173-174, states that this letter was sent at Cowley's suggestion and he refers to it as a "coup de théâtre" which proved decisive. Prince Clemens Metternich urged Buol to conclude the discussions as quickly as possible since the longer they lasted, the more they played into the hands of

Napoleon and presented dangers to all friends of peace. (Burckhart, *op. cit.*, 202-203, no. 144, Vienna, June 2, 1858.)

88   HHSA no. 18 C res., Paris, February 10, 1859, Hübner to Buol.

89   HHSA no. 85 K, Paris, August 20, 1858, Hübner to Buol.

90   Fr. Doc., vol. 472, no. 160, Vienna, November 30, 1858, Bainville to Walewski.

91   *Ibid.*, extract of a confidential note, December 1858, Bourqueney to Walewski.

92   Buol was convinced that the Serbian uprising was the result of Pan Slav propaganda aimed at the dismemberment of Turkey. By intervening, he hoped to prevent the insurgents from driving the Turkish garrison out of the fortress of Belgrade.

93   HHSA no. 2 A-O, Paris, January 2, 1859, Hübner to Buol.

94   *Ibid.*

95   HHSA no. 5 A-B, Paris, January 8, 1859, Hübner to Buol.

96   *Ibid.*

Chapter Seven: THE ITALIAN QUESTION, 1856-1859. FROM THE CONGRESS OF PARIS TO THE CONCLUSION OF THE FRANCO-PIEDMONTESE ALLIANCE

1   See the article by Anatole Leroy-Beaulieu, "La Politique du Second Empire," in *Revue des Deux Mondes*, vol. 98, March-April 1872, 536-572. *Cf.* G. I. Bratianu: *Napoléon III et les nationalités*, Paris, 1934.

2   Generally opposed to the Emperor's Italian policy were the Empress, who had strong clerical sympathies, Count Walewski, the Duc de Gramont, French Minister at Turin, a large part of the *Corps Législatif*, and a majority of the Senate. On the other hand, Napoleon was supported by various liberal and anti-clerical groups which favored any attacks aimed at Austria and the Papacy.

3   A. Pingaud, "Napoleon III et ses Projets de Confédération Italienne," *Revue Historique*, vol. 155, 1927, 333.

4   *Cavour E. L'Inghilterra*, I, no. 251, 194, Cavour to Victor Emmanuel, Paris, February 27, 1856.

5   See chapter 6, p. 117.

6   *Cavour E. L'Inghilterra*, I, no. 322, 259, memorandum dated March 5, 1856.

7   See chapter 5, pp. 109-110.

8   HHSA no. 32 B, Paris, April 28, 1856, Hübner to Buol.

9   *Ibid.*

10   HHSA no. 41 A-C, Paris, May 17, 1856, Hübner to Buol.

11   *Ibid.*

12   Fr. Doc., vol. 464, no. 49, Vienna, May 14, 1856, de Serre to Walewski.

13   *Ibid.*

14   HHSA no. 46 C, Paris, May 24, 1856, Hübner to Buol.

15 "Above all," wrote Buol to Hübner, "it is a question of reaffirming the principle of authority at Naples." (HHSA PL, Vienna, July 6, 1856.) This was also the view of Franz Joseph, who disapproved of any advice to the King not given in his interest and in a friendly manner. (HHSA Nachlass Buols, Laxemberg, July 15, 1856, Franz Joseph to Buol.)

16 HHSA no. 46 C, Paris, May 24, 1856, Hübner to Buol.

17 Napoleon's secret aim was to dethrone the Bourbons in Naples and restore the Muratists but realizing that England would never agree to this, he had decided not to engage himself beyond the presentation of identical notes demanding an amnesty for the political prisoners of Naples. Moreover, financiers and merchants of Paris, as well as some of the Emperor's intimate advisers, were opposed to French intervention. (*Cf.* Boutenko, *loc. cit.*, 309 and C. Vidal, "Le Second Empire et Ferdinand II de Naples, 1852-1859," *Rassegna Storica Del Risorgimento,* Anno XXXIX, Fasc. IV, Ottobre-Dicembre 1952, 843.)

18 HHSA no. 88 A res., Compiègne, October 22, 1856, Hübner to Buol.

19 HHSA no. 89 E, Compiègne, October 27, 1856, Hübner to Buol.

20 Though Ferdinand Maximilian, the brother of the Emperor, was personally attractive and entertained plans for reform, he soon discovered that his authority was limited and that all decisions were made in Vienna. His position grew steadily more uncomfortable and on April 20, 1859, he was replaced by General Count Gyulai. (*Cf.* Egon Caesar Corti: *Maximilian and Charlotte of Mexico,* 2 vols., New York, 1928, I, 71.)

21 P. Matter: *Cavour et l'Unité Italienne,* 3 vols., Paris, 1922-27, III, 12.

22 Whyte, *op. cit.,* 234. *Cf.* Matter, *op. cit.,* III, 13 and Stern, VIII, 273.

23 HHSA Sardaigne, Rapports, Expéditions, Varia, 1856-1857, vol. XI/48, Milan, February 10, 1857.

24 Whyte, *op. cit.,* 235. To the English and French ministers at Turin, Count Paar declared that if Cavour's reply was not satisfactory, Austria would break off diplomatic relations. (*Cavour E. L'Inghilterra,* II, no. 675, 103, Cavour to E. d'Azeglio, Turin, February 18, 1857.)

25 Dated Turin, February 20, 1857.

26 HHSA no. 1, Vienna, March 3, 1857, Buol to Hübner.

27 HHSA, Sardaigne, vol. XI/48, Vienna, March 16, 1857, Buol to Paar.

28 HHSA no. 17 chiffre, Paris, February 24, 1857, Hübner to Buol. In London, Clarendon gave a similar warning to Karolyi, stressing the bad effect on Anglo-Austrian relations. (HHSA no. 14 B, London, February 25, 1857, Karolyi to Buol.)

29 HHSA no. 20 A-C, Paris, March 7, 1857, Hübner to Buol.

30 *Ibid.* Hübner was opposed to the rupture of diplomatic relations between Austria and Piedmont, fearing that it would give Napoleon an excuse to intervene. (*Neuf Ans,* II, 16.)

31 HHSA no. 25 B, Paris, March 29, 1857, Hübner to Buol.

32   *Cavour E. L'Inghilterra,* II, no. 688, London, March 23, 1857, E. d'Azeglio to Cavour, reporting a conversation with Clarendon.

33   *Ibid.,* no. 697, Cavour to E. d'Azeglio, Turin, April 17, 1857.

34   *Ibid.* Cavour believed that the move was inspired by Cowley under Hübner's influence.

35   *Il Carteggio Cavour-Nigra,* I, no. 6, 46, Salmour to Cavour, Plombières, July 27, 1857.

36   In September 1857, Gramont was transferred from Turin to Rome but Cavour did not trust his successor, Prince de La Tour d'Auvergne.

37   *Carteggio Cavour-Salmour,* Bologna, 1936, 125-127, 129 and 131. *Cf. Il Carteggio Cavour-Nigra,* I, no. 6, 45-46, Salmour to Cavour, Plombières, July 27, 1857.

38   *Carteggio Cavour-Salmour,* 127.

39   *Il Carteggio Cavour-Nigra,* I, no. 6, 45.

40   *Ibid.,* 46.

41   *Carteggio Cavour-Salmour,* no. 78, 133, August 1, 1857.

42   Matter, *op. cit.,* III, 42.

43   The inspiration for the letter came from Pietri, Prefect of Police, who visited Orsini in prison and told him of Napoleon's generous plans for Italy. (La Gorce, II, 350 and Whyte, *op. cit.,* 250.)

44   Stern, VIII, 292.

45   *Il Carteggio Cavour-Nigra,* I, no. 13, General Della Rocca to Victor Emmanuel, Paris, February 5, 1858. Napoleon was also furious at England for permitting the right of asylum to Italian revolutionaries. Orsini had spent some time in England.

46   Napoleon employed the same arguments in a conversation with Villamarina. "What are the real advantages," he asked, "which the English alliance can offer you? Not material support, that goes without saying, for England has no army, and what is more, she will have India and China on her back for a long time yet." The only alliance for Piedmont was with France but the Emperor declared that if England persisted in defending the treaties of 1815 as she had been doing since the Paris Congress, he might find himself compelled to seek Austrian support, "and once entered into this orbit, I would have to renounce everything which until now has been the subject of my thoughts and the desire of my heart. I, who have always wished the happiness and independence of Italy, will be forced to ally myself with a cabinet for which I have always felt and feel at this moment, the greatest repugnance." (*Ibid.,* no. 14, 41, Villamarina to Cavour, Paris, February 6, 1858.)

47   *Ibid.,* no. 23, Paris, February 22, 1858.

48   *Neuf Ans,* II, 97.

49   *Ibid.,* 103. *Cf.* HHSA no. 17 A-D, Paris, February 7, 1858, Hübner to Buol.

50   HHSA no. 10 C, Paris, January 21, 1858, Hübner to Buol.

51   Fr. Doc. vol. 470, no. 9, Vienna, January 20, 1858, Bainville to Walewski.

52 *Ibid.,* no. 14, Vienna, February 11, 1858, Bourqueney to Walewski. Bourqueney declared to Hübner that Napoleon had decided not to undertake anything in Italy without first consulting with Austria. (*Neuf Ans,* II, 108.)

53 Matter, *op. cit.,* III, 84.

54 HHSA no. 37 A-B, Paris, April 7, 1858, Hübner to Buol.

55 HHSA PL, no. 1, Paris, April 9, 1858, Hübner to Buol.

56 *Ibid.*

57 HHSA no. 47 secret, Paris, May 2, 1858, Hübner to Buol.

58 *Ibid.*

59 In this connection Hübner's comment is *à propos:* "The Emperor Napoleon by his secret diplomacy himself treated the affairs of high external policy. The man least initiated into the views of his master was ordinarily his Minister of Foreign Affairs. No one was less (initiated) than Count Walewski." (*Neuf Ans,* II, 155.)

60 HHSA Nachlass Rechbergs, 524, PL, Vienna, March 9, 1858, Buol to Hübner.

61 HHSA no. 11 res., Vienna, April 19, 1858, Buol to Hübner.

62 HHSA no. 7, Vienna, May 12, 1858. During a visit to Vienna early in May 1858, Hübner complained to Franz Joseph about the irritating tone adopted by Buol in the latter's dealings with the French Government. (*Neuf Ans,* II, 158-159.)

63 HHSA no. 54 A-K, Paris, May 23, 1858, Hübner to Buol.

64 HHSA no. 54 B, Paris, May 23, 1858, Hübner to Buol.

65 Whyte, *op. cit.,* 250.

66 *Il Carteggio Cavour-Nigra,* I, no. 5, 42, Paris, July 11, 1857, Salmour to Cavour.

67 *Ibid.,* no. 27, 84, Paris, March 31, 1858.

68 *Ibid.,* no. 29, 85, Cavour to Dr. Conneau, Turin, May 6, 1858.

69 *Ibid.,* no. 33, 87, Nigra to Cavour, Paris, May 9, 1858.

70 *Ibid.,* no. 34, 87, Nigra to Cavour, Paris, May 10, 1858. Nigra added that such a division also had the approval of the Empress.

71 *Ibid.,* no. 39, 90, Cavour to Villamarina. The latter was warned not to inform Walewski or anyone else about the interview in Turin.

72 Cavour wrote to Salmour, authorizing him to inform Prince de La Tour d'Auvergne, the French Minister at Turin, about the invitation to visit Plombières. (*Carteggio Cavour-Salmour,* 160.)

73 The interview on July 21st lasted eight hours. Cavour brought with him a memorandum and a draft treaty. Details of the interview were set forth by Cavour in a letter which he wrote to Victor Emmanuel from Baden-Baden on July 24th, 1858. (*Il Carteggio Cavour-Nigra,* I, no. 51, 103-113.)

74 Résumé des points concertés à Plombières, sent by Cavour to Napoleon on August 3, 1858. (*Il Carteggio Cavour-Nigra,* I, 123. *Cf.* L. Chiala: *Lettere edite e inedite di Camillo Cavour,* 6 volumes, Turin 1882-1887, II, 566-567.)

75 *Neuf Ans,* II, 199-200, July 30, 1858.

76 HHSA no. 78 D, Paris, July 29, 1858, Hübner to Buol.

77   *Neuf Ans,* II, 220-221.

78   *Ibid.,* 221.

79   HHSA no. 4, Vienna, August 4, 1858, Buol to Hübner.

80   Prince Napoleon Joseph Charles Paul Bonaparte, son of the ex-King Jerome of Westphalia, was born in Trieste, September 9, 1822, and was educated in Italy, Switzerland and Germany. He served in the Constituent Assembly in 1849 where he displayed markedly republican sentiments. In 1852 he was made a Prince of the Imperial Family and entered the Senate. During the Crimean War he was general of a division but remained in the war zone only a short time. He was President of the Commission of the Universal Exposition of 1855, was charged with a diplomatic mission relative to the Neufchâtel affair in 1857, and acted as Minister of Algeria and the Colonies from June 1858 to March 1859. During the Italian campaign of 1859 he was placed at the head of the Fifth Army Corps and took part in the negotiations leading to the Truce of Villafranca.

81   Ernest d'Hauterive: *Napoléon III et le Prince Napoléon. Correspondance inédite,* Paris, 1925, v.

82   "If things continue thus," wrote Hübner, "my position will become untenable. I will be obliged to demand my recall; my departure will be one more step, and a great step, toward the rupture and back of the rupture, there would only be war. This is what one wishes at the Palais Royal (home of Prince Napoleon), where the 'Presse' is written." (*Neuf Ans,* II, 240, December 23, 1858.) On December 26, 1858, Cowley wrote to Malmesbury about Hübner: "The Emperor had now taken a personal dislike to him and treats him very ill. This goes to Hübner's heart, who has not *sang froid* or independence enough to hide it, and if I dared give advice on so delicate a matter, I should recommend him to ask to be removed elsewhere. Until that is done, Austria will have no influence here." (Wellesley and Sencourt, 155.) Malmesbury told Apponyi that so long as Hübner remained at Paris, there would be no improvement in Austro-French relations. (HHSA secret, London, January 1, 1859, Apponyi to Buol.)

83   HHSA no. 104 E, Paris, November 29, 1858, Hübner to Buol.

84   *Il Carteggio Cavour-Nigra,* I, no. 133, 196, November 21, 1858, Napoleon III to Cavour.

85   *Ibid.,* no. 166, 241, December 13, 1858, Cavour to Nigra.

86   *Ibid.,* no. 135, 198, November 3, 1858, Prince Napoleon to Cavour.

87   G. Rothan, "Napoléon III et l'Italie," *Revue des Deux Mondes,* vol. 151, January-February 1899, 774.

88   *Il Carteggio Cavour-Nigra,* I, no. 180, 258, December 24, 1858, Cavour to Villamarina.

89   In 1857 the Duke of Saxe-Coburg detected a change in England's attitude toward Italy. "Whilst the ideas of Italian independence," he wrote, "have formerly met with undivided sympathy in that country, people now observed a rather cool demeanour there towards everything that appeared to be connected with Cavour's policy. If the influence

of French policy in Italy was formerly looked upon as too reactionary, it had now fallen into disfavour because it was beginning to turn against the treaties of Europe." The Duke added that "the imperialistic flirtation with detested Russianism cast a drop, bitter as wormwood, into the alliance of the Western Powers." (*Memoirs of Ernest II*, II, 237.)

90 HHSA PL, London, April 30, 1858, Apponyi to Buol.

91 HHSA PL, London, December 8, 1858, Apponyi to Buol.

92 Malmesbury, *op. cit.*, II, 147, Malmesbury to Cowley, January 7 and 11, 1859.

93 Prince Albert referred to this support in a letter to Baron Stockmar on May 17, 1857. "The anxiety to flatter Prussia in the Neufchâtel affair, and to support her through thick and thin, the visit of Prince Napoleon to Berlin in return for that of Fritz Wilhelm, before that of the Archduke Max, which was earlier in date, was returned in Vienna, excites comment both there and in Berlin. Is it that it was thought desirable to make sure of Prussia before attacking Austria?" (Martin, *op. cit.*, IV, 51.)

94 By articles XXXVI and XXXVII of the Vienna Act of 1820 the obligations of the confederate states in case of war were defined. An attack on one would be regarded as an attack on the confederation. However, where an attack was made on the territory of a member state which was outside the confederation, the Diet would decide by majority vote if the attack threatened the security of the confederation as a whole. An affirmative vote in the Diet obligated all members to assist. Austria was therefore entitled to call for such assistance in the event of an attack against Lombardy-Venetia. Since it was known that Austria could obtain a majority vote, Prussia announced that if it were taken without her approval, she would refuse to be bound by it. (R. C. Binckley: *Realism and Nationalism, 1852-1871*, New York and London, 1935, 209.)

95 Binckley, *op. cit.*, 208. In the summer of 1858 Prussia was anxious to form an alliance with England which, considering the Anglo-Austrian *rapprochement*, appeared to depend upon friendship with Austria. King Leopold of Belgium was active in promoting good relations between Berlin and Vienna. He said to Apponyi that Napoleon would not think of fighting Austria if she had allies. (HHSA PL, London, June 30, 1858, Apponyi to Buol.) For details concerning Leopold's activities, see Sybel, II, 356.

96 On Pepoli's mission, see Stern, VIII, 301.

97 For details of the negotiations see, above all, the excellent article by B. H. Sumner, "The Secret Franco-Russian Treaty of 3 March 1859" in *Eng. Hist. Rev.*, XLVIII, 1933, 65-83. In addition, there is an article by Ernest d'Hauterive, "Mission du Prince Napoléon à Varsovie, 1858" in *Revue des Deux Mondes*, vol. 45, 7th per., May-June 1929, 823-54, based upon an account written by Prince Napoleon in 1868 entitled, "Récit du Prince Napoléon, 28 septembre 1868. Note sur la politique qui à amené la guerre d'Italie en 1859," and another by A. Pingaud, "Un projet d'alliance franco-russe en 1858" in *Séances et Travaux de l'Académie des Sciences Morales et Politiques*, July-August 1928, 471-86.

Sumner cites a Russian article in *Veka,* "Iz istorii russko-frantsuzskikh otnoshenii" based on documents from the secret archives of Gortchakoff. *Cf.* Martens, *op. cit.,* XV, 296-306 for Franco-Russian relations, 1856-1858 and Rothan, *loc. cit.,* 769-72.

98　d'Hauterive, *loc. cit.,* 831 and Sumner, 68.

99　Walewski was merely informed by the Emperor that Prince Napoleon was leaving for Warsaw in order to give a new demonstration of friendship toward the Tsar. (F. Charles-Roux, "La Russie, la France et la question d'Orient après la Guerre de Crimée," *Revue Historique,* vol. 109, 1909, 290-91.

100　*Ibid.,* 291.

101　d'Hauterive, *loc. cit.,* 837. The Prince wrote: "Russia was a woman whom I wished to compromise by letters if need be, while in any case refusing to marry her." (*Ibid.,* 838.)

102　*Ibid.,* 844-45.

103　The idea of setting up an independent Hungarian state was the subject of negotiations between Napoleon and Cavour. In December 1858, Cavour invited Klapka, the Hungarian revolutionist, to visit Turin. "Since it is a matter of raising against Austria the nationalities which she oppresses under her yoke, why should we not make use of the Rumanians, who detest the Austrians as much as we? I spoke at some length on this subject with M. Bratianu, who stopped yesterday at Turin on his way to Paris. He assured me that the Principalities are ready to rise *en masse* in order to extend the hand to the Rumanians of the Banat, Bukowina and Transylvania. If this insurrection breaks out, it will give an immense force to the Hungarian insurrection which, assured of its rear, will concentrate all its forces in order to strike a great blow at the very heart of the Empire. Besides, the example of the Austrian Rumanians will be followed by the Austrian Serbs and perhaps even by the Croats." (*Il Carteggio Cavour-Nigra,* I, no. 172, 252, Cavour to Nigra, December 7, 1858.) Later Cavour informed Nigra that he had seen Klapka and was satisfied with the scheme to create a Hungarian uprising. (*Ibid.,* no. 209, 283, January 7, 1859.) Klapka went to Paris in order to submit plans for the insurrection to Napoleon. In February 1859 Cavour was informed by Prince Napoleon that the scheme had progressed and that Klapka had been given funds by Napoleon. (*Ibid.,* II, no. 262, 20, Paris, February 18, 1859.) In June 1859 Napoleon promised Kossuth to finance a revolt in Hungary if the Magyar leader would raise an army. (L. Chiala: *Politica Segreta di Napoleone III e di Cavour in Italia e in Ungheria, 1858-1861,* Turin, 1895, 55.) This little volume is almost entirely devoted to the Hungarian problem and gives letters and conversations of the Hungarian leaders, Kossuth, Klapka, Teleky and Szarvody with Cavour, Bixio and Napoleon.

104　*Il Carteggio Cavour-Nigra,* I, no. 104, 163, Paris, October 6, 1858, Nigra to Cavour.

105　d'Hauterive, *loc. cit.,* 845.

106　The first of the draft treaties provided for the benevolent neutrality of Russia in the coming Italian war, the deployment of Russian

·

troops on the Galician frontier sufficient to immobilize 150,000 Austrian troops, the stationing of Russian warships at Spezia and Toulon, a promise by Russia to guarantee France against Prussia and the German states and a similar promise by France to guarantee Russia against England. In the second draft treaty provision was made for Russia's approval of the cession of Nice and Savoy to France, the establishment of a Kingdom of Upper Italy comprising 10,000,000 inhabitants, and the promise by the two powers not to oppose the erection of an independent Hungarian state. Napoleon would support the abrogation of the Black Sea Clause and Russia would break off diplomatic relations with Austria. (Sumner, *loc. cit.*, 72.)

107 d'Hauterive, *loc. cit.*, 845, Pingaud, *loc. cit.*, 152-53 and Sumner, 72. The date of Gortchakoff's letter to Prince Napoleon was 15/27 November 1858.

108 *Il Carteggio Cavour-Nigra*, I, no. 191, Paris, January 1, 1859, Nigra to Cavour.

109 The terms are given by Sumner, 78 and Pingaud, *loc. cit.*, 161. *Cf. Il Carteggio Cavour-Nigra*, II, no. 338, 120-21, Paris, March 19, 1859, Nigra to Cavour.

110 *Il Carteggio Cavour-Nigra*, I, no. 120, 178, Turin, October 25, 1858.

111 *Ibid.*, no. 133, 196, Compiègne, November 2, 1858, Napoleon III to Cavour.

112 *Ibid.*, no. 203, 280, Paris, January 4, 1859, Nigra to Cavour. The latter regretted that Napoleon informed Walewski and that he had found it necessary to use his services in formulating the treaties. "He (Walewski) will try to harm us as much as possible." (*Ibid.*, no. 209, 283, January 7, 1859, Cavour to Nigra.)

113 They included a political treaty of alliance, a military convention, a financial convention, and a convention relating to the marriage of Prince Napoleon and Princess Clothilde.

114 The treaties were dated Turin, December 22nd and Paris, December 16th. (*Il Carteggio Cavour-Nigra*, I, 311-315.) They were antedated, as Napoleon explained in a letter to his cousin on January 26, 1859, in order that it should not appear that the marriage between the Prince and Princess Clothilde was a mere bargain obtained in return for a treaty. (E. d'Hauterive, "Corréspondance Inédite de Napoléon III et du Prince Napoléon," *Revue des Deux Mondes*, vol. 19, January-February 1924, 83.) *Cf.* Matter, *op. cit.*, III, 132-36 for details concerning dates of the treaties.

115 Text of treaties given in *Il Carteggio Cavour-Nigra*, I, 311-15 and Matter, III, 137-39.

Chapter Eight: DRIFTING TOWARD WAR, 1859

1   HHSA no. 1, Paris, January 1, 1859, Hübner to Buol.

2   Hübner: *Neuf Ans,* II, 245. Cowley referred to the severe tone used by Napoleon and the disquietude in the public mind. (BB, XXXII, nos. 1 and 3, Paris, January 3 and 7, 1859, Cowley to Malmesbury.)

3   Napoleon had read the alarming dispatches sent by the French Chargé d'Affaires in Vienna on December 27 and 30, 1858: Fr. Doc. vol. 472, Bainville to Walewski. *Cf.* Matter, III, 126.

4   La Gorce, II, 380.

5   Baron Napoleon Beyens: *Le Second Empire. Vu par un Diplomate Belge,* 2 vols., Paris, 1925, II, 144. The author was the son of the Belgian Minister to Paris.

6   HHSA no. 3 A-C, Paris, January 3, 1859, Hübner to Buol.

7   *Ibid.*

8   Hübner: *Neuf Ans,* II, 246.

9   HHSA no. 3 A-C.

10   As Cowley wrote to Malmesbury, this statement had the opposite effect as people asked why it was so guarded and why more positive assurances were not given. (BB, XXXII, no. 16, Paris, January 10, 1859.)

11   HHSA Vienna, January 8, 1859, Buol to Hübner. Buol explained the dispatch of the army corps as a precaution taken because of anarchist activities. *Cf.* BB, XXXII, no. 16, Vienna, January 12, 1859, Loftus to Malmesbury.

12   In a letter to Prince Napoleon referring to the effect produced by the Emperor's remarks in Italy, Cavour wrote: "The most moderate already see the French crossing the Po and sweeping away the Austrians. This state of affairs has a good side since it proves to Europe that Austrian domination will always be detested in Italy." (*Il Carteggio Cavour-Nigra,* I, no. 210, 286, Turin, January 7, 1859. The British Minister at Turin wrote that the words expressed by Napoleon to Hübner were "likely to be considered as tantamount to a declaration of war." BB, XXXII, no. 4, Turin, January 3, 1859, Hudson to Malmesbury.)

13   BB, XXXII, no. 19, Turin, January 10, 1859, Hudson to Malmesbury, enclosure: copy and translation of speech. Cavour sent a draft of the speech to Nigra with instructions to get the views of Napoleon. (*Il Carteggio Cavour-Nigra,* I, no. 186, December 31, 1858 and Whyte, *op. cit.,* 271.) The Emperor deleted the last part of it and added a paragraph beginning with the words, "our country though small in size . . ." (Whyte, 271.)

14   *Cavour E. L'Inghilterra,* II, no. 878, 248, London, January 15, 1859, Lord Shaftesbury to E. d'Azeglio.

15   BB, XXXII, no. 11, FO, January 13, 1859.

16   Matter, III, 153.

17   Malmesbury, *op. cit.,* II, 280, February 3, 1859.

18   BB, XXXII, no. 5, Malmesbury to Cowley, FO, January 10 and no. 8, Malmesbury to Loftus, FO, January 12, 1859.

19   HHSA no. 6 B, London, January 19, 1859, Apponyi to Buol.

20 *Ibid.*

21 HHSA PL, Vienna, January 27, 1859, Buol to Apponyi and BB, XXXII, no. 26, Vienna, January 20, 1859, Loftus to Malmesbury.

22 HHSA PL, Vienna, February 6, 1859.

23 Matter, III, 151. As Hübner sized up the situation, war was favored by the army and the radicals and opposed by the financial, commercial and industrial groups as well as by the Catholic party. (HHSA no. 8 A-C res., Paris, January 14, 1859, Hübner to Buol.)

24 HHSA no. 2 res., Paris, January 2, 1859, Hübner to Buol.

25 HHSA no. 8 B, Paris, January 14, 1859, Hübner to Buol.

26 HHSA no. 7 chiffre, Paris, January 12, 1859, Hübner to Buol.

27 HHSA no. 8 A-C res., Paris, January 14, 1859, Hübner to Buol.

28 *Ibid.*

29 *Ibid.*

30 HHSA no. 10 A-G, Paris, January 19, 1859, Hübner to Buol.

31 *Ibid.*, no. 10 F res.

32 *Ibid.*

33 HHSA no. 14 E res., Paris, January 31, 1859, Hübner to Buol.

34 *Ibid.* Hübner reported that most of the French journals were anti-Austrian and that only one, the *Univers,* representing the Catholic party, had the courage to proclaim sympathy with Austria and to demand an alliance with her. (HHSA no. 8 A-C res., Paris, January 14, 1859, Hübner to Buol.)

35 *Ibid.*, no. 14 E res.

36 *Ibid.*

37 The brochure was written by M. Arthur de La Guéronnière at the request of the Emperor. According to La Gorce, II, 386, the principal ideas were furnished by Eugène Rendu, while La Guéronnière prepared the brochure under the supervision of Napoleon, who read the proof and made certain revisions. A full account is given in Case, *op. cit.,* pp. 58-60. *Cf.* L. Chiala: *Lettere edite e inedite di Camillo Cavour,* III, appendix, 385ff. and Matter, III, 153-54.

38 Chiala, III, 385ff. and Matter, III, 153.

39 La Gorce, II, 396.

40 HHSA no. 18 A-D and 18 C res., Paris, February 10, 1859, Hübner to Buol. (*Cf.* Stern, VIII, 309, who states that the speech did not make a good impression either in France or in foreign countries.)

41 Hübner: *Neuf Ans,* II, 287.

42 HHSA no. 18 C res., Paris, February 10, 1859.

43 BB, XXXII, no. 9, Malmesbury to Crampton, FO, January 12 and no. 10 Malmesbury to Bloomfield, FO, January 12, 1859.

44 HHSA no. 6 B, St. Petersburg, 4 February/23 January 1859, Szechenyi to Buol and BB, XXXII, no. 72, Crampton to Malmesbury, St. Petersburg, January 26, 1859. In his conversation with Crampton, Gortchakoff was bitter in his denunciation of Austria.

45 G. Rothan, "Napoléon III et l'Italie," *Revue des Deux Mondes,* vol. 152, 334. *Cf.* Martin, *op. cit.,* IV, 367.

46 *Ibid.*, date of letter February 14, 1859. *Cf.* Martin, IV, 368-71.

47 BB, XXXII, no. 62, Malmesbury to Cowley. In his dispatch, Malmesbury referred to Cowley's special qualifications for the mission: his excellent knowledge of the French court and his personal intimacy with Buol.

48 *Ibid.,* no. 65, Paris, February 16, 1859, Cowley to Malmesbury. Cowley was convinced of the Emperor's sincerity and of his desire for peace. (*Ibid.,* no. 66, Paris, February 18, 1859, Cowley to Malmesbury.)

49 *Ibid.,* no. 70, FO, February 22, 1859, Malmesbury to Cowley.

50 *Il Carteggio Cavour-Nigra,* II, no. 249, 809, February 10, 1859.

51 HHSA no. 1, Vienna, March 11, 1859, Buol to Hübner.

52 BB, XXXII, no. 106, Vienna, March 9, 1859, Cowley to Malmesbury, giving account of mission to Vienna.

53 *Ibid.* Buol made the same statement to the French Ambassador. (Fr. Doc. vol. 473, no. 22, Vienna, February 22, 1859, Bainville to Walewski.)

54 In a letter to Apponyi, Buol wrote that Cowley left Vienna in the best mood and apparently satisfied with his visit. "He appeared to me to be very much under the charm of the French Emperor but I believe that I succeeded in changing his judgment a little." (HHSA PL, Vienna, March 10, 1859.)

55 HHSA, London, March 4, 1859, Apponyi to Buol.

56 BB, XXXII, no. 106.

57 *Ibid.*

58 *Ibid.,* no. 110, London, March 14, 1859, Cowley to Malmesbury.

59 Fr. Doc. vol. 473, no. 25, Vienna, March 2, 1859, Bainville to Walewski.

60 *Ibid.*

61 According to Rothan, *loc. cit.,* 343-44, the English mediation worked to the detriment of Austria, since the latter was prepared while her adversaries were not. Cowley's mission checked Austria at a moment when she could have defeated Piedmont without much risk. "In paralyzing her by negotiations which were complicated and without result, her enemies were permitted to precipitate in turn their armaments and to operate them in conjunction."

62 *Ibid.,* 347. Regarding the article in the *Moniteur,* Hübner wrote: "What a disavowal of his own conduct! What a contradiction, what a confession, what denials and what language! After having denied (January 24th) in the same *Moniteur,* in a Jewish manner, the reports of the existence of an offensive and defensive alliance with Sardinia, he admitted that a defensive treaty had been concluded in the midst of badly founded fears. He denied preparations which everyone knows have been made in view of the eventuality of war. And in order to exonerate himself, he accuses the whole world of malevolence, credulity and stupidity! However, the effect produced by the article was immense. The French public, so impressionable by nature, considers it as an abandonment of the policy of war." (HHSA no. 34 A-H res., Paris, March 19, 1859, Hübner to Buol.)

63   Matter, III, 159. Napoleon raised no objections and actually approved the proclamation of March 9th after it was drawn up.

64   *Il Carteggio Cavour-Nigra,* II, no. 304, 86, Paris, March 12, 1859, Nigra to Cavour. Both Napoleon and Walewski warned Cowley that preparations for war in the German states would force France to arm. (BB, XXXII, no. 133, Paris, March 18, 1859, Cowley to Malmesbury.)

65   Matter, III, 160.

66   Martin, IV, 405, March 18, 1859. In a letter to Prince Albert on March 22nd, Clarendon expressed the belief that Russia's aim in proposing the congress was to bring about a misunderstanding between England and France. (*Ibid.,* 407.)

67   BB, XXXII, no. 120, FO, March 19, 1859, Malmesbury to Loftus.

68   *Ibid.,* no. 137, St. Petersburg, March 21, 1859, Crampton to Malmesbury.

69   According to the French Chargé d'Affaires, Buol displayed much ill-humor when he learned of the proposal. Prince Clemens Metternich was consulted and urged acceptance. (Fr. Doc. vol. 474, no. 35, Vienna, March 22, 1859, Bainville to Walewski.)

70   BB, XXXII, no. 172, Vienna, March 21, 1859, Loftus to Malmesbury.

71   *Il Carteggio Cavour-Nigra,* II, no. 333, 112, Turin, March 18, 1859, Cavour to Nigra.

72   *Ibid.,* no. 336, 118, March 19, 1859, Cavour to Napoleon III. Cavour reminded the Emperor that the Italians had suffered too much from congresses and had not forgotten Troppau, Laibach and Verona.

73   *Ibid.,* no. 344, 127, March 22, 1859, Cavour to Nigra.

74   *Ibid.,* no. 347, 129, March 22, 1859, Cavour to Nigra.

75   *Ibid.,* no. 352, 135-36, Palais de Tuileries, March 23, 1859.

76   *Ibid.*

77   d'Hauterive, *op. cit.,* 150, letter dated March 18, 1859.

78   *Ibid.,* 151, letter dated March 22, 1859.

79   *Ibid.,* 156, letter to Prince Napoleon.

80   HHSA no. 36 B confid., Paris, March 26, 1859, Hübner to Buol. In telegrams to Malmesbury dated March 17 and 21, Cowley stated that Napoleon had agreed to the disarmament of Piedmont as preliminary to the deliberations of the congress. (BB, XXXII.)

81   *Ibid.*

82   *Ibid.*

83   HHSA no. 36 G, Paris, March 26, 1859, Hübner to Buol.

84   HHSA no. 36 H secret, Paris, March 26, 1859, Hübner to Buol.

85   Émile Lesueur: *Le Prince de La Tour d'Auvergne et le secret de l'Impératrice,* Paris, 1930, 117-18. Letter of Walewski to La Tour d'Auvergne, March 30, 1859. *Cf.* Matter, III, 165 and Rothan, *loc. cit.* 599.

86   *Il Carteggio Cavour-Nigra,* II, no. 358, 141, Paris, March 28, 1859, Cavour to Victor Emmanuel.

87 *Ibid.*

88 *Ibid.,* no. 364, 147-48, Paris, March 1859, Cavour to Napoleon III, plan soumis à l'Empéreur par le Comte de Cavour.

89 *Ibid.*

90 *Ibid.,* no. 359, 142, Turin, March 28, 1859.

91 *Ibid.,* 142-43, Paris, March 29, 1859.

92 *Ibid.,* no. 361, Paris, March 30, 1859.

93 *Carteggio Cavour-Salmour,* 187.

94 Hübner was informed by persons close to the Emperor, such as General Fleury and Baron Heeckeren, that Cavour was greatly discouraged and no longer counted upon France, while Walewski told him that the Piedmontese statesman was embarrassed, almost humble. (HHSA PL, Paris, March 29, 1859, Hübner to Buol.)

95 BB, XXXII, no. 190, FO, March 30, 1859.

96 *Ibid.,* nos. 209 and 211, Vienna, March 31, 1859, Loftus to Malmesbury.

97 *Ibid.,* no. 210, Vienna, March 31, 1859, Loftus to Malmesbury.

98 HHSA PL, Vienna, March 29, 1859.

99 BB, XXXII, no. 200, FO, April 2, 1859, Malmesbury to Cowley.

100 Fr. Doc., vol. 474, telegram, Paris, April 12, 1859, Walewski to Bainville. This proposal was mentioned by Walewski to Cavour during the latter's visit to Paris.

101 HHSA no. 34 A-H, London, April 6, 1859, Apponyi to Buol.

102 BB, XXXII, no. 189, FO, March 30, 1859, Malmesbury to Loftus.

103 Fr. Doc., vol. 474, telegram, Paris, April 12, 1859, Walewski to Bainville. A Russian proposal to hold the congress without Austria was rejected by England and Prussia. (HHSA no. 37 E, London, April 13, 1859, Apponyi to Buol and BB, XXXII, no. 218, Bloomfield to Malmesbury, Berlin, April 2, and no. 257, Malmesbury to Cowley, FO, April 9, 1859.)

104 BB, XXXII, no. 270, FO, April 11, 1859, Malmesbury to Loftus and HHSA no. 37 B, London, April 13, 1859, Apponyi to Buol.

105 *Ibid.,* no. 260, FO, April 9, 1859, Malmesbury to Loftus.

106 BB, XXXII, no. 295, FO, April 12, 1859, Malmesbury to Cowley. "If Sardinia," he wrote, "refuses disarmament now and Austria makes it a *casus belli,* accompanying it with a note showing her cruel position in being made to wait and bleed to death, or till her enemies are ready, I believe public opinion will be with her." (Malmesbury, *op. cit.,* II, 171.)

107 *Ibid.,* no. 304, FO, April 13, 1859, Malmesbury to West. Malmesbury threatened to withdraw from all further negotiations if Cavour rejected the proposal.

108 Matter, III, 174.

109 *Ibid.*

110 BB, XXXII, no. 348, Turin, April 18, 1859, West to Malmesbury, enclosure: statement of Cavour in *Piedmontese Gazette,* April 18th.

111 HHSA no. 45 A-D, Paris, April 15, 1859, Hübner to Buol.

112 *Ibid.*

113 *Ibid.*

114 Ollivier, *op. cit.*, III, 537-40. The date of the memoir is February 1859.

115 BB, XXXII, no. 314, Cowley to Malmesbury, Paris, April 15, 1859.

116 *Ibid.*, no. 343, Malmesbury to Cowley, FO, April 18, 1859.

117 Matter, III, 178.

118 *Ibid.*, 178-79.

119 d'Hauterive, *loc. cit.*, 520.

120 *Ibid.*, Prince Napoleon to Cavour, April 20, 1859.

121 Matter, III, 179. This information was conveyed in a telegram sent by Cavour to Prince Napoleon on April 18th.

122 BB, XXXII, no. 360, Paris, April 19, 1859, Cowley to Malmesbury, enclosure: copy of telegram from Turin.

123 Josef von Paić, "Zur politischen Vorgeschichte des Feldzuges 1859 nach offiziellen Quellen," *Mitteilungen des österreichischen Instituts für Geschichtsforschung an der Wiener Universität*, XLIII Band, 3 und 4 Heft, 1929 Universitäts-Verlag Wagner, Innsbruck, 376-90, discussion of April 19th meeting is found on p. 380ff. This important article is based on minutes of the ministerial meetings, January 5, 28, February 19, April 6, 19 and 27, found in the Archiv der Militär-Zentral Kanzlei, Vienna.

124 *Ibid.*

125 Mayr, *op cit.*, 505. *Cf.* Paić, 380ff. and Srbik, *op cit.*, footnote, 619.

126 Paić, 378f.

127 Paić, 382ff.

128 *Ibid.* French public opinion was strongly opposed to war before the dispatch of the ultimatum. (Lynn M. Case: *French Opinion on War and Diplomacy during the Second Empire,* Univ. of Penn. Press, 1954, p. 70.) It is conceivable that this situation could have influenced the Emperor to exert pressure on Piedmont.

129 In connection with the Franco-Russian treaty, it is interesting to note that Napoleon assured Cowley that there was no foundation whatever for the reports of such a treaty and that he could so inform his government. (BB, XXXII, no. 477, Paris, April 29, 1859, Cowley to Malmesbury.)

130 Paić, 382ff.

131 HHSA.

132 BB, XXXII, no. 384, FO, April 23, 1859, Malmesbury to Loftus, which mentions the telegram.

133 *Ibid.*, nos. 396 and 415, FO, April 23 and 25, 1859.

134 *Ibid.*, nos. 435 and 456, Paris, April 24 and 26, 1859, Cowley to Malmesbury.

135 *Ibid.*, no. 476, Paris, April 28, 1859, Cowley to Malmesbury

and HHSA rapport teleg. no. 2160/9893, Paris, April 28, 1859, Hübner to Buol.

136   The best account of Prussia's attitude and of Austria's attempts to win her support is found in the excellent study by H. Kentmann, "Preussen und die Bundeshilfe an Österreich im Jahre 1859," *Mitteilungen des österreichischen Instituts für Geschichtsforschung,* XII Band, 1933, Universitäts-Verlag Wagner, Innsbruck, 297-415. This is based on Austrian and Prussian documents.

137   *Ibid.,* 327-33. *Cf.* Stern, VIII, 315.

138   *Ibid. Cf.* Stern, VIII, 558-63 for Albrecht's reports, April 13, 15 and 16 taken from HHSA.

139   HHSA, instructions for Count Karolyi, Vienna, April 16, 1859. *Cf.* F. Engel-Jánosi: *Graf Rechberg. Vier Kapitel zu seiner und Österreichs Geschichte,* Munich, 1927, 37-38.

140   HHSA no. 1 F, St. Petersburg, 6 May/24 April 1859, Karolyi to Buol.

141   *Ibid.*

142   *Ibid.*

143   HHSA PL, St. Petersburg, 6 May/24 April 1859.

144   HHSA no. 1 B, St. Peterburg, 6 May/24 April 1859, Karolyi to Buol.

145   HHSA chiffre teleg., St. Petersburg, April 30, 1859, Karolyi to Buol.

146   HHSA chiffre teleg., St. Petersburg, May 1, 1859, Karolyi to Buol.

147   HHSA no. 1 E, St. Petersburg, 6 May/24 April 1859, Karolyi to Buol.

148   HHSA no. 43 B, London, April 23, 1859, Apponyi to Buol. The Austrian Ambassador reported that Malmesbury had received a telegram from Loftus giving this information.

149   Beust, Friedrich Ferdinand Graf von: *Aus drei Vierteljahrhunderten. Erinnerungen und Aufzeichnungen,* 2 vols., Stuttgart, 1887. II, 356.

150   Franz Joseph acted upon the advice of Prince Clemens Metternich in appointing Rechberg. (Bibl, II, 251 and Srbik, *op. cit.,* II, 509.)

Chapter Nine: THE WAR FOR ITALIAN INDEPENDENCE AND THE TRUCE OF VILLAFRANCA

1   HHSA PL, Verona, June 9, 1859, Metternich to Rechberg.

2   *Ibid.*

3   *Ibid.*

4   d'Hauterive, *op. cit.,* 227.

5   HHSA London, June 7, 1859.

6   *Il Carteggio Cavour-Nigra,* II, no. 473, 231, July 1, 1859, Cavour to Prince Napoleon. While Cavour encouraged the plan for an uprising in Hungary, he also did his best to prevent Austria from obtaining

Prussian support. (*Cf.* F. Valsecchi, "La Politica di Cavour e la Prussia nel 1859," *Archivio Storico Italiano,* 1936, Anno XCIV, 37-66.)

7 Kentmann, *loc. cit.,* 351-58 on mission of Willisen and 352 on his instructions. *Cf.* Schweinitz, General Hans Lothar von: *Denkwürdigkeiten des Botschafters General von Schweinitz,* 3 vols., Berlin, 1927, I, 129, Stern, VIII, 344, Sybel, II, 373 and Engel-Jánosi, *op. cit.,* 46-49.

8 Kentmann, 367 and Stern, VIII, 344.

9 Kentmann, 376-77.

10 Matter, III, 227, citing Russell to English Minister at Berlin, June 28, 1859.

11 Engel-Jánosi, *op. cit.,* 49.

12 Kentmann, 382f. and Engel-Jánosi, *op cit.,* 49.

13 Kentmann, 393-95 and Engel-Jánosi, *op. cit.,* 52-53.

14 Kentmann, 395.

15 On July 12th Windischgrätz telegraphed Rechberg that an alliance could be concluded within twenty-four hours. (Kentmann, 396 and Engel-Jánosi, *op. cit.,* 53.)

16 HHSA PL, London, May 21, 1859.

17 HHSA confid., May 1859, instructions from Rechberg to Esterhazy.

18 *Ibid.*

19 HHSA PL, London, June 7, 1859.

20 HHSA PL, Vienna, June 12, 1859, Rechberg to Apponyi.

21 HHSA.

22 Charles-Roux, *op. cit.,* 258, Gortchakoff to Kisseleff.

23 *Ibid.*

24 In connection with his decision to leave the war, Napoleon made overtures to Prussia. At the end of June he sent Gudin, the well-known artist to Berlin with instructions to urge upon the Prince Regent a declaration of neutrality. While nothing came of this, Gudin was able to report that the Prince Regent did not plan war against France. (Engel-Jánosi, *op. cit.,* 55-56.)

25 M. B. Urban: *British Opinion and Policy on the Unification of Italy, 1856-1861,* New York, 1938, 245. *Cf.* HHSA teleg. chiffre, London, July 7, 1859, Apponyi to Rechberg.

26 *Ibid. Cf.* Ollivier, IV, 225.

27 They objected to an archduke placed over Venetia.

28 Urban, 246.

29 HHSA résumé of negotiations at Villafranca, 1859. *Cf.* Comte Fleury: *Souvenirs du General Cte. Fleury,* 3rd ed., 2 vols., Paris, 1897-98, II, 110-111, letter dated Valeggio, July 7, 1859.

30 Fr. Doc., vol. 474, Valeggio, July 10, 1859, Napoleon to Prince Alexander of Hesse.

31 *Ibid.*

32 An account of what took place is given in *Il Carteggio Cavour-Nigra,* II, 237-52, Fleury, *op. cit.,* II, 111-24, and in an article by Prince Napoleon, "Les Préliminaires de la Paix, 11 juillet 1859," *Revue des Deux Mondes,* August 1, 1859.

33   Napoleon also told Franz Joseph that England and Prussia intended to deprive Austria of Venetia. (*Cf.* Engel-Jánosi, *op. cit.,* 57.)

34   HHSA résumé of the negotiations at Villafranca, Franz Joseph to Napoleon III, July 12, 1859.

35   Charles-Roux, *op. cit.,* 269.

36   HHSA no. 70, London, July 14, 1859. A detailed account of England's reactions is given in Urban, *op. cit.,* 235ff.

37   HHSA PL, London, July 19, 1859, Esterhazy to Buol.

38   *Cavour E. L'Inghilterra,* II, no. 1039, 347, London, July 13, 1859.

39   HHSA no. 76 A-F, London, July 27, 1859, Apponyi to Rechberg. Russell wrote to Cowley that the terms were not satisfactory because they did not fulfill the intentions which England and France had proclaimed in common at the Paris Congress on April 8, 1856. (BB, LXVIII, no. 30, FO, July 25, 1859.)

40   La Gorce, III, 109.

41   *Cavour E. L'Inghilterra,* II, no. 1041, 349-50, July 16, 1859.

42   HHSA Napoleon to Franz Joseph, St. Cloud, July 24, 1859.

43   *Ibid.*

44   HHSA Vienna, August 2, 1859, Franz Joseph to Napoleon III. Metternich did not actually become Ambassador until December 1859. See H. Salomon: *L'Ambassade de Richard de Metternich,* Paris, 1931, especially the first 100 pages for Metternich's work during the period 1859-1864.

45   *Ibid.*

46   HHSA Vienna, August 3, 1859, Rechberg to Colloredo and Meyenbug.

47   HHSA no. 1 A-B, Paris, August 7, 1859, Metternich to Rechberg.

48   Debidour, *op. cit.,* II, 200.

49   HHSA no. 1 B, Paris, August 7, 1859, Metternich to Rechberg.

50   HHSA no. 2 A-C, Paris, August 13, 1859, Metternich to Rechberg.

51   *Ibid.*

52   HHSA teleg. chiffre, no. 7, Paris, August 16, 1859, Metternich to Rechberg.

53   *Ibid.*

54   HHSA no. 4 A-D, Paris, August 16, 1859, Metternich to Rechberg.

55   HHSA PL, Paris, August 17, 1859, Metternich to Rechberg.

56   HHSA no. 1, Vienna, August 19, 1859, Rechberg to Metternich, enclosure: letter of Franz Joseph to Napoleon III, Laxemberg, August 18, 1859.

57   HHSA PL, Paris, August 23, 1859, Metternich to Rechberg.

58   HHSA no. 7 I, Paris, August 25, 1859, Metternich to Rechberg.

59   Russell insisted on the principle of non-intervention and held that Austria should retain Venetia but let the rest of Italy govern itself.

(BB, LXVIII, nos. 88, FO, August 16 and 101, FO, August 24, 1859, Russell to Fain, at Vienna.)

60 HHSA PL, Paris, August 25, 1859, Metternich to Rechberg.

61 *Ibid.*

62 HHSA PL, Vienna, August 30, 1859, Rechberg to Metternich.

63 HHSA no. 2 res., Vienna, August 3, 1859, Rechberg to Apponyi.

64 *Ibid.*

65 HHSA PL, Vienna, August 3, 1859, Rechberg to Apponyi.

66 HHSA no. 80 A-G, London, August 12, 1859, Apponyi to Rechberg and BB, LXVIII, no. 75, FO, August 11 and no. 84, FO, August 16, 1859, Russell to Cowley. Russell would not approve a congress where the use of force would be sanctioned to restore a government in Italy. (*Ibid.*, no. 130, FO, September 17, 1859, Russell to Cowley.)

67 HHSA no. 80 B, London, August 12, 1859, Apponyi to Rechberg.

68 HHSA PL, London, August 12, 1859, Apponyi to Rechberg.

69 *Ibid.*

70 HHSA PL, Paris, September 5, 1859, Metternich to Rechberg.

71 *Ibid.*

72 *Ibid.*

73 HHSA St. Saveur, August 26, 1859, Napoleon to Franz Joseph.

74 *Ibid.*

75 HHSA no. 8 A-C, Paris, September 5, 1859, Metternich to Rechberg.

76 *Ibid.*

77 *Ibid.*

78 HHSA Laxemberg, September 14, 1859, Franz Joseph to Napoleon III.

79 *Ibid.*

80 HHSA annex to no. 11, Biarritz, September 27, 1859, Metternich to Rechberg. The memorandum is referred to by Engel-Jánosi, *op. cit.,* 66-67.

81 HHSA Biarritz, September 27, 1859, Metternich to Rechberg.

82 HHSA PL, Biarritz, September 27, 1859, Metternich to Rechberg.

83 HHSA no. 12 B, Paris, October 23, 1859, Metternich to Rechberg.

84 *Ibid.*

85 *Ibid.*

86 HHSA PL, Paris, October 23, 1859, Metternich to Rechberg. Count Arese had been sent by the Piedmontese Government to Napoleon to inquire about an Austro-French alliance. (Comte J. Grabinski: *Un Ami de Napoléon III. Le Comte Arese et la Politique Italienne sous la Second Empire,* Paris, 1897, 177.)

87 HHSA PL, November 5, 1859, Rechberg to Metternich.

88 HHSA no. 2, Vienna, November 5, 1859, Rechberg to Metternich.

89 HHSA teleg. 5707/3135 chiffre no. 57, Compiègne, November 9, 1859, Metternich to Rechberg.

90 Apponyi reported that there was a growing hatred for Napoleon in England and that the English public thought of a war with France. (HHSA London, November 26, 1859, Apponyi to Rechberg.) In another report, he wrote: "The attention here is directed not to the congress or the Italian question but to the possibility of war with France." (HHSA, London, November 28, 1859, Apponyi to Rechberg.)

91 At the end of September, Napoleon sent Colonel Reille on a mission to St. Petersburg presumably to get Russian approval for his policy regarding the Italian duchies. But neither the Tsar nor Gortchakoff approved; they merely resigned themselves to a *fait accompli*. (Charles-Roux, *op. cit.,* 271.)

92 HHSA PL, Paris, November 15, 1859, Metternich to Rechberg.

93 *Ibid.*

94 HHSA no. 16 A-B, Paris, November 16, 1859, Metternich to Rechberg.

95 *Ibid.*

96 HHSA no. 16 B, November 16, 1859, Metternich to Rechberg.

97 *Ibid.*

98 HHSA Paris, November 6, 1859, Metternich to Rechberg.

99 HHSA no. 5, Vienna, November 24, 1859, Rechberg to Metternich.

100 HHSA no. 18 A-B très secrète, Paris, November 26, 1859, Metternich to Rechberg.

101 HHSA no. 1, Vienna, December 9, 1859, Rechberg to Metternich.

102 BB, LXVIII, nos. 197 and 203, Vienna, November 19 and 24, 1859, Loftus to Russell and no. 209, Paris, November 29, 1859, Cowley to Russell.

103 *Ibid.,* no. 214, FO, December 3, 1859, Russell to Cowley.

104 *Ibid.,* no. 212, St. Petersburg, November 22, 1859, Crampton to Russell. Gortchakoff informed Crampton that Alexander II and the Prince Regent had reached an agreement at Breslau. Moreover, he stated that Russia would not agree to rule out the use of force in all circumstances.

105 *Ibid.,* no. 235, Vienna, December 12, 1859, Loftus to Russell.

105a Case, *op. cit.,* 110.

106 R. H. Edelston: *Napoleon III and Italy. A Brief Historical Survey,* Darlington, 1922, 113.

107 HHSA PL confid., London, December 30, 1859, Apponyi to Rechberg.

108 This was the opinion of Cowley. (BB, LXVIII, no. 251, Paris, January 1, 1860, Cowley to Russell.)

109 Fr. Doc., vol. 476, no. 2, Vienna, December 28, 1859, de Moustier to Walewski.

110 HHSA no. 2 E res., Paris, December 27, 1859, Metternich to Rechberg.

111 HHSA PL, Vienna, December 31, 1859, Rechberg to Metternich.

112 *Ibid.*

113 Even the Pope, in accepting the invitation to the congress, had not considered it necessary to make reservations concerning the territorial integrity of his states since this seemed incontestable. (HHSA no. 1 A-F, Rome, January 6, 1860, Bach to Rechberg.)

114 HHSA no. 1 A-D, Paris, January 3, 1860, Metternich to Rechberg.

115 HHSA PL très secrète, Paris, January 3, 1860, Metternich to Rechberg.

116 *Ibid.*

117 *Ibid.*

118 HHSA no. 2 A-B, Paris, January 9, 1860, Metternich to Rechberg.

119 HHSA PL, Vienna, January 8, 1860, Rechberg to Metternich.

120 Fr. Doc., vol. 476, no. 6, Paris, January 9, 1860, Baroche to de Moustier.

121 HHSA no. 5, London, January 13, 1860, Apponyi to Rechberg.

122 *Ibid.,* enclosure.

123 HHSA no. 6 A-D, London, January 19, 1860, Apponyi to Rechberg. To the Piedmontese statesman, Il Desambrois-Dabormida, Napoleon told of his efforts to reach an agreement with England for the purpose of upholding the principle of non-intervention in Italy. (*Il Carteggio Cavour-Nigra,* III, no. 500, 11, Paris, January 9, 1860.) Apponyi learned that in his overtures to London, Napoleon represented Austria as being on the point of recommencing the war. (HHSA PL, London, January 10, 1860, Apponyi to Rechberg.)

124 HHSA no. 7 A-B, London, January 23, 1860, Apponyi to Rechberg.

125 HHSA teleg. chiffre 8, Paris, January 16, 1860, Metternich to Rechberg.

126 BB, LXVII, FO, January 14, Russell to Loftus and FO, January 15, 1860, Russell to Cowley.

127 HHSA no. 3 secrète, Vienna, January 30, 1860. Rechberg complained to Loftus that England had apparently abandoned her policy of neutrality in Italy to become an active participant. (BB, LXVII, no. 24, Vienna, January 24, 1860, Loftus to Russell.) The English plan was submitted to Franz Joseph, who rejected the first point but raised no objections to the others. (*Ibid.,* no. 31, Vienna, January 30, 1860, Loftus to Russell.)

128 L. Thouvenel: *Le Secret de l'Empéreur. Corréspondance confidentielle et inédite échangée entre M. Thouvenel et le Duc de Gramont et le General Comte de Flahaut, 1860-1863,* Paris, 1889, 2 vols., I, 7-11, annex to letter of January 1860.

129 Fr. Doc. vol. 476, no. 11, Paris, January 31, 1860.

130 BB, LXVII, no. 21, Paris, January 27, 1860, Cowley to Russell.

131 Fr. Doc. vol. 476, no. 13, Vienna, February 11, 1860, de Moustier to Thouvenel.

132 HHSA PL, Vienna, February 11, 1860, Rechberg to Metternich.

133 *Il Carteggio Cavour-Nigra,* III, no. 531, 45-47, for Cavour's instructions to Nigra, February 7, 1860, and no. 532, 49, for his instructions to Arese, February 8, 1860.

134 *Ibid.,* no. 553, 69-70, Paris, February 15, 1860, Nigra to Cavour.

135 *Ibid.,* no. 543, 60-61, Paris, February 13, 1860, Nigra to Cavour. *Cf.* F. Valsecchi, "Toscana ed Austria nel 1859 nei documenti diplomatici austriaci," *Archivio Storico Italiano,* 1936, Anno XCIV, 37-55.

136 *Ibid.,* no. 544, 62, Paris, February 13, 1860, Nigra to Cavour.

137 *Ibid.,* no. 601, 116, Paris, February 27, 1860, Nigra to Cavour.

138 *Ibid.,* 142-143, Turin, March 5, 1860, Cavour to General Durando, Ambassador at Constantinople.

139 *Ibid.*

140 HHSA PL, Vienna, March 6, 1860, Rechberg to Metternich.

141 *Ibid.*

142 HHSA no. 1, Vienna, March 7, 1860, Rechberg to Metternich.

143 HHSA no. 15 A-H, Paris, March 9, 1860, Metternich to Rechberg.

144 *Ibid.*

145 *Ibid.*

146 *Ibid.*

147 HHSA no. 15 B, Paris, March 9, 1860, Metternich to Rechberg.

148 Fr. Doc. vol. 476, PL, Paris, March 9, 1860, Thouvenel to de Moustier.

149 *Ibid.,* no. 31 confid., Vienna, March 13, 1860, de Moustier to Thouvenel.

150 HHSA PL, Paris, March 9, 1860, Metternich to Rechberg.

151 *Ibid.*

152 HHSA no. 32 B, London, March 10, 1860, Apponyi to Rechberg. *Cf.* Urban, *op. cit.,* 397-400 on the British reaction to the cession of Nice and Savoy.

153 HHSA no. 48 B confid., London, May 15, 1860, Apponyi to Rechberg.

154 HHSA no. 1, Vienna, May 24, 1860, Rechberg to Apponyi. As a matter of fact, Apponyi reported to Rechberg, April 6th, that Russell's Italian sympathies had lost none of their force. (*Ibid.,* no. 41 C.)

155 HHSA no. 20, Paris, March 20, 1860, Metternich to Rechberg.

156 Fr. Doc. vol. 476, no. 40, Paris, March 21, 1860, Thouvenel to de Moustier.

157 HHSA no. 22 A-B, Paris, March 27, 1860, Metternich to Rechberg.

158 *Il Carteggio Cavour-Nigra,* III, no. 726, 227, Paris, March 27, 1860, Nigra to Cavour.

159 *Ibid.,* no. 732, 230, Paris, March 29, 1860, Nigra to Cavour.

Chapter Ten: ROME, NAPLES AND VENETIA, 1860-1861

1 H. von Srbik (ed.): *Deutsche Geschichtsquellen des 19 Jahrhunderts.* Herausgegeben durch die Historische Kommission bei der Bayerischen Akademie der Wissenschaften. *Quellen zur deutschen Politik Österreichs, 1859-1866,* vols. I and II, Berlin 1934, for these negotiations. *Cf.* R. Ibbeken (ed.): *Die auswärtige Politik Preussens, 1858-71. Diplomatische Aktenstücke,* vol. II, Oldenburg, 1932.

2 *Ibid.,* I, no. 69 PL, Berlin, January 27, 1860, Karolyi to Rechberg.

3 *Ibid.,* no. 75, 4 B, February 4th and no. 72, telegram, Berlin, January 28, 1860, Karolyi to Rechberg.

4 *Ibid.,* no. 74, 4 C vertraulich, Karolyi to Rechberg, Berlin, February 4, 1860.

5 *Ibid.,* no. 78, PL, Vienna, February 10, 1860, Rechberg to Karolyi.

6 HHSA no. 3 B, St. Petersburg, 3 February/22 January 1860.

7 HHSA no. 3 A-E, St. Petersburg, 3 February/22 January 1860, Thun to Rechberg.

8 *Ibid.,* 3 B.

9 See chapter 12, pp. 290-291.

10 Srbik, *Quellen,* I, no. 100, Berlin, March 15, 1860, Karolyi to Rechberg.

11 HHSA no. 24 A-G confid., Paris, April 10, 1860, Metternich to Rechberg.

12 HHSA PL, Vienna, April 10, 1860, Rechberg to Metternich.

13 HHSA PL, Vienna, April 14, 1860, Rechberg to Metternich.

14 *Ibid.*

15 HHSA Vienna, February 10, 1860, Rechberg to Apponyi.

16 HHSA PL, London, March 10, 1860, Apponyi to Rechberg.

17 HHSA PL, Vienna, March 19, 1860, Rechberg to Apponyi.

18 On the Roman question see L. M. Case: *Franco-Italian Relations, 1860-1865. The Roman Question and the Convention of September.* (Phila., Univ. of Penn. Press, 1932.)

19 Fr. Doc., vol. 477, no. 50, Paris, April 7, 1860, Thouvenel to de Moustier.

20 *Ibid.,* no. 40, Vienna, April 11, 1860, de Moustier to Thouvenel.

21 Debidour, II, 211.

22 Charles H. Pouthas, "La médiation de Napoléon III entre le Roi de Naples, les Siciliens et le gouvernement piemontais, mai-août 1860." *Rassegna Storica Del Risorgimento,* Anno XXXIX, Fasc. IV, Ottobre-Dicembre 1952, 765. This article throws new light on Napoleon's role in the Neapolitan affair.

23 *Ibid.,* 766, May 30th.

24 *Ibid.,* 767, June 3rd.

25 *Ibid.,* 768, June 4th.

26 *Ibid. Cf.* HHSA no. 54 A-I, London, June 4, 1860, Apponyi to Rechberg.

27 *Ibid.,* 768.

28 *Ibid.*

29 *Ibid.,* 771.
30 *Ibid.,* 772.
31 *Ibid.,* 773.
32 *Ibid.,* 774.
33 *Ibid.,* 776-77.
34 HHSA PL, Paris, June 11, 1860, Metternich to Rechberg.
35 *Ibid.*
36 HHSA PL, Vienna, June 12, 1860, Rechberg to Metternich.
37 Srbik, *Quellen,* I, no. 170, Baden, June 17th, Trauttmansdorff to Rechberg and no. 195 PL, Baden, June 27, 1860, Prince Regent to Franz Joseph.
38 HHSA no. 45 A-F, Paris, July 9, 1860, Metternich to Rechberg.
39 HHSA no. 45 C, Paris, July 9, 1860, Metternich to Rechberg.
40 HHSA PL, Paris, July 10, 1860.
41 *Ibid.*
42 *Ibid.*
43 HHSA PL, Vienna, July 16, 1860, Rechberg to Metternich.
44 Srbik, *Quellen,* I, no. 233, Vienna, July 22, 1860, Rechberg to Franz Joseph.
45 *Ibid.,* no. 234, Denkschrift des Freiherrn von Biegeleben, July 22, 1860. On the rivalry between Biegeleben and Rechberg see Clark, *op. cit.,* 7-12.
46 *Ibid.,* nos. 231, 233, 234, 236, 237, 238, 239, 247, 256 and 258. *Cf.* Clark, 8-9, H. Oncken (ed.): *Grossherzog Friedrich I von Baden und die deutsche Politik von 1854-1871. Briefwechsel, Denkschriften, Tagebücher.* Hersg. von der badischen historischen Kommission, 2 vols., Stuttgart, 1927, I, 197-202, and Freiherr von Hegelmuller, "Graf Alois Karolyi," *Deutsche Revue,* XXXVIII, 1913, Heft 2, 281-283.
47 Srbik, *Quellen,* I, nos. 237, 239.
48 *Ibid.,* no. 236, Teplitz, July 26, 1860.
49 HHSA PL, Paris, July 26, 1860, Metternich to Rechberg.
50 *Ibid.*
51 King Leopold of Belgium was told by Russell that England would support Austria in case of an attack on Venetia. (HHSA no. 60 secret, London, July 2, 1860, Apponyi to Rechberg.)
52 *Il Carteggio Cavour-Nigra,* IV, nos. 1012, 113 and 1031, 135, Paris, July 29 and August 5, 1860, Nigra to Cavour.
53 Fr. Doc. vol. 477, no. 78, Vienna, August 12, 1860, de Moustier to Thouvenel.
54 L. Thouvenel: *Le Secret de l'Empéreur,* I, 192.
55 France. Archives des Affaires Étrangères, Paris, Papiers Thouvenel, vol. 9, PL, Rome, September 20, 1860, Gramont to Napoleon III.
56 *Ibid.,* PL confid., Rome, October 6, 1860, Gramont to Thouvenel. On August 29th Napoleon gave his approval to a plan submitted by Cavour for the invasion of Umbria and the Marches. (*Il Carteggio Cavour-Nigra,* IV, no. 1079, 186, Cavour to Nigra.)
57 *Il Carteggio Cavour-Nigra,* IV, no. 1127, 219, Paris, September 20, 1860, Nigra to Cavour.

58 On Russia's attitude see Charles-Roux, "La Russie et la Politique Italienne de Napoléon III," *Revue Historique*, 1910-11, 288 and G. Pagès, "Les Relations de la France et de la Russie en 1860," *Revue d'Histoire du Sud-Est Européen*, V, 1928, 277-87. Rechberg was much disappointed by Prussia's attitude. (Srbik, *Quellen*, I, no. 263, PL, Vienna, September 18, 1860, Rechberg to Chotek.)

59 HHSA instructions for Lt. Gen. Count Mensdorff, Vienna, September 24, 1860.

60 HHSA no. 1 res., Vienna, June 29, 1860, Rechberg to Apponyi. Rechberg was referring to an understanding of July 1859.

61 *Il Carteggio Cavour-Nigra*, IV, no. 1167, 252, October 16, 1860.

62 *Ibid.*, no. 1159, 245, Paris, October 10, 1860, Prince Napoleon to Nigra.

63 *Ibid.*

64 HHSA no. 32 A-C, St. Petersburg, 14/2 September 1860, Thun to Rechberg. From Berlin came the report that Bismarck was working for an alliance of Prussia, Russia and France. (Srbik, *Quellen*, I, no. 192, Berlin, June 23, 1860, Karolyi to Rechberg.)

65 HHSA no. 33, St. Petersburg, 28/16 September 1860, Thun to Rechberg.

66 HHSA no. 34 B, St. Petersburg, 5 October/23 September 1860, Thun to Rechberg.

67 HHSA no. 73 C secrète, Paris, October 2, 1860, Mülinen to Rechberg.

68 HHSA teleg. 3520/18032 chiffre no. 123, Paris, October 12, 1860, Mülinen to Rechberg.

69 *Ibid.*

70 HHSA no. 32 A-C, St. Petersburg, 14/2 September 1860, Thun to Rechberg.

71 Fr. Doc. vol. 477, no. 93, Vienna, October 13, 1860, de Moustier to Thouvenel.

72 *Ibid.*

73 The plebiscite in Sicily was held on the 21st and likewise favored Piedmont.

74 HHSA Varia: Résumé rédigé à l'usage de S. M. Empéreur pour l'entrévue de Varsovie, Vienna, October 18, 1860.

75 These were prepared for Napoleon by Thouvenel. HHSA Warsaw, October 23, 1860, enclosure.

76 HHSA confid., Warsaw, October 20, 1860.

77 HHSA, Rémarques sur les 4 propositions françaises rémies par l'Empéreur Alexandre à S. M. I. R. A. et au Prince Regent de Prusse, Varsovie, 23 octobre, 1860.

78 In a dispatch to Metternich, Rechberg explained that he had accepted the French proposals out of regard for the Tsar, whose good will it was necessary to cultivate in order to offset the liberalism of Gortchakoff. (HHSA no. 2 res., Vienna, November 12, 1860.)

79 L. Thouvenel: *Le Secret de l'Empéreur*, I, 283, St. Petersburg, November 3, 1860, Duc de Montebello to Thouvenel.

80 *Ibid.*

81 *Ibid.*

82 Matter, III, 410, Cavour to Nigra, Turin, October 30, 1860.

83 HHSA no. 82 A-B, Paris, October 29, 1860, Metternich to Rechberg, résumé of a conversation between Hübner and Napoleon.

84 HHSA teleg. 3309/19405 chiffre no. 132, Paris, November 3, 1860, Metternich to Rechberg.

85 *Ibid.*

86 HHSA PL, Paris, November 5, 1860, Metternich to Rechberg.

87 *Ibid.*

88 HHSA no. 84 D, Paris, November 5, 1860, Metternich to Rechberg.

89 HHSA PL, Vienna, November 12, 1860, Rechberg to Metternich.

90 *Ibid.*

91 HHSA PL, Vienna, November 28, 1860, Rechberg to Metternich.

92 *Ibid.*

93 HHSA no. 86 A-D, Paris, November 15, 1860, Metternich to Rechberg.

94 HHSA no. 86 B, Paris, November 15, 1860, Metternich to Rechberg.

95 HHSA PL, Paris, December 9, 1860, Metternich to Rechberg.

96 HHSA no. 90 B, Paris, December 9, 1860, Metternich to Rechberg.

97 HHSA no. 1 res., Vienna, December 17, 1860, Rechberg to Metternich.

98 *Il Carteggio Cavour-Nigra*, IV, no. 1178, 264, Paris, October 27, 1860.

99 *La Questione romana negli anni 1860-1861. Carteggio de Conte di Cavour.* A cura della Commissione Reale Editrice, 2 vols., Bologna, 1929, I, 135, Turin, December 16, 1860, Cavour to Victor Emmanuel.

100 *Il Carteggio Cavour-Nigra*, IV, no. 1183, 268, Paris, November 3, 1860.

101 HHSA no. 38 A-C, St. Petersburg, 8 December/26 November 1860, Thun to Rechberg.

102 The brochure was written by M. Isaac Pereire, a French banker who was interested in Austrian finances. It is likely that Napoleon had a hand in its preparation.

103 Edelston, *op. cit.*, 262-63, letter of Queen Victoria to Russell, December 10, 1860. *Cf.* Martin, *op. cit.*, V, 278.

104 Metternich reported to Rechberg that Napoleon opposed the cession of Venetia. (HHSA no. 97 B, Paris, December 21, 1860.) About the same time, Cowley informed Thouvenel that the English Cabinet considered the moment inopportune to approach Austria on the subject. He added that Napoleon shared this opinion. (L. Thouvenel: *Le Secret de l'Empéreur*, I, 333, Thouvenel to Flahaut, Paris, December 27, 1860.) Cowley was opposed to Italian unification as contrary to British interests

and did not believe it could be brought about. (Maxwell, *op. cit.*, 231, Cowley to Clarendon, Chantilly, December 6, 1860.)

105 HHSA no. 1, Vienna, December 23, 1860, Rechberg to Metternich.

106 HHSA PL, London, January 2, 1861, Apponyi to Rechberg, enclosure: letter of Palmerston, Broadlands, December 27, 1860.

107 *Ibid.*, letter to Palmerston, January 2, 1861.

108 Maxwell, *op. cit.*, 234.

109 HHSA, letter dated December 31, 1860.

110 HHSA PL, London, January 3, 1861, Apponyi to Rechberg, enclosure: letter from Clarendon dated January 1, 1861.

111 HHSA no. 11 A-E, London, February 8, 1861, Apponyi to Rechberg.

112 Maxwell, *op cit.*, 234.

Chapter Eleven: RECOGNITION OF THE KINGDOM OF ITALY, 1862

1 HHSA PL, Paris, January 8, 1862, Metternich to Rechberg, enclosure: draft of a private and confidential letter, Metternich to Rechberg.

2 HHSA PL, Paris, January 8, 1862.

3 HHSA PL, Vienna, January 22, 1862 and PL confid., Vienna, January 22, 1862.

4 *La Questione Romana*, I, no. 93, 132-33.

5 HHSA no. 32 A-B, Paris, April 25, 1861, Metternich to Rechberg.

6 HHSA no. 39, Paris, June 8, 1861, Metternich to Rechberg, enclosure: note of Thouvenel to Metternich, June 6th.

7 Frederick A. Wellesley: *Secrets of the Second Empire. Private Letters from the Paris Embassy. Selections from the Papers of Henry Richard Charles Wellesley, First Earl Cowley, Ambassador at Paris, 1852-1867*, New York, 1929, 233.

8 *Ibid.*, 235.

9 See article by Alfred Stern, "Georg Klindworth. Ein politischer Geheimagent des neunzehnten Jahrhunderts," *Historische Viertel Jahrsschrift*, vol. 25, 430-58 and note 695-96.

10 *Ibid.*, 430.

11 *Ibid.*, 445. *Cf.* Engel-Jánosi, *op. cit.*, 101 and H. Friedjung: *Der Kampf um die Vorherrschaft in Deutschland, 1859-1866*, 2 vols., Stuttgart and Berlin, 1902, II, 583.

12 Ernst Freiherr von Plener: *Erinnerungen*, 2 vols., Stuttgart, 1911, I, 35.

13 Stern, *loc. cit.*, 445. In a private letter to Rechberg, Apponyi expressed appreciation of Klindworth's services and urged that the latter be given more money to enable him to visit London more frequently. "Klindworth," he added, "is an unusual man because of his connections and his aptitude. I have known him intimately for too long a time to have any illusions concerning his morality." (HHSA PL, London, March 11, 1861.)

14   HHSA no. 4 C, Paris, January 20, 1862, Metternich to Rechberg, enclosure: dispatch, Paris, January 11, 1862, Thouvenel to Lavelette.

15   *Ibid.,* enclosure: Rome, January 18, 1862, Lavelette to Thouvenel.

16   HHSA no. 7 B, Paris, February 3, 1862, Metternich to Rechberg.

17   *Ibid.*

18   HHSA no. 2, Vienna, February 8, 1862, Rechberg to Metternich.

19   *Ibid.*

20   HHSA no. 3 res., Vienna, February 8, 1862.

21   Engel-Jánosi, *op. cit.,* 75, declares that as long as Rechberg remained in office, he was convinced that Austria would regain her Italian territory.

22   Fr. Doc., vol. 481, no. 4 confid., Vienna, January 31, 1862, Gramont to Thouvenel.

23   HHSA no. 16 A-G, Paris, March 9, 1862, Metternich to Rechberg.

24   *Ibid.*

25   HHSA no. 12 A-B, Paris, February 23, 1862, Metternich to Rechberg.

26   HHSA no. 17 B, Paris, March 14, 1862, Metternich to Rechberg.

27   *Ibid.*

28   HHSA PL, Paris, March 19, 1862, Metternich to Rechberg.

29   HHSA no. 1, Vienna, March 20, 1862, Rechberg to Metternich.

30   HHSA PL, Vienna, April 14, 1862.

31   *Ibid.*

32   Fr. Doc., vol. 481, no. 19, Vienna, April 15, 1862, Gramont to Thouvenel.

33   *Ibid.,* no. 20 confid., Vienna, April 23, 1862, Gramont to Thouvenel. *Cf.* Case, *op. cit.,* 173-74.

34   Stern, *loc. cit.,* 445, mentions that Palmerston sent his letters to Rechberg not through the English Ambassador but through Klindworth.

35   Fr. Doc., vol. 481, no. 24 confid. and secret, Vienna, May 1, 1862, Gramont to Thouvenel. During the year 1862 Rechberg employed Klindworth quite frequently. At first, he gave the secret agent a certain latitude because the latter apparently had influenced Palmerston in Austria's favor. (HHSA PL, Vienna, February 21, 1862, Rechberg to Apponyi.) Indeed, the English Prime Minister promised to defend Austria *à toute outrance* if she were attacked, without provocation in Dalmatia, the mouths of Cattaro or the Hungarian littoral. (HHSA PL, London, February 15, 1862, Apponyi to Rechberg, from a report by Klindworth.) Klindworth also suggested that Austria enter into close relations with Delane of the London *Times.* (HHSA PL, Vienna, February 21, 1862, Rechberg to Apponyi.) Apponyi was able to report that the articles in the *Times* had become more friendly toward Austria and that some of the articles could have been edited in Vienna. (HHSA PL, London, March 31, 1862, Apponyi to Rechberg.) Later on Rechberg found it necessary to exercise a strict surveillance over the agent. Russell had learned that Klindworth told Palmerston that Rechberg

would be quite agreeable in the question of Venetia provided England guaranteed to Austria the possession of Dalmatia. (HHSA Nachlass Rechbergs, secrète, London, May 21, 1862, Apponyi to Rechber.) Rechberg regarded this as a betrayal and thereafter arranged that Klindworth be placed under the direction of the Austrian Embassy in London.

36 HHSA no. 29 A-C, Paris, April 28, 1862, Metternich to Rechberg. Though hostile to Italian unity, the Empress expressed much sympathy for the Poles and Hungarians. (*La Questione Romana,* II, no. 436, 190, Paris, May 11, 1861, Vimercati to Cavour.)

37 HHSA PL, May 10, 1862, Metternich to Rechberg.

38 HHSA no. 31 G, Paris, May 10, 1862, Metternich to Rechberg, enclosure: letters from Hübner.

39 *Ibid.,* enclosure no. 1.

40 *Ibid.,* enclosure no. 3.

41 *Ibid.,* enclosure no. 5.

42 HHSA no. 31 B, Paris, May 10, 1862, Metternich to Rechberg.

43 HHSA PL, Paris, May 12, 1862, Metternich to Rechberg.

44 HHSA no. 32 C res., Paris, May 16, 1862, Metternich to Rechberg.

45 Fr. Doc., vol. 481, letter of Napoleon III, May 20, 1862.

46 S. Jacini: *Il Tramonte de Portere Temporale. Nelle Relazione degli Ambasciatore austriaci a Rome, 1860-1870,* Bari, 1931, 90-91, no. 11 C, Rome, June 14, 1862, Bach to Rechberg.

47 HHSA no. 36 A-E, Paris, June 9, 1862, Metternich to Rechberg.

48 *Ibid.*

49 HHSA PL, Paris, June 9, 1862, Metternich to Rechberg.

50 HHSA PL, Fontainebleau, June 30, 1862, Metternich to Rechberg.

51 HHSA no. 43 B, Paris, July 7, 1862, Metternich to Rechberg.

52 *Ibid.*

53 HHSA PL, Paris, February 9, 1862, Metternich to Rechberg.

54 HHSA no. 3 secrète, Vienna, May 30, 1862, Rechberg to Metternich. *Cf.* Beyens, I, 321.

55 Papiers Thouvenel, IX, Vienna, May 30, 1862, Gramont to Thouvenel. *Cf.* E. von Wertheimer: *Bismarck im politischen Kampf,* Berlin, 1930, 78.

56 HHSA no. 3 secrète, Vienna, May 30, 1862, Rechberg to Metternich.

57 *Ibid.* Beyens, I, 321 states that Metternich was given *carte blanche* to take such action as he deemed necessary, even to advance in the direction of an alliance with France. This appears to be an exaggeration. Rechberg made no mention of such an alliance.

58 HHSA PL, Vienna, May 30, 1862. Rechberg expressed the same fear to Thun at St. Petersburg. (HHSA no. 2 res., Vienna, June 5, 1862.)

59 HHSA no. 36 B, Paris, June 9, 1862, Metternich to Rechberg.

60 Revertera reported from St. Petersburg that Budberg was a dangerous rival of Gortchakoff and wanted to supplant the latter. He learned that Budberg had gone to Paris in order to discover the intentions of

France concerning a solution of the Italian question. (HHSA no. 17 B, St. Petersburg, 13/1 June 1862, Revertera to Rechberg.)

61 HHSA no. 36 B, Paris. Wertheimer, *op. cit.*, 80, denies that Thouvenel solicited Bismarck's appointment.

62 *Ibid.*

63 *Ibid.*

64 HHSA no. 1 res., Vienna, June 23, 1862, Rechberg to Metternich.

65 HHSA no. 2 res., Vienna, July 11, 1862, Rechberg to Metternich.

66 At first Gortchakoff opposed recognition. In April 1861 he refused a request from Lord Napier, the English Ambassador, to bring pressure on Prussia in order to induce the latter to extend recognition. Instead, he declared that Russia would employ her influence to dissuade other powers, particularly Prussia, from an act he regarded as a flagrant violation of existing treaties. (HHSA no. 23 G, St. Petersburg, 28/16 April 1861, F. Thun to Rechberg.) He informed Bismarck in January 1862 that Russia would not extend recognition and would never desert the cause of Francis II of Naples. (HHSA no. 3, St. Petersburg, 23/11 January 1862, F. Thun to Rechberg.) Some weeks later, Gortchakoff told Thun that conditions in Italy were such that it would be folly to extend recognition. (HHSA no. 12 A-C, St. Petersburg, 20/8 March 1862, F. Thun to Rechberg.) The Tsar likewise revealed his opposition and desired a solid front of the rulers against revolutionary tendencies. (HHSA no. 13 D, St. Petersburg, 16/4 April 1862, F. Thun to Rechberg, reporting audience with the Tsar.) With the mission of Budberg to Paris, however, Austria was prepared for Russia's action.

67 Fr. Doc., vol. 482, no. 44, Vienna, July 15, 1862, Gramont to Thouvenel.

68 HHSA PL, Trouville, July 16, 1862, Metternich to Rechberg.

69 At Berlin Bernstorff explained that Prussia extended recognition after reaching an understanding with Russia and after receiving assurances from Turin regarding Rome and Venetia. (Srbik, *Quellen*, II, no. 823, Berlin, July 12, 1862, Karolyi to Rechberg.)

70 HHSA no. 21 A-F, St. Petersburg, 5 July/23 June 1862, Revertera to Rechberg.

71 HHSA no. 2, Vienna, July 20, 1862, Rechberg to Metternich. Cavour died on June 6, 1861.

72 HHSA no. 46 A-F, Paris, July 24, 1862, Metternich to Rechberg.

73 *Ibid.*

74 *Ibid.*

75 HHSA PL, Vienna, August 5, 1862, Rechberg to Metternich.

76 Fr. Doc., vol. 482, no. 49 confid., Vienna, August 16, 1862, Gramont to Thouvenel.

77 *Ibid.*, no. 53 confid., Vienna, August 30, 1862, Gramont to Thouvenel.

78 *Ibid.*

79 HHSA no. 50 A-C secret, Paris, September 1, 1862, Metternich to Rechberg.

80   Debidour, *op. cit.*, II, 243.
81   HHSA no. 51 A-B, Paris, September 4, 1862, Metternich to Rechberg.
82   *Ibid.*
83   HHSA PL, Vienna, October 21, 1862, Rechberg to Mülinen.
84   HHSA PL A, Paris, October 30, 1862, Metternich to Rechberg.
85   *Ibid.*
86   HHSA PL B confid., Paris, October 30, 1862, Metternich to Rechberg.
87   *Ibid.*
88   *Ibid.*
89   HHSA no. 70 F, Paris, December 30, 1862, Metternich to Rechberg.
90   *Ibid.*

Chapter Twelve: THE QUESTION OF AN *ENTENTE* ON EASTERN AFFAIRS, 1859-1863

1   HHSA Nachlass Rechbergs. PL, St. Petersburg, 27/15 September 1859, Szechenyi to Rechberg.
2   Rechberg wrote to Szechenyi at St. Petersburg that Prince Alexander had reported that there was a good chance of effecting a *rapprochement*. (HHSA no. 1, Vienna, November 1, 1859.) On the other hand, Gortchakoff told Montebello, the French Ambassador, that Prince Alexander had sought to resurrect the Holy Alliance and declared that the Tsar would never consent to it. (Charles-Roux, *op. cit.*, 279.)
3   HHSA Punktation für S. Kais. Hoheit den Erzherzog Albrecht, Vienna, October 11, 1859, and Points d'instruction pour Son Excellence, Monsieur Baron de Werner, Vienna, October 17, 1859.
4   HHSA no. 4, Warsaw, October 21, 1859, Werner to Rechberg.
5   *Ibid.*
6   HHSA no. 2 res., Vienna, October 19, 1859, Rechberg to Metternich.
7   HHSA telegram 5366/27973 chiffre no. 50, Paris, October 29, 1859, Metternich to Rechberg.
8   HHSA no. 13 A-E secret, Paris, October 29, 1859, Metternich to Rechberg.
9   *Ibid.*
10   HHSA PL, Paris, October 24, 1859, Metternich to Rechberg.
11   *Ibid.*
12   HHSA no. 3 secrète, Vienna, October 30, 1859.
13   *Ibid.*
14   *Ibid.*
15   *Ibid.*
16   HHSA PL, Vienna, November 5, 1859, Rechberg to Metternich.
17   *Ibid.*
18   HHSA no. 15 A-F secret, Paris, November 6, 1859, Metternich to Rechberg.

19 *Ibid.*

20 HHSA no. 15 B secret, Paris, November 6, 1859, Metternich to Rechberg.

21 HHSA no. 15 D, Paris, November 6, 1859, Metternich to Rechberg.

22 HHSA Nachlass Rechbergs 524 d, PL, Vienna, November 18, 1859, Rechberg to Szechenyi.

23 According to a letter which Kisseleff sent to Gortchakoff and which the latter read to Thun, the Austrian Ambassador, it was Metternich who approached the Russian envoy in regard to the proposed *entente* and declared that inasmuch as Rechberg was so much occupied with internal problems, he had been given *carte blanche* for the conduct of political affairs. Metternich added that he was anxious to reach an understanding with Kisseleff, that he had already spoken to Walewski but the latter had cut him short. Metternich therefore suggested to Kisseleff that it was advisable to let the matter rest for the moment. (HHSA no. 1 B, St. Petersburg, 20/8 December 1859, Thun to Rechberg.)

24 HHSA no. 1 res., Vienna, November 24, 1859, Rechberg to Metternich.

25 *Ibid.*

26 HHSA no. 2 secret, Vienna, November 24, 1859, Rechberg to Metternich.

27 *Ibid.*

28 *Ibid.*

29 HHSA PL, Paris, November 26, 1859, Metternich to Rechberg.

30 HHSA no. 3, Vienna, January 10, 1860, Rechberg to Metternich.

31 HHSA PL, Vienna, April 20, 1860, Rechberg to Metternich.

32 *Ibid.*

33 *Ibid.*

34 *Ibid.*

35 HHSA PL, Paris, April 23, 1860, Metternich to Rechberg.

36 *Ibid.*

37 HHSA no. 33 A-E res., Paris, May 10, 1860, Metternich to Rechberg.

38 HHSA no. 33 B confid., Paris, May 10, 1860, Metternich to Rechberg.

39 HHSA no. 1 B, St. Petersburg, 20/8 December 1859, Thun to Rechberg.

40 HHSA no. 4 A-D, St. Petersburg, 30/18 December 1859, Thun to Rechberg.

41 HHSA PL, St. Petersburg, 13/1 February 1860, Thun to Rechberg.

42 HHSA no. 19 A-E, St. Petersburg, 16/4 May 1860.

43 *Ibid.*

44 HHSA no. 19 B, St. Petersburg, 16/4 May 1860.

45 HHSA no. 38 B, Paris, June 6, 1860.

46 HHSA no. 19 A-E, St. Petersburg, 16/4 May 1860, Revertera to Rechberg

47 HHSA no. 42 C, Fontainebleau, June 25, 1860, Metternich to Rechberg.

48 HHSA PL, Vienna, July 6, 1860, Rechberg to Metternich.

49 In January 1861 Metternich informed Rechberg of a conversation with the Empress Eugénie. It was the first since September 1859, when Napoleon forbade the Empress to discuss political affairs with the Austrian Ambassador. That she did so now was because the Emperor approved. In any case, she warned Metternich that Austria's policy was in danger in view of the ambitions of Piedmont and the situation in the east. (HHSA Nachlass Rechbergs, 524, secret, Paris, January 21, 1861.)

50 HHSA no. 45 B, Paris, July 9, 1860, Metternich to Rechberg. Metternich noted that Napoleon forgot to add that he himself was revolutionary everywhere.

51 HHSA PL, Vienna, August 27, 1860, Rechberg to Thun.

52 HHSA no. 6 A-E, St. Petersburg, 28/16 January 1861, Thun to Rechberg.

53 HHSA no. 19 confid., St. Petersburg, 7 April/26 March 1861.

54 *Ibid.*

55 HHSA no. 1, Vienna, February 13, 1861, Rechberg to Thun.

56 HHSA no. 2 secrète, Vienna, February 8, 1861, Rechberg to Metternich.

57 HHSA no. 16 A-E, Paris, February 21, 1861, Metternich to Rechberg.

58 HHSA no. 15 B, Paris, February 15, 1861, Metternich to Rechberg.

59 *Ibid.*

60 HHSA no. 21 C, Paris, March 12, 1861.

61 HHSA no. 21 D, Paris, March 12, 1861, Metternich to Rechberg.

62 HHSA no. 1, Vienna, March 17, 1861.

63 HHSA PL, Vienna, March 17, 1861, Rechberg to Metternich.

64 HHSA no. 72 B, Paris, December 22, 1861, Metternich to Rechberg.

65 HHSA no. 72 C, Paris, December 22, 1861, Metternich to Rechberg.

66 HHSA PL, Vienna, December 16, 1861, Rechberg to Metternich.

67 *Ibid.*

68 HHSA no. 1 A-C, Paris, January 8, 1863, Metternich to Rechberg.

69 HHSA no. 2 res., Paris, January 13, 1863, Metternich to Rechberg.

70 HHSA no. 6 C, Paris, January 24, 1863, Metternich to Rechberg.

71 HHSA no. 6 D secret, Paris, January 24, 1863, Metternich to Rechberg.

72 HHSA no. 1, Vienna, January 30, 1863, Rechberg to Metternich.

73 HHSA no. 3, Vienna, January 30, 1863, Rechberg to Metternich.

74 Fr. Doc., vol. 483, no. 9, Vienna, January 30, 1863.

75 *Ibid.*
76 HHSA, St. Petersburg, 18/6 January 1863, Thun to Rechberg.
77 *Ibid.*
78 *Ibid.*
79 *Ibid.*
80 HHSA PL, Vienna, February 5, 1863, Rechberg to Thun.
81 HHSA no. 7 E res., Paris, February 7, 1863, Metternich to Rechberg.
82 HHSA no. 9, Paris, February 26, 1863, Metternich to Rechberg.
83 *Ibid.*
84 *Ibid.*

Chapter Thirteen: THE POLISH QUESTION, 1863

1 HHSA PL, Paris, January 22, 1861, Metternich to Rechberg.
1a Case, *French Opinion on War and Diplomacy during the Second Empire,* 179, mentions that French opinion was universally sympathetic to the Polish cause throughout 1863.
2 For details of the negotiations leading up to the Convention and for the part played by Bismarck see the excellent article by Robert H. Lord, "Bismarck and Russia in 1863," *Am. Hist. Rev.,* vol. 29, October 1923, 24-48.
3 Napoleon apparently suspected that the Convention contained a secret article concerning France or Italy. (M. Julian Klaczko: *Études Diplomatie Contemporaines. Les Cabinets de l'Europe en 1863-1864,* Paris, 1866, 59.)
4 T. Filipowicz, ed.: *Confidential Correspondence of the British Government Respecting the Insurrection in Poland, 1863,* London, 1914, 81, no. 74, Paris, February 21, 1863, Drouyn de Lhuys to Baron Gros, and Fr. Doc., vol. 483, no. 17, Paris, February 21, 1863, Drouyn de Lhuys to Gramont. *Cf.* BB, LXXV, no. 64, FO, March 2, 1863, Russell to Cowley, enclosures: Drouyn de Lhuys to Baron Gros, Paris, February 21, 1863 and Baron Gros to Russell, London, March 2, 1863.
5 Ollivier, *op. cit.,* VI, 110, quoting statement by Russell on March 26, 1862 and speech by Palmerston, April 4, 1862. For the English position in regard to the Polish revolt see the article by Dr. Henryk Wereszycki, "Great Britain and the Polish Question in 1863," *Eng. Hist. Rev.,* vol. L, 1935, 78-108.
6 Klaczko, 73.
7 For Austria's position see Klaczko, S. Kosmian: *Das Jahr 1863. Polen und die europäische Diplomatie,* Vienna, 1896, and Dr. Hanns Schlitter, "Die Frage der Wiederherstellung Polens im österreichischer Ministerrat 1863," *Österreichische Rundschau,* vol. 58, January-March 1919, 63-69.
8 Klaczko, 87-88 for details.
9 Fr. Doc., vol. 483, no. 17, Vienna, February 27, 1863, Gramont to Drouyn de Lhuys.
10 *Ibid.* Russell was rather pleased with the stand taken by Rech-

berg. (Filipowicz, 143, no. 135, FO, March 5, 1863, Russell to Cowley, and BB, LXXV, no. 68, FO, March 5, 1863, Russell to Cowley.)

11 "From early March onward, by a kind of general tacit agreement, the Alvensleben Convention was consigned to oblivion." (Lord, *loc. cit.,* 35.)

12 D'Hauterive, *op. cit.,* 351-365, "Note à l'Empéreur sur les affaires de Pologne." *Cf.* Engel-Jánosi, *op. cit.,* 92, who correctly points out that the memorandum was dated January 22nd and that Napoleon replied on February 20th.

13 HHSA no. 8 B, Paris, February 22, 1863, Metternich to Rechberg. A good brief summary of the alliance negotiations is given by Stern, *op. cit.,* IX, 164-167 and by Engel-Jánosi, *op. cit.,* 92-96.

14 HHSA no. 8 D, Paris, February 22, 1863, Metternich to Rechberg.

15 HHSA no. 8 G, Paris, February 22, 1863, Metternich to Rechberg.

16 HHSA PL, Paris, February 22, 1863, Metternich to Rechberg. *Cf.* the article by A. Stern, "L'Insurrection polonaise de 1863 et l'Impératrice Eugénie," *Revue Historique,* vol. 137, 1921, 66-74, and by E. C. Corti, "Les Idées de l'Impératrice Eugénie sur le redressement de la carte de l'Europe d'après les rapports de Prince Richard de Metternich," *Revue des Études Napoléoniennes,* September 1922, 147-155.

17 So boundless was Napoleon's enthusiasm for the alliance that Cowley feared that unless Austria and England went part way to satisfy him, the Emperor would throw himself into the arms of Russia. (HHSA telegram, Paris, February 26, 1863, Metternich to Rechberg.)

18 HHSA nos. 1, 2, 3 and 4 res., and PL, Vienna, February 27, 1863.

19 HHSA PL très secrète, Paris, March 5, 1863, Metternich to Rechberg.

20 *Ibid.*

21 HHSA très secrète, Paris, March 5, 1863, Metternich to Rechberg, enclosure: letter dated March 2, 1863.

22 Filipowicz, 88, no. 82, Paris, February 25, 1863, Cowley to Russell. Metternich kept Cowley informed of the alliance negotiations.

23 *Ibid.,* 233, no. 222, Paris, March 17, 1863, Cowley to Russell.

24 HHSA PL, très secrète, Paris, March 5, 1863.

25 HHSA chiffre, Vienna, March 8, 1863, Rechberg to Metternich.

26 HHSA PL, Paris, March 9, 1863, enclosure dated March 8, 1863.

27 This letter is not in the Austrian archives. *Cf.* Stern, *op. cit.,* IX, 167.

28 HHSA no. 20 A-E, London, March 18, 1863, Apponyi to Rechberg.

29 Fr. Doc., vol. 483, no. 23 très confid., Vienna, March 19, 1863, Gramont to Drouyn de Lhuys.

30 *Ibid.*

31 *Ibid.*

32   HHSA Pièces rélatives au voyage du Prince Metternich à Vienne en mars 1863.

33   HHSA PL, Vienna, March 21, 1863.

34   HHSA, March 21, 1863.

35   HHSA, Paris, March 28, 1863.

36   HHSA Instructions secrètes et personnelles pour le Prince Metternich, Vienna, March 21, 1863.

37   Klaczko, 105, on the importance of Galicia to Austria.

38   HHSA no. 2 res., Vienna, March 12, 1863, Rechberg to Apponyi. *Cf.* Filipowicz, 186, no. 188, Vienna, March 12, 1863, Bloomfield to Russell and BB, LXXV, no. 88, Vienna, March 8, 1863, Bloomfield to Russell.

39   HHSA no. 12 B, Paris, March 29, 1863, Metternich to Rechberg.

40   HHSA telegram, Paris, March 26, 1863, Metternich to Rechberg.

41   HHSA no. 4, Vienna, March 27, 1863, Rechberg to Metternich.

42   Fr. Doc., vol. 483, no. 28 confid., Vienna, March 31, 1863, Gramont to Drouyn de Lhuys. *Cf.* Filipowicz, 297, no. 285, Vienna, March 29, 1863, Bloomfield to Russell.

43   HHSA Vienna, March 31, 1863, Rechberg to Metternich and Apponyi.

44   HHSA no. 21 A-C, London, March 27, 1863, Apponyi to Rechberg.

45   HHSA PL, Vienna, March 31, 1863, Rechberg to Metternich.

46   *Ibid.*

47   HHSA no. 12 B, Paris, March 29, 1863, Metternich to Rechberg.

48   *Ibid.*

49   HHSA no. 8, St. Petersburg, 22/10 March 1863, F. Thun to Rechberg.

50   HHSA no. 15, Paris, April 17, 1863, Metternich to Rechberg.

51   HHSA PL, Paris, April 17, 1863, Metternich to Rechberg.

52   HHSA no. 16 A-D, Paris, April 22, 1863, Metternich to Rechberg.

53   HHSA PL no. 2, Vienna, April 30, 1863, Rechberg to Apponyi.

54   HHSA no. 18 A-D, Paris, May 7, 1863, Metternich to Rechberg.

55   HHSA PL, Paris, May 7, 1863, Metternich to Rechberg.

56   HHSA telegram, Vienna, May 9, 1863, Rechberg to Metternich.

57   Schlitter, *loc. cit.,* 65 and Engel-Jánosi, *op. cit.,* 102, citing Ministerprotokoll of May 19, 1863.

58   Lord, *loc. cit.,* 44, Stern, IX, 173, La Gorce, IV, 460 and Charles-Roux, *op. cit.,* 354.

59   HHSA no. 3, Vienna, May 11, 1863, Rechberg to Metternich.

60   *Ibid.*

61   Fr. Doc., vol. 484, no. 43 confid., Vienna, May 10, 1863, Gramont to Drouyn de Lhuys.

62   This program was approved by the Austrian Council of Ministers on June 10th. *Cf.* Schlitter, *loc. cit.,* 66.

63   HHSA Vienna, May 10, 1863, Rechberg to Metternich and Apponyi.

64 HHSA no. 6, Vienna, May 23, 1863, Rechberg to Metternich, enclosure: FO, London, May 19, 1863, Russell to Bloomfield. Both Russell and Palmerston suggested the establishment of an independent Poland with an Austrian archduke as king. Rechberg instructed Apponyi to combat this suggestion. (HHSA nos. 36 E and 38 C, London, May 18 and June 1, 1863, Apponyi to Rechberg, and no. 3, Vienna, May 23, 1863 and PL, Vienna, June 4, 1863, Rechberg to Apponyi.)

65 HHSA no. 2, Vienna, May 23, 1863, Rechberg to Metternich, enclosures: nos. 41 and 42, Paris, May 13, 14, 1863, Drouyn de Lhuys to Gramont.

66 HHSA PL, Paris, May 20, 1863, Metternich to Rechberg.

67 HHSA no. 3 confid., Vienna, May 23, 1863, Rechberg to Metternich.

68 HHSA no. 4, Vienna, May 23, 1863, Rechberg to Metternich.

69 HHSA no. 3, Vienna, May 23, 1863, Rechberg to Metternich. Among the papers left behind by Rechberg after his resignation in 1864 is a document which gives an excellent analysis of the probable effects on Austria of the reëstablishment of an independent Polish kingdom. Rechberg did not deny that such a kingdom might prove a valuable buffer state against Russia but he asked if it could exist without internal strife and without becoming the pawn of the great powers. Furthermore, he expressed the fear that it would become the center of agitation against Austria, a second Piedmont waiting to take advantage of Austria's first serious embarrassment in order to obtain Galicia, and a vassal of France. (HHSA In den Papieren des Grafen Rechberg nach dessen Rücktritt gefunden.)

70 In other words, England and France demanded that the six points in the Austrian program be submitted to the conference after an armistice had been arranged.

71 HHSA no. 2 confid., Vienna, June 12, 1863, Rechberg to Metternich.

72 At a meeting of the Austrian Council of Ministers on June 15th, Franz Joseph supported Rechberg's opposition to an armistice. (Engel-Jánosi, *op. cit.,* 105.)

73 Fr. Doc., vol. 484, no. 53 confid., Vienna, June 16, 1863, Gramont to Drouyn de Lhuys.

74 Notes of England and France dated June 17th, that of Austria June 18th. The last made no mention of an armistice.

75 HHSA no. 21 A-E, St. Petersburg, 13/1 June 1863, Thun to Rechberg.

76 HHSA no. 26, Paris, June 22, 1863, Metternich to Rechberg and Fr. Doc., vol. 484, no. 54, Paris, June 20, 1863, Drouyn de Lhuys to Gramont.

77 HHSA no. 27 B, Paris, June 26, 1863, Metternich to Rechberg.

78 HHSA no. 1, Vienna, June 19, 1863, Rechberg to Metternich and Apponyi, enclosure: St. Petersburg, 13/1 July 1863, Gortchakoff to Balabine.

79 Fr. Doc., vol. 484, no. 59, Vienna, July 18, 1863, Gramont to Drouyn de Lhuys.

80 HHSA no. 3 res., Vienna, July 19, 1863, Rechberg to Metternich and Apponyi.

81 HHSA telegram 9593/875 chiffre no. 70, Paris, July 28, 1863, Metternich to Rechberg. Curiously enough England made the same proposal a few weeks later but again Austria refused though France was prepared to cooperate.

82 HHSA no. 4, Vienna, November 17, 1863, Rechberg to Metternich, annex: report of the Ministerial Council, November 1, 1863. (*Cf.* Engel-Jánosi, *op. cit.,* 114-116, Schlitter, *loc. cit.,* 68-69 and Kosmian, *op. cit.,* 300ff.)

83 HHSA no. 4, Vienna, November 17, 1863, enclosure: Exposé de la situation, November 1, 1863.

84 HHSA no. 43 B, Paris, October 12, 1863, Mülinen to Rechberg.

85 *Ibid.*

86 HHSA no. 45, Paris, November 5, 1863, Mülinen to Rechberg, enclosure: Discours prononcé par Sa Majesté l'Empéreur à l'ouverture de la session Législatif. (*Cf.* La Gorce, IV, 461-63, Ollivier, VI, 355ff. and Stern, IX, 180.)

87 HHSA no. 46 C, Paris, November 7, 1863, Mülinen to Rechberg.

88 Fr. Doc., vol. 485, no. 96, Vienna, November 8, 1863, Gramont to Drouyn de Lhuys.

89 *Ibid.,* no. 98, Vienna, November 14, 1863, Gramont to Drouyn de Lhuys.

90 HHSA no. 2 res., Vienna, November 17, 1863.

91 HHSA Vienna, November 6, 1863.

92 HHSA telegram 4350/1730 chiffre no. 53, London, November 8, 1863.

93 HHSA telegrams, Vienna, November 9, 12, 1863, Rechberg to Wimpffen, and no. 1, Vienna, December 8, 1863, Rechberg to Metternich, enclosure: FO, November 12, 1863, Russell to Cowley.

94 HHSA PL, London, November 22, 1863, Apponyi to Rechberg, repeating oral instructions.

95 HHSA no. 86 A-C, London, November 18, 1863, Apponyi to Rechberg.

96 HHSA no. 86 C, London, November 18, 1863, Apponyi to Rechberg.

97 Fr. Doc., vol. 485, no. 96, Paris, November 15, 1863.

98 *Ibid.*

99 HHSA telegram 4523/281 chiffre no. 104, Paris, November 20, 1863, Metternich to Rechberg.

100 Napoleon learned that Austria had encouraged England to take the initiative of a refusal. (HHSA no. 54 A-F, Paris, November 27, 1863, Metternich to Rechberg.) In his reply to Napoleon, dated Tsarkoe Selo, 18/6 November 1863, the Tsar accepted the congress but requested France to specify its bases. Gortchakoff informed Thun that Russia could

not refuse since he himself had previously advocated the idea of a congress. (HHSA no. 41 A-E, St. Petersburg, 25/13 November 1863, G. Thun to Rechberg.)

101 HHSA no. 1, Vienna, December 8, 1863.

102 HHSA PL, Vienna, December 8, 1863.

103 HHSA no. 2 res., Vienna, December 8, 1863, Rechberg to Metternich.

104 Fr. Doc., vol. 485, no. 112, Vienna, December 15, 1863, Gramont to Drouyn de Lhuys.

105 HHSA no. 59 B, Paris, December 14, 1863, Metternich to Rechberg.

106 *Ibid.*

107 HHSA PL, Paris, December 14, 1863, Metternich to Rechberg.

Chapter Fourteen: CONCLUSIONS

1 Professor Case in his excellent study: *French Opinion on War and Diplomacy during the Second Empire,* shows that Napoleon III was kept informed of French public opinion through the reports of procureurs general and prefects. These reports, unlike the press, constituted a fairly reliable index concerning the public attitude in the important questions, domestic and foreign.

Bibliography

Unpublished Documents

Austria. *Haus-, Hof-, und Staatsarchiv,* Vienna. (Cited as HHSA)
  Correspondence with Paris, January 1851 to end of December 1863
  Correspondence with London, January 1852 to end of December 1863
  Correspondence with St. Petersburg, January 1852 to end of December 1863
  Correspondence with Berlin, especially for years 1852, 1854, 1855 and 1859
  Correspondence with Rome, 1860-1861
  Correspondence with Turin, 1856-1857
  Nachlass Buol-Schauenstein
  Nachlass Rechberg, 524 C, 524 D
  Nachlass Wimpffen (11 letters from Count Wimpffen to Baron Oldenburg, London 1863)
  Kabinettsarchiv, protocols of the Council of Ministers, especially since 1854
Austria. *Kriegsarchiv,* Vienna, miscellaneous documents, particularly for 1859.
France. *Archives des Affaires Étrangères,* Paris. (Cited as Fr. Doc.)
  Correspondence with Vienna, January 1851 to end of November 1863
  Mémoires et Documents, volume II: Italie, 1860-1863; volume IX: Papiers Thouvenel (letters addressed to Thouvenel)

Published Documents

Carteggio Cavour-Salmour. A cura della Reale Commissione Editrice, Bologna, 1936.
Cavour E. *L'Inghilterra. Carteggio con V. E. d'Azeglio,* 2 volumes, Bologna, 1926.
Filipowicz, T. (editor). *Confidential Correspondence of the British Government Respecting the Insurrection in Poland, 1863,* London, 1914.
Great Britain. *Accounts and Papers. Blue Books.* (Cited as BB)
  LXXI (1854) Eastern Papers

LX (1854-55) State Papers (Crimean War)
LXI (1856) State Papers (Paris Congress)
LIX (1857-58) State Papers (Naples, Sardinia)
LXI (1857-58) State Papers (Moldavia, Wallachia)
XXXII (1859) State Papers (Italy)
XIII (1859) State Papers (Italy)
LXVII (1860) State Papers (Italy, Savoy, Nice)
LXVIII (1860) State Papers (Italy, Naples)
LXVII (1861) Italy, correspondence
LXIII (1862) Italy
LXXV (1863) Poland

Ibbeken, Rudolf (editor). *Die auswärtige Politik Preussens 1858-1871. Diplomatische Aktenstücke,* volumes 1-3, Oldenburg, 1932.

Il Carteggio Cavour-Nigra. Dal 1858 al 1861. A cura della Reale Commissione Editrice, 4 volumes, Bologna, 1926.

La Questione Romana. Negli anni 1860-1861. Carteggio de Conte di Cavour. A cura della Commissione Reale Editrice, 2 volumes, Bologna, 1929.

Lutostanski, C. (editor). *Recueil des actes diplomatiques et documents conçernant la Pologne,* 2 volumes, Lausanne, 1920.

Martens, F. F. (editor). *Recueil des traités et conventions conclus par la Russie avec les puissances étrangères,* 15 volumes, St. Petersburg, 1874-1909.

Martens, G. (editor). *Nouveau Recueil Général des traités, conventions et autres transactions rémarquables, servant à la connaisance des rélations étrangères des puissances et états dans leurs rapports mutuels.* Continuation du grand recueil de G. Martens par Charles Samiver, 20 volumes, Goettingue, 1843-1875.

Poschinger, H. R. von (editor). *Preussens auswärtige Politik 1850 bis 1858. Unveröffentliche Dokumente aus dem Nachlasse des Minister-Präsidenten Otto Frh. von Manteuffel,* 3 volumes, Berlin, 1902.

Srbik, Heinrich Ritter von (editor). *Deutsche Geschichtsquellen des 19 Jahrhunderts.* Herausgegeben durch die Historische Kommission bei der Bayerischen Akademie der Wissenschaften. *Quellen zur deutschen Politik Österreichs 1859-1866,* volumes 1-2, Verlag Gerhard Stalling, Oldenburg-Berlin, 1934-1935.

Zaïonchkovskii, A. M. *Vostochnaia Voina 1853-1856. G. V. Sziazi & Sovremenoi ei Polititicheskoi Obstonovskoi,* 2 volumes bound in 5, St. Petersburg, 1908-1913.

Secondary Works

Albe, Duc d'. *Lettres familières de l'Impératrice Eugénie,* 2 volumes, Paris, 1935.

Andreas, W. *Peter von Meyendorff. Ein russischer Staatsmann der Restaurationszeit. Jahrbuch der Charakterologie*, 2, 3, Berlin, 1926.

Andreas, W. *Die russische Diplomatie und die Politik Friedrich Wilhelms IV von Preussen.* Abhandlungen der preussischen Akademie der Wissenschaft, 1926.

Arneth, A. von. *Aus meinem Leben*, 2 volumes, Vienna, 1891-92.

Ashley, E. *Life of Henry John Temple, Viscount Palmerston, 1846-1865,* 2nd edition, 2 volumes, London, 1876.

Aubry, O. *The Phantom Emperor*, New York, 1929.

Auvergne, E. B. F. d'. *Napoléon III*, Paris, 1929. Also in English translation, London, 1929.

Bac, F. S. B. *Napoléon III inconnu*, Paris, 1932.

Bagger, E. *Francis Joseph*, New York, 1927.

Bailly, R. *Histoire de l'amitié franco-polonaise*, Paris, 1926.

Balfour, Lady Frances. *Life of the Earl of Aberdeen*, London, 1922.

Bapst, E. *Les origines de la guerre de Crimée. La France et la Russie de 1848 à 1854*, Paris, 1912.

Bapst, G. *Le maréchal Canrobert. Souvenirs d'un siècle*, Paris, 1898-99.

Barail, General du. *Mes Souvenirs*, 2 volumes, Paris, 1894-96.

Bastgen, H. *Die römische Frage. Dokumente und Stimmen*, 3 volumes, Freiburg, 1919.

Beauregard, Comte de. *Étude et revue de l'histoire de l'Empéreur Napoléon III*, Nice, 1903.

Beer, A. *Die orientalische Politik Österreichs seit 1774*, Prague, 1883.

Beer, A. *Die Finanzen Österreichs in XIX Jahrhundert. Nach archivalischen Quellen*, Prague, 1877.

Beer, A. *Fürst Schwarzenbergs deutsche Politik bis zu den Dresdener Konferenzen*, Histor. Taschenbuch, Leipzig, 1891.

Benson, A. and Esher, Viscount. *The Letters of Queen Victoria. A Selection from Her Majesty's Correspondence between the Years 1837 and 1861*, 3 volumes, volume III, New York, 1907.

Bell, H. C. F. *Lord Palmerston*, 2 volumes, New York, 1936.

Berger, A. F. *Felix, Fürst zu Schwarzenberg*, Leipzig, 1853.

Bernhardi, L. *Zur Polenpolitik des Königreichs Preussen*, Berlin, 1923.

Beust, Friedrich Ferdinand Graf von. *Aus drei Vierteljahrhunderten. Erinnerungen und Aufzeichnungen*, 2 volumes, Stuttgart, 1887.

Beyens, Baron Napoleon Eugene. *Le Second Empire vu par un Diplomate Belge*, 2 volumes, Paris, 1925.

Bianchi, N. *La politique du Comte de Cavour, 1852-1851*, Paris, 1885.

Bibl, V. *Der Zerfall Österreichs. Von Revolution zu Revolution*, 2 volumes, Vienna, 1921.

Biegeleben, R., Freiherr von. *Ludwig Freiherr von Biegeleben. Ein Vorkämpfer des Grossdeutschen Gedanken*, Vienna, 1930.

Binckley, R. *Realism and Nationalism, 1852-1871. The Rise of Modern Europe Series,* New York, 1935.

Bloomfield, Baroness Georgiana. *Reminiscences of Court and Diplomatic Life,* 2 volumes, New York, 1883.

Borries, K. *Preussen im Krimkrieg, 1853-1856,* Stuttgart, 1930.

Boulenger, M. *Le Duc de Morny,* Paris, 1925.

Bourgeois, E. *Manuel historique de la politique étrangère.* Volume III: *Le Temps Présent,* Paris, 1905.

Bourgeois, E. and Clermont, E. *Rome et Napoléon III, 1849-1870,* Paris, 1907.

Bratianu, G. I. *Napoléon III et les nationalités,* Paris, 1934.

Brooks, G. *Napoleon III,* London, 1933.

Buckle, G. E. (editor). *The Letters of Queen Victoria. Second Series. A Selection from Her Majesty's Correspondence and Journal between the years 1862 and 1878,* 2 volumes, volume I, New York, 1926.

Buddeus, A. *Russland unter Alexander II Nikolojewitsch. Zur innern Geschichte und äussern Politik von Thronwechsel bis auf die Gegenwart,* Leipzig, 1860.

Bulle, C. *Geschichte des zweiten Kaiserreichs und des Königreichs Italien,* Berlin, 1890.

Burckhardt, C. J. *Briefe des Staatskanzlers Fürsten Metternich-Winneburg an den österreichischen Minister des Allerhöchsten Hauses und des Äussern, Grafen Buol-Schauenstein aus den Jahren 1852-1859,* Munich and Berlin, 1934.

Cahuet, A. *La question d'Orient dans l'histoire contemporaine, 1821-1905,* Paris, 1905.

Carette, Mme. A. *Souvenirs intimes de la cour des Tuileries.* Volume III, Paris, 1891.

Case, L. M. *Franco-Italian Relations, 1860-1865. The Roman Question and the Convention of September,* Phila., Univ. of Penn. Press, 1932.

Case, L. M. *French Opinion on War and Diplomacy during the Second Empire,* Phila., Univ. of Penn. Press, 1954.

Cassagnac, A. Granier de. *Souvenirs du Second Empire,* Paris, 1879.

Cassagnac, A. Granier de. *L'Empéreur, la Pologne et l'Europe,* Paris, 1863.

Chambrier, J. de. *Second Empire. Avant et après Sadowa,* Paris, 1910.

Chapelle, Comte de la (editor). *Napoléon III. Oeuvres posthumes autographes et inédits,* London, n. d.

Chapman, Mrs. M. *Imperial Brother: The Life of the Duc de Morny,* New York, 1931.

Charles-Roux, F. *Alexandre II, Gortchakoff et Napoléon III,* Paris, 1913.

Charmatz, R. *Österreichs Innere Geschichte,* Leipzig, 1918.

Charmatz, R. *Kaiser Franz Joseph I,* Leipzig, 1917.

Charmatz, R. *Minister Freiherr von Bruck, der Vorkämpfer Mitteleuropas,* Leipzig, 1916.

Charmatz, R. *Geschichte der auswärtigen Politik Österreichs im 19 Jahrhundert,* Leipzig, 1914.

Chiala, L. *Lettere edite e inedite di Camillo Cavour,* 6 volumes, Turin, 1882-87.

Chiala, L. *Politica segreta di Napoleone III e di Cavour in Italia e in Ungheria, 1858-1861,* Turin, 1895.

Cilibrizzi, S. *Storia parlamentare, politica e diplomatica d'Italia da Novarra e Vittoria Veneto,* 3 volumes, Milan, 1923-29. Volume I.

Clark, C. W. *Franz Joseph and Bismarck. The Diplomacy of Austria before the War of 1866,* Cambridge, Harvard Univ. Press, 1934.

Corti, Count Caesar E. *Elizabeth of Austria,* London, 1936.

Corti, Count Caesar E. *Maximilian and Charlotte of Mexico,* 2 volumes, New York, 1928.

Czartoryski, W. *Le Rhin et la Vistula,* Paris, 1861.

Czartoryski, W. *Affaires de Pologne,* Paris, 1863.

Darimon, A. *Histoire de douze ans, 1857-1869,* Paris, 1863.

Daudet, L. *L'Inconnu, l'Impératrice Eugénie,* Paris, 1922.

Debidour, A. *Histoire des rapports de l'Église et de l'État en France de 1789 à 1870,* Paris, 1898.

Debidour, A. *Histoire Diplomatique de l'Europe, 1814-1878,* 2 volumes, Paris, 1891.

East, W. G. *Union of Moldavia and Wallachia,* New York, 1929.

Ebeling, A. *Napoleon III und sein Hof, 1851-1870,* 3 volumes, Cologne, 1891-1894.

Eckardt, J. von. *Russland vor und nach dem Krimkrieg,* Leipzig, 1879.

Eckardt, J. von. *Berlin und St. Petersburg. Preussische Beiträge zur Geschichte der russisch-deutschen Beziehungen,* Leipzig, 1880.

Eckardt, J. von. *Von Nikolai zu Alexander III,* Leipzig, 1886.

Eckhart, F. *Die deutsche Frage und der Krimkrieg. Deutsche Gesellschaft zum Studium Osteuropas. Osteuropäische Forschungen,* Heft 9, Berlin, 1931.

Edelston, R. H. *Napoleon III and Italy. A Brief Historical Survey,* Darlington, 1922.

Egelhaaf, G. *Geschichte des neuzehnten Jahrhunderts vom Wiener Kongress bis zum Frankfurter Frieden,* 2 volumes, Stuttgart, 1925.

Elliott, Sir Henry. *Some Reflections and Other Diplomatic Experiences,* London, 1922.

Engel-Jánosi, F. *Graf Rechberg. Vier Kapitel zu seiner und Österreichs Geschichte,* Munich, 1927.

Engel-Jánosi, F. *Der Freiherr von Hübner, 1811-1892,* Innsbruck, 1934.

Ernest II. *Memoirs of Ernest II, Duke of Saxe-Coburg-Gotha.* Trans. by P. Andreae, 4 volumes, London, 1888-90.

Ernst, Otto (editor). *Franz Joseph in seinen Briefen,* Vienna, 1924.

Espagny, Comte M. H. de Laire d'. *Mémoires du duc de Persigny. Publiés avec des documents inédits, un avant-propos et un épilogue,* 3rd ed., Paris, 1896.

Esslinger, Elisabeth. *Kaiserin Eugenie und die Politik des zweiten Kaiserreichs,* Stuttgart, 1932.

Fischel, A. *Der Panslawismus bis zum Weltkrieg,* Stuttgart and Berlin, 1919.

Fleury, Comte (editor). *Memoirs of the Empress Eugenie,* 2 volumes, New York, 1920.

Fleury, Comte. *Souvenirs du General Comte Fleury,* 3rd ed., 2 volumes, Paris, 1897-98.

Friedjung, H. *Österreich von 1848 bis 1860,* 2 volumes, Stuttgart and Berlin, 1912.

Friedjung, H. *Der Krimkrieg und die österreichische Politik,* 2nd ed., Stuttgart and Berlin, 1911.

Friedjung, H. *Historische Aufsätze,* 2 volumes, Stuttgart, 1919.

Friedjung, H. *Der Kampf um die Vorherrschaft in Deutschland, 1859-1866,* 2 volumes, Stuttgart and Berlin, 1902.

Friese, C. *Russland und Preussen vom Krimkrieg bis zum polnischen Aufstand. Osteuropäische Forschungen. Im Auftrage der deutschen Gesellschaft zum Studium Osteuropas.* Herausgegeben von Otto Hoetzsch, volume XI, Berlin, 1931.

Gallavresi, G. *Italia e Austria, 1859-1914,* Milan, 1923.

Geffcken, F. H. *Zur Geschichte des orientalischen Krieges, 1853-1856,* Berlin, 1881.

Gooch, G. P. (editor). *The Later Correspondence of Lord John Russell, 1840-1878,* 2 volumes, London, 1925.

Gooch, G. P. and Ward, A. W. (editors). *Cambridge History of British Foreign Policy, 1783-1919,* 3 volumes, London, 1922-23, volume II.

Gordon, Arthur. *The Earl of Aberdeen,* London, 1893.

Goriainov, S. *Le Bosphore et les Dardanelles,* Paris, 1910.

Gourdon, E. *Histoire du Congrès de Paris,* Paris, 1857.

Grabinski, Comte J. *Un ami de Napoléon III. Le Comte Arese et la politique italienne sous la Second Empire,* Paris, 1897.

Guedalla, P. *Palmerston,* New York, 1927.

Guedalla, P. *The Second Empire,* London, 1932.

Guerard, A. L. *Napoleon III,* Cambridge, Harvard Univ. Press, 1943.

Guichen, Vicomte E. de. *Les Grandes Questions Européennes et la Diplomatie des Puissances sous la Seconde République Française,* 2 volumes, Paris, 1929, volume II.

Guichen, Vicomte E. de. *La Guerre de Crimée (1854-1856) et l'attitude des Puissances Européennes,* Paris, 1936.

Hagg, H. T. *The Congress of Paris of 1856,* typed thesis, Univ. of Iowa, 1936.

Harcourt, Comte Bernard d'. *Diplomatie et Diplomates. Les quatre ministères de M. Drouyn de Lhuys,* Paris, 1882.

Hauterive, Ernest d'. *Napoléon III et le Prince Napoléon. Corréspondance inédite,* Paris, 1925.

Hazen, C. D., Thayer, W. R. and Lord, R. H. *Three Peace Congresses,* Cambridge, Harvard Univ. Press, 1917.

Heller, Oberst Dr. Edward. *Mitteleuropa Vorkämpfer, Fürst Felix zu Schwarzenberg,* Vienna, 1933.

Hover, E. *Der polnische Aufstand 1863 im Lichte neuerer Erfahrungen,* Berlin, 1904.

Hübner, J. A., Graf von. *Neuf ans de souvenirs d'un ambassadeur d'Autriche à Paris sous le second empire, 1851-1859. Publiés par son fils Le Comte Alexander de Hübner,* 2 volumes, Paris, 1904. Also in German: *Neun Jahre Erinnerungen eines österreichischen Botschafters in Paris, 1851-1859,* 2 volumes, Berlin, 1904.

Hübner, J. A., Graf von. *Ein Jahr meines Lebens, 1848-1849,* Leipzig, 1891.

Jacini, S. *Il Tramonte del Portere Temporale. Nelle Relazione degli Ambasciatore austriaci a Rome, 1860-1870,* Bari, 1931.

Jomini, Alexander. *Études diplomatiques sur la guerre de Crimée, 1852-1856,* 2 volumes, St. Petersburg, 1878. Also English edition: *Diplomatic Study of the Crimean War,* 2 volumes, London, 1882.

Jorga, N. *Geschichte des osmanischen Reiches,* volume V, Gotha, 1913.

Kaiser, K. *Napoleon III und der polnische Aufstand von 1863,* Berlin, 1932.

Klaczko, J. *Études de diplomatie contemporaine. Les cabinets de l'Europe en 1863-1864,* Paris, 1866.

Knorr, E. *Die polnischen Aufstände seit 1830,* Berlin, 1880.

Kosmian, S. *Das Jahr 1863. Polen und die europäische Diplomatie,* Vienna, 1896.

Kunau, H. *Die Stellung der preussischen Konservativen zur äussern Politik während des Krimkrieges,* Halle, 1914.

Kunze, H. *Die Usedom-Wedellsche Mission im Winter 1854-1855. Abhandlung zur Geschichte der preussischen Politik während des Krimkrieges,* Leipzig, 1922.

La Gorce, P. de. *Histoire du Second Empire,* 4th ed., 7 volumes, Paris, 1899-1905.

La Gorce, P. de. *Au temps du Second Empire,* Paris, 1935.

Lano, P. de. *La secret d'un Empire,* 3 volumes, Paris, 1891-93.

La Roncière Le Noury. *Corréspondance intime avec sa femme et sa fille,* Paris, 1928.

Lesueuer, E. *Le Prince de La Tour d'Auvergne et le secret de l'Impératrice. Contribution à l'histoire diplomatique du Second Empire,* Paris, 1930.

Ley, H. *Die italienische Einung und die englische Politik, 1859-1861,* Berlin, 1935.

Loftus, Lord A. *Diplomatic Reminiscences. First Series, 1837-1862,* London, 1892. *Second Series, 1862-1879,* London, 1894.

Lord, T. de. *Histoire du Second Empire, 1848-1870,* 6 volumes, Paris, 1868-1875.

Lucius, H. *Rôle politique de la Prusse pendant la guerre de Crimée,* Paris, 1903.

Malmesbury, Third Earl of. *Memoirs of an Ex-Minister,* 2nd ed., 2 volumes, London, 1884.

Margutti, A. A. V. *The Emperor Francis Joseph and His Times,* London, 1921.

Martin, Theodore. *The Life of His Royal Highness, The Prince Consort,* 5 volumes, New York, 1875-1881.

Mataja, H. *Österreichische Politik im 19 und 20 Jahrhundert. Ein Geschichtlicher Überblick. (Berichte zur Kultur und Zeitgeschichte,* volume X, nos. 225-226, Vienna, 1935.)

Matter, P. *Cavour et l'Unité Italienne,* 3 volumes. Volume III: 1856-1861, Paris, 1927.

Maurain, J. *La politique ecclésiastique du Second Empire de 1852 à 1869,* Paris, 1931.

Maurain, J. *Un bourgeois français au XIX siècle. Baroche Ministre de Napoléon III d'après ses papiers inédits,* Paris, 1936.

Maxwell, Sir H. *The Life and Letters of George Wm. Fred., Fourth Earl of Clarendon,* 2 volumes, London, 1913.

Mayr, Josef Karl (editor). *Das Tagebuch des Polizeiministers Kempen von 1848 bis 1859,* Vienna, 1931.

Mazziotti, M. *Napoleone III e l'Italia,* Milan, 1925.

Metternich-Sandor, Princess Pauline. *Souvenirs de la Princesse Pauline de Metternich, 1859-1871,* Paris, 1922.

Meyendorff, P. von. *Ein russischer Diplomat an den Höfen von Berlin und Wien. Politischer und privater Briefwechsel, 1826-1863.* Hersg. und eingeleitet von O. Hoetzsch, 3 volumes, Berlin, 1923.

Meyer, A. O. *Bismarcks Kampf mit Österreich am Bundestag zu Frankfurt,* Berlin, 1927.

Morny, Duc de. *Extrait des Mémoires. Une Ambassade en Russie 1856,* Paris, 1892.

Mülinen, Comte de. *Les Finances de l'Autriche. Étude historique et statistique*, Paris, 1875.

Muller, R. *Die Partei Bethmann-Hollweg und die orientalische Krise, 1853-1856*, Halle, 1926.

Munster, G. H. Count. *Political Sketches of the State of Europe from 1814 to 1867*, Edinburgh, 1868, trans. from the German.

Musulin, Freiherr von. *Das Haus am Ballplatz. Erinnerungen eines österreich-ungarischen Diplomaten*, Munich, 1924.

Nesselrode, Comte A. de. *Lettres et Papiers du Chancelier Comte de Nesselrode, 1760-1856. Extrait des Archives*, 11 volumes, Paris, n. d.

Ollivier, E. *L'Empire Libérale. Études, Récits, Souvenirs*, 17 volumes, Paris, 1895-1915.

Oncken, H. (editor). *Grossherzog Friedrich I von Baden und die deutsche Politik von 1854-1871. Briefwechsel, Denkschriften, Tagebücher.* Hersg. von der badischen historischen Kommission, 2 volumes, Stuttgart, 1927.

Paléologue, M. *The Tragic Empress*, New York, 1928.

Palm, F. C. *England and Napoleon III. A Study of a Utopian Dictator*, Duke University Press, 1944.

Pinon, Réné. *Histoire Diplomatique 1515-1928.* (In *Histoire de la Nation Française*, volume IX, Paris, 1929.)

Plener, E. Freiherr von. *Erinnerungen*, 2 volumes, Stuttgart, 1911.

Prokesch-Osten, Graf von. *Aus den Briefen des Grafen von Prokesch-Osten, K. K. Botschafters und Feldzeugmeisters, 1849-1855*, Vienna, 1896.

Pradier-Fodère, P. L. *M. Drouyn de Lhuys*, Laval, 1871.

Puryear, V. J. *England and the Straits Question, 1844-1856*, Univ. of California Press, 1931.

Redlich, Josef. *Emperor Francis Joseph of Austria*, New York, 1929.

Redlich, Josef. *Das österreichische Staats-und-Reichsproblem. Geschichtliche Darstellung der inneren Politik der Habsburgischen Monarchie von 1848 bis zum Untergang des Reiches*, 2 volumes, Leipzig, 1920-1926.

Reiset, Comte de. *Mes Souvenirs*, 3 volumes, Paris, 1902-1903.

Rheindorff, K. *Die Schwarze Meer (Pontus) Frage vom Pariser Frieden 1856 bis zum Abschlusse der Londoner Konferenz von 1871*, Berlin, 1925.

Ricasoli, Baron Bettino. *Lettere e documenti del Baron Ricasoli.* Edited by Tabarrini and Gotti, 10 volumes, Florence, 1874ff.

Riker, T. W. *The Making of Roumania. A Study of an International Problem, 1856-1866*, London, 1931.

Rothan, G. *Souvenirs Diplomatiques. L'Europe et l'avenement du Second Empire*, Paris, 1892.

Rothan, G. *La Prusse et son Roi pendant la guerre de Crimée*, Paris, 1888.

Saint-Arnaud, Imbert de. *France and Italy, 1852-1870*, New York, 1899.

Salata, F. *Per la Storia diplomatica della questione Romano. Da Cavour alla Triplice Alleanza*, Milan, 1929.

Salomon, H. *L'Ambassade de Richard de Metternich à Paris*, Paris, 1931.

Satow, Sir Ernest. *An Austrian Diplomat in the Fifties*, Cambridge, 1908. Based on Hübner's journal.

Schiemann, T. *Geschichte Russlands unter Kaiser Nikolaus I*, 4 volumes, Berlin, 1904-1919.

Schlitter, Hanns. *Aus der Regierungszeit Kaiser Franz Joseph I*, Vienna, 1919.

Schnürer, E. (editor). *Briefe Kaiser Franz Josephs I an seine Mutter, 1838-1872*, Munich, 1930.

Schule, E. *Russland und Frankreich vom Ausgang des Krimkrieges bis zum Italienischen Krieg, 1856-1859* (*Osteuropäische Forschungen*, volume 19, Berlin, 1935).

Schwarzenberg, A. *Prince Felix zu Schwarzenberg. Prime Minister of Austria, 1848-1852*, New York, 1946.

Schweinitz, General Hans Lothar von. *Denkwürdigkeiten des Botschafters General von Schweinitz*, 3 volumes, Berlin, 1927.

Seignobos, C. *Le déclin de l'Empire et l'établissement de la 3e République, 1859-1875*, Paris, 1921. Volume VII of Lavisse: *Histoire de la France contemporaine*.

Sencourt, R. *The Life of the Empress Eugenie*, New York, 1931.

Sencourt, R. *Napoleon III. The Modern Emperor*, London, 1934.

Senior, N. W. *Conversations with M. Thiers, M. Guizot and other distinguished persons during the Second Empire*, 2 volumes, London, 1878.

Senior, N. W. *Conversations with distinguished persons during the Second Empire, 1860-1863*, 2 volumes, London, 1880.

Silva, P. *La politica di Napoleone III in Italia*, Milan, 1927.

Simpson, F. A. *Louis Napoleon and the Recovery of France, 1848-1856*, New York, 1923.

Simpson, F. A. *The Rise of Louis Napoleon*, London, 1925.

Sosnosky, T. von. *Die Balkanpolitik Österreich-Ungarns seit 1866*, 3 volumes, Vienna, 1913-1914. Volume I.

Springer, A. *Geschichte Österreichs seit dem Wiener Frieden 1809*, volumes I and II, Leipzig, 1863-1865.

Srbik, H. von. *Metternich der Staatsmann und der Mensch*, 2 volumes, Vienna, 1925.

Srbik, H. von. *Deutsche Einheit. Idee und Wirklichkeit vom Heiligen Reich bis Königgrätz*, 3 volumes, Munich, 1935-42.

Steefel, L. D. *The Schleswig-Holstein Question*, Harvard University Press, 1932.

Steinitz, Eduard Ritter von (editor). *Erinnerungen an Franz Joseph I*, Berlin, 1931.

Stern, A. *Geschichte Europas seit den Verträgen von 1815 bis zum Frankfurter Frieden von 1871*, 10 volumes, Stuttgart, 1894-1924.

Sybel, H. von. *The Founding of the German Empire by William I*, 7 volumes, New York, 1890-98, volume II.

Taylor, A. J. P. *The Hapsburg Monarchy, 1815-1918*, London, 1941.

Taylor, A. J. P. *The Struggle for Mastery in Europe, 1848-1918*, Oxford History of Modern Europe, vol. II, New York, 1954.

Temblaire, C. E. (editor). *Oeuvres de Louis Napoléon Bonaparte*, 3 volumes, Paris, 1848.

Temperley, H. *England and the Near East. The Crimea*, London, 1936.

Temperley, H. and Penson, L. M. (editors). *A Century of Diplomatic Blue Books, 1814-1914*, Cambridge, University Press, 1938.

Thouvenel, L. *Nicholas I et Napoléon III, 1852-1854*, Paris, 1891.

Thouvenel, L. *Trois années de la question d'Orient, 1856-1859*, Paris, 1897.

Thouvenel, L. *Pagès de l'histoire du Second Empire, 1854-1866*, Paris, 1903.

Thouvenel, L. *Le secret de l'Empéreur. Corréspondance confidentielle et inédite échangée entre M. Thouvenel, le duc de Gramont et le Général Comte de Flahaut, 1860-1863*, 2 volumes, Paris, 1889.

Trotka, T. W. *Der polnische Aufstand 1863*, Berlin, 1895.

Tschuppik, Karl. *Franz Joseph I*, Dresden, 1928.

Urban, Miriam B. *British Opinion on the Unification of Italy, 1856-1861*, New York, 1938.

Valsecchi, Franco. *L'Alleanza di Crimea. Il Risorgimento e L'Europa*, Arnoldo Mondadori Editori, 1948.

Viel-Castel, Comte Horace de. *Mémoires sur le règne de Napoléon III, 1851-1864*, 6 volumes, Paris, 1883-1884.

Vitzthum von Eckstädt, Karl Friedrich Graf. *Berlin und Wien in den Jahren 1845-1852. Politische Privatbriefe mit einem Vorwort von F. Muller*, 2nd ed., Stuttgart, 1886.

Vitzthum von Eckstädt, Karl Friedrich Graf. *London, Gastein und Sadowa, 1864-1866. Denkwürdigkeiten*, Stuttgart, 1889.

Vitzthum von Eckstädt, Karl Friedrich Graf. *St. Petersburg and London in the Years 1852-1864*, London, 1887.

Walpole, Sir Spencer. *The Life of Lord John Russell*, 2nd ed., 2 volumes, London, 1891.

Wellesley, Hon. F. A. (editor). *Secrets of the Second Empire: Private Letters from the Paris Embassy. Selections from the Papers of Henry Richard Charles Wellesley, First Earl Cowley*, New York, 1929.

English edition: *The Paris Embassy during the Second Empire: Selections from the Papers of the first Earl Cowley,* London, 1928.

Wellesley, Sir Victor and Sencourt, R. (editors). *Conversations with Napoleon III. A collection of documents mostly unpublished and almost entirely diplomatic.* Selected and arranged with introductions by Sir Victor Wellesley and Robert Sencourt, London, 1934.

Wertheimer, E. von. *Bismarck im politischen Kampf,* Berlin, 1930.

Whyte, A. J. *The Political Life and Letters of Cavour, 1848-1861,* London, 1930.

Wolfsgruber, C. *Joseph Othmar Kardinal Rauscher, Fürstbischof von Wien. Sein Leben und sein Wirken,* Freiburg im Breisgau, 1888.

Woodward, E. L. *Three Studies in European Conservatism. Metternich: Guizot: The Catholic Church in the Nineteenth Century,* London, 1929.

Articles

Boutenko, V. "Un projet d'alliance franco-russe en 1856 d'après des documents inédits des Archives Russes." *Revue Historique,* vol. 155 (1927), pp. 277-325.

Charles-Roux, F. "La Russie et la Politique Italienne de Napoléon III." *Revue Historique,* vol. 105 (1910), pp. 35-62.

Charles-Roux, F. "La France et l'Entente Russo-Prussienne après la guerre de Crimée." *Revue Historique,* vol. 112 (1913), pp. 28-61.

Charles-Roux, F. "La Russie et l'Alliance Anglo-Française après la guerre de Crimée." *Revue Historique,* vol. 101 (1909), pp. 272-315.

Charles-Roux, F. "La Russie, La France et la question d'Orient après la guerre de Crimée." *Revue Historique,* vol. 109 (1912), pp. 272-306.

Corti, Count Caesar E. "Les Idées de l'Impératrice Eugénie sur le redressement de la carte de l'Europe d'après les rapports de Prince Richard de Metternich." *Revue des Études Napoléoniennes,* II (1922), pp. 147-155.

Daniels, E. "Die politische Vorgeschichte des Krieges von 1859." *Preuss. Jahrb.,* vol. 206 (1926), pp. 1-18.

East, W. G. "The Osborne Conference and Memorandum of August 1857." *English Historical Review,* vol. XLIII (1928), pp. 409-412.

Goriainov, S. "Les étapes de l'alliance franco-russe, 1853-1861." *Revue de Paris,* vol. XIX (1912), pp. 1-29, 529-544, 755-776.

Hallberg, C. W. "La France et l'Autriche en 1857. Un memorandum du Comte Buol." *Revue d'Histoire Diplomatique* (Oct.-Dec. 1939), pp. 353-360.

Handelsman, M. "La Guerre de Crimée. La question polonaise et les origines du problème Bulgare." *Revue Historique,* vol. 169 (1932), pp. 271-315.

Hauterive, Ernest d'. "Corréspondance inédite de Napoléon III et du Prince Napoléon." *Revue des Deux Mondes,* vol. 18, 7th per. (Nov.-Dec. 1923), pp. 763-796; vol. 19, 7th per. (Jan.-Feb. 1924), pp. 51-84, 519-545.

Hauterive, Ernest d'. "Mission du Prince Napoléon à Varsovie (1858)." *Revue des Deux Mondes,* vol. 45, 7th per. (May-June 1928), pp. 823-854.

Henderson, G. B. "The Diplomatic Revolution of 1854." *American Historical Review,* vol. XLIII, no. 1 (Oct. 1937), pp. 22-50.

Hengelmüller von Hengelvar, L. Freiherr von. "Graf Alois Karolyi. Ein Beitrag zur Geschichte der österreichisch-ungarischen Diplomatie." *Deutsche Revue,* vol. XXXVIII, heft 1, 2 (1913), vol. XXXIX (1914) and vol. XL (1915).

Kentmann, H. "Preussen und die Bundeshilfe an Österreich im Jahre 1859." *Mitteilingen des österreichischen Instituts für Geschichtsforschung,* XII Band, 1933, Universitäts-Verlag Wagner, Innsbruck, pp. 297-415.

Leroy-Beaulieu, A. "La Politique du Second Empire." *Revue des Deux Mondes,* vol. 98, 2nd per. (Mar.-April 1872), pp. 536-572.

Leroy-Beaulieu, A. "Le Roi Victor Emmanuel et la Monarchie Italienne." *Revue des Deux Mondes,* vol. 238, 3rd per. (Mar.-April 1878), pp. 837-870.

Lord, R. H. "Bismarck and Russia in 1863." *American Historical Review,* vol. 29 (Oct. 1923), pp. 24-48.

Masson, F. "L'Italie Libérée (1857-1882). Lettres et Dépêches du Roi Victor Emmanuel II et du Comte de Cavour au Prince Napoléon." *Revue des Deux Mondes,* vol. 13, 7th per. (Jan.-Feb. 1923), pp. 39-73, 550-573, 845-861.

Matter, P. "Cavour et la Guerre de Crimée." *Revue Historique,* vol. 145 (1924), pp. 161-202.

Mosse, W. E. "The Triple Treaty of 15 April 1856." *English Historical Review,* vol. LXVII, no. 263 (April 1952), pp. 203-229.

Pagès, G. "Les Rélations de la France et de la Russie en 1860." *Revue d'Histoire du Sud-Est Européen,* vol. V (1928), pp. 277-287.

Paić, Josef von. "Zur politischen Vorgeschichte des Feldzuges 1859 nach offiziellen Quellen." *Mitteilungen des österreichischen Instituts für Geschichtsforschung an der Wiener Universität,* XLIII Band, 3 und 4 Heft, 1929, Universitäts-Verlag Wagner, Innsbruck, pp. 376-390.

Pingaud, A. "La Politique Extérieure du Second Empire." *Revue Historique,* vol. 156 (1927), pp. 41-68.

Pingaud, A. "Napoléon III et ses Projets de Confédération Italienne." *Revue Historique,* vol. 155 (1927), pp. 333-336.

Pingaud, A. "Un Projet de désarmament de Napoléon III 1863." *Institut de France. Acad. des Sciences Morales et Politique. Science et Travaux,* Paris (Nov.-Dec. 1931), pp. 471-486.

Pouthas, Charles H. "La médiation de Napoléon III entre le Roi de Naples, les Siciliens et le gouvernement piemontais, mai-août 1860." *Rassegna Storica Del Risorgimento,* Anno XXXIX, Fasc. IV, Ottobre-Dicembre 1952, pp. 762-779.

Reinsch, J. "Napoléon III et la Paix." *Revue Historique,* vol. 136 (1921), pp. 161-219.

Riker, T. W. "The Concert of Europe and Moldavia." *English Historical Review,* vol. XLII (1927), pp. 227-244.

Riker, T. W. "The Pact of Osborne." *American Historical Review,* vol. XXXIV (1927), pp. 237ff.

Rothan, G. "Souvenirs Diplomatique. L'Entrévue de Stuttgart." *Revue des Deux Mondes,* vol. 90 (Nov.-Dec. 1888), pp. 505-586.

Rothan, G. "Napoléon III et l'Italie." *Revue des Deux Mondes,* vol. 151 (Jan.-Feb. 1899), pp. 529-561, vol. 152 (Mar.-April 1899), pp. 333-359.

Salomon, R. "Die Anerkennung Napoleon III." *Zeitschrift für Osteuropäische Geschichte,* vol. II (1912), pp. 312-366.

Schlitter, Dr. Hanns. "Die Frage der Wiederherstellung Polens im österreichischen Ministerrat 1863." *Österreichische Rundschau,* vol. 58 (Jan.-Mar. 1919), pp. 63-69.

Schmitt, B. E. "The Diplomatic Preliminaries of the Crimean War." *American Historical Review,* vol. XXV (Oct. 1919), pp. 36-67.

Schnerb, Robert. "Napoleon III and the Second Empire." Bibliographical article. *Journal of Modern History,* vol. 8 (1936), pp. 338-355.

Srbik, H. Ritter von. "Franz Joseph I. Charakter und Regierungsgrundsätze." *Historische Zeitschrift,* vol. 144 (1931), pp. 509-526.

Stern, A. "L'Insurrection Polonaise de 1863 et l'Impératrice Eugénie." *Revue Historique,* vol. 137 (1921), pp. 66-73.

Stern, A. "Georg Klindworth, ein politischer Geheimagent des XIX Jahrhunderts." *Historische Viertel-Jahrsschrift,* vol. 25 (1930), pp. 430ff., 696.

Sumner, B. H. "The Secret Franco-Russian Treaty of 3 March 1859." *English Historical Review,* vol. XLVIII (1933), pp. 65-83.

Temperley, H. "More Light on the Pact of Osborne, 9 August 1857." *Cambridge Historical Journal,* vol. 5 (1937), pp. 315-323.

Temperley, H. "The Treaty of Paris and Its Execution." *Journal of Modern History,* vol. 4 (1932), pp. 387-415, 523-543.

Valsecchi, F. "La Politica di Cavour e la Prussia nel 1859." *Archivio Storico Italiano,* disp. I, 1936, Anno XCIV, pp. 37-66.

Valsecchi, F. "Toscana ed Austria nel 1859 nei documenti diplomatici austriaci." *Archivio Storico Italiano.* disp. II, 1936, Anno XCIV, pp. 37-55.

Vidal, Cesar. "Le Second Empire et Ferdinand II de Naples, 1852-1859." *Rassegna Storica Del Risorgimento,* Anno XXXIX, Fasc. IV, Ottobre-Dicembre 1952, pp. 835-844.

Wereszycki, Dr. H. "Great Britain and the Polish Question in 1863." *English Historical Review,* vol. L (1935), pp. 78-108.

Woodward, E. L. "The Diplomacy of the Vatican under Popes Pius IX and Leo XIII." *Journal of the Royal Inst. of Int. Aff.* (May 1924), pp. 113-138.

Index